ASPECTS of MOD

Railway Electrics

Ian Morton

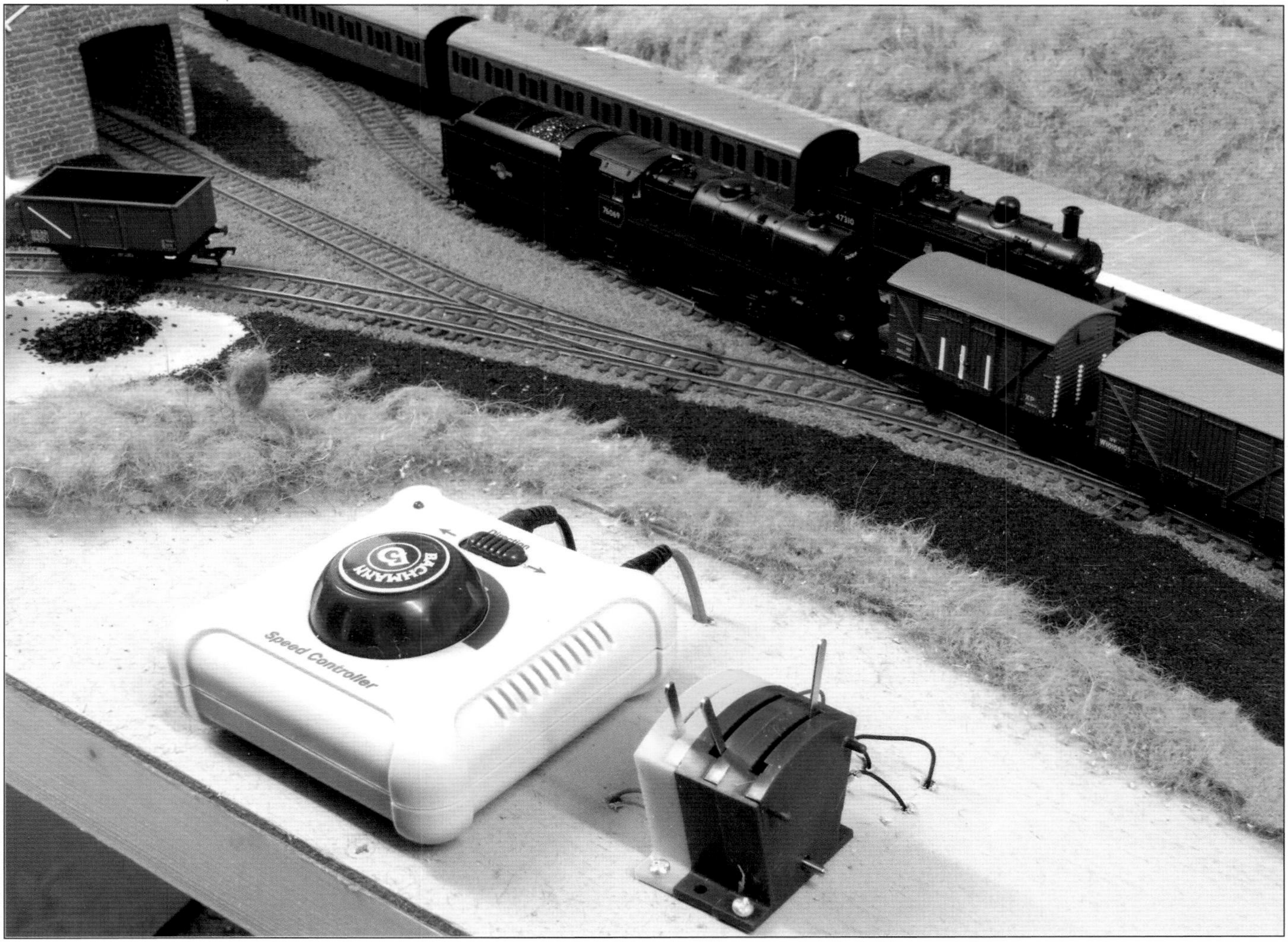

First published 2009

ISBN 978 07110 3343 6

Published by Ian Allan Publishing Ltd

an imprint of Ian Allan Publishing Ltd, Hersham, Surrey KT12 4RG.
Printed by Ian Allan Printing Ltd, Hersham, Surrey KT12 4RG.

Code: 0911/B1

Visit the Ian Allan Publishing web site at: www.ianallanpublishing.com

Contents

Introduction

Model railway electrics – a topic to make otherwise rational people start to tremble and break out in a sweat. Many modellers say that they are baffled by the electrics under their layout or even can't build a layout because they don't understand how to wire it up. Fear not, this book will guide you gently through the ideas and techniques that you need in order to become a proficient model railway electrician.

The electrical knowledge and skills that you need to successfully wire up a model railway are limited and easy to acquire. Don't be fooled into thinking that because there are hundreds of wires beneath a layout that it must all be terribly complicated, it isn't. It is the same few simple circuits repeated many times over.

Those of a technical disposition may well like to complicate the wiring of their model railway, that is their choice and something that they enjoy. If you are, or aspire to be, a technical whizz kid then you ought to join MERG, the Model Electronic Railway Group, which caters for those of us who like playing with circuits – details can be found on their website www.merg.org.uk.

I shall assume that you know nothing about model railway electrics to start with, if you do then feel free to skim or even skip the basics with the exception of the golden rules, these are important points that need to be read and acted on.

A Note On DCC

Many people may think that a book such as this is rendered obsolete by the widespread adoption of DCC (Digital Command Control). DCC allows the control of multiple locomotives on the same piece of track and can control hundreds of accessories such as point motors and lights from your controller with no need for a complex control panel – all with only two wires running around the layout.

Whilst it is true that DCC can vastly reduce the amount of wiring needed for a layout, none the less you still have to connect track to the controller, fit point motors and wrestle with reverse loops – all of which are explained in this volume. DCC specific information is marked with DCC in the margin.

For a fuller explanation of what DCC is and how to use it please refer to my book '*Aspects of Modelling – Digital Command Control*'.

The Golden Rules

Rule 1. **No mains electricity.**
Buy a professionally made power supply for your model railway and only use low-voltage (12V to 16V) outputs. Do not be tempted to run a mains cable along your layout. Mains voltage can, and does, kill. Don't take any chances with it; I'd hate to lose a reader.

Rule 2. **Use the correct tools.**
Using the correct tool ensures that the task is done effectively and efficiently. As an example, use a wire stripper to strip the insulating sleeve off lengths of wire. Do not use a craft knife, however tempting it may seem. The knife may slip and cut you; it will most likely cut off some of the wire strands and lead to a weakened connection that may well fail at a later date.

Rule 3. **Colour code your wiring.**
A simple colour code can make it much easier to work out what wire goes where. If your track feeds are all red for one side and black for the other it makes it much harder to introduce a short circuit by connecting different rails together.

Rule 4. **Keep it tidy.**
It is so tempting just to run a couple of wires "to see if it works" and then a couple more until you have something that resembles a bird's nest under the layout. Keeping your wiring tidy will help you when it comes to locating faults or making changes.

Rule 5. **Keep notes.**
Along with Rules 3 and 4 this is all about making it easy for yourself in future. You may know what the green and purple striped wire that you used because you didn't have any of the correct colour does now, but you won't remember when a length of track mysteriously goes dead in nine months time. Make sketches of the wiring noting where the wires go and what they do. Ideally you should number each end of each wire with a sticky label so that if they are ever disconnected, either by design or accident, you can establish where they should go.

Rule 6: **Every length of rail, however long or short, needs to be connected to the controller.**
Every length of rail, however long or short, needs to be connected to the controller, either directly or via a switch, if you want to run a train on it. The connection can either be by a wire or by a metal rail joiner from another piece of track, but it must be connected.

Remember:
Never connect model railway equipment directly to the mains.
Always follow the manufacturer's instructions

IF IN DOUBT ALWAYS CONSULT A QUALIFIED ELECTRICIAN.

CHAPTER

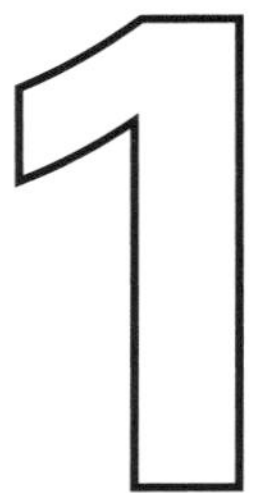

Electrickery

As Arthur C Clarke pointed out, any sufficiently advanced technology is indistinguishable from magic. Today we are surrounded by advanced technology in our daily lives so the trivial matter of a model railway locomotive moving doesn't warrant a second glance, but we need to understand what is going on in order to be able to make it work effectively.

For the moment I shall assume that we are looking at a standard 12V DC locomotive, it can be any scale or gauge. Inside there is an electric motor connected to the track. For the purpose of this exercise we will assume that there is a standard model railway controller connected to the track. If you have a DCC (Digital Command Control) controller and DCC equipped locomotive then the details are a little different, but the principle is the same.

As we turn the knob on the controller from OFF to MAXIMUM the motor in the locomotive will run faster and faster. When we turn the knob back to OFF the motor stops. If we then change the direction switch and move the knob again the motor runs in the opposite direction. This allows us to control the direction and speed of our model, but how does the magic actually work?

Each of the rails is connected to the controller. The wheels of the locomotive are electrically connected to the motor. With the locomotive standing on the track the controller is connected via the rails and wheels to the motor.

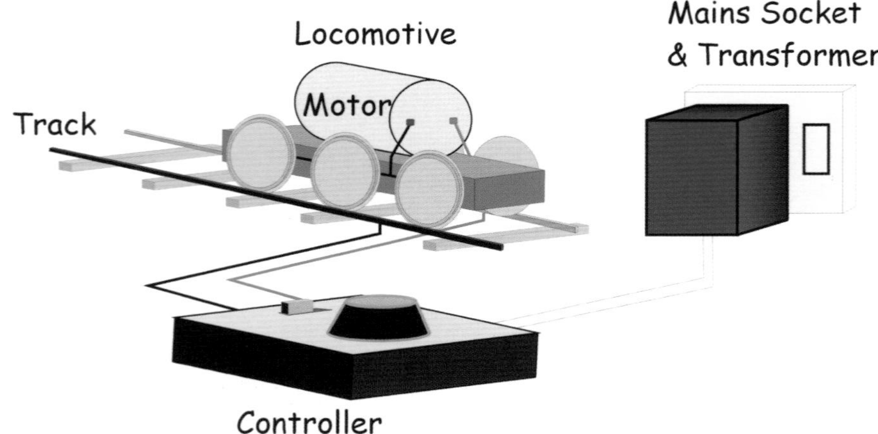

This diagram shows the electrical connections needed to make a model locomotive move. A transformer is plugged into a mains socket. The transformer converts the mains voltage electricity into something safer for us to use. The transformer powers the controller which has a knob to control the locomotive's speed and a switch to control its direction. Two wires from the controller run to the rails, one each side of the track. The locomotive has metal wheels that pick up electricity from the track and they, in turn, are connected to the locomotive's motor.

The controller puts a VOLTAGE across the two rails. This is what causes the motor to run. As the voltage increases from 0 (OFF) to 12 Volts (MAXIMUM) the motor goes faster. If we change the direction switch then the voltage is applied the other way around and goes from 0 (OFF) to -12 Volts (MAXIMUM – in reverse).

A convention has arisen that the locomotive will move forward if the right-hand rail is positive and backwards if it is negative. This ensures that if two locomotives are being run by one controller they will both travel in the same direction.

If you lift the locomotive travelling 'up the page' on the diagram off the track, turn it around and replace it, it will carry on moving 'up the page' So if we have a controller connected to an oval of track and we put two locomotives on the track they will both run clockwise, or anti-clockwise, at the same time.

DCC

With DCC things are a little more complicated. The controller puts a constant AC voltage on the track and adds a high frequency control signal to it. This signal is picked up by a special circuit, called a decoder, in the locomotive which controls the speed and direction of the motor. This allows you to control many different locomotives on the same piece of track.

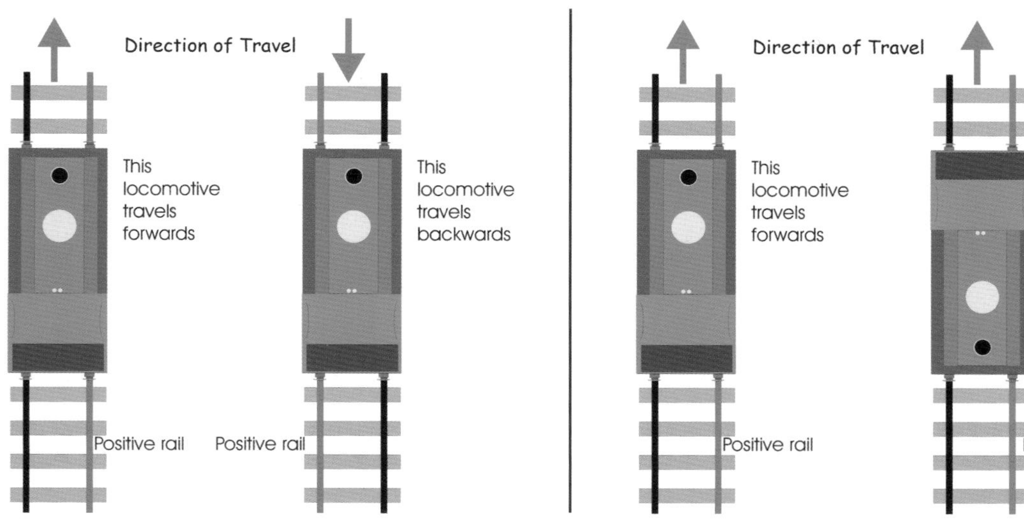

LEFT: *If you physically turn a locomotive around it will still carry on travelling in the same direction.*

ABOVE LEFT: *A moving locomotive always has the positive rail on the right. If you change the direction switch on the controller this will swap the positive connection to the other rail and the locomotive will change direction.*

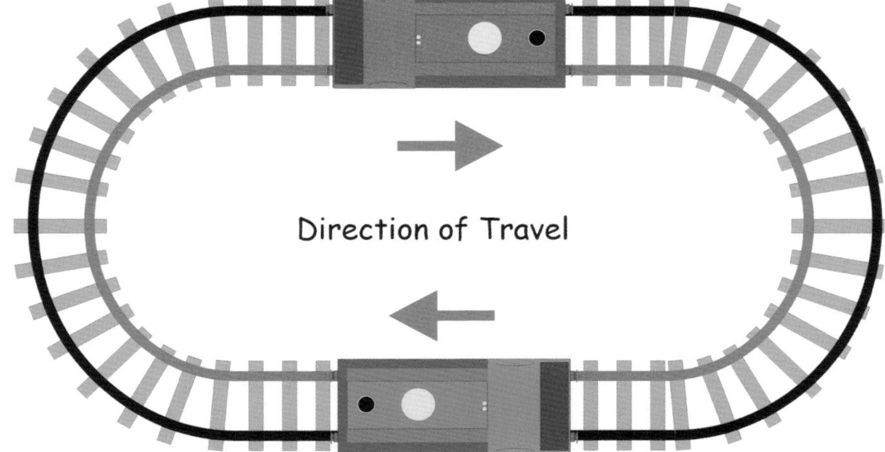

LEFT: *Two locomotives being controlled by one controller will always move in the same direction.*

Two (or more) locomotives

The problem with having two locomotives on the same track is that they both move at once and probably at different speeds. A common requirement on model railways is the ability to stop a locomotive responding to the controller. Users of DCC can skip the next section as they can control multiple locomotives independently on the same track, but for conventional controllers we need to use a switch. These are just like light switches, they can stop the electricity flowing to part of the layout and thus stop any locomotives on that section responding to the controller.

Let's assume we now have two ovals of track, with a locomotive on each. Both ovals are connected to the same controller and thus both locomotives run at the same time.

If we put a switch in the red wire leading to the right-hand oval we can have both trains running if the switch is on, or just the left-hand train running if the switch is off. If we were to put another switch in the red wire leading to the left-hand oval we could then choose to have either of the trains running on their own, both running at the same time or both stopped no matter how much we twiddle the controller's knob. This is called isolating and is the key to being able to have more than one locomotive on the rails at a time.

You only need to put a switch in one of the wires, not both. Breaking the electrical circuit at any point stops the electricity flowing. Whilst this has the

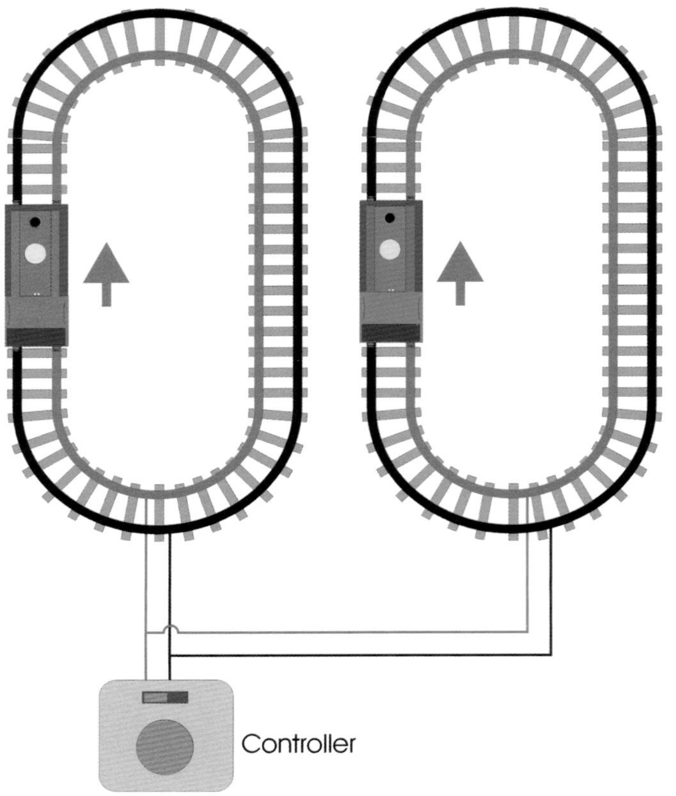

Locomotive does not move when the switch is off

On/Off Switch

Controller

Controller

Two ovals of track connected to the same controller. Both locomotives will run at the same time.

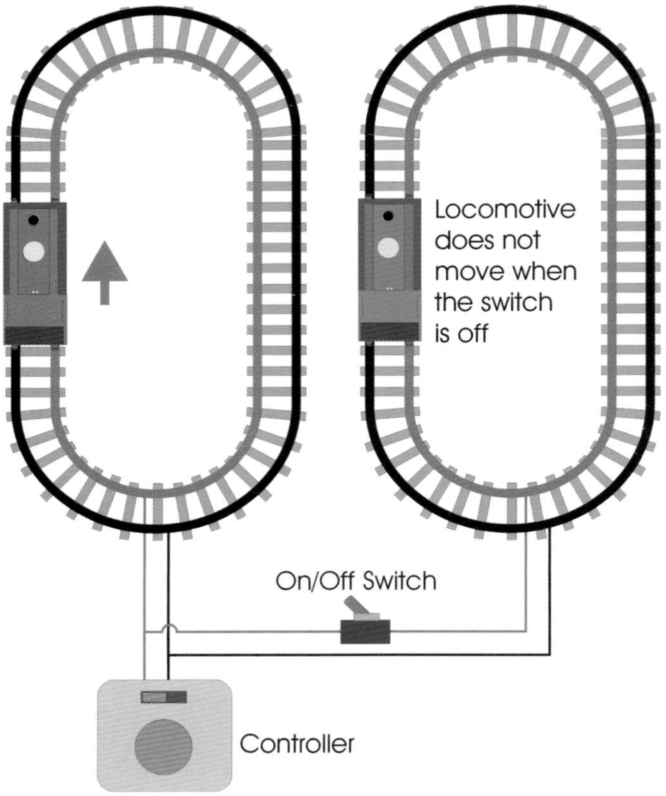

With an on/off switch in one of the wires we can stop one of the locomotives, regardless of the controller's setting.

advantage that it makes it easier to arrange isolated sections of track, the downside is that if any wire comes loose then something will stop working. This is why it is so important to keep the wiring neat, colour code it and keep notes of which wire does what.

So how do we make isolating sections? Imagine a layout made up of three straight sections of track. On one rail (the rail connected to the controller's black wire) we use metal rail joiners. On the other (the rail connected to the controller's red wire) we use plastic insulating rail joiners. We then connect one wire (the controller's black wire) to the black rail and three red wires, one to each length of track, to the red rail. The red wire from the middle section goes straight to the controller; the other two go through switches and then to the controller.

Let's start off with both switches off and a locomotive at each end of the track. Turn the controller up and nothing will happen as both locomotives are isolated.

Now turn switch A on and turn the controller up. The locomotive on the left will move and can run up and down the track. The locomotive on the right is still isolated and will not move.

With both locomotives on isolated sections of track neither will move regardless of how the controller is set.

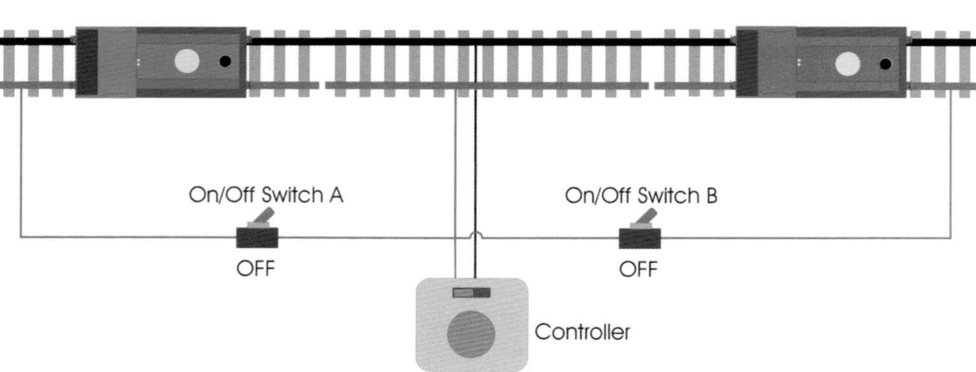

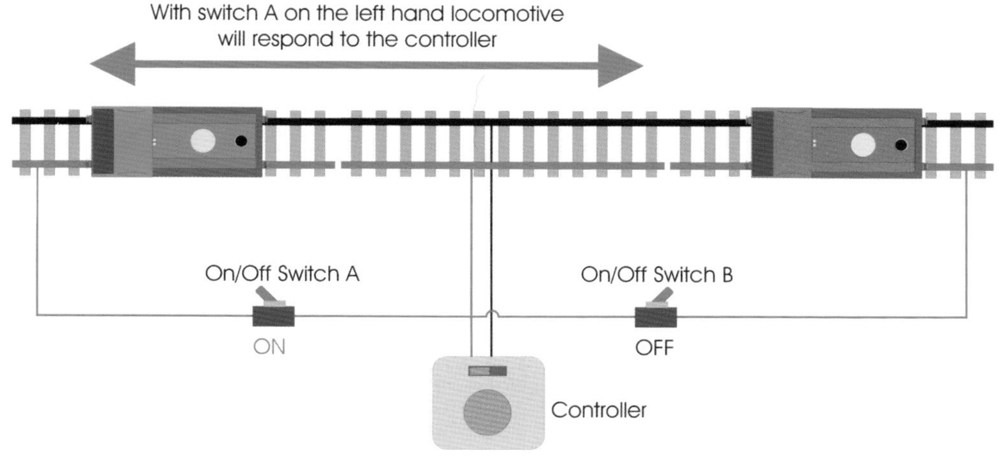

With switch A turned on, the left-hand locomotive will respond to the controller. The right-hand locomotive will remain stationary.

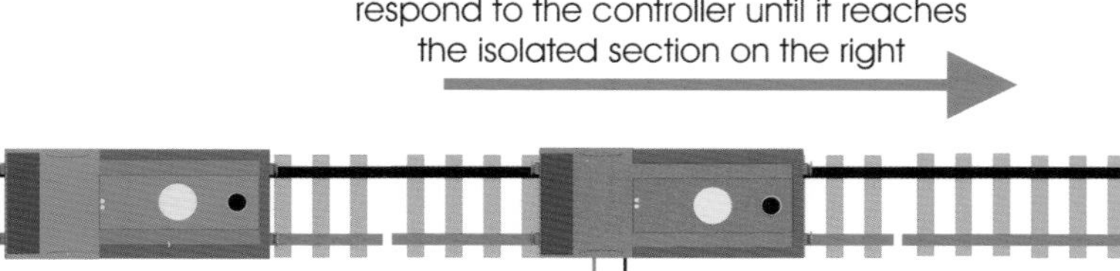

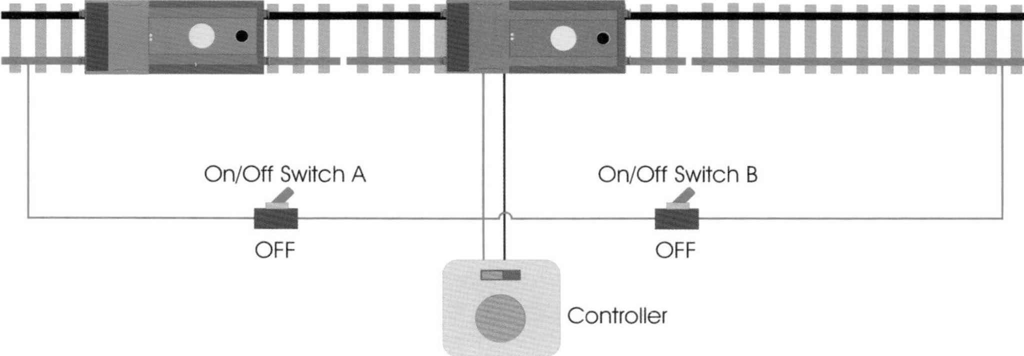

The red locomotive will stop when it reaches the isolated section on the right.

Return the locomotive to the left-hand end of the layout, turn switch A off and switch B on. The locomotive on the right will move and the one on the left is isolated.

If you turn switch B off whilst the locomotive is on the centre section of track it will still run until it reaches the isolated section. You can use this technique to automatically stop trains at the end of sidings – especially useful if you have hidden sidings on your layout.

What will happen if you run your locomotive into the isolated section on the left? As the first wheel of the moving locomotive enters the isolated section the locomotive bridges the gap between the two sections and electricity starts to flow in the isolated section. The left hand locomotive will start to move, in the same direction as the other locomotive. If the right-hand locomotive continues to run in to the isolated section both locomotives will continue to move until all its wheels are within the isolated section, at which point both locomotives will stop. This situation is best avoided as it is embarrassing and can lead to damage when a locomotive takes off unexpectedly.

Now, what happens if we make the track into an oval? The two isolating sections are now joined together and both switches need to be off to isolate the section. To make the isolating sections operate as before we need to add an extra insulating rail joiner in the red rail on the far side of the oval.

If we put two insulating joiners in the far side with the intention of being able to isolate the curves but always have power on the straights something strange happens. Our locomotive will always move in section 1, will move in section 2 if

Using switches and insulating rail joiners we can have two locomotives on the same oval of track and one or both of them moving.

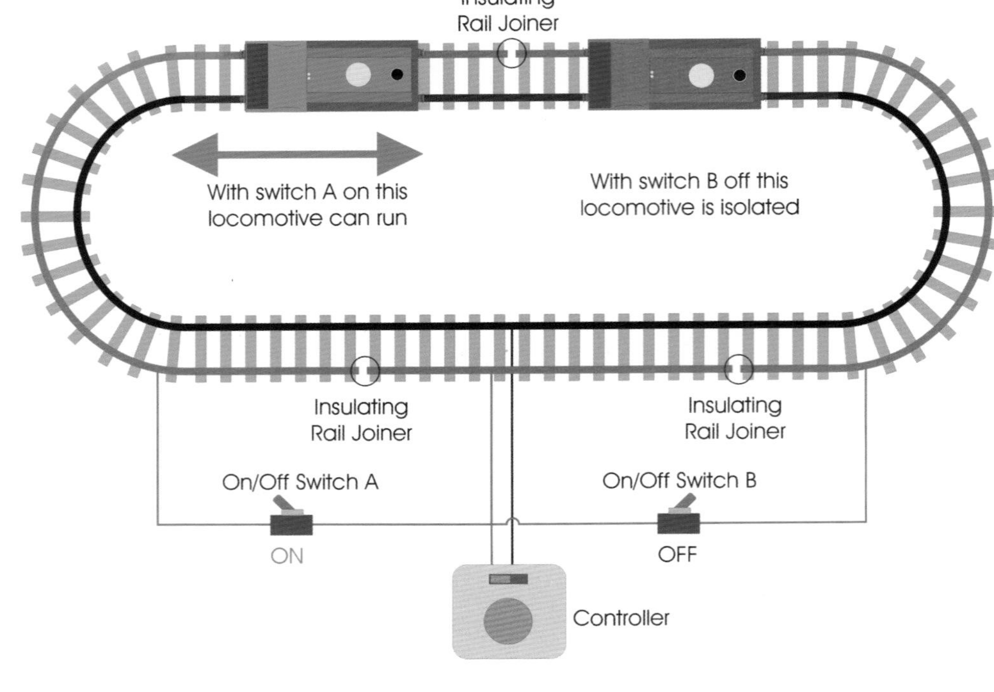

You should make sure that every section of track is connected to the controller otherwise, as at the top of the oval here, you will end up with somewhere that trains just will not run.

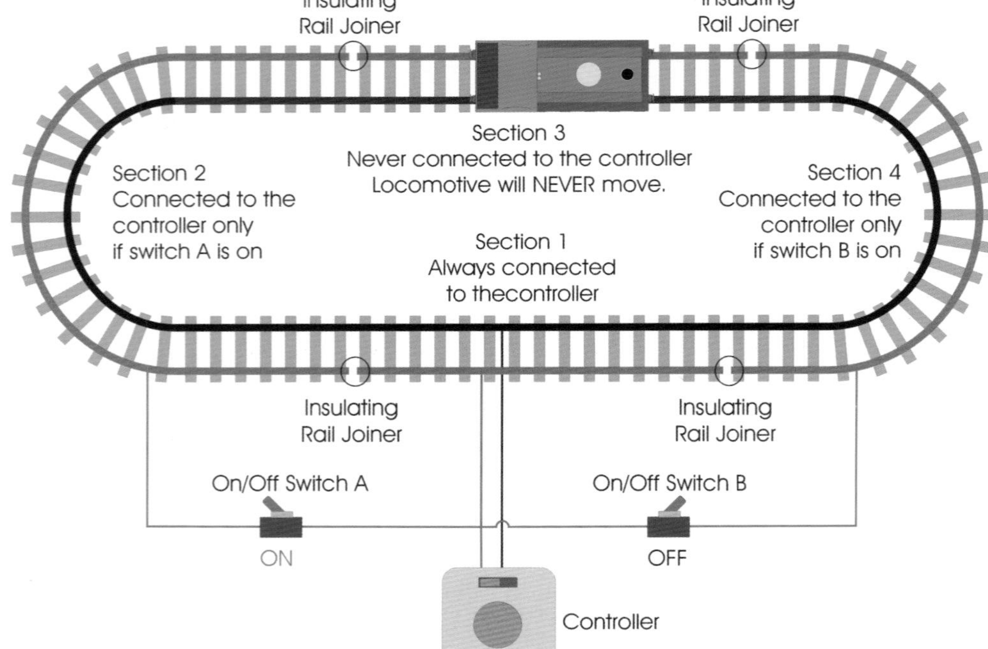

switch A is on, will move in section 4 if switch B is on but no matter what we do it will not move in section 3. Why? Because there is no way for electricity to get to the red rail in section 3. We need to connect an extra wire from the controller to the red rail in section 3 for it to work. Remember Rule 6: **Every length of rail, however long or short, needs to be connected to the controller.**

Every length of rail, however long or short, needs to be connected to the controller, either directly or via a switch, if you want to run a train on it. The connection can either be by a wire or by a metal rail joiner from another piece of track, but it must be connected.

To make wiring up as easy as possible always use the same rail for your isolating sections, the red rail. It doesn't matter which one you choose to be the red rail, but once you have chosen stick to it.

You should place isolating sections anywhere where you might need to park a locomotive on your layout. They should be at least as long as a locomotive – if they are shorter then the locomotive will pick up power from the adjacent powered section and move – regardless of how you set the switch.

These diagrams show how isolating sections are normally shown on a track plan. The top siding shows one method, a line representing a break in the red rail with a link to the powered section. The bottom siding shows how this would be wired. Note that the isolating section by the buffers is fed from the section next to it. This means that it can only be powered if both the switches are on. This is a useful feature in a locomotive depot as it stops unexpected movements if switches are accidentally left on.

If switch A is off then both the sections on the bottom siding are isolated regardless of how switch B is set. You could park a locomotive in each section.

If switch A is on and switch B is off the section of the bottom siding nearest the point is powered and the section nearest the buffers is not. A locomotive parked by the buffers will stay still whilst you can drive another locomotive into or out of the other section.

If both switches A and B are on then the whole siding is powered and you can drive a locomotive all the way along it.

Controllers

The controller is a key element in your layout – however simple or complex your system is, nothing is going to move very far without some sort of controller. Whilst various enhancements and improvements have been made to them over

BELOW LEFT: *Isolating sections shown on a track plan and, on the bottom siding, how they would actually be wired.*

BOTTOM LEFT: *If switch A is off then it doesn't matter if switch B is on or off, no power will get to the siding.*

BELOW RIGHT: *With switch A on a locomotive can travel halfway along the siding. With switch B off a locomotive could be isolated at the end of the siding.*

BOTTOM RIGHT: *With both switches on a locomotive can run right to the end of the siding.*

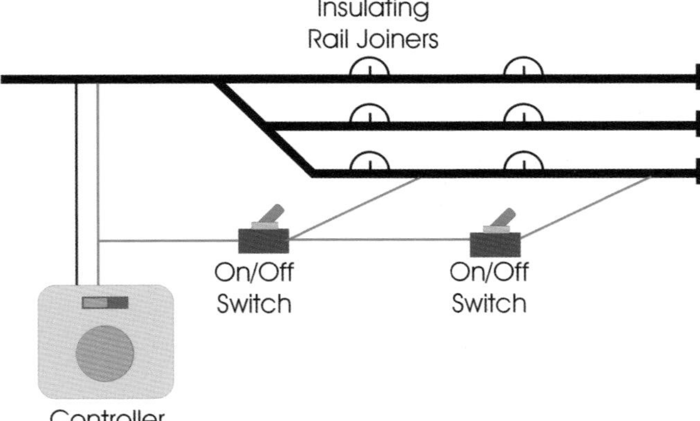

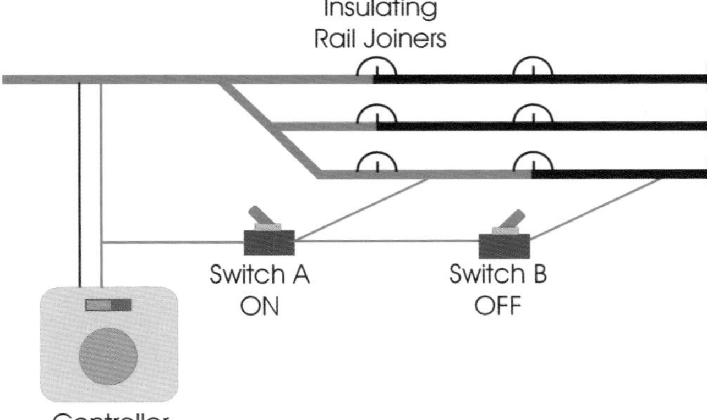

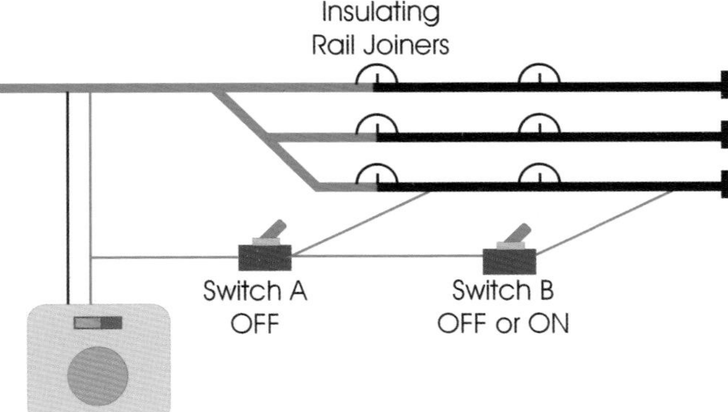

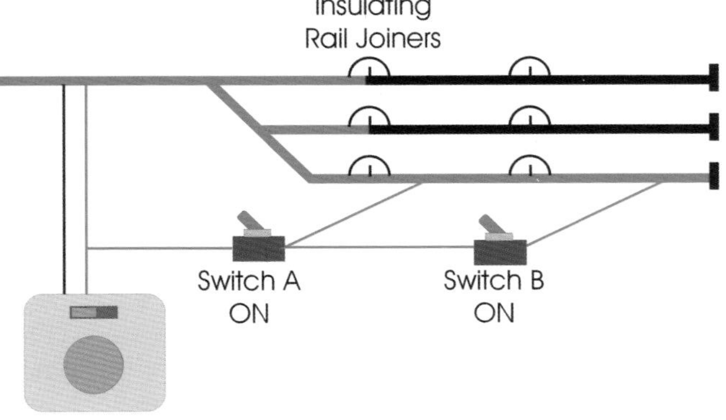

the years the typical controller of today looks remarkably similar to one of fifty years ago. There is a speed control, almost always a knob, and a direction control, usually a separate switch. There are two wires running to the track and a cable running to a mains plug. Over the years many different controllers have been produced by a variety of manufacturers and given that a controller can last for many years you will often find them available secondhand. This chapter gives a brief outline of the major types of controller that you may encounter.

Back in the mists of time controllers were either resistance or variable transformer types. The resistance controller was simply a large variable resistor, the higher the resistance the less of the voltage from the transformer was available to the train. The disadvantage of the resistance controller is that an electric motor at rest has a higher resistance than one in motion, so as soon as the motor starts its resistance drops significantly. With a resistance controller this means that the current flowing in the circuit suddenly increases, making the motor speed up. The practical upshot of this was that you needed to turn the controller up to start the locomotive and then immediately turn it down a little to stop the locomotive sprinting off. The variable transformer was more refined in that it varied the voltage from the transformer and so the 'startled rabbit' effect was reduced.

Both types of controller provided full-wave rectified DC (direct current). This was not the pure DC that you would get from a battery but a more 'lumpy' version (see diagram). This gave rise to the first form of pulse power which was known as half-wave – basically half the cycles were thrown away. This had the effect of providing jolts of power to push sticky motors around and roughly halved the track voltage for a given controller setting. This was very popular for shunting operations, despite the fact that it made motors run hot and noisily.

Many variable transformer controllers are still in use today. Hammant & Morgan (usually referred to as H&M) produced a range of metal cased controllers that were virtually indestructible and they can often be obtained cheaply on the secondhand market. The Clipper, Safety Minor and Duette are the most common and all have additional 16V AC and 12V DC outputs for powering

These diagrams show the different forms of electricity used by controllers:

This is pure DC (direct current). The voltage remains constant as time passes. This is the sort of voltage you get from a battery or some controllers.

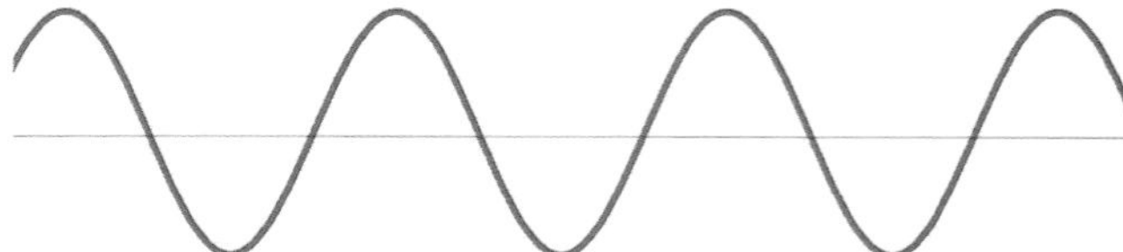

This is pure AC (alternating current). The voltage rises and falls as time passes. This is the sort of voltage you get from mains sockets. Above the line the voltage is positive, below it is negative. If you attempted to run a locomotive using AC it would just sit still as the motor jigged backwards and forwards until it heated up and burnt out.

This is full-wave rectified DC. The negative half of the AC cycle has been converted to a positive value giving a 'lumpy' version of DC. The voltage will vary between zero and the maximum set by the control knob. This should give an average voltage of about three-quarters the maximum value, around 12V for a 16V AC supply.

This is half-wave rectified DC. The negative half of the AC cycle has been thrown away giving jolts of power.

Somewhat battered, but still going strong, this H&M Safety Minor variable transformer controller is over 30 years old. The control knob is a centre-off type and the slide switch is to select half or full wave rectification.

other controllers and accessories.

In the late 1960s and early 1970s technology caught up with model railways and the first transistorised controllers were introduced. These use electronics rather than brute force to control the speed of a locomotive. The lighter components made hand-held units a possibility and with additional components the output could be made a smoother DC.

The transistorised controllers also enabled the introduction of inertia simulation or momentum. This is extra circuitry which imitates the way a real train behaves – the train accelerates or decelerates gently to the speed set on the controller. A variation on this is to have separate regulator and brake controls - to start the train the brake is off and the required speed is set on the regulator. The train accelerates until the correct speed is reached. If you increase the regulator setting the train will accelerate again. If you reduce the regulator setting there will be no immediate effect on the train's speed, it will decelerate very slowly. To slow or stop the train you need to put the brake on. The further on the brake goes, the faster the train will stop. Another variation is to have push buttons to accelerate and brake. You push the accelerate button until the train is going at your chosen speed and then press the brake button to slow down or stop. If you have an inertia simulation controller then an emergency stop button is a remarkably useful facility, it will enable you to stop the train dead if you have misjudged your speed or stopping distance.

Inertia simulation is best suited to layouts with a main line run. It can be difficult for shunting and most controllers provide the ability to turn it off and

Modern controllers, like this Bachmann example, are transistorised. Here the switch controls the direction and the knob controls speed.

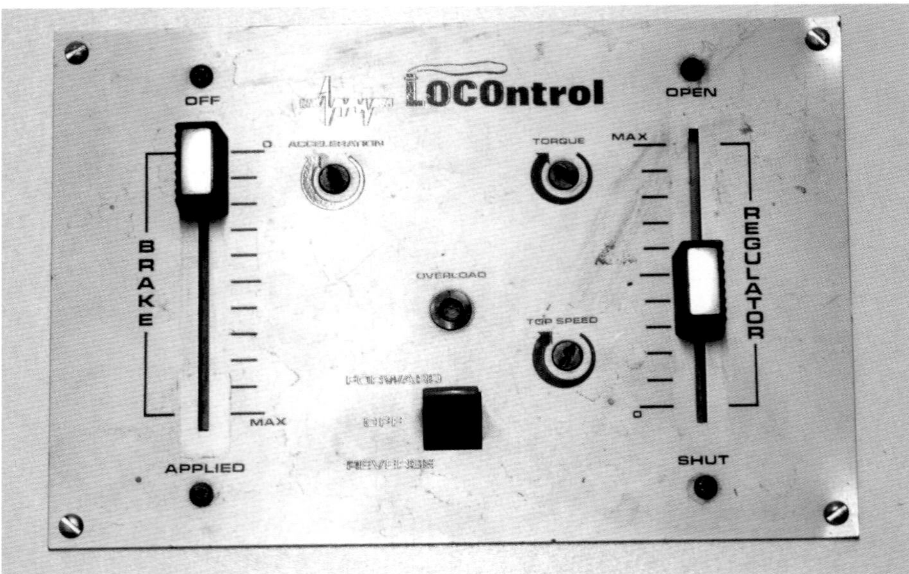

An early panel-mounted controller with inertia simulation. The regulator is on the right and the brake on the left. The direction switch has a centre off position and there are three small controls to set the throttle's characteristics – maximum speed, torque and acceleration rate.

have direct control of the locomotive's speed with the regulator knob.

Many controllers have a switch to control the direction of travel. Some have a centre off position which allows the track to be disconnected from the controller – useful for ensuring that nothing can be moved by accidentally knocking the speed control knob. Some, including the H&M variable transformer units have the direction control built into the speed control knob. The knob's centre position is off. Rotating the knob anti-clockwise from the centre increases the speed in one direction and clockwise increases it in the other. The variable transformer units have a click that you can feel in the off position, transistorised units that work in a similar way do not which can be very awkward if you are watching the locomotive rather than the controller.

Of course controllers with fancy features like inertia showed up the poor motors in many of the commercial locomotives of the time. The first attempt to compensate for this was another form of pulse power known as pulse width modulation (PWM). With a PWM controller the power is output in 12V pulses. The longer the pulse the faster the locomotive will go. The advantage of PWM is that it provides full power which overcomes any stickiness in the motor or gears. The disadvantage is that like half-wave rectification it makes the motor noisy and heats it up.

With transistorised pulse-power controllers you can add feedback to improve performance even more. These sense the speed at which the motor is turning and increase or decrease the size of the pulses to compensate. So if the motor speeds up, for example if the locomotive is going downhill, then the controller will decrease the power to keep the speed constant. Similarly if the motor slows down, for example due to muck in the gearbox, the controller will increase the power. A good feedback controller will enable a model locomotive to crawl along at remarkably slow speeds – certainly slower than a real locomotive could achieve.

Whatever type of controller you have it will be fitted with some form of cut-out. This is a device which turns the output off if you short circuit it. The usual reason for short-circuits is a derailment but anything from a screwdriver left across the rails to incorrect wiring can cause them and the cut-out will turn the power off before it can do much damage. Older units will probably have a thermal cut-out which is operated by the increased current heating a strip up which then bends and breaks the circuit. You will have to wait for the strip to cool down again before the controller will operate again. Transistorised controllers have electronic cut-outs that will reset as soon as the fault is cleared.

For wiring purposes it doesn't matter what sort of controller you have, all we are interested in is the two wires that run to the track. If you change your controller for a more sophisticated model it will not affect your layout wiring.

Two (or more) Controllers

CHAPTER

By using on/off switches we can isolate locomotives so that only one moves at a time. But what happens when we want to have two (or more) locomotives moving at once? Well, we need two (or more) controllers. The snag is that we can't just wire a number of controllers to the rails and let them fight it out between them – this would result in overload cut-outs tripping and quite possibly some expensive, short-lived fireworks. We can connect different controllers to separate isolated sections of track but that lacks flexibility and can lead to problems as trains pass from one controller's area to another. What we need are switches that can connect different controllers to different sections of track.

Common Return

Before we look at the switches, a word about controllers and common return. Common return is a method of wiring up a model railway that can save money on switches and wiring. Basically each controller's 'red' wire is connected to the 'red' rails on the layout via whatever switches you need. The 'black' wire of each controller is connected directly to the 'black' rails on the layout, thus the 'black' wires (the 'returns') are grouped together (in 'common') saving on wiring on the black side of the circuit. You don't need any rail breaks in the 'black' rails (except for reversing loops, live-frog points and other nasties that we will discuss later in the book) and you don't need any switches either. The only snag is that each controller must have its own mains plug. You cannot feed a number of controllers from one transformer and use common return wiring.

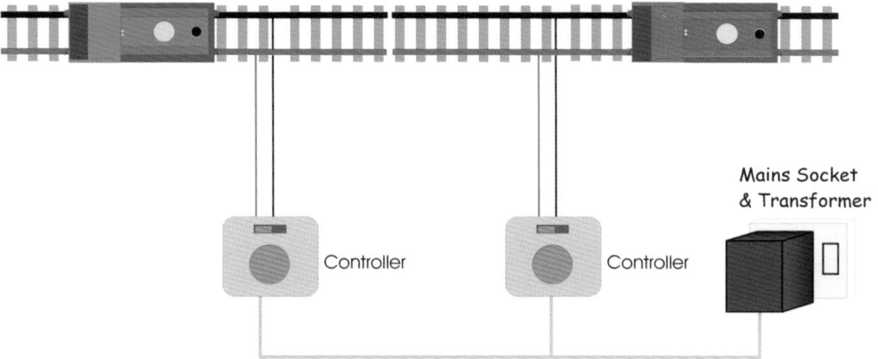

Independent controllers. Each electrical section is isolated by gaps in both the red and black rails. two controllers can share a transformer if necessary.

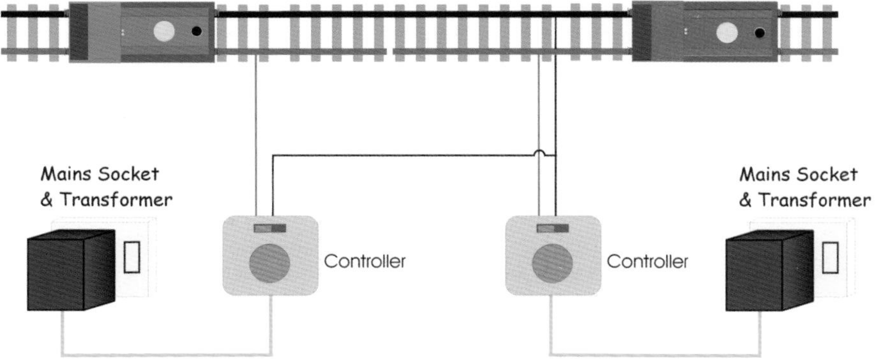

Common return wiring. Each electrical section is only isolated by gaps in the red rail. The black rail is common to all electrical sections. The controllers must each have their own transformer.

Circuit diagram for a SPST (single pole single throw) or on/off switch.

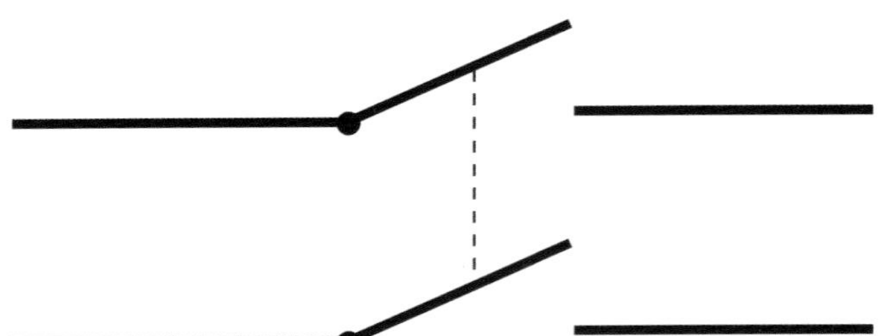

Circuit diagram for a DPST (double pole single throw) switch which can turn two independent circuits on or off at the same time.

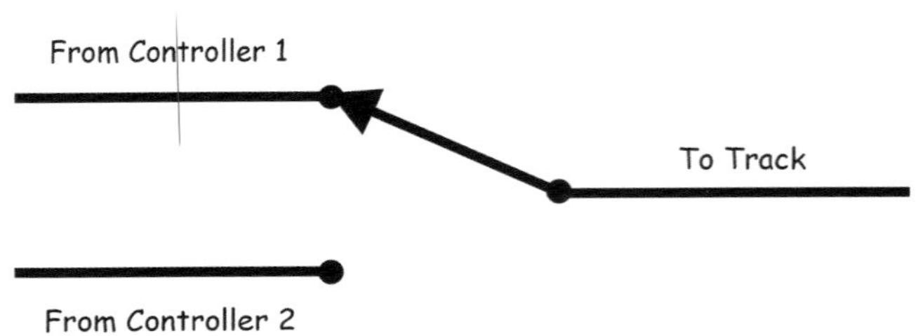

A SPDT (single pole double throw) or changeover switch allows you to select one of two controllers to be connected to an electrical section.

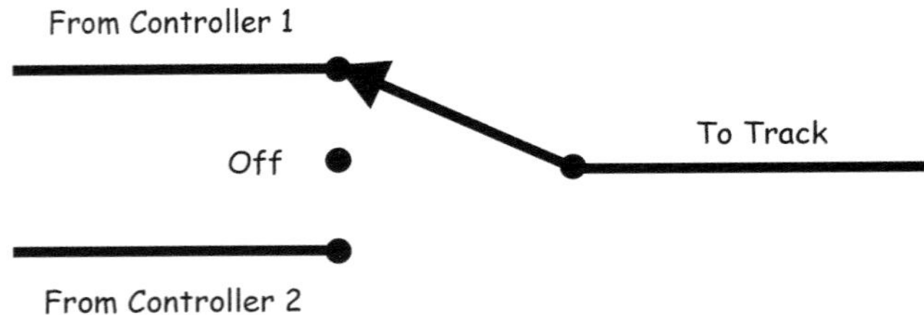

A SPDT c/off (single pole double throw centre off) switch allows you to select one of two controllers to be connected to an electrical section or disconnect both controllers so that the section is isolated.

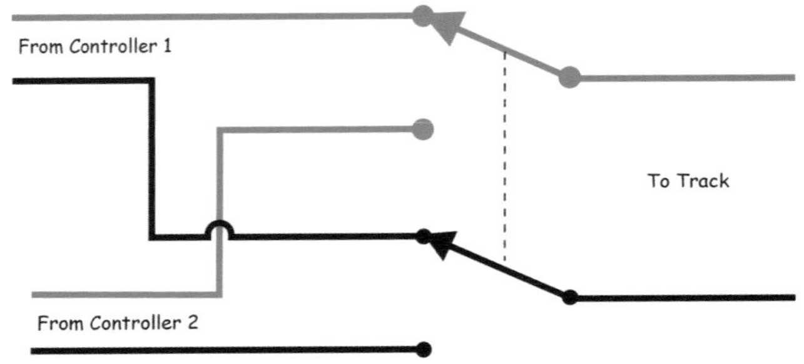

If you don't use common return wiring then you will need to use a DPDT switch in place of the SPDT switch shown in the previous diagrams.

Right, back to switches. In the previous chapter I introduced you to the 'on-off' switch which could be used to isolate a locomotive by cutting off the power. This is normally known as a 'single throw' switch, often abbreviated to ST. Where the switch only has contacts to turn one wire on or off it is called a 'single pole' switch, abbreviated to SP. Thus a single pole, single throw, or SPST, switch is a simple on-off switch. Where the switch has contacts that can turn two separate wires on or off at the same time it is called a 'double pole' switch, abbreviated to DP. Thus a DPST switch (double pole single throw) will turn two wires on or off at the same time. This type of switch could be used to illuminate a light on the control panel at the same time as it supplies power to the track.

You could use a number of SPST switches to select which of a number of controllers is connected to a section of track. Apart from the cost this would also leave the problem that it would be possible to connect a section of track to more than one controller at once.

Changeover switches, also known as 'double throw' (abbreviated to DT) allow you to connect a wire to one of two connections. These switches can be used to select which of two controllers are connected to a section of track. As a bonus they are also available in 'centre-off' versions which have a central 'off' position where the track is not connected to either controller.

If you do not use common return wiring then instead of a SPDT switch you will need to use a double pole double throw (DPDT) switch and wire the switch to both the red and black rails.

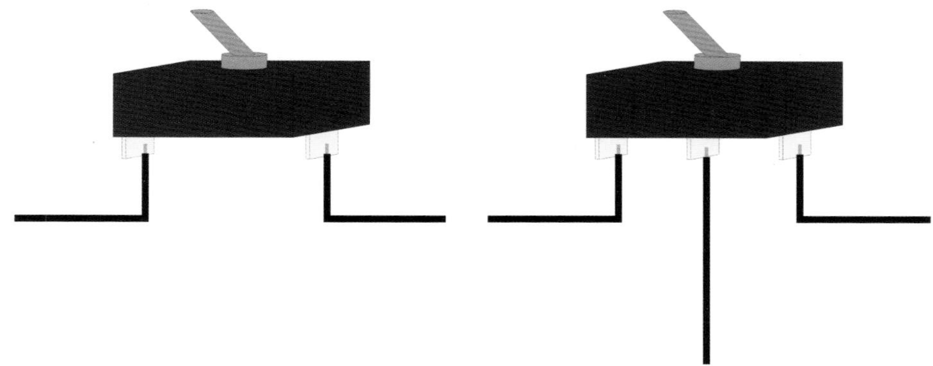

A SPST (on/off) toggle switch showing the electrical connections.

A SPDT (changeover) toggle switch showing the electrical connections. The centre terminal is connected to either the terminal on the left or the one on the right, depending on the position of the switch.

Switches come in various designs and sizes. The most common types used for model railways are toggle switches of various sizes and slide switches. Toggle switches are the easiest of the types to mount, they just need a suitably sized hole drilling in your control panel.

Two other types of switch that are commonly encountered on model railways are push buttons and rotary switches. Push buttons normally only allow current to pass whilst the button is actually being pressed. As soon as the button is released the contact is broken. These are useful for sections of track, such as the end of sidings, where you don't want power to be left on by accident and for operating things like point motos, where a short burst of current is all that is needed. Rotary switches allow multiple poles to be switched between multiple outputs. To change the switch you rotate a knob. Rotary switches come in a variety of configurations: 1 pole 12 way, 2 pole 6 way, 3 pole 4 way and 4 pole 3 way.

A selection of switches. From left to right: a 4-pole 3-way rotary, two toggle switches, two push buttons and a slide switch.

Points

Plain track is nice and simple, we just add feeds to the track to get power in and insulated rail joiners to stop it going where we don't want it. Unfortunately a layout that consists purely of plain track is of limited operational interest, to be able to shunt and swap trains you need points.

One problem with points is that the 'red' and 'black' powered rails can meet and, left to their own devices, this would cause a short circuit. A short circuit is where the electricity can find an easy way to get from the controller's 'red' terminal to the 'black' terminal without having to do any work, like powering an electric motor. This causes a big surge in the current flowing and will result in the controller's cut-out operating to switch the power off before anything gets damaged. There are two ways to approach this problem, which are covered in Chapter 4.

A Quick Guide To The Switches We Have Discussed

Abbreviation	*In Full*	*Number of contacts*	*Function*
SPST	Single Pole Single Throw	2	On/Off
SPDT	Single Pole Double Throw	3	Select between two controllers
SPDT c/off	Single Pole Double Throw Centre Off	3	Select between two controllers and also off
DPST	Double Pole Single Throw	4	On/Off for 2 separate wires
DPDT	Double Pole Double Throw	6	Select between two controllers when not using common return wiring
DPDT c/off	Double Pole Double Throw Centre Off	6	Select between two controllers and also off when not using common return wiring
PB	Momentary Push Button (Normally Open)	2	Allows current to flow only whilst the button is pressed
Rotary	Various configurations available. 1 pole 12 way 2 pole 6 way 3 pole 4 way 4 pole 3 way	Varies	Switch multiple poles between multiple connections.

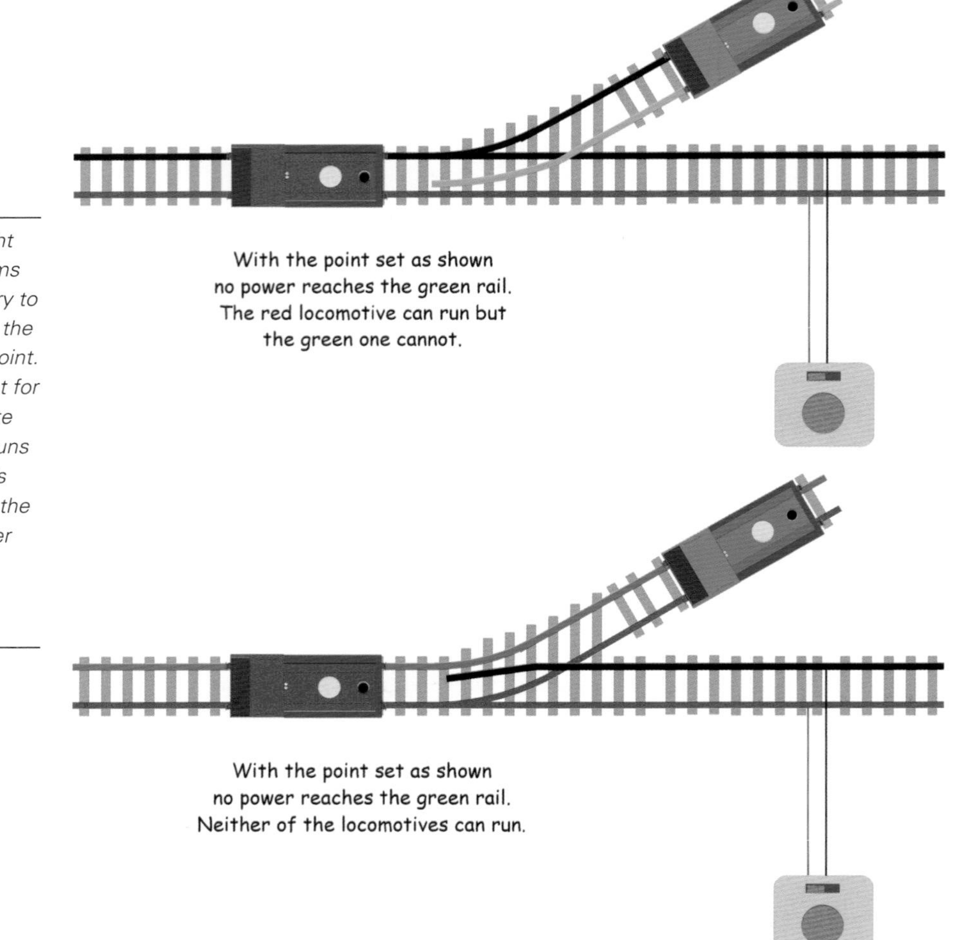

The diagrams right show the problems that arise if you try to feed power from the wrong end of a point. With the point set for the powered route one locomotive runs whilst the other is isolated but with the point set the other way both locomotives are isolated.

The other problem with points is that if you have a power feed on the exit from one side of the point, power can't reach the other exit. As a result you should always put feeds at the single-track (toe) end of a point so that both the exit tracks can be powered.

This need to feed power from the toe of a point can mean that you need to provide extra power feeds, depending on your track plan.

The easiest way to decide if you need an extra power feed is to apply what I call the Huskisson Test. Place, or imagine, a locomotive on the siding that you wish to test. Place a model figure over each of the power feeds. If the locomotive

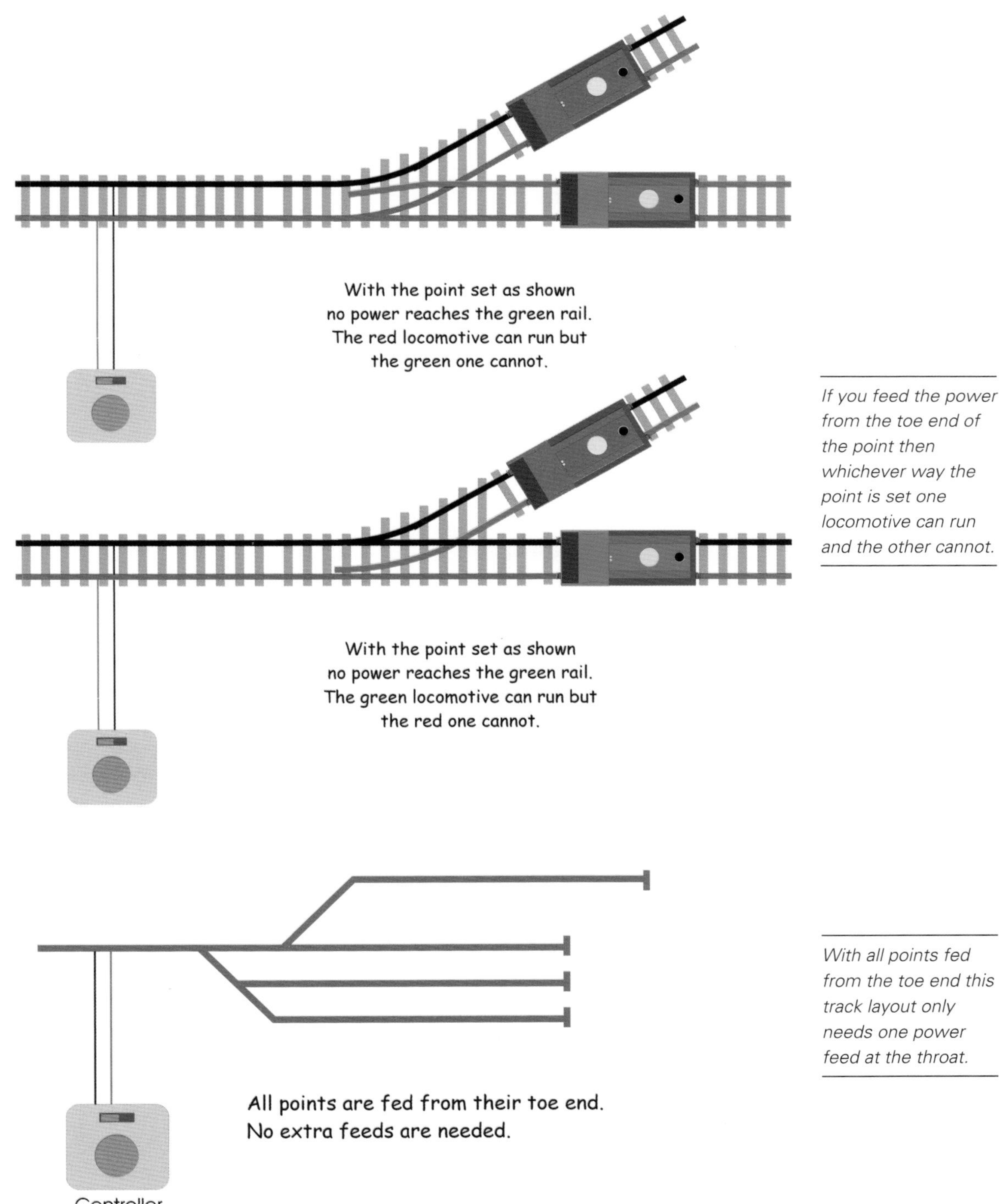

If you feed the power from the toe end of the point then whichever way the point is set one locomotive can run and the other cannot.

With all points fed from the toe end this track layout only needs one power feed at the throat.

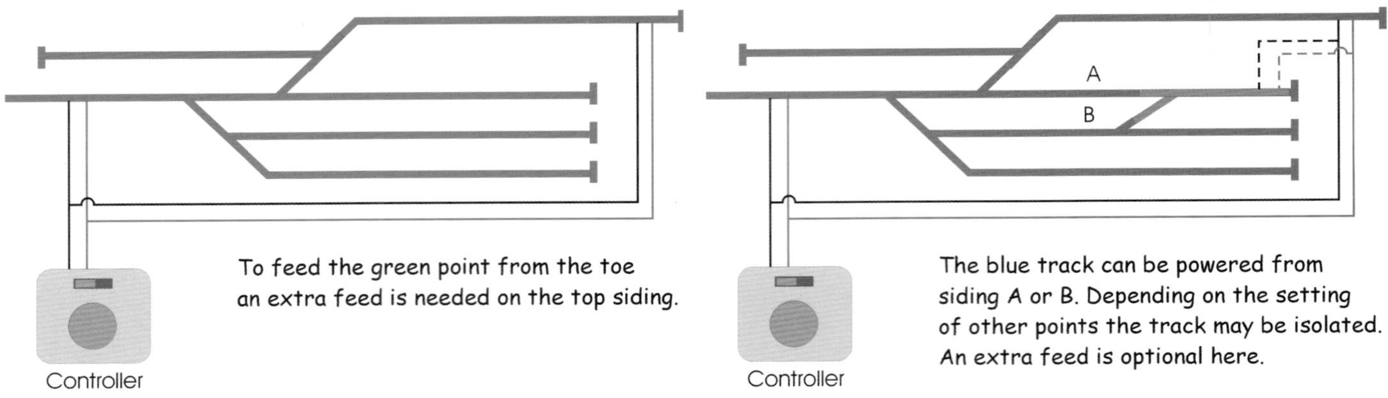

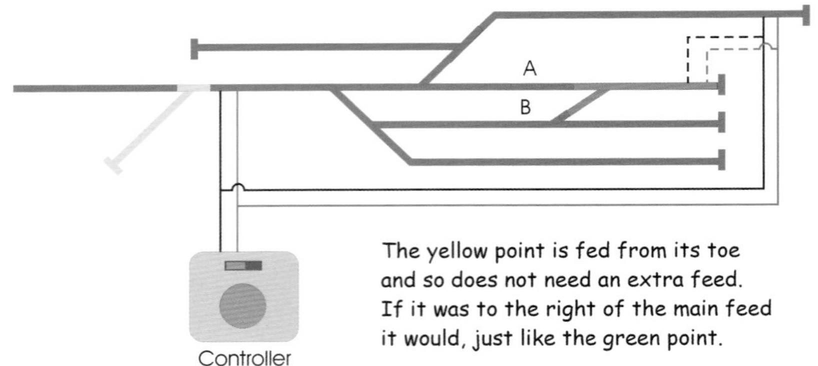

TOP LEFT: *The point marked in green that faces in the other direction needs an extra power feed.*

TOP RIGHT: *The point marked in blue can either be powered from its own feed or through sidings A and B.*

LEFT: *The point marked in yellow has its toe pointing towards the main power feed and thus is powered when set for either the main line or the siding.*

could run one of the figures over without changing direction then it will be powered, if it cannot then you need an extra feed. (The test is named after William Huskisson who died after being run over by a locomotive during the opening of the Liverpool and Manchester Railway in 1830.)

Reverse Loops

Reverse loops and their relation the wye are one of the nightmares of model railway wiring. For those using clockwork, live-steam, battery power or even old three-rail track they are not a problem and can be scattered about the layout like confetti, but for those of us who use conventional 2-rail wiring, both DC and DCC, they are a problem.

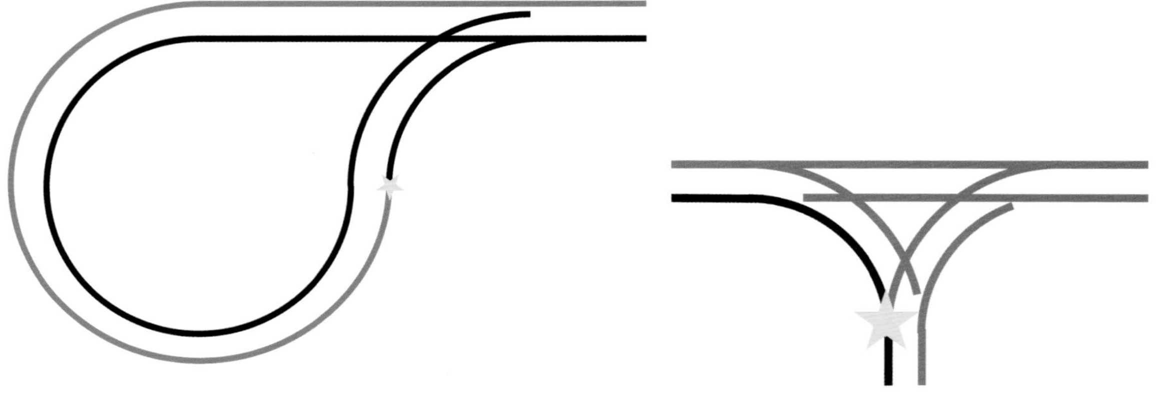

RIGHT: *A reverse loop always causes a short circuit when the black and red rails meet.*

FAR RIGHT: *Similarly a wye configuration will cause a short circuit on one leg.*

When you have a reverse loop or wye configuration no matter how you arrange things sooner or later a 'red' powered rail will meet a 'black' powered rail and cause a short circuit. Whilst placing insulated rail joiners somewhere on the loop will solve the short, you won't actually be able to run anything around the loop because as soon as a metal wheel crosses the join the short will reappear as the two sides are connected through the wheel or locomotive.

With DC controllers the normal solution is to feed the loop through a DPDT switch that can reverse the power connections to the rails. In operation you set the switch one way, run the train into the loop and stop, throw the switch, reverse the direction switch on the controller and then bring the train out of the other end of the loop. Your locomotive is now facing the other way when the controller is set to 'forwards'.

Some people use a switch linked to the point motor or point lever at the entrance to the loop to ensure that the power is set correctly for the direction chosen. This has the advantage that you won't get a sudden short if the power switch is set the wrong way for a train moving into or out of the loop, but can have an interesting effect if the point is changed whilst the train is in motion as the loco will suddenly change direction.

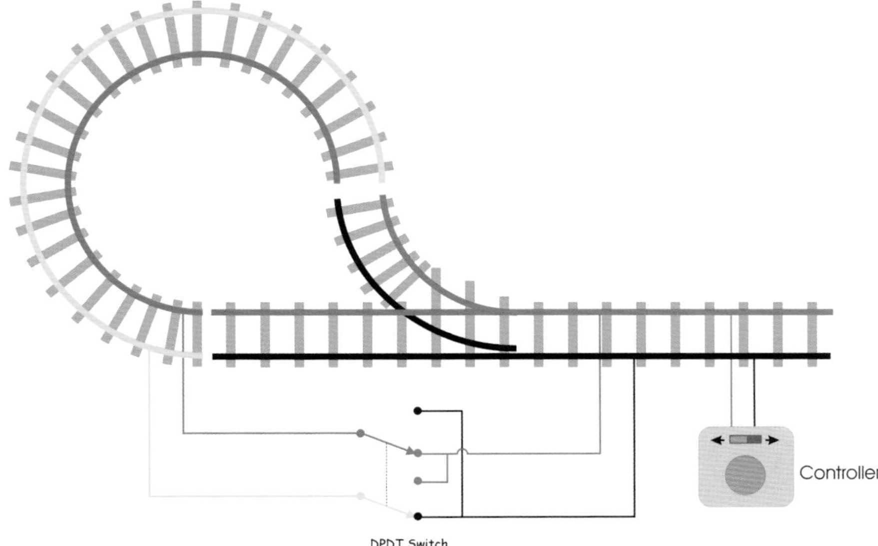

The reverse loop must be insulated on both rails at both ends, a total of four insulated rail joins. The insulated joins must be in the same place on both the black and red rail to avoid the possibility of short circuits. The power feeds for the reverse loop are connected to the rest of the layout through a DPDT (double-pole double-throw) switch.

DCC

The good news is that the switch method still works with DCC with the advantage that as locomotive direction is controlled by the on-board decoder your locomotive will still go forwards when you select forward on the controller. The disadvantage of using the switch system is that if you don't set it correctly you will get a short and, given the lack of switches needed with DCC it is easy to forget. If you are using sound decoders it is possible for the brief break in supply whilst you throw the switch to cause them to reset and you will need to turn the sound on again.

A far more elegant solution is offered by the automatic reverse loop units available from various manufacturers. You can use any manufacturer's reverse loop unit, regardless of which DCC controller you have. These are, in essence, specialised versions of the power district units.

When the reverse loop unit detects a short circuit instead of cutting the power it tries reversing the power connections, if the short circuit is still there then it cuts the power. This is achieved in a matter of thousandths of a second so the locomotive decoder doesn't notice that the interruption to the power supply. The decoder doesn't care which rail is 'red' or 'black' so carries on doing whatever it was doing before the power connections were reversed.

The practical upshot of this is that you can drive a locomotive into a reverse loop that is connected to an automatic reverse loop unit without worrying about which way a switch is set, throw the point with the locomotive still moving and exit from the loop without slowing down. Alternatively you could run into the loop and then reverse out. The reversing loop becomes just like any other length of track as far as operation is concerned.

To use the reverse loop you first set the point and the DPDT switch to the entrance position and then drive the train into the loop.

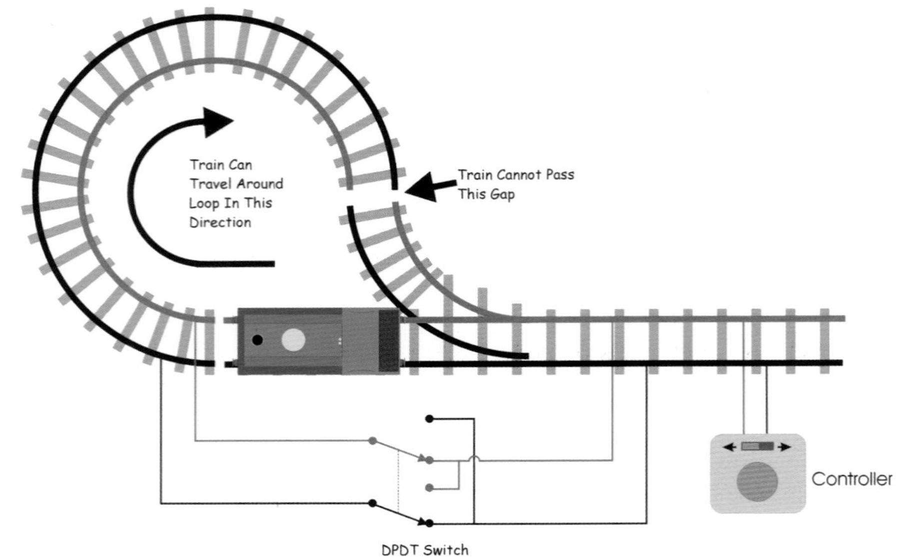

When the train is completely in the loop, stop the train and set the DPDT switch and point to the exit position.

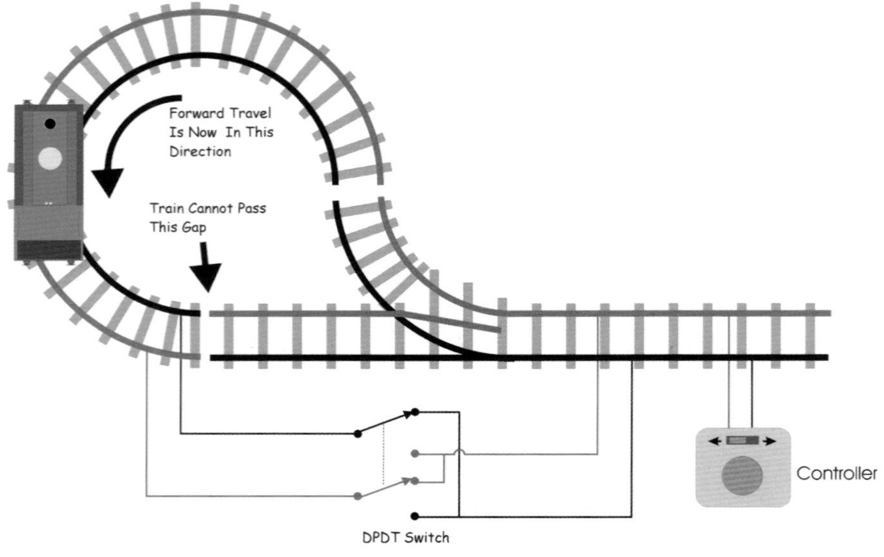

You can now reverse the direction switch on the controller and drive the train out of the loop.

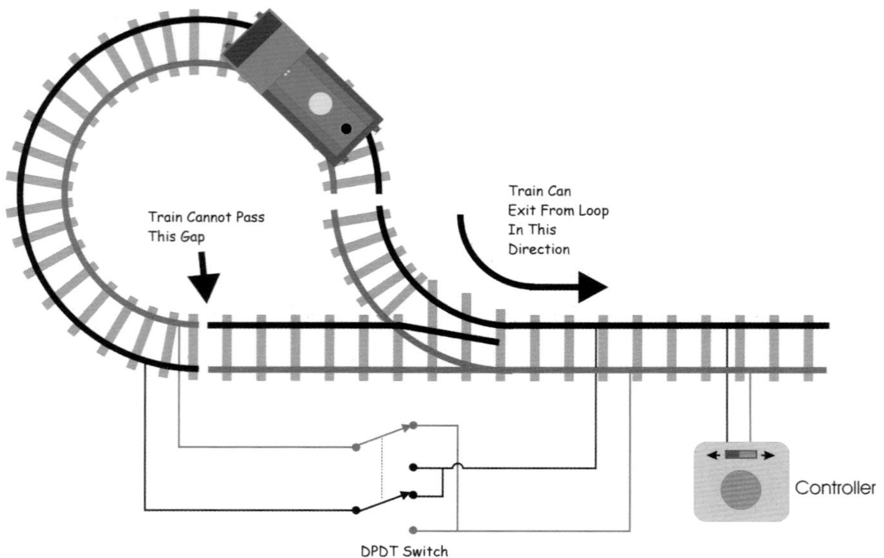

A Simple Example

So how does this work in practice?

Imagine the simple layout below. It has two separate ovals and a goods yard so it is possible that three locomotives could be running at once. Assuming that you are using common return wiring then by dividing the layout into ten sections, each fed from a SPDT c/off switch, you can operate three locomotives in a railway-like manner. By providing sections 1 and 5 trains can be held in the tunnel which represents the rest of the railway system. Section 9 allows a locomotive arriving in the goods yard to be isolated whilst section 10 serves the same purpose for the shunting locomotive.

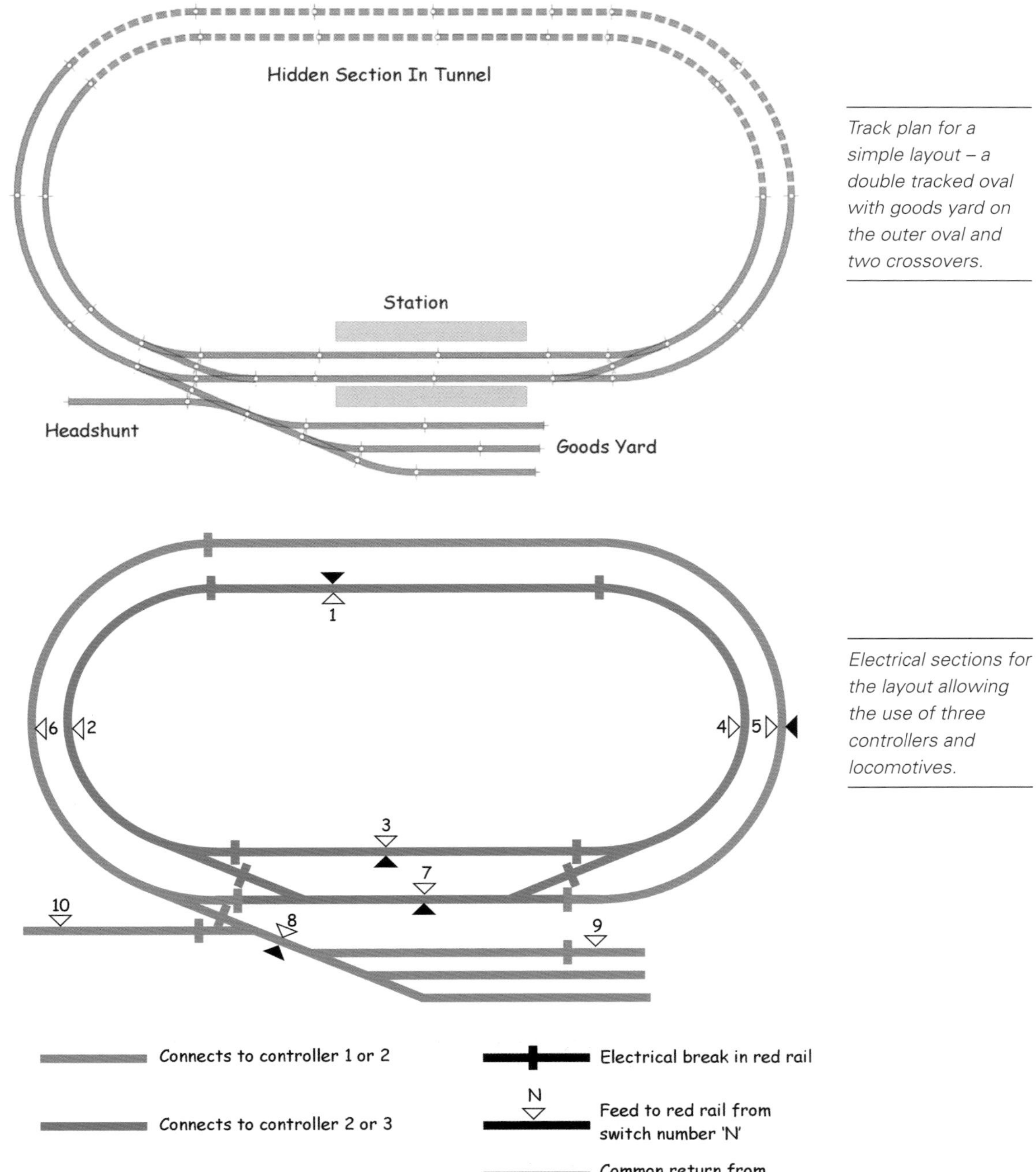

Track plan for a simple layout – a double tracked oval with goods yard on the outer oval and two crossovers.

Electrical sections for the layout allowing the use of three controllers and locomotives.

For normal operation the inner loop would be operated by controller 3, the outer loop by controller 2 and the goods yard by controller 1.

Imagine a clockwise freight ready to depart from the goods yard for a lap of the outer loop. The shunting loco would be isolated in the headshunt (section 10) and the goods yard switched over to controller 2 along with sections 5, 6 and 7.

Once the train has left the goods yard, switching sections 8, 9 and 10 to controller 1 allows the shunter to continue with its work.

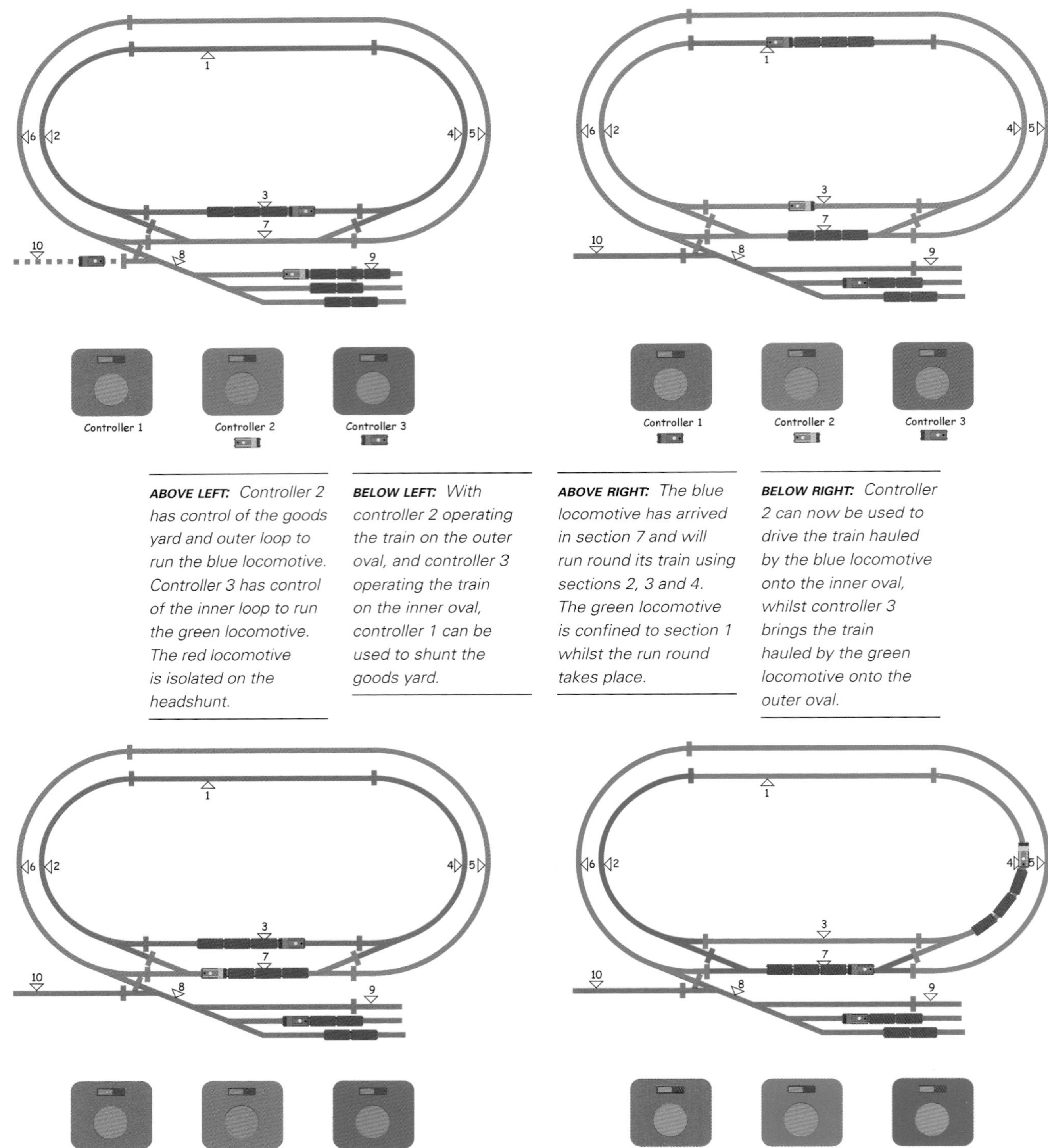

ABOVE LEFT: *Controller 2 has control of the goods yard and outer loop to run the blue locomotive. Controller 3 has control of the inner loop to run the green locomotive. The red locomotive is isolated on the headshunt.*

BELOW LEFT: *With controller 2 operating the train on the outer oval, and controller 3 operating the train on the inner oval, controller 1 can be used to shunt the goods yard.*

ABOVE RIGHT: *The blue locomotive has arrived in section 7 and will run round its train using sections 2, 3 and 4. The green locomotive is confined to section 1 whilst the run round takes place.*

BELOW RIGHT: *Controller 2 can now be used to drive the train hauled by the blue locomotive onto the inner oval, whilst controller 3 brings the train hauled by the green locomotive onto the outer oval.*

On arrival in section 7 the locomotive can run round its train using sections 2, 3, 4 and 7. The train on the inner loop could be isolated in section 1 whilst this takes place.

Controller 2 can now be used to drive its train onto the inner loop. Once it is clear of section 7 sections 2 and 7 can be switched to controller 3 and the train held in section 1 can then be driven onto the outer loop,

With both trains stationary the outer loop sections 5, 6 and 7 can be switched back to controller 2, giving it control of the green locomotive. The inner loop sections 1, 2, 3 and 4 can be switched to controller 3, giving that control of the blue locomotive. You will notice that the two controllers are now controlling different trains to the ones that they were operating earlier.

The red locomotive is then parked in the headshunt and isolated, after which the goods yard can be switched to controller 2 ready for the train on the outer loop to arrive.

Switching section 9 off will isolate the green locomotive and then switching section 10 on will give controller 2 control of the red locomotive to shunt the newly arrived train.

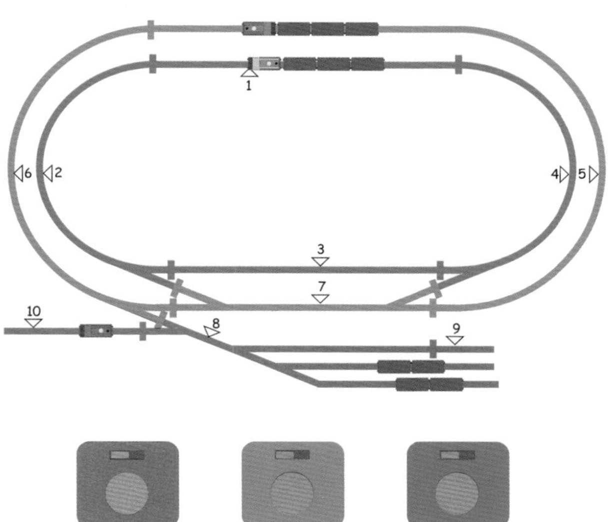

With a few switches we have transformed a simple train set type layout into an operable model railway. Now let's look at how to put the theory into practice, and first we need to look at wire. Wire is the key ingredient in wiring a layout. So far we have looked at what wire does, the things that you connect it to and what happens when you do, but not at the wire itself.

LEFT: *With both trains stationary the outer loop sections 5, 6 and 7 can be switched back to controller 2, giving it control of the green locomotive. The inner loop sections 1, 2, 3 and 4 can be switched to controller 3, giving that control of the blue locomotive.*

BELOW LEFT: *With the red locomotive isolated in the headshunt the goods yard can be switched to controller 2 for the green locomotive's train to arrive.*

BELOW RIGHT: *With the green locomotive isolated in section 9 the red locomotive can shunt its train.*

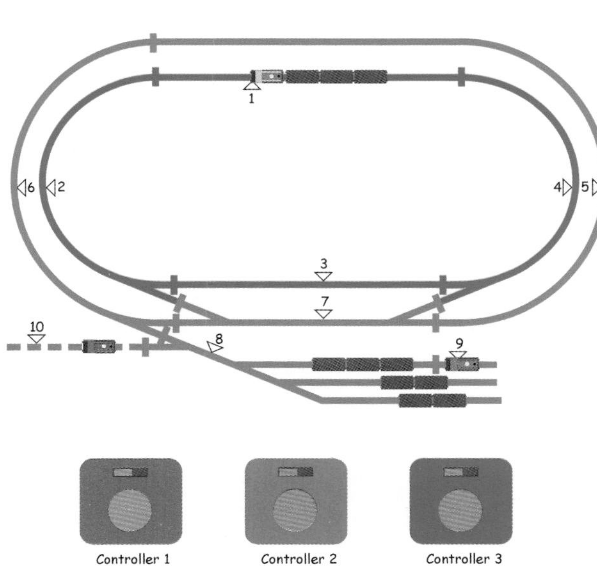

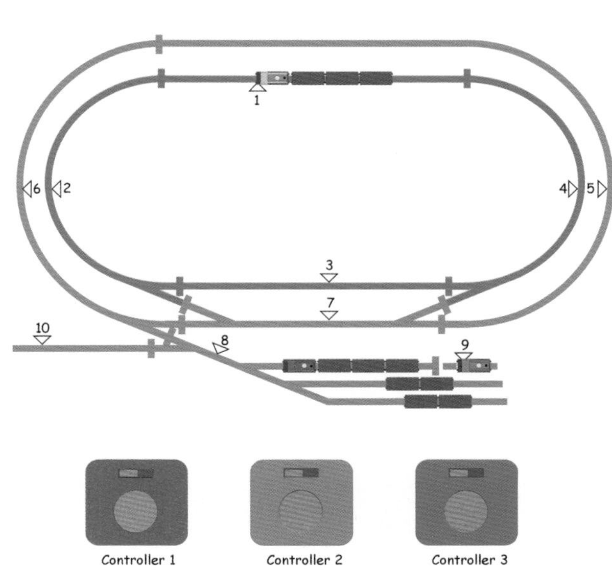

CHAPTER 3 The Basic Ingredients – Wire and Solder

Electrical wire comes in a bewildering variety of types, sizes and colours. Given a catalogue or internet store which lists hundreds of different sorts you could be forgiven for just picking one at random, on the basis that as long as it will carry electricity it will do the job. In fact the different types of wire are all for specific purposes and, as with any tool or material, choosing correctly will get the best out of your wiring.

The good news is that we don't need to use specially designed, and thus expensive, types of wire. We aren't carrying audio signals or computer data, we're not dealing with high voltages, large currents or long distances so we can use nice, simple, ordinary and cheap wire – typically called equipment wire. This consists of one or more copper wires inside an insulating plastic coat.
Our wire comes in two basic types: single core and multi-strand.

- Single core wire is a single copper wire. The advantages of single-core wire are that it keeps its shape when bent and is easy to solder to rails and terminals. The disadvantage is that if it is bent or moved a lot the copper wire will break leading to mysterious electrical failures.
- Multi-strand wire is made from a number of thin strands of copper wire twisted together. The advantage of multi-strand wire is that it can be bent and flexed without the copper wires breaking. The disadvantages are that it doesn't keep its shape when bent and it can be difficult to solder it neatly to rails.

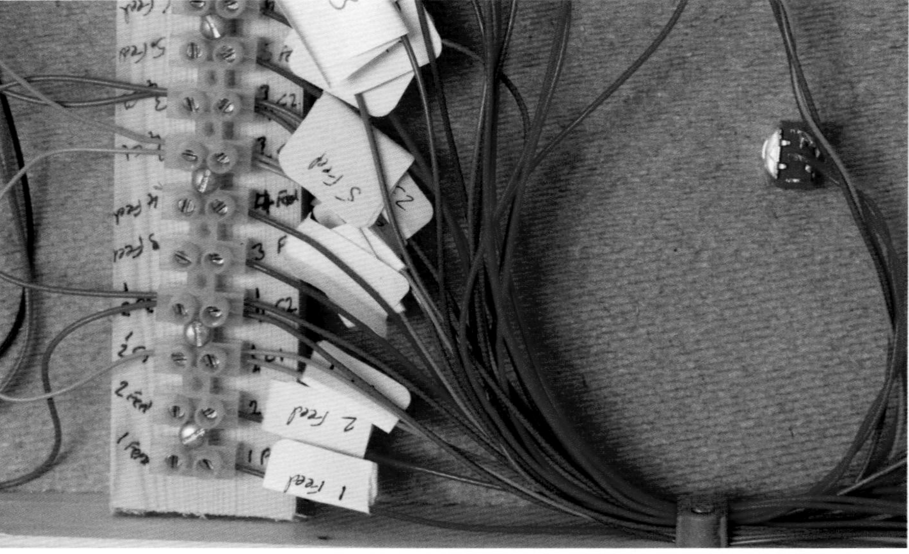

RIGHT: *In this chapter we unravel the mysteries of wire. Using different coloured wires for different purposes helps when it comes to fault-finding or altering things. Labelling the wires helps too. Keeping things orderly with cable clips, cable ties and staples helps to keep wires from getting caught up in things and possibly being pulled out.*

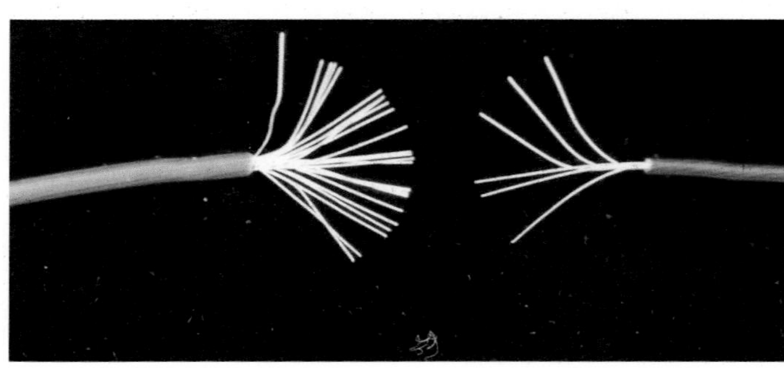

BELOW LEFT: *Two different types of multi-strand wire, on the left is 24/0.2 with 24 individual strands of wire inside the insulating coat, on the right is 7/0.2 with only 7 wires of the same size.*

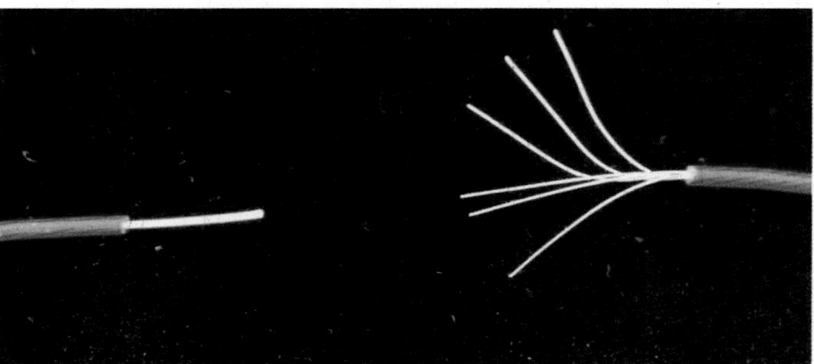

BELOW RIGHT: *On the left is some single core (1/0.6) wire compared to multi-strand (7/0.2) on the right. Despite both wires being 1.2mm in diameter on the outside the single core wire can carry a higher current as there is more copper inside the insulating coat.*

Single core wire is usually described in terms of its cross-sectional area, for example 0.6mm². Sometimes it is described using either Standard Wire Gauge (SWG) or American Wire Gauge (AWG).

Multi-core wire is usually described in terms of the number of strands and their cross-sectional area, for example 7/0.2mm² which is 7 strands, each of 0.2mm² cross-section.

Do not confuse multi-strand wire with multi-way cables. Multi-way indicates that there are a number of different individual wires encased in an outer sheath. A mains lead is an example of a multi-way cable, having three multi-strand wires, each encased in its own coloured coat, all within an outer sheath.

The larger the wire (bigger cross-section or more strands), the more current it can carry. This is important if you are powering solenoid point motors or a DCC layout with many locomotives in use. It is also advisable to use thicker wire on long runs between the control panel and the track or point motor. Over long runs the wire's own resistance means that the voltage at the far end drops a little. Using a thicker wire reduces this tendency. For our purposes a long run is anything above about 12′ (4m).

Typical wire sizes:

Type	*Designation*	*Overall diameter (including insulation)*	*Max. current*
Multi-strand	10/0.1	1.1mm	0.5A
Multi-strand	7/0.2	1.2mm	1.4A
Multi-strand	16/0.2	1.6mm	3.0A
Multi-strand	24/0.2	2.3mm	4.5A
Multi-strand	32/0.2	2.6mm	6.0A
Single core	1/0.6 (22AWG, 23SWG)	1.2mm	1.8A

These wires are available in a variety of colours as well as striped versions which enable your wiring to be colour-coded. This will help you when you need to modify the wiring or trace a fault.

Typical uses:

Solenoid point motors – short run	16/0.2
Solenoid point motors – long run or powered by capacitor discharge unit	24/0.2
Solenoid point motors – long run and powered by capacitor discharge unit	32/0.2
DC track feed – short run with modern N or OO locomotives	7/0.2
DC track feed – short run with O or older OO locomotives	16/0.2
DC track feed – long run with modern N or OO locomotives	16/0.2
DC track feed – long run with O or older OO locomotives	24/0.2
DC common return – small to medium layout	24/0.2
DC common return – medium to large layout	32/0.2
DCC track bus – 3A booster	16/0.2
DCC track bus – 5A booster	24/0.2
LED or low-voltage bulbs	7/0.2

Single-core wire has the advantage that it keeps its shape when bent. This can be very useful but the drawback is that you cannot use it anywhere where the wire might be subjected to regular movement.

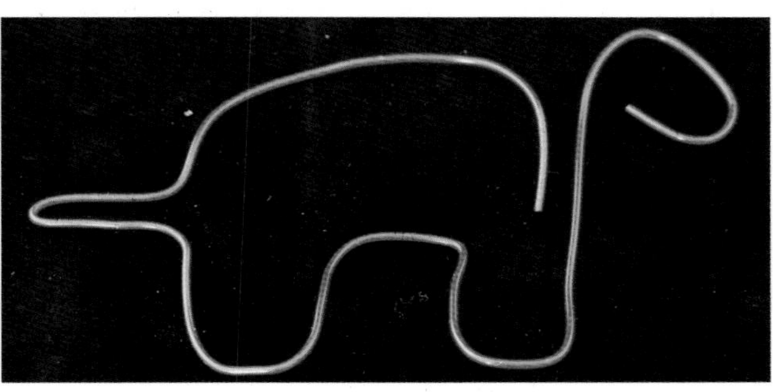

Single core wire is best used inside control panels and for the last few inches connecting a track feed to the track. Solder a few inches of single core wire to the rails, drop it through a hole in the baseboard to a terminal and connect it to a length of multi-strand cable for the run to the control panel.

For wiring inside locomotives thin multi-strand wire is available from suppliers like Express Models. This five-

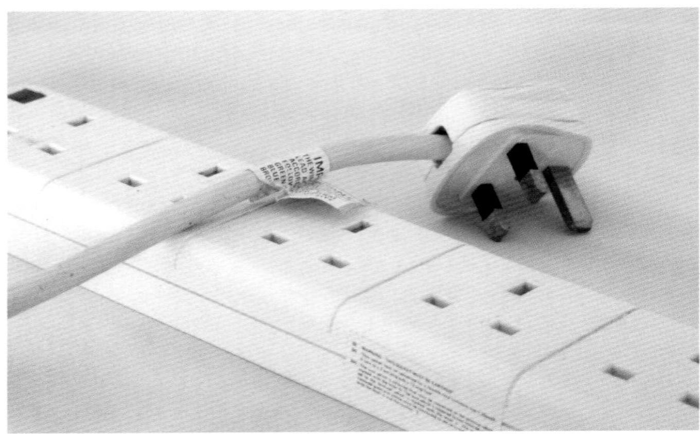

Wire comes in a wide variety of colours, which makes it easy to colour-code your layout wiring. It also comes on reels, very useful as even a small layout can use up a lot of wire.

However tempting it is, don't use mains wires or fittings for your layout wiring. Connecting your layout wiring to the mains could have fatal consequences – and I don't want to lose any readers!

strand wire is only 0.6mm in diameter, including the insulation and is sufficiently thin and flexible to fit in and around the inside of a model.

Suitable wire is available from specialist model railway suppliers such as AllComponents as well as general electronic suppliers such as Maplin or Rapid Electronics. It is well worth buying a reel of each of the colours that you intend to use as even a modest layout will swallow a surprisingly large amount of wire.

One last word of advice: never use mains cable (or connectors). Apart from the difficulties that come with its size, there is always the chance that someone will confuse the model mains wiring with real mains wiring and connect one to the other – with potentially fatal results.

Soldering

Now you need to learn how to solder. This is a means of making electrical connections that is vital if you are to progress beyond the rather ugly terminal clips used to connect controllers to train sets. Soldering model railway wiring is not difficult; it is a skill that can be mastered quickly.

The Tools

You will need a soldering iron, typically an 18 or 25 Watt electric one. These can be obtained cheaply from electronics retailers such as Maplin Electronics, some model railway suppliers and specialists such as Brewsters. Purchase a stand with your iron, do not be tempted to try and save money by using a mug or something equally unsuitable as a holder – it will end with something getting burnt – probably you.

You will need some electrical solder. This looks like thick wire and comes in various thicknesses. Try and buy a large reel of thin solder, that way you shouldn't run out in the middle of a job and won't have difficulty soldering closely spaced contacts on small switches. Suitable solder can be purchased from the same place as your soldering iron. The reel illustrated is 500g of 20 SWG (0.9mm diameter) solder.

You will cut and strip a lot of wires when you build a model railway so a set of good wire strippers is a wise investment. Again, they can be purchased from your soldering iron supplier. Do not attempt to strip the insulation from small wires using a knife. Apart from the obvious risk of injuring yourself you will almost certainly damage the wire, possibly leading to a mysterious failure later.

The final ingredients are a good light and a work-surface that will stand up to a bit of abuse, an off-cut of melamine-coated shelving is ideal.

The Golden Rules of Soldering

The three key elements to a good soldered joint are:

- Cleanliness
- Heat
- No movement

Tools for soldering: wire strippers, solder, electric soldering iron and stand, a good light and a work surface.

Cleanliness really is next to godliness as far as soldering is concerned. Freshly stripped wire and newly purchased switches should be okay, but anything that has been around for a while, or used before needs a quick rub down with some wet and dry paper or a glass-fibre pencil.

Heat is vital. The molten solder will not flow over cold metal so you need to make sure that both the items that you intend to join are heated up by the soldering iron. If you are joining really big bits of metal, you'll need a powerful iron but for wires, switches and most model rails 25 Watts should be sufficient.

No movement. If the wire moves whilst the solder is solidifying then you will need to solder the joint again. Even if the joint looks good, it may be weak inside and could fail leading to one of those mysterious, intermittent problems that are very difficult to solve.

How To Solder

The process itself is simple and with a little practice you'll be able to make a good joint nearly every time.

The first step in a soldered joint is to make a good mechanical joint. Here a wire has been looped through the tag on a switch.

Step1. Make a good mechanical join. When joining a wire to a switch there is a tag that it can be looped through or around. If you are joining two wires they can be twisted together. For a wire to rail join you are reliant on the wire being held in position whilst you solder the join so you will probably need a weight or clamp close to, but not on, the join to stop the wire moving.

Step 2. Ensure that the items being soldered are not going to move. Blu-tack is a remarkably useful tool in this respect and will hold both switches and wires in place. Be warned that it doesn't like getting hot, so make sure that it is well out of the way of the soldering iron.

Step 3. Make sure that the bit on your soldering iron is up to temperature and clean. Your soldering iron stand should have a damp sponge or similar that you can wipe the bit on to ensure that there is no grot on it.

Step 4. Place the bit so that it heats both of the parts to be joined. If you heat one but not the other the solder will not flow properly and you will get a bad joint, if you get one at all.

The soldering iron bit is touching, and heating, both the wire and the switch. The solder is in my other hand ready to be applied to the join.

Step 5. After a few seconds the join should be hot enough to apply the solder. Continue holding the soldering iron in place and with your other hand feed some solder onto the join by the tip of the iron. It should melt and flow freely. If the solder does not melt, but forms a ball then the join is not hot enough. If the solder melts but only flows freely on one part of the join then it has not been heated evenly. When sufficient solder has melted to make a good join you can remove both the solder and then the iron. The solder will then start to solidify.

Step 6. Wipe the soldering iron on the sponge and then put it back in its stand. Examine the join and make sure that it looks smooth and even – if it is lumpy then it wasn't hot enough. If you need to remake the join then do so, you'll need to add a little bit more solder to get some more flux on the join.

Depending on what you have joined and where it is going to be used you may want to cover the joint with some heat-shrink tubing to insulate it from the rest of the world, this will stop any accidental short circuits in the future. Heat-shrink tubing can be obtained from electronic suppliers and is cut to length, slipped over the join and shrunk by holding the thick section of the soldering iron bit close to it.

Three wires soldered to a toggle switch. The switch is now ready to be installed in a control panel.

Wiring The Control Panel and Track

CHAPTER

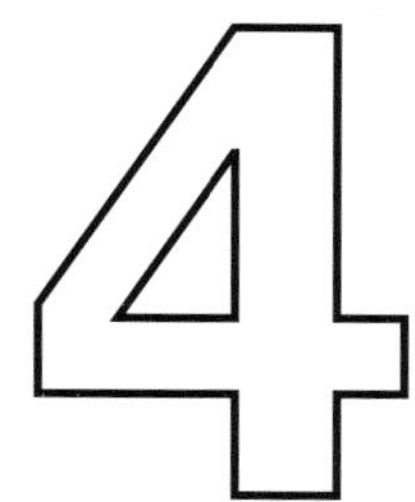

Model railway wiring looks complex. This is because there can be hundreds of wires underneath a medium-sized layout. The key thing to remember is that it is the same few simple circuits repeated many times.

Our simple layout from chapter 3 will serve as an example of how to wire a layout. It uses four simple circuits, and two of those are the same circuit, just connected to different things.

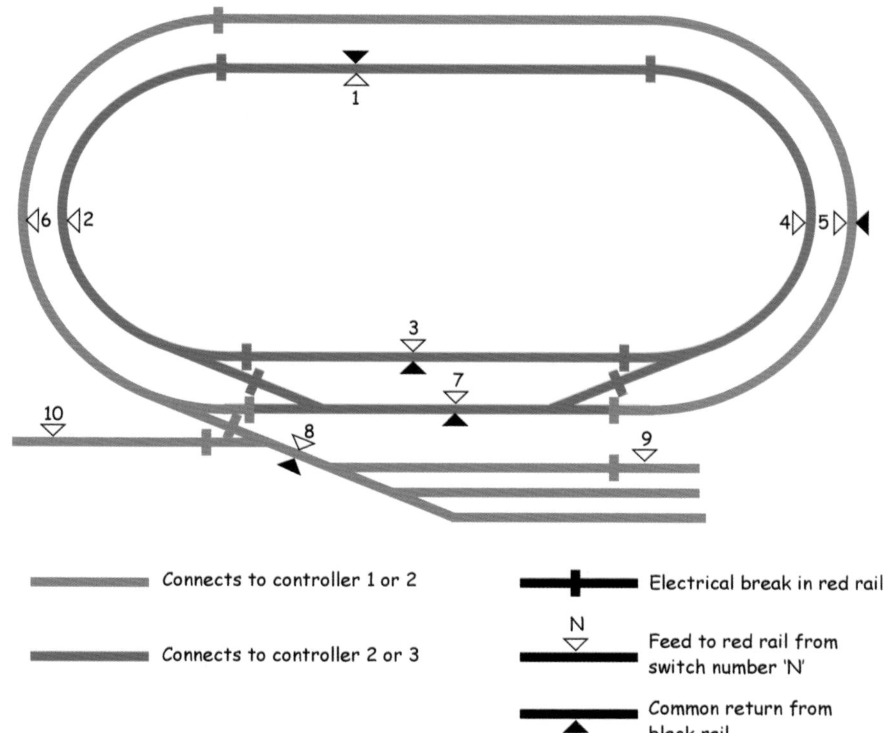

Our simple layout from chapter 2 will serve as an example of how to wire a layout.

Compiling The Circuit Diagram

Switches 1, 2, 3, 4 and 7 use a SPDT centre off switch connected to controllers 2 and 3 with the centre tag going to the red rail of the track section it controls.

Switches 5, 6 and 8 use the same circuit, but connected to controllers 1 and 2.

Switches 9 and 10 are just on/off (SPST) switches connected between the feed for the red rail of section 8 and the red rail of the track section they control.

The diagrams show the individual circuits and what it looks like when you combine all the switches on one circuit diagram.

Building The Control Panel

To build the control panel I first cut a piece of white faced hardboard 24″ x 12″ and glued and pined lengths of 1¼″ x ¾″ timber along three sides on the back. I also fixed a length of timber on its side along the centre on the back.

Turning the control panel over I drew a schematic layout diagram on the front in pencil. This does not have to be to scale, it just needs to be clear and leave sufficient space between the tracks so that you can mount and operate the switches. I used a track spacing of about 1″. While I was at it I cut out an opening for one of the controllers, an elderly panel mounting unit.

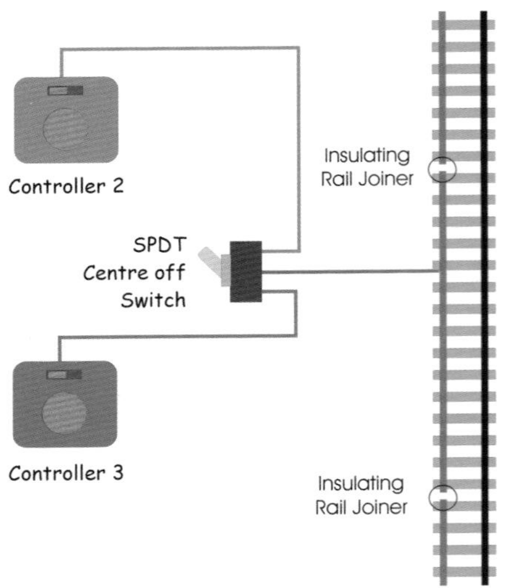

The top section of the diagram shows how sections 1, 2, 3, 4 and 7 are physically connected up. The bottom section shows how this is represented on a circuit diagram.

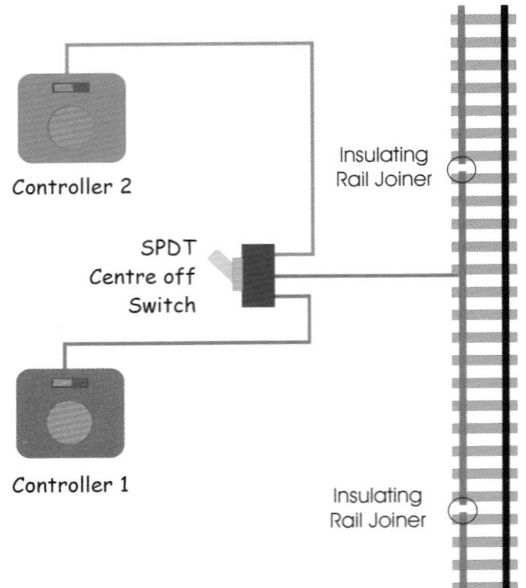

Switches 5, 6 and 8 use the same circuit, but connected to controllers 1 and 2.

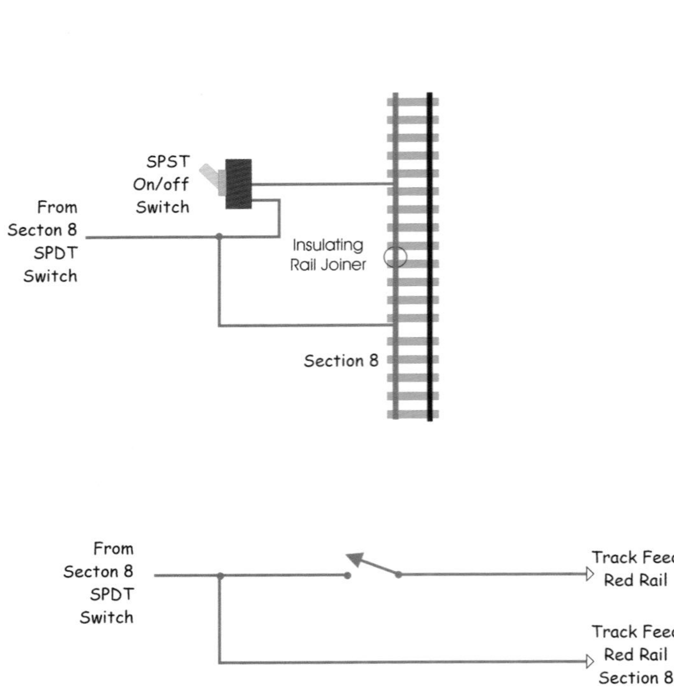

The two places where locomotives are isolated in the goods yard have simple on/off (SPST) switches connected to the goods yard's electrical section.

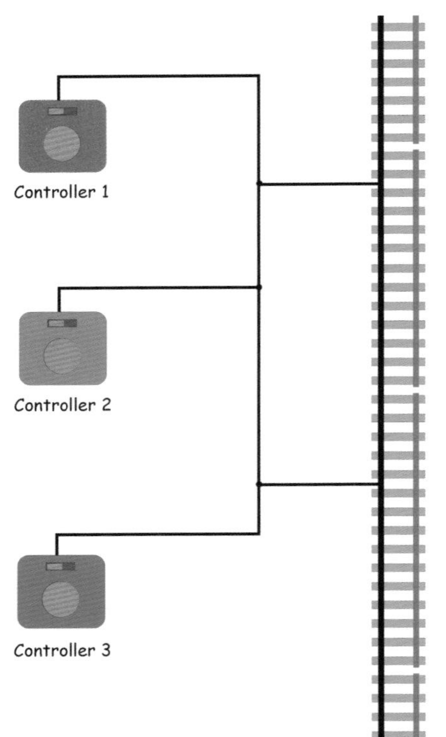

With the common return system all the black rail feeds and the black wires from each controller are connected together.

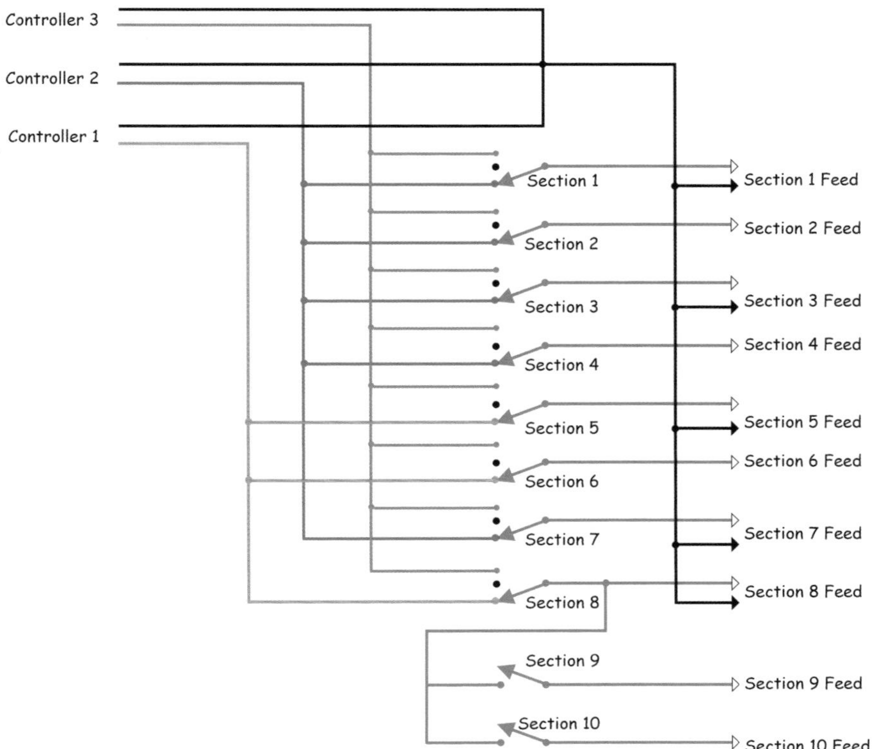

Combining the circuits for all the sections results in what appears to be a complicated circuit diagram, but it is just the individual circuits we have already seen repeated a number of times.

The layout diagram was drawn out in pencil in schematic form on the front of the panel.

Car lining tape was stuck down over the pencil lines.

I used car lining tape, which I purchased from Halfords, to create the lines for the control panel. This self-adhesive tape is laid covering the pencil lines and can be cut with a craft or Stanley knife. Once the tape was all in position I moved on to drilling holes for the switches.

I drilled $\frac{1}{4}$" holes for the toggle switches that I was using. The holes were drilled roughly in the middle of each section of track. The holes were then cleaned up with a knife ready for the switches to be fitted.

All ten switches had the necessary wires soldered in place as a batch job. The wires were cut well over-length. I adopted a simple colour code for the wires on the control panel as follows:

- Wires going to section track feeds – Red
- Wires coming from controller 1 – Yellow
- Wires coming from controller 2 – Blue
- Wires coming from controller 3 – Green
- Common return wires – Black

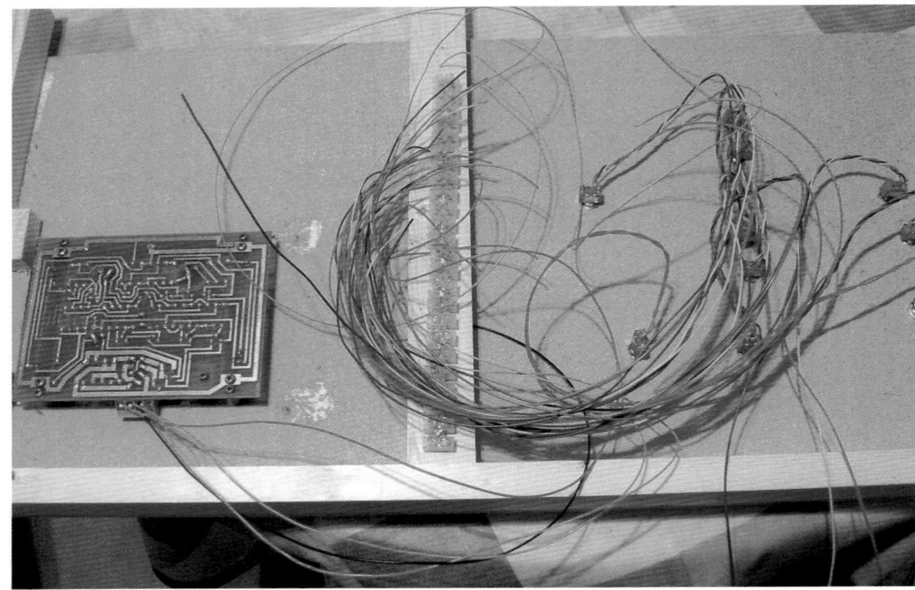

The toggle switches had wires soldered in place before mounting on the control panel. The wires were trimmed to length as they were connected up.

It is far more economical to buy colours that you will use a lot of, such as red and black, by the 100m reel rather than in shorter lengths. Even a small model railway can eat up a lot of wire.

I screwed down two lengths of 5A terminal blocks to the centre timber strip. This is where the bulk of the wiring will take place. Each of the switch wires was connected to a terminal. The wire was cut to length, stripped, labelled and then the terminal screwed tight. The labels identified each wire using a simple code:

e.g. **1 C2** indicates section 1, feed from Controller 2
2 Feed indicates section 2, red track **Feed**

To reduce the number of terminal blocks I needed I ran two wires to each of the controller feeds. So the feed from controller 3 goes to a terminal that feeds switches 1 and 2, then on to one that feeds switches 3 and 4 and finally on to one that feeds switch 7.

With all the wires from the switches to the terminal block in place I nailed down two cable clips to keep them neat and started daisy-chaining the wires on the controller side of the block. Starting with the blue feed from controller 2 this

Each wire should be labelled to identify it. This will make fault-finding and any later changes a lot easier.

The terminal block was wired up in stages, testing as I went.

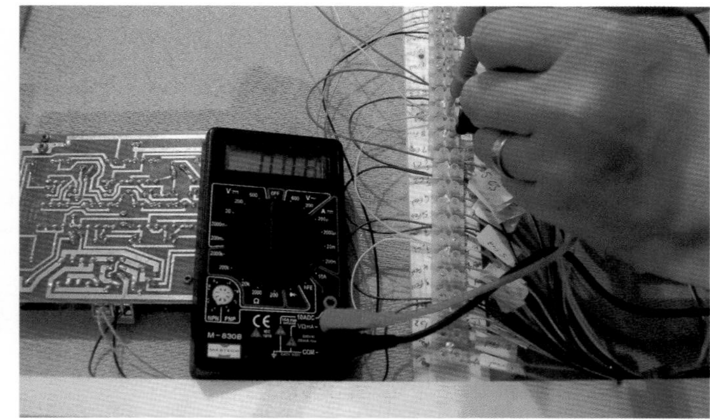

Using an electrical meter set on the resistance (Ω) scale to test the electrical continuity of a circuit.

was connected to the first of the blue wires on the switch side with a short link to the next one, another short link to the next, and so on. I then did the same for the yellow feed from controller 1 and green feed from controller 3, both of which will be on the layout.

It is always a good idea to check your wiring before you go any further. Check that each track feed connects to the correct controller in each switch position. To do this you need to use a test meter or continuity meter. Test meters are available for under ten pounds from suppliers such as Maplin Electronics and are invaluable for testing and fault-finding.

Set the meter to the Ω (Ohm or Resistance) range and place the probes on the track feed connected to a switch and one of the controller feeds connected to the same switch. With the switch one way you should see a low resistance (very close to 0) and with the switch in the other two positions you should see an infinite resistance – usually shown as a '1' on the left of the display. Work through the various feed and switch combinations until you are confident that the control panel is working correctly.

Wiring The Track

Having created the control panel we must now turn our attention to wiring up the track. Those who started with a train set are probably familiar with the various types of power clip available from the manufacturers such as Hornby and Peco which are manufactured for this purpose. Whilst they are ideal for layouts that are regularly set up, changed and broken down they leave a lot to be desired on a model railway as they are obtrusive and don't resemble anything found on the prototype.

For model railways the usual scheme is to solder wires directly to the rails, either the outer side or base, and then drop the wires through holes in the baseboard. An alternative method is to solder the wires to the fishplates that connect two lengths of track together. By now soldering will hold no terror for you but there are some things that you need to bear in mind.

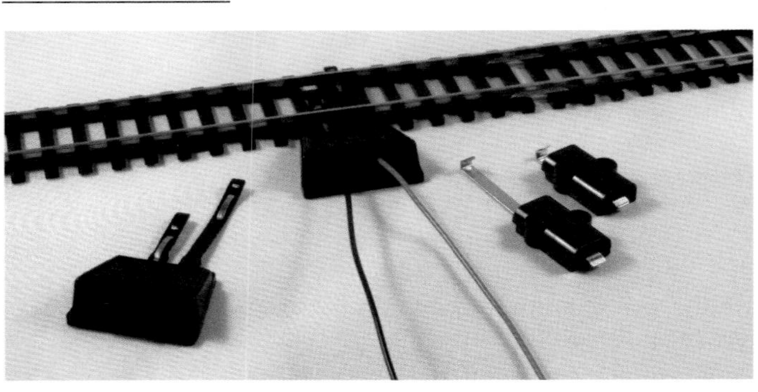

Commercial power connectors are ideal for train sets but are not suitable for model railways. These examples are by Hornby (left) and Peco (right).

Cable clips come in a variety of sizes and are useful where you have a lot of wires. Unfortunately hammering them in can disrupt the layout by dislodging scenery and derailing stock.

- Ideally you should use single core wire instead of multi-strand.
- Clean the rail with an abrasive cleaner such as wet and dry paper, a glass fibre pencil or a track cleaning rubber.
- Be careful not to melt the plastic sleepers and rail fixings – clean and quick are the watchwords.

Single core wire is a very different animal to the multi-core type that we have been using up until now. Once bent it will retain its shape, which is very useful for this job. The down-side is that if it is bent or moved too often the wire can break inside its sleeve leading to mysterious circuit failures. The technique is to solder a short length of wire to the rail which drops through the baseboard to a connector underneath. The standard multi-core wire is then run from the connector to the control panel.

To keep wires in order underneath the baseboard you need some means of keeping them in position. Wires that hang loosely are an invitation for something to catch in them and rip one or more out of their connectors. Whilst you can buy cable clips from your local D-I-Y store they need to be hammered into position which can disrupt things on top of the baseboard – especially if you are altering the wiring on a layout that has already had the scenery installed. I find that a staple gun is a wonderful tool for the job – the staples are cheap, can easily be removed if you wish to change the wiring, the gun can be used on its side or upside down and the whole process is quick.

You simply hold the wires in place with one hand, place the staple gun on top of them, check that the staple won't pierce any of the wires and fire the staple in. Job done.

Staples are a cheap and easy way of keeping wires under control. You can use a staple gun on its side or upside down with ease which makes for a quick and easy job.

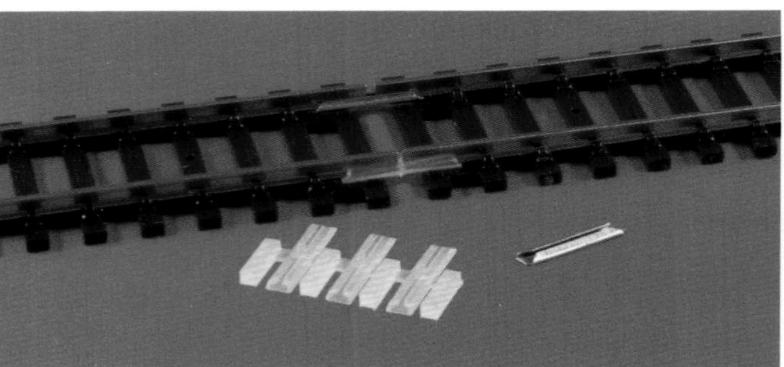

To isolate different sections you need to replace the metal rail joiners with plastic insulating ones. These normally need to be cut from a strip, like the one shown on the left, before use. On sectional track you will need to use a pair of pliers to pull the metal rail joiner off the track. If you are careful you will be able to remove it without damaging it and save it for re-use later.

To isolate the electrical sections from each other you will need to put insulating rail-joiners in the track. These are plastic versions of the standard metal rail joiner. If you are using sectional track you will need to pull the existing metal joiner off using pliers. Grab it on the sides and pull gently. If you are careful you will be able to save it for reuse. If you grab it by the top and bottom you will crush it and it will only be fit for the bin. Remember that for common return wiring you only need to put an insulating rail joiner in the rail on the 'red' side of the track.

If your layout is on a single board or is permanently fixed in place with no prospect of ever having to be moved or dismantled then you can run the wire from the track dropper to the control panel as a single run. However if you may need to separate one or more baseboards at some point then you will need some form of electrical connector at the baseboard joins.

For a layout that is rarely disturbed then the same type of terminal blocks that we used on the control panel will suffice. Screw one to each baseboard and then join them with short lengths of wire. When the baseboards need to be separated just disconnect the link wires from one of the terminal blocks.

For layouts that are moved frequently, either for storage or exhibitions, you will need a proper plug and socket. The standard 25-way 'D' connector used on computers is a popular choice as it is relatively cheap and easily available. You

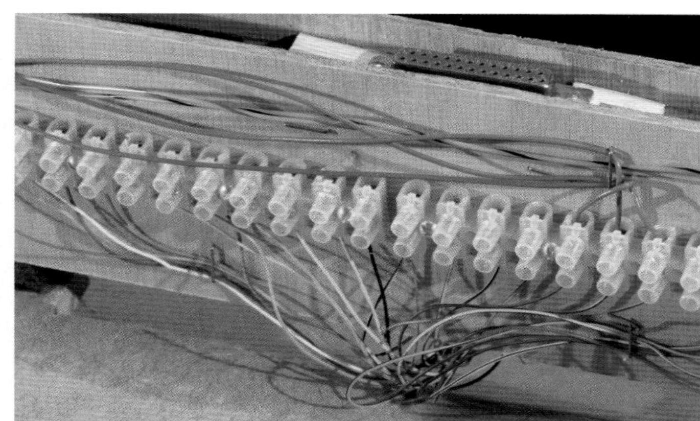

ABOVE: *The standard computer 25-way 'D' connector provides a useful electrical connector for model railways. At the back is a ready-made cable whilst at the front is half a cable that has had both the outer sheath stripped from the cable and the casing removed from the socket.*

do need to be careful though as the contacts are rated for a maximum of about 7A each. If you are running heavy current users such as large scale locomotives, multi-locomotive DCC or solenoid point motors you may need to use two (or more) contacts for each connection. Other types of connector, such as the 4 and 5 way DIN audio plugs and sockets, are available from electronics and model railway suppliers but bear in mind that you should never use mains style connectors – someone might plug them into the mains by mistake. Similarly you should never mix mains and layout wiring on the same connector – it is an accident waiting to happen.

When wiring multi-way connectors such as 25 way D-plugs or DIN plugs you should always cover the soldered connection for each wire with heat shrink sleeving before moving on to solder the next wire. This will ensure that no stray strands of wire can accidentally bridge two connections and will avoid splashes of solder doing the same and causing mysterious short circuits and faults later.

ABOVE: *Having stripped back one end of a 25-way cable, the socket has been screwed in place and the wires connected to two terminal strips. Wires are then run around the baseboard to their various destinations.*

ABOVE: *When soldering the connections in place on any multi-way connector always insulate the wires using heat shrink sleeving as you go. This will prevent any mysterious short circuits later due to stray strands of wire bridging two connections.*

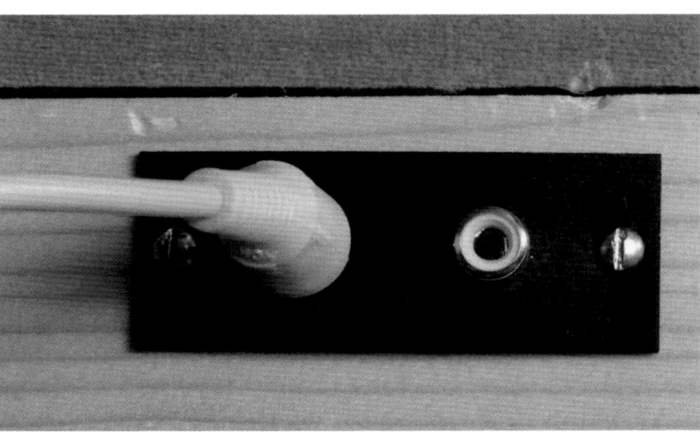

ABOVE: *Audio DIN plugs and sockets are frequently used for connecting handheld controllers to the layout. They can also be useful where a small number of wires need to cross between baseboards.*

LEFT: *Audio phono plugs and sockets are ideal for connecting DCC bus wires between baseboards. Each plug, like the yellow one shown on the left, carries two connections.*

CHAPTER

Point Motors

Just when you thought it was safe to venture back underneath the baseboards it is time to turn our attention to solenoid point motors. Before we begin I should explain that most of them aren't actually motors at all; actuators would be a better term but, they have been known as point motors since the dawn of time, so we're stuck with the term.

Twin-Solenoid Point Motors

The basic twin-solenoid point motor consists of two electro-magnets and a metal bar. Turn one of the electromagnets on and it magnetically attracts the bar, pulling the bar towards it. Turn the other electromagnet on and the bar is pulled the other way. All we need to do is connect the bar to a point and we can move the blades from side to side.

Commercial point motors come with various extras such as electrical switches, the ability to hold the blades firmly at each end of their travel and devices to make connecting the motor to the point easier.

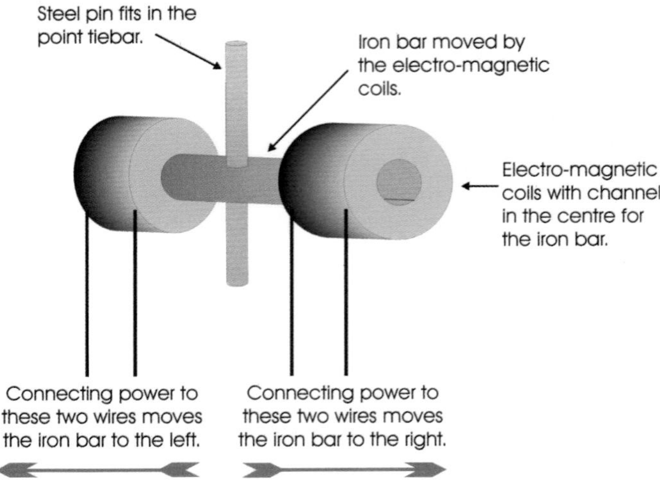

Typical construction and operation of a twin-solenoid point motor.

Whilst manufacturers such as Hornby and Peco supply devices to mount point motors on top of the baseboard most layout builders opt to put them below the baseboard. Both Peco and Hornby point motors can be fitted directly to the underside of their points, given a suitable hole in the baseboard. Use of other makes of motor or point requires that the motor be fixed to the baseboard itself. Regardless of which motors and points you use it is important that when they are installed the point motor's bar should be in its centre position when the point blades are centred. In addition the point blades should be able to be moved easily by pushing the point motor's bar from side to side and should go fully home in both directions. Any mechanical stiffness or misalignment can lead to unreliability.

This Peco point motor has an optional switch mounted underneath. The yellow wires operate the point motor whilst the black ones are for the switch.

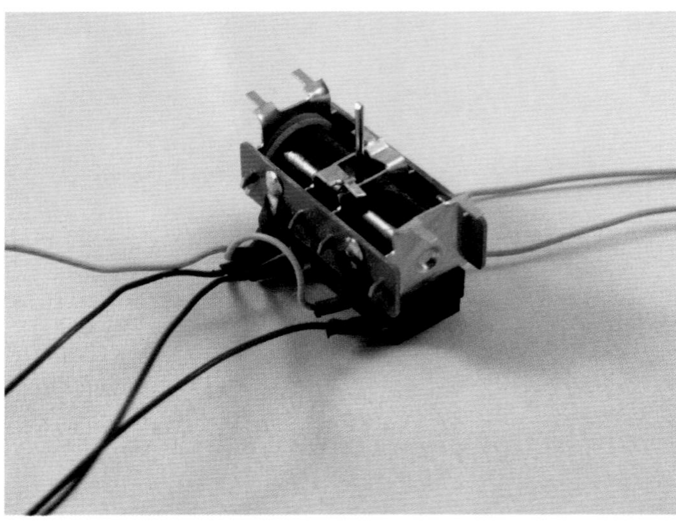

Point motors need a short burst of current to operate them. This will generate a magnetic field and pull the bar to one end of its travel. Keeping the current on after this point serves no useful purpose and, in fact, will shorten the life of the motor. The two electro-magnets, or solenoids, are made of many turns of thin copper wire. Whilst the power is on they carry a large current and if the power is left on the copper wire heats up and burns off its insulating coat leading to a short circuit, a burning smell and the need to get a new point motor.

To avoid leaving the power to a point motor on a number of different solutions have been devised:

- Using push buttons or switches that only pass current whilst they are being pressed
- Using a probe and stud system where the power is only on whilst the handheld probe is in contact with a stud on the control panel
- Using a switch on the point motor to cut off the power once it has moved
- Using a capacitor discharge unit which provides a short burst of power.

Push buttons and switches

Special switches for point motor operation are available in the Peco and Hornby ranges, Hornby's resembles a signal box lever. Standard electrical push buttons and passing contact switches can also be used, but bear in mind that they do need to carry a heavy current so miniature switches and push buttons should be avoided. You can mount the switches on a central control panel or local panels close to the points that they control. The panel can either have switches laid out in a row, like a manual signal box, or on a track diagram which makes it easier to see what each switch does.

As with power to the track the circuit for a single point motor is simple. The complication comes when you have a number of them.

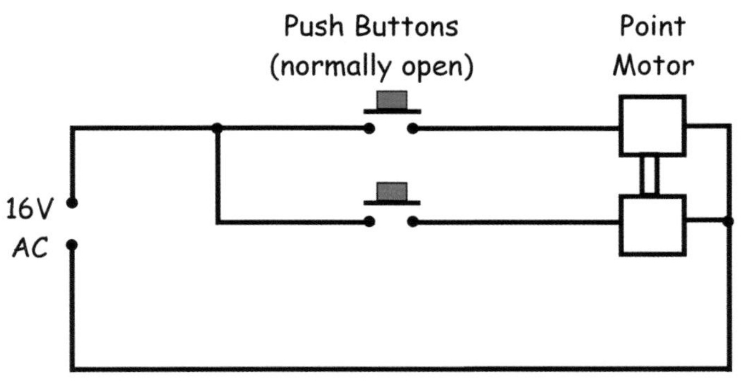

Using two push buttons to operate a point motor.

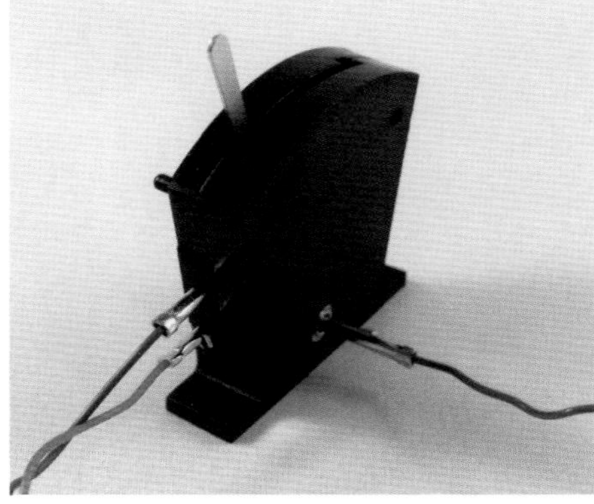

Hornby's point motor switch is designed to look like a real signal box lever. They can be joined in a row.

Probe and stud

The probe and stud system is a variation on the push button method. A handheld probe which is connected to the power supply is touched against metal studs on the control panel. The studs are connected to the point motors and when the probe touches them the circuit is completed and current flows. When the probe is removed from the stud the circuit is broken and current stops flowing.

You can make your own probe using the plastic section of a ball point pen with studs from brass screws or bolts. Alternatively Peco include suitable items in their range.

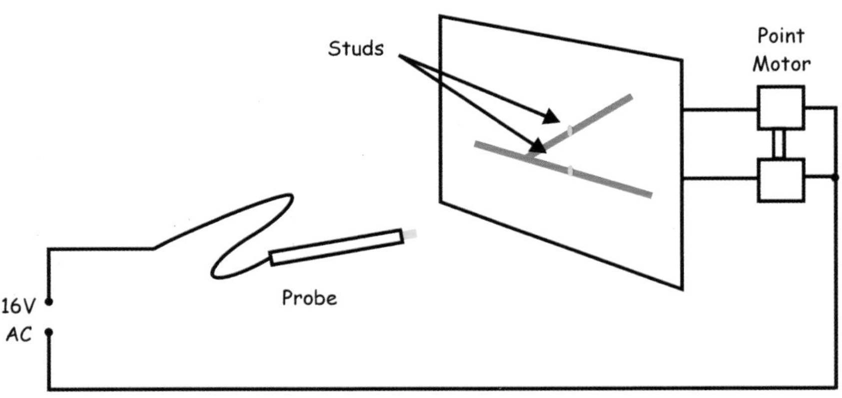

Using a probe and studs to operate a point motor.

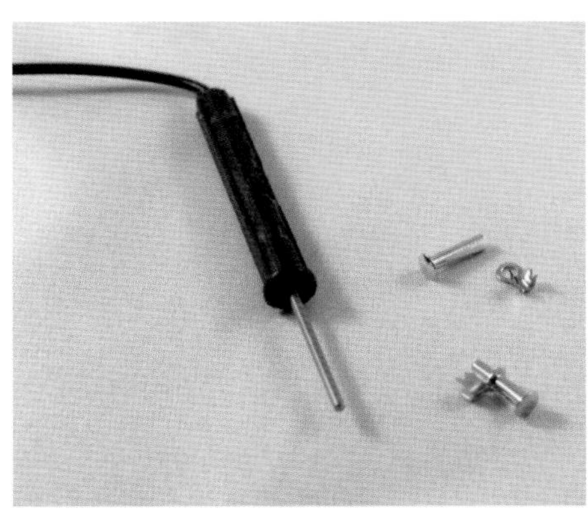

Peco have both a probe and suitable studs in their range.

Switch on the point motor

At first glance using a switch on the point motor to break the circuit seems to be an ideal solution, however it has some drawbacks. If the point motor fails to throw, for example when an item of rolling stock stops the point blades moving, current will continue to flow until the point motor burns out. If the switch cuts the power before the point blades are fully home then trains can be derailed. In addition point motor operated switches are often more usefully employed for other purposes such as switching track power, controlling signals or lights on the control panel to show which route is set.

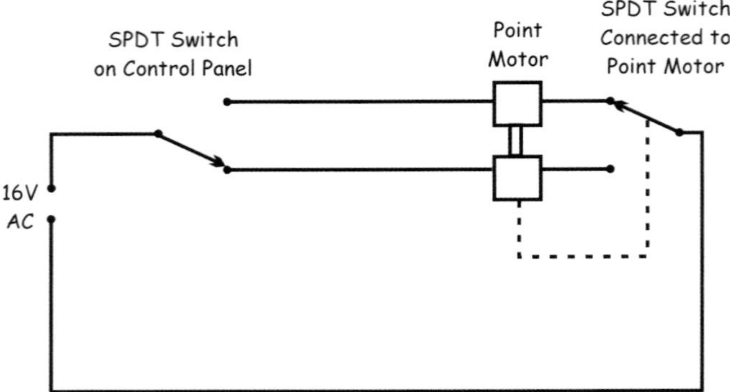

Using a switch mounted on the point motor to cut off the current.

Capacitor discharge unit

A capacitor discharge unit (CDU) is an electronic device that is designed to overcome some of the twin-solenoid point motor's idiosyncrasies. It charges up from a power supply and then releases a large, quick pulse of power when you operate a point motor. The pulse ensures that your point motors won't get burnt out if a switch gets stuck on and, as a bonus, not only does it enable you to operate a number of point motors at once but helps to ensure that even sticky motors throw all the way and don't get stuck half-way.

The ability to operate more than one point motor at a time means that you can operate both the points on a crossing at once or even set up a route with a single button. I shall cover this in a later chapter. Another way to use a CDU is to select the point or points to be operated using a rotary switch. When you have selected the points you press a button and they all throw at once.

With the reduction in price of many electronic components a new method has appeared where individual point motors have their own CDU. This means that ordinary switches can be used on the control panel, with extra poles if necessary for route indication or other purposes. An example of this is the DCC Concepts MASTERswitch V2 available from Bromsgrove Models and DCC Supplies in the UK.

BELOW: *When you use a capacitor discharge unit (CDU) you can either use two push buttons to operate each point motor or use a rotary switch to select which point motor operates when you press the button. CDUs can operate more than one point motor at a time.*

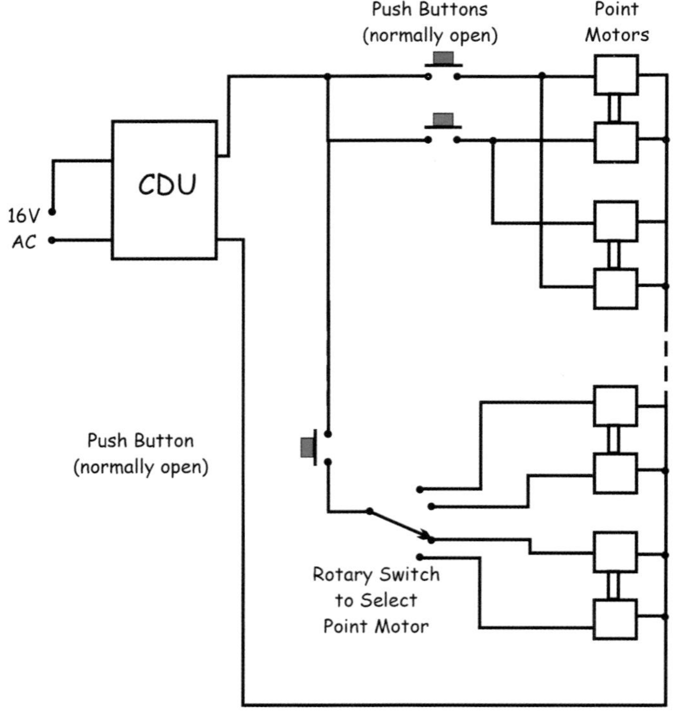

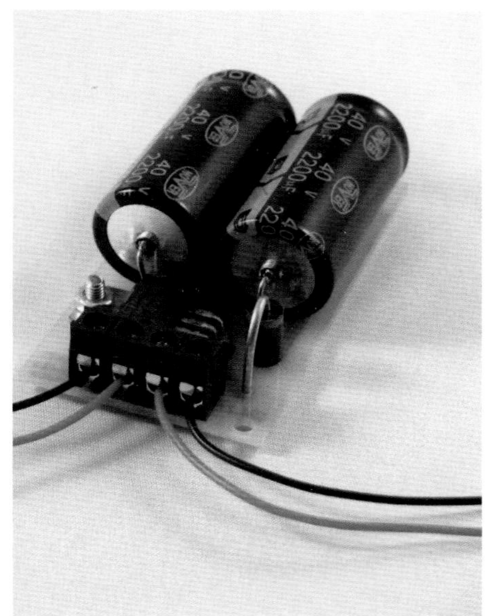

Gaugemaster produce this capacitor discharge unit which is capable of operating up to six point motors simultaneously. One pair of wires is connected to a 24V AC power supply, the other to the switches and point motors.

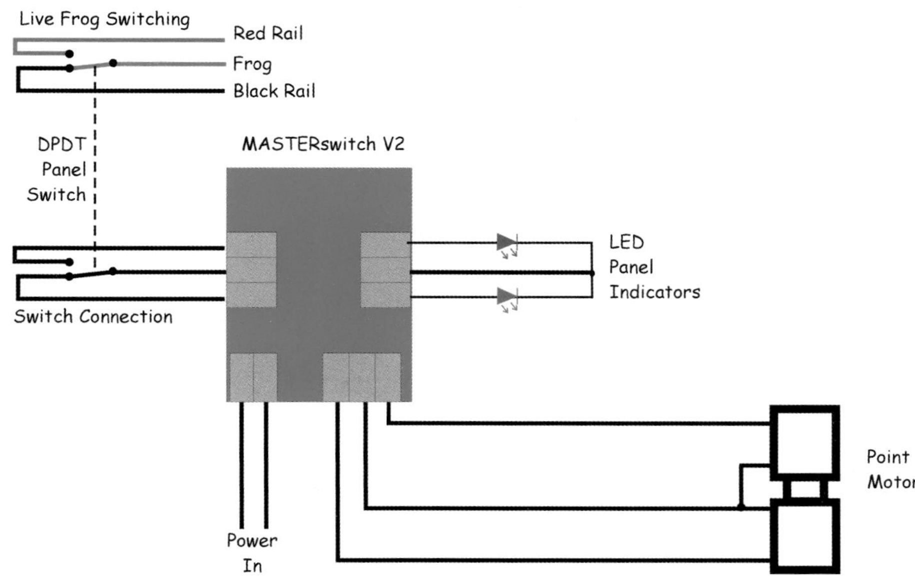

ABOVE: *The DCC Concepts MASTERswitch V2 is a localised capacitor discharge unit that can control up to four twin-solenoid point motors moved in unision. It also incorporates circuitry to operate LED panel indicators and the panel switch can also be used to switch the polarity of live frogs.*

Mounting Twin-Solenoid Point Motors

Now that you know how to connect up point motors, I shall move on to the job of mounting them underneath the baseboard. If you are using Peco or Hornby track then you will find that the points come with fittings built-in so that you can easily add under-baseboard mounted point motors. If you use track made by other manufacturers you may need to use other methods or adapt these.

Both Peco and Hornby produce similar point motors that are designed to fit underneath their points. Peco offer variants for low-current and specialist mounting along with accessories such as mounting bases and switches operated by the motor. Seep also produce solenoid point motors which can be used in the same way.

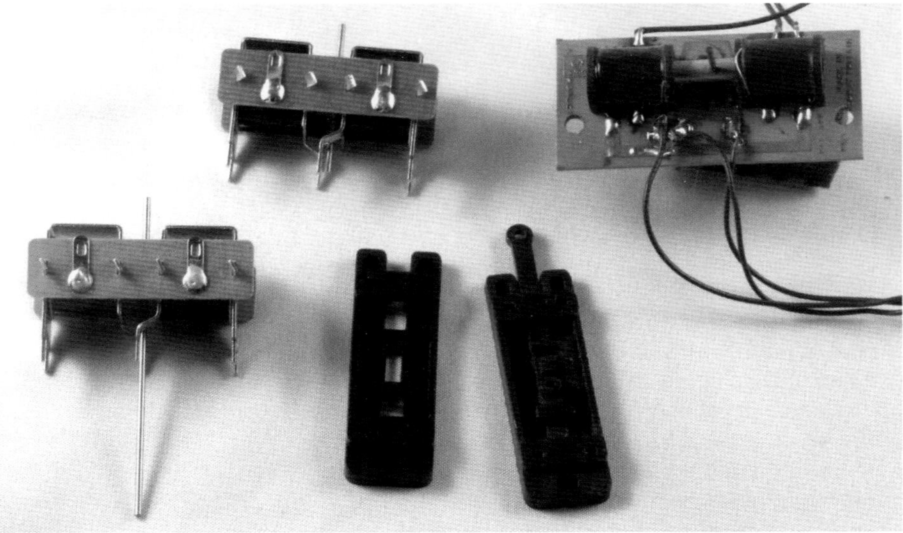

RIGHT: *A selection of point motors and accessories. Top left – a standard Peco point motor, top right – a Seep point motor with built-in switch. Bottom left – a Peco point motor with extended operating arm, bottom centre – a Peco under-baseboard mounting plate, bottom right – a Peco above baseboard mounting plate.*

Method One

This method involves clipping the point motor to the underside of the point. For OO gauge track you need to bend down the centre legs on the point motor and plug the end lugs into the holes either side of the tiebar. Make sure that the circular arm on the point motor fits into the hole in the middle of the tiebar.

ABOVE: *Hornby and Peco point motors simply clip in to four holes, two either side of the point. The operating arm fits into a hole in the middle of the tiebar.*

The standard Peco or Hornby point motor just clips in place on the bottom of their OO scale points. The centre legs are not needed for OO track need to be bent up.

RIGHT: *To stop the point motor falling off the point you need to use a pair of pliers to twist the four metal legs that poke out through about 45 degrees.*

Check that the point still operates freely when moved by hand. Each of the small sections of lug that protrudes above the sleepers needs to be twisted through about 45 degrees using a pair of pliers. This will stop the point motor falling out when it is operated!

For N gauge track the point motor is wider than the point. This time you need to fold down one pair of end lugs and insert the middle and other end lugs into the holes either side of the tiebar. Make sure that the circular arm on the point motor fits into the hole in one end of the tiebar. You can fit the motor so that it juts out either side - this may need some forethought in areas where you have a number of points otherwise you may find two motors that need to fit in the same space.

Having fitted the point motor you need to create a hole for it. These motors require a 40mm x 25mm

BELOW: *The standard Peco point motor is wider than an N gauge point and so it sticks out to one side. You use the centre legs and one set of end legs to fix it in place. This point motor also has an optional electrical switch fitted.*

The hole needed for a point motor fixed directly underneath the point is large and awkward.

In N gauge the hole for the point motor will be wider than the track. This can cause problems where you have a number of points in close proximity. Careful thought may need to be given when selecting which side of the motor is fixed to each point.

Using an offcut of brown envelope sandwiched between the point motor and point enables the large hole needed for motors fixed directly to the point to be disguised.

The brown paper covers the hole and enables the track to be ballasted as normal. The edges should be stuck down otherwise they will wrinkle up like this.

rectangular hole. Establish where the hole needs to be and mark it out on the baseboard. Drill an 8-10mm diameter hole and use that as the starting point to cut the opening out with an electric jigsaw.

This method does leave a large and unsightly hole in the baseboard but it can be disguised by cutting out a section of brown envelope slightly larger than the opening. Cut a small hole for the point motor's circular arm so that it can move from side to side. Place the arm through the hole and then push the mounting lugs through the envelope before mounting on the point. When you put the point in place the envelope will neatly cover the hole and a little PVA glue around the edge will stop the paper from lifting.

This method is only really suitable for point motors that are fitted at the same time as the track is laid. It is virtually impossible to get the lugs and tiebar in place through a small hole once the track has been fixed down.

Method Two

By attaching the point motor to the baseboard rather than the point we gain the advantage of being able to fit point motors after the track has been laid and the ability to easily replace a motor should it fail. In addition some types of point motor, such as those produced by Seep, can only be fitted this way.

When you lay the track you need to make a small hole for the point motor arm. This can either by a single hole about 5mm in diameter or two holes about 2mm diameter joined together to make a slit 5mm long. Either way the resulting hole must be sufficiently large that the hole for the point motor's arm in the

TOP: *Seep point motors just need a small hole for the operating arm to pass through the baseboard. To fit them you simply cut the operating arm to length and then screw the motor in place. This is the view from underneath the baseboard.*

ABOVE: *The Peco adaptor base allows you to mount a Peco extended arm point motor under the baseboard. The point motor fits in the base in exactly the same way that it is fitted to a point. The unit is then screwed in place under the baseboard.*

ABOVE: *Point motors with long operating arms need to have the arm trimmed to length. Place the point motor in position, mark the length, remove the motor and trim the arm with a razor saw or small hacksaw. This point also shows the improved appearance that can be obtained by trimming back the tie-bar and removing the point motor fixings on a Peco Streamline point.*

tiebar is over the opening at both ends of its travel. There is no need to disguise the opening in the baseboard as it will be under the point's tiebar and sleepers.

If you are using a Seep point motor then the first step is to hold it in position with the operating arm through the baseboard and hole in the tiebar. Mark the operating arm where it projects through the tiebar, remove the motor and then trim the operating arm to length with a razor saw. Replace the point motor, making sure that the motor is parallel to the tiebar and use two screws to fix it in place. Check that the point still operates freely by hand - if you have difficulty moving it then the point motor will too. The usual causes of stiff operation are that the operating arm is rubbing on the side of the hole or that the point motor is mounted at an angle to the tiebar.

Peco offer a special adaptor for under-baseboard mounting. This is a plastic moulding with similar fixings to their points. Fold up the centre legs, fit the motor to the plate and twist the lugs to secure it in place. You will need to use the extended pin version of the Peco point motor as the operating arm has to pass through the baseboard. The standard version of the point motor does not have a long enough arm to do this. Temporarily mount the point motor

LEFT: *You can mount extended arm Peco point motors underneath the baseboard by simply bending the two sets of end legs outwards and fixing them in place with screws and cup washers.*

assembly under the baseboard, mark the length of the arm, remove and cut the arm to length. The assembly can then be screwed in place on the baseboard.

For those of a more economical disposition you can dispense with the adaptor base and screw the point motor directly to the baseboard. To do this you need to bend the end legs outwards and trap them under the screw using cup washers. Again you will need to use the extended pin version of the Peco point motor.

Slow-motion Point Motors

Now whilst the twin solenoid point motors have served the hobby well for many years they do have a number of drawbacks and disadvantages. One alternative that is increasing in popularity is the slow-motion point motor. These consist of an electric motor that drives an actuator arm. The advantages of this type of motor are that it is gentle in operation, quiet, holds the point blades firmly closed and doesn't need such thick wires and large power supplies. One of the most common types used in the UK is the Circuitron Tortoise™.

The Tortoise™

When you unpack the Tortoise™ the first thing that strikes you is its size. It is much larger than the twin-solenoid point motors that we are accustomed to. It comes in a sealed green plastic case and tinkering with the innards will void the warranty - so leave them well alone. On the outside there is an electrical connector and an arm. You also get a length of wire, a plastic fulcrum and a screw. The motor is 5.6mm wide, 5cm deep and 8.2cm tall so you do need at least 3½" below the baseboard to fit the motor. For awkward situations you can purchase a kit to allow the motor to be mounted away from the point that it operates. The kit can also be configured so that you can operate two points at once, typically both sides of a crossover. Surprisingly enough this does not offer a significant cost saving and, provided that you have the room, it is easier to fit a second motor.

The motor is designed to be mounted underneath the baseboard with the wire providing the movement. To do this you need a small hole in the point tie-bar and a larger hole underneath it (for OO gauge a ¼" hole in the baseboard is about right). The wire is bent according to the instructions supplied and the fulcrum fitted to the plastic guides on the motor. Using the template supplied with the instructions four holes are drilled on the underside of the baseboard for four No.4 ½" screws (12 x

The motor comes with a bag that contains the plastic fulcrum, operating wire and screw that fixes the wire to the operating arm. The screws to attach the motor to the baseboard are not supplied.

The motor mounted underneath a Peco OO gauge curved point. The actuating wire needs to be trimmed to length and the electrical connections made.

2.5mm) which are used to fix the motor in position. The hole in the plastic fulcrum needs to be directly under the hole in the baseboard. With the motor at the centre of its travel, and the wire going straight up, the point tie-bar should be centred.

If you are using Peco or Hornby points with built-in springs these should be removed. The motor provides plenty of force to keep the point blades in position and the 'snap' action of the spring can lead to the point moving at a different time to the built-in switch contacts changing over. This can cause a short circuit with live frog points.

The Tortoise™ comes with two built-in SPDT switches for use with live-frog points (see Chapter 6) and signalling systems. These change as the motor goes through its central position. The motor can either be used with an edge-connector plug or by soldering wires directly to the connections on the motor. There are eight connections: two for the motor and three for each of the built-in switches. If you solder the wires in place it is strongly advised that you run the wires to nearby screw terminals so that you can easily reverse the direction if the motor moves the wrong way when you apply the power.

The Tortoise™ can be run from either a DC or an AC power supply. As the motor draws less than 20mA you don't need to use heavy wires and a 500mA supply will typically run up to 30 Tortoises™. For a DC supply the voltage should be 12V or less, the lower the voltage the slower the motor will run. The motor will not be damaged by connecting it to an AC supply. With the current flowing one way through the motor it will move to one side and when the current it reversed it will move to the other.

Using a single DC supply, such as a 9V wall-mounted transformer, you need to use DPDT switches to control the motors. The positive and negative wires from the power supply are run to each of the switches and then two wires run from each switch to the motor that it controls (figure 1).

If you use two DC supplies then you can use SPDT switches. The positive from one power supply and the negative from the other run to each switch. The other negative and positive terminals are connected and run as a common return to one terminal of each Tortoise™. A single wire then links each switch to its motor (figure 2).

With an AC supply you should use a slightly higher voltage, up to 16V. Here you connect two diodes, facing in opposite directions, to one of the power supply terminals. The diodes are then connected to the switches. The other terminal on the power supply is run as a common return to one terminal of each Tortoise™. A single wire then links each switch to its motor (figure 3).

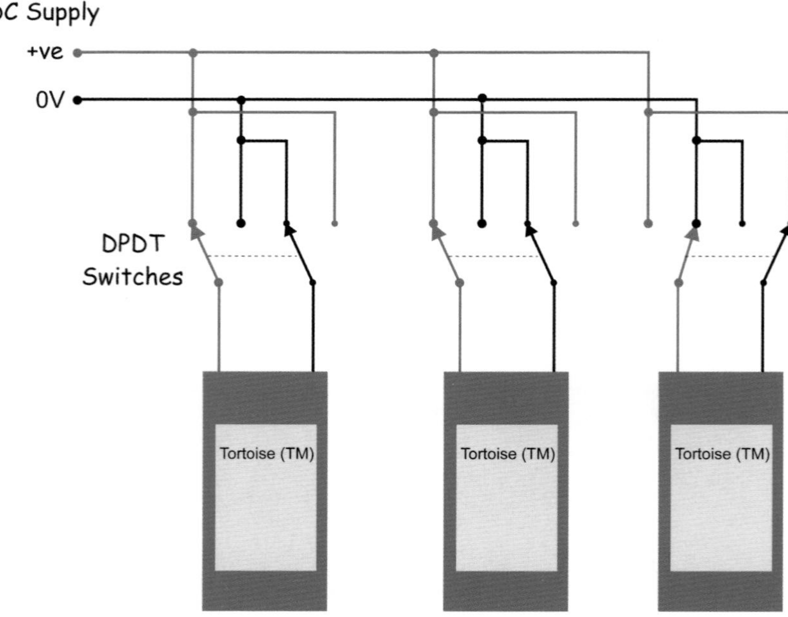

FIGURE 1 *- Wiring Tortoise™ point motors with a DC power supply and DPDT switches.*

As an added bonus when you use SPDT switches you can add LEDs to indicate which way the point is set without tying up one of the built in switches. Simply connect a pair of LEDs between the control panel switch and the Tortoise™. The motor acts as a suitable current limiting resistor. When it is stalled one of the LEDs will be lit, whilst it is moving the LEDs will be dim (figure 4).

The Tortoise™ is available from many UK retailers and typically costs £12-13.

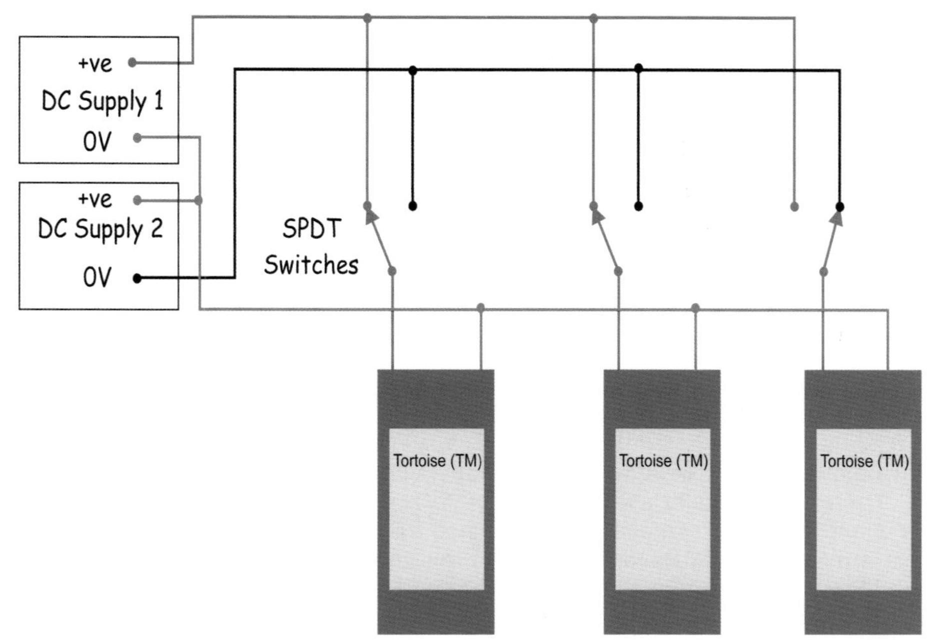

***FIGURE 2** - Wiring Tortoise™ point motors with a pair of DC power supplies and SPDT switches.*

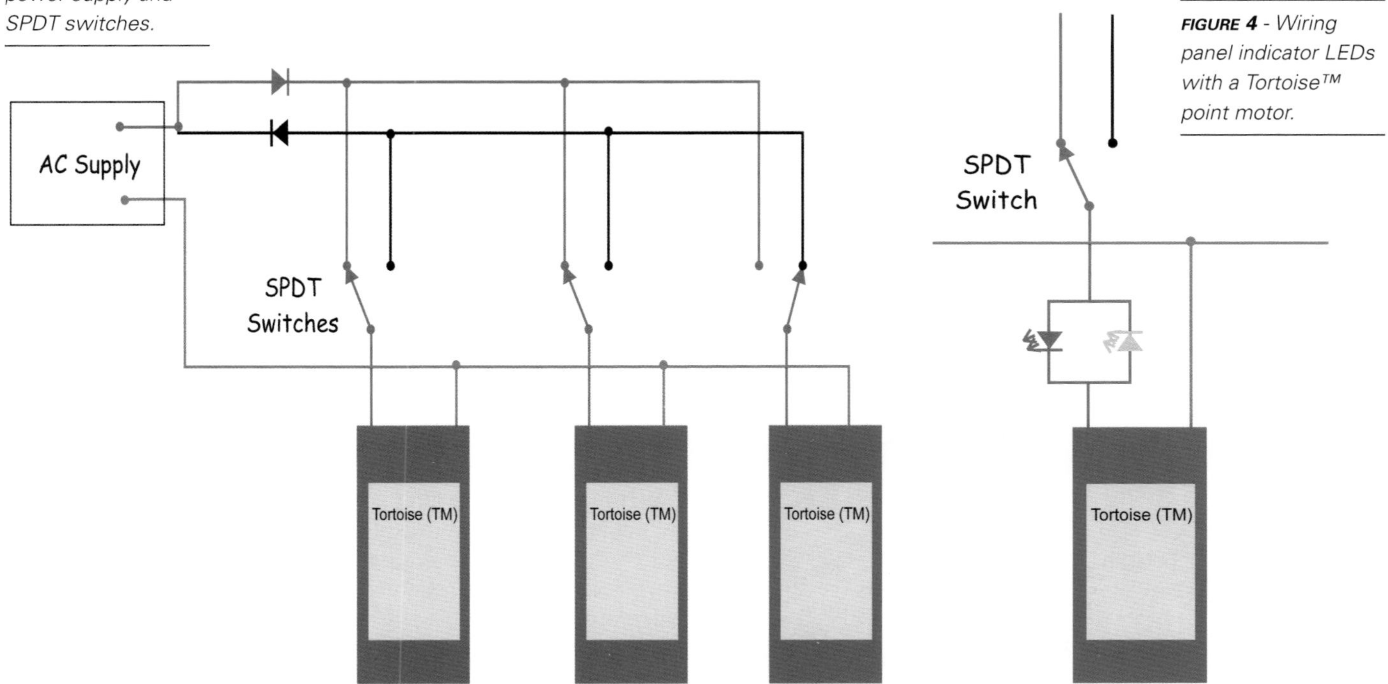

***FIGURE 3** - Wiring Tortoise™ point motors with an AC power supply and SPDT switches.*

***FIGURE 4** - Wiring panel indicator LEDs with a Tortoise™ point motor.*

CHAPTER

Frogs – Dead or Alive

One of the stranger terms that you will come across in the model railway world is 'frog'. People talk of track with 'dead frogs' or getting better running by using 'live frogs'. This is all very mystifying to the uninitiated and conjures up visions of small amphibians being squashed by model locomotives or dressed up in an engine driver's uniform.

To put you out of your misery the term 'frog' is used to describe the part where the rails come together at a point. People involved with real railways call it a crossing but on model railways it has always been a frog. That is the simple part. Things get complicated because we insist on powering our models by means of electricity fed through the rails. In previous chapters I have used the terms 'red' and 'black' to describe the rails connected to each terminal of the controller. Now when you connect a 'red' rail to a 'black' rail you get a short circuit and everything stops, and this is just what will happen at a frog if it is left to its own devices as shown on the first diagram. If the point is set for the siding then the 'red' rail must cross the 'black' one.

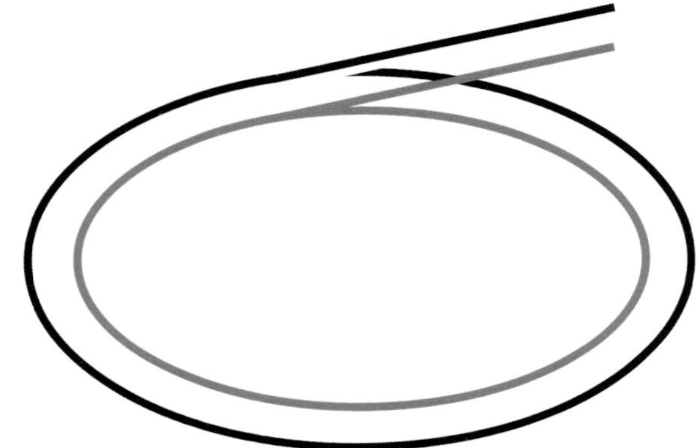

One of the problems with our electrically powered models is how to deal with the place in pointwork where the two rails meet, known as the frog in model railway circles. Where the red and black rails meet you will get a short circuit which will stop anything running.

There are basically two methods of solving this problem, known as 'dead frog' and 'live frog' respectively. With 'dead frog' points a small section of rail at the frog is electrically dead. This solves the problem of short circuits but can lead to locomotives stalling on the dead section of track, especially if you use small tank locomotives or larger locomotives that only pick up current on a few wheels. With 'live frog' points a larger section of rail is electrically isolated from the rest of the layout and connected to whichever rail the point is set for. Whilst this involves extra work when you lay and wire the track it provides a continuous electrical path through the point which prevents any unscheduled stops.

Dead Frogs

Most commercial trackwork is supplied with dead frog points. These can simply be laid without worrying about extra wiring for the frog. Looking at the second diagram we can see that the point blades are connected to the rails on the other side of the frog by wires built into the underside of the point. In the diagram the point is set for the straight route. The top point blade is against the red rail and picks up power from it. The wire passes the power to the red rail on the left hand side allowing a locomotive to pass along that route. Now let's look at the diverging route. The red rail has power but the black rail is connected to the lower point blade which is not touching the black rail, thus the lower point blade can't pick up any power and the diverging route isn't powered. This means that if the diverging route isn't connected to a black power feed at some place further down the line, any locomotive parked on the diverging route will not receive any power and be isolated. This simple trick allows you to isolate locomotives at many places around the layout without any extra wiring.

This is a standard dead frog point. The black areas are plastic and are electrically dead. It solves the problem of short circuits but can cause locomotives to stall.

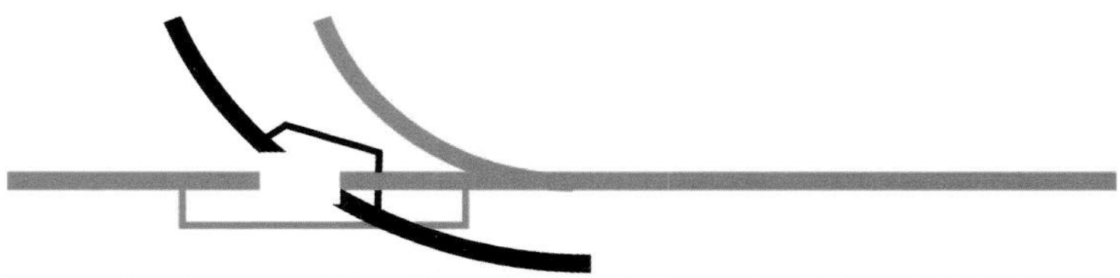

Wires built into the point connect the point blades to the rails on the other side of the frog. They pass current to the exit selected by the point blades and isolate the other exit.

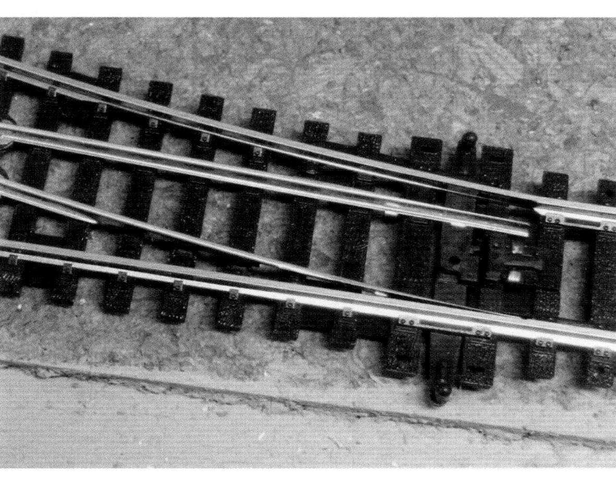

With dead frog points you are reliant on the point blades to pass electrical power along the layout unless you add extra feeds.

You are, of course, reliant on the point blades to pick up the current so if they are dirty or not fully in position you will get intermittent running. If you don't need the ability to isolate a locomotive, either because you use DCC or have switched isolating sections, then you can add feeds on the exit rails which will pass power back to the point blades ensuring that they are always powered. The dead frog will ensure that the red and black are kept apart.

Whilst I am on the subject of points I should like to emphasise the fact that each point needs electrical power at the toe (the single track) end if you are to be able to run trains on both the exit tracks. This is something that it is easy to overlook, even in simple track plans, ending up with a layout where sections only get power if a point some distance away is set correctly.

In the simple terminus shown the track feed at D is needed to get power to the goods yard. If you want to be able to isolate a locomotive in the loop then the easiest solution will be to run a feed to the black rail only, leaving the red rail fed from feed A via point B. Of course this means that point B must be set for the loop if you want to shunt the goods yard.

A more complex solution would be to feed both red and black rails at feed D and put a break in the red rail at C. This would allow you to put a switch in the red feed at D allowing you to isolate the loop and goods yard.

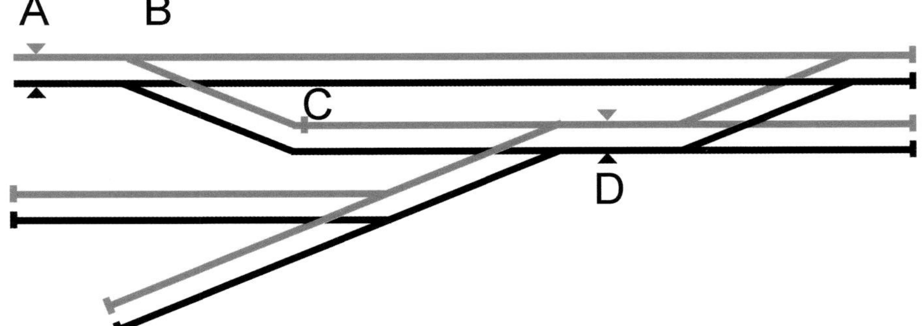

Even a simple track layout needs extra electrical feeds to ensure that electrical power can reach all the tracks.

Live Frogs

Live frog points, such as those marketed by Peco under the name 'Electrofrog', need a bit more work when you lay and wire the track but will reward you with better running. You can use the point blades to pass power to the frog but this does seem rather a short-sighted technique, any gains in performance from the live frog will be offset by the possibility of a poor power connection at the point blade. If you must do it this way then you need to put insulating rail joiners on the rails that lead away from the frog and provide power feeds to the track beyond the joiners. The only exceptions to this are dead end sidings. When the point is set against them then both rails are the same 'colour' and thus any locomotive standing in them is effectively isolated. So for a simple 'Inglenook' style shunting layout you can, if you wish, use live frog points without any extra work.

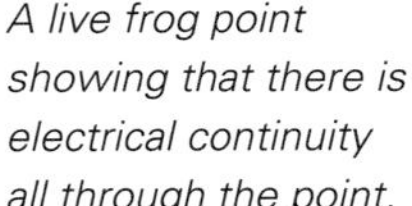

A live frog point showing that there is electrical continuity all through the point.

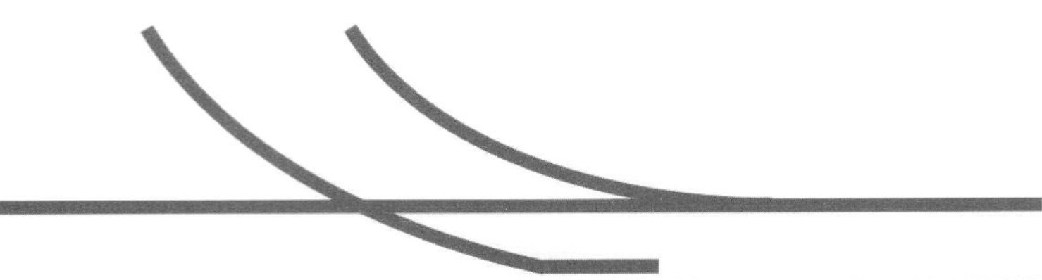

With dead-end sidings there is no need to put insulating rail joiners on the exit roads and, as you can see on the diverging route, the siding is isolated when the point is set against it.

As one of the main benefits of live frog points is that you have electrical pick-up throughout the point it is normal to provide some form of electrical switch to route power to the frog rather than rely on the point blades to do the job. With motorised points this is normally performed by a single pole double throw (SPDT) switch attached to the point motor. Some point motors, like the slow-motion Tortoise, come with switches built in others, like those produced by Peco, require a switch to be fitted. Where points are manually operated a switch needs to be provided in the operating linkage. One thing to avoid is having a switch that is not mechanically linked to the point – it would be all to easy for the point to be set one way and the switch the other, leading to a short circuit.

Given that the frog area can be connected to either the red or black rail depending on how the point is set it is vital to put insulated rail joiners in the two rails leading away from the frog. You will need to provide electrical feeds for the rails beyond the point and these can be run from the rails at the toe side of the point, a section switch on the control panel or your DCC power bus – whichever is appropriate. The one exception is where you have a dead-end siding that you do not mind being electrically dead when the point is set against in. In this case you do not need to install the insulated rail joiner and jumper on that rail.

As the point blades are electrically live you can encounter problems with wheels that are out of gauge. It is not uncommon to find ready-to-run stock, particularly locomotives, where one or more pairs of wheels are too close together on their axle. Apart from the obvious problem that incorrectly gauged wheels can lead to derailments when they run through a live frog point it is possible for them to touch the open point blade causing a short circuit. In extreme cases this can happen with correctly gauged wheels if you run long wheelbase locomotives round sharp radius points. The solution to this is to connect the point blades to their adjacent running rail and have them electrically

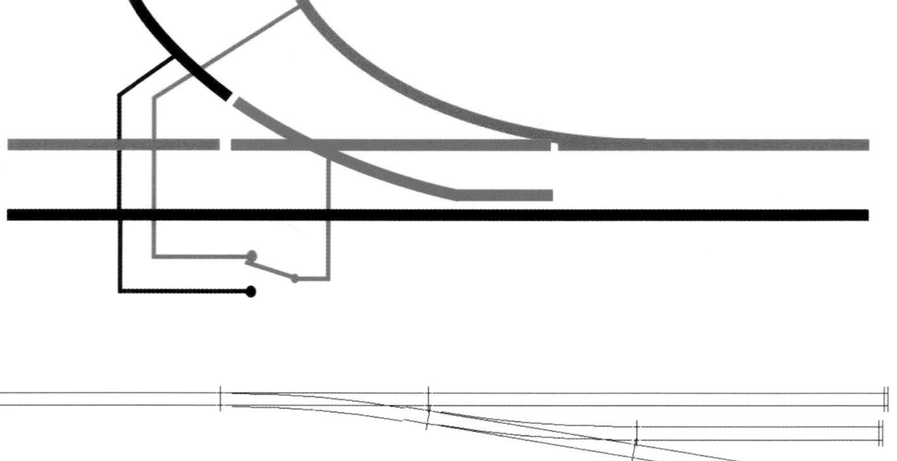

***RIGHT TOP:** The full installation for a live frog point. The point blades and frog are switched between the two running rails depending on how the point is set. Insulating rail joiners are used on the rails leaving the frog and the rails beyond are connected to the appropriate power feed.*

***LEFT BOTTOM:** The classic 'Inglenook' plan. Because all the points are fed from the toe and there are no loops then you can, if you wish, use live frog points without any special wiring. More complex layouts with loops or a continuous run need extra work if you wish to use live frog points.*

isolated from the frog area. Fortunately this doesn't require any extra switches, just extra wires. Peco Electrofrog points come with the point blades connected to the frog, however their OO points can easily be converted to having the blades connected to the running rails by breaking two connections and soldering jumper wires in place.

Things start to get awkward when you use more complex trackwork. Single and double slips require two switches, one for the frog at each end, as do diamond crossings. It may seem strange having to electrically switch a diamond crossing when it has no moving parts, but it is a price that has to be paid. Usually the switches can be linked to another point that sets the route into the crossing.

You can, if you wish, use a mixture of dead and live frog points on a layout. This is especially useful if you are upgrading to live frogs over a period or want to extend an existing dead frog layout using live frog points. Unlike DC and DCC there are no compatibility problems running the two side by side – except that once you have tried them you will probably like them so much that you will want to replace all the dead frog points. After all, frogs don't bite!

Diamond Crossings

Crossings spring up in various locations on railways; the most straightforward, although rare, is where two completely unrelated lines cross each other on the level. Sometimes they can be found in stations where two sidings cross each other, but the most common, certainly in model railway terms is at a double-track junction. These situations are all illustrated in figure 1.

With dead frog (or, 'Insulfrog' as Peco call them) crossings no special wiring is needed as the two paths through the crossing are electrically separate. The first photo shows a dead frog crossing, and the second shows the electrically live sections for the route running from top left to bottom right. Whilst this is simple to install it can cause problems due to the dead sections on the crossing – remember your locomotive needs to have at least one pick-up on the black rail and one on the red to keep moving. The longer the crossing, like this one, the bigger the dead sections get, and the harder it is to get small locomotives, or ones with limited power pick-ups across.

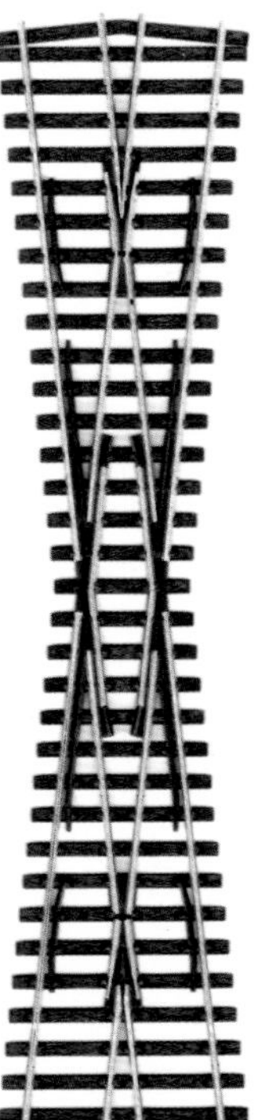

BELOW LEFT: *This is a Peco Code 75 OO gauge long crossing with dead frogs.*

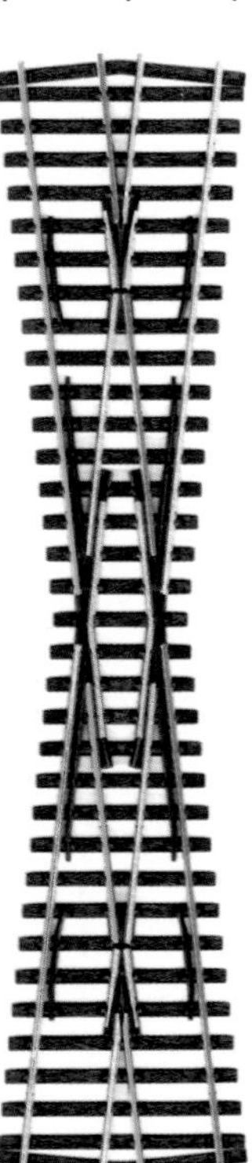

BELOW MIDDLE: *This photo shows the electrically live rails for a train travelling from the top left to bottom right. Note the large areas where there is no power to be picked up. This can cause problems for small locomotives and those which don't pick up power on many wheels.*

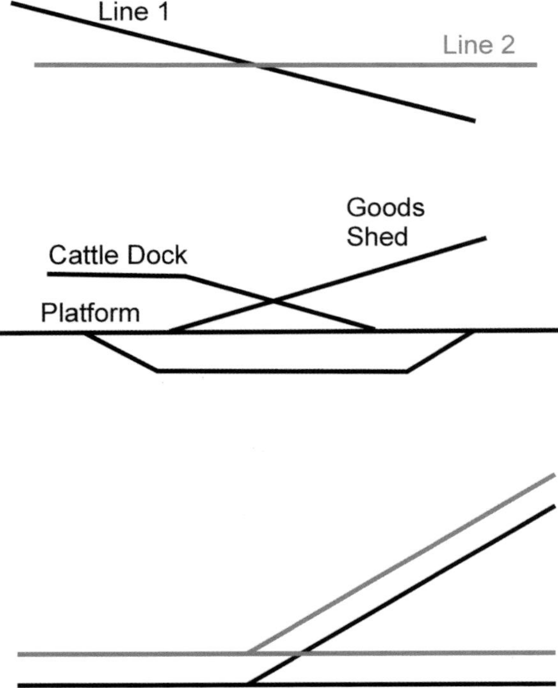

FIGURE 1 *- Crossings can crop up in a number of places on railways, both real and model. These include where two unrelated lines cross on the level (top), in stations (middle) and at double track junctions (bottom).*

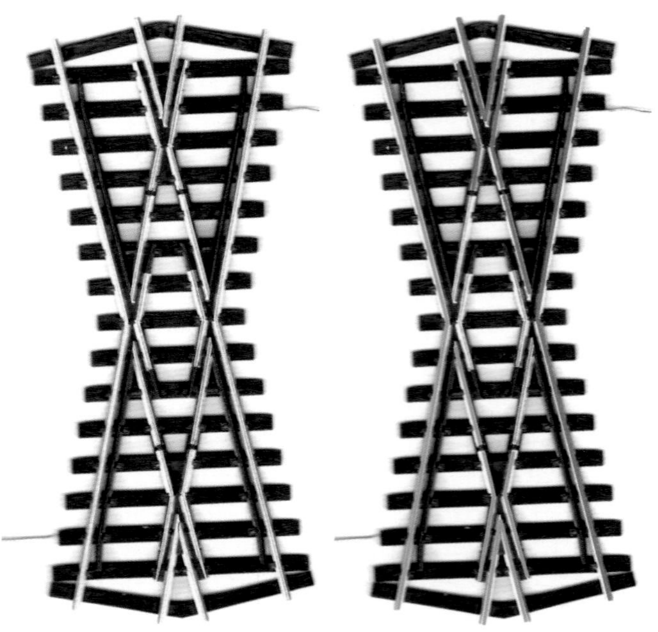

ABOVE LEFT: This is a Peco Code 75 gauge short crossing with live frogs.

ABOVE RIGHT: This photo shows the electrically live rails for a train travelling from top left to bottom right. Whilst the electrically dead sections have been minimised note the effect on the route from top right to bottom left – you can't run a train along that.

To solve this problem on points we can adopt live frogs and the same is true for crossings. The third photo shows a live-frog crossing and the fourth shows the electrically live sections for a train running from top left to bottom right again. See how few electrically dead gaps there are, so that there is virtually no loss of power as a locomotive traverses the crossing – even at slow speeds. This is good news as far as running is concerned, but comes at a price.

Take another look at the fourth photograph. Note how the rails on the other route through the crossing, from top right to bottom left, are also connected to the power. Whilst we could drive a train through on either route with a dead frog crossing only one route on a live frog crossing can be powered at a time. This means that the crossing needs to be switched from one route to another, just as if it was a point.

This causes great confusion as many people cannot see why they need to switch a crossing electrically if none of the track physically moves. To make things worse unless you have some very clever route-setting electronics, the crossing must be switched manually as the route cannot be set in reference to a point.

As an example, take the station plan in figure 1. It would seem sensible to link the crossing to the two points that feed the sidings – but this won't work. Imagine what would happen if both points were set to the sidings at the same time: you would get a short circuit. Similarly on the double track junction, the red line could be set to go straight across and the black line to go up the junction – again you'd get a short circuit. In both cases the only way to avoid this would be to ensure that the conflicting routes cannot be set which is easier said than done. Of course, if there is no point that you can link to then you don't have the option – imagine a simple figure '8' layout.

Where the two routes are both fed from the same section or controller, such as in the station plan, a double-pole double-throw (DPDT) switch is needed to switch the crossing. Referring to figure 2 and the annotated photo. The two wires that are supplied attached to the crossing connect to the frogs (coloured

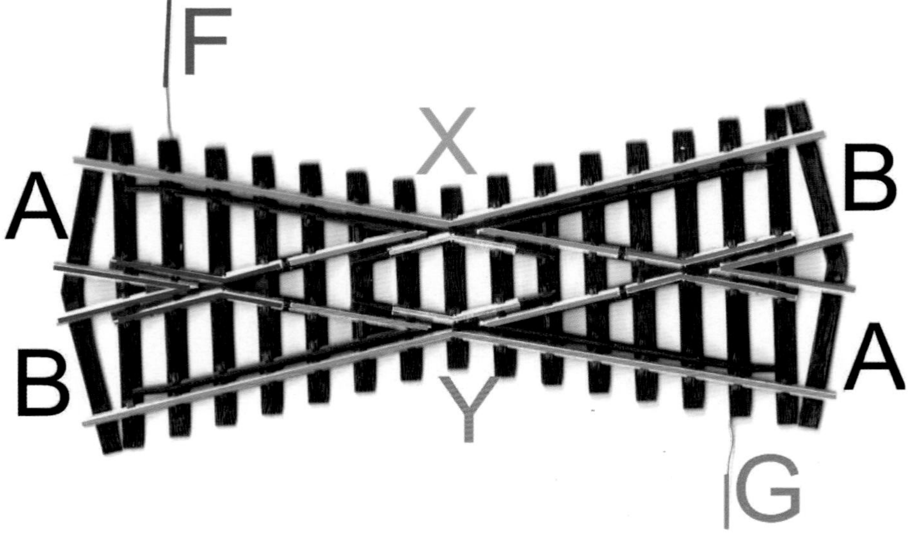

This is the short crossing again, this time showing its electrical sections.

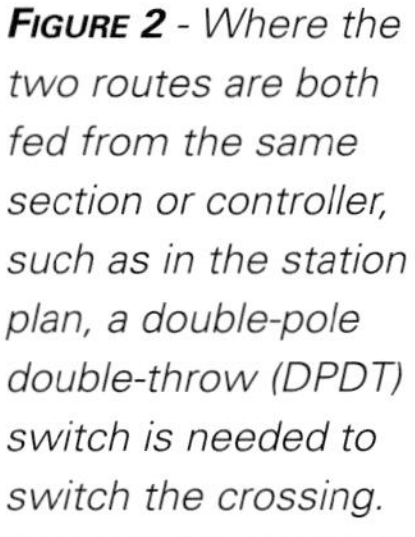

Figure 2 *- Where the two routes are both fed from the same section or controller, such as in the station plan, a double-pole double-throw (DPDT) switch is needed to switch the crossing.*

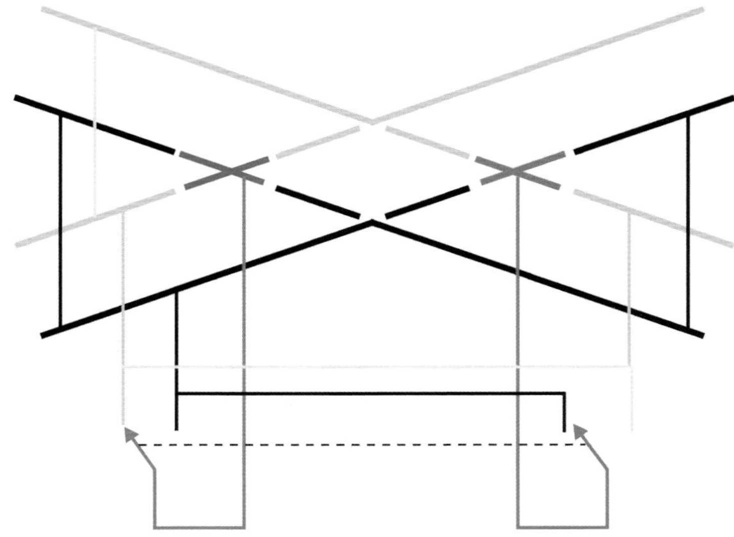

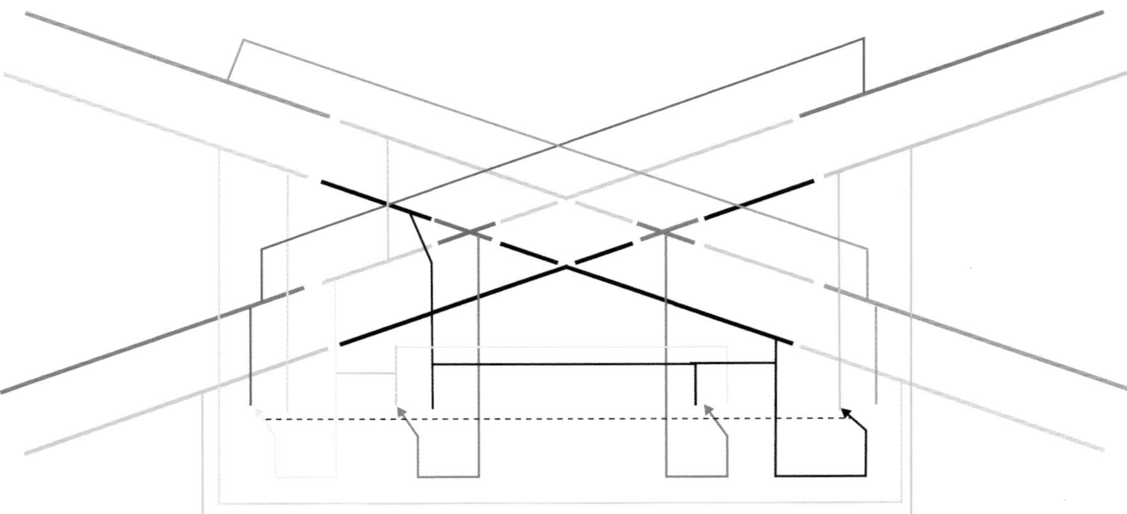

Figure 3 *- If the two routes are fed from different sections, controllers or have the red and black rails on opposite sides (for example on a figure '8') then you need to use either two DPDT switches or a 4-pole double-throw switch (4PDT).*

blue and red in the photo). You need to place insulated rail joiners where the frogs connect to the rest of the layout. The other rails (green and purple) use standard rail joiners. Note that you have to provide two wires to connect the plain track either side of the crossing.

For a train travelling in direction A-A, frog F (blue) needs to be connected to rail Y (purple) and frog G (orange) to rail X (green). For a train travelling in direction B-B frog F (blue) needs to be connected to rail X (green) and frog G (orange) to rail Y (purple).

If the two routes are fed from different sections, controllers or have the red and black rails on opposite sides (for example on a figure '8') then you need to use either two DPDT switches or a 4-pole double-throw switch (4PDT). The wiring becomes more complex as the green and purple rails now need to be switched as well as the frogs. In addition you now have four jumpers to connect the plain track at either side of the crossing and all the places where it joins the rest of the layout need insulating rail joiners. If you use two DPDT switches then you will need to use one to switch the frogs, as per figure 2, and one to switch the controller/section. Figure 3 is drawn for a 4PDT switch, if you use two DPDT switches then one should be connected up with the blue and red switches from figure 3 and the other with the grey and black ones.

Single and Double Slips

A slip is a crossing that has point blades built in so that as well as going straight across a train can be routed onto the other leg of the crossing. With a single slip only one side of the crossing has this facility, whilst on a double slip both sides of the crossing can be switched. Hopefully the diagram will make this clear.

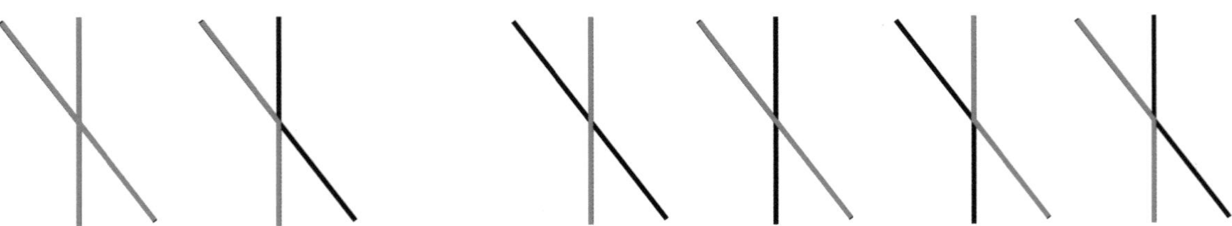

With a single slip you can either run trains straight across, just like a standard crossing or you can divert down one leg.

Double slips let you divert down either leg. With Peco's double slip you cannot have both straight routes set simultaneously.

With the point blades set for the straight routes the slip will behave just like a crossing and if you have live frogs then you have the same problems with keeping opposite polarities apart. If one or both of the point blades are set for the diverting route then only one route is passable through the crossing – the other line will be blocked.

Starting with a dead frog example, to keep things simple, the secret is to treat it as two points laid end to end. As long as the red and black rails have feeds everything else will fall into place. If you are using the slip to let two electrically separate tracks cross or join then you will need to arrange isolating sections and a switch to select the power source, just as if it was a pair of points. By giving the slip its own power feed it can be connected to the correct controller as required.

When it comes to live frog slips, thinking of them as two points back to back helps to simplify matters. The power from the controller is fed to the outer rails, coloured blue and red in the illustration. The two frogs, coloured green and yellow, have their own feeds which need to be connected to either the blue or red feed depending on how the point blades are set.

In the illustration the point blades are set so that a train can go from the lower left line to the lower right, or vice versa. Thus both the green and yellow feeds need to be connected to the blue feed. If the point blades were set so that the train went from upper left to lower right then the green feed would need to be connected to the red feed and the yellow to the blue. What you will find is that the frog feed depends on how the point blades at the other end of the slip

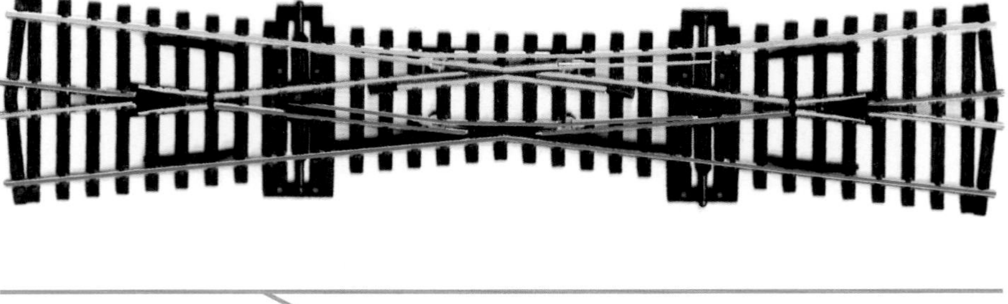

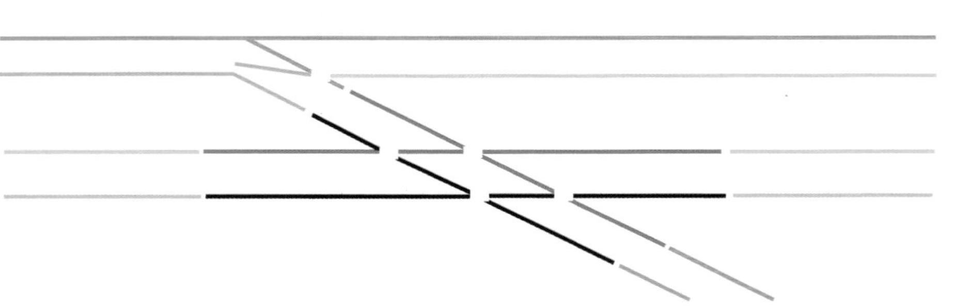

RIGHT TOP: *A dead frog single slip showing the electrically connected rails. As long as the red rails are connected to one side of the controller and the green rails to the other everything will work properly. The same is true for a dead frog double slip.*

BOTTOM: *Where a slip is used to cross an electrically separate line you need to isolate it from all the connecting lines and giving it its own power feeds (red and black rails).*

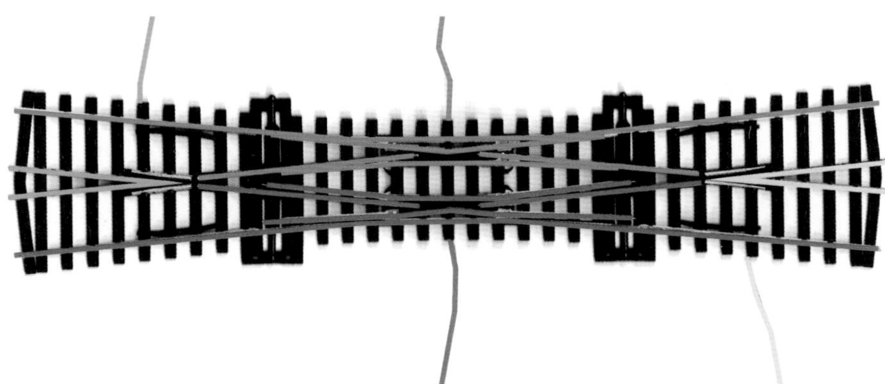

A live frog double slip showing the electrical feeds and the rails to which they are connected.

are set. If the right-hand tiebar is in the up position in the illustration then the green feed needs to be connected to the blue feed, if it is down it should be connected to the red one. Similarly if the left-hand tiebar is in the up position the yellow feed should be connected to the blue feed and to the red if it is down. These feeds can be switched by an accessory switch fitted to the slip's point motors (don't forget you'll need two – even for a single slip) if you use them, just like an ordinary live frog point. Don't forget that the green and yellow rails will need to be isolated from the rest of the layout, just like you would with a live frog point.

Passing Loops

We've looked at both dead frog and live frog points as individual items so now we'll look at what happens when you use them in a passing or run-round loop. Loops can be found on virtually all layouts and are used so that locomotives can run around their trains or for one train to pass another.

Starting with dead frog points and no extra wiring we get figure 1 – if both points are set to the same line, in this case the upper one, then a train can run through that line whilst another train is held isolated on the bottom one. This is the loop at its simplest: it relies on the points to route power to the selected line and isolate the other one.

It may look like a station, but it is just a loop with a few sidings hung off it. In this section we'll look at ways to wire loops with both dead and live frogs.

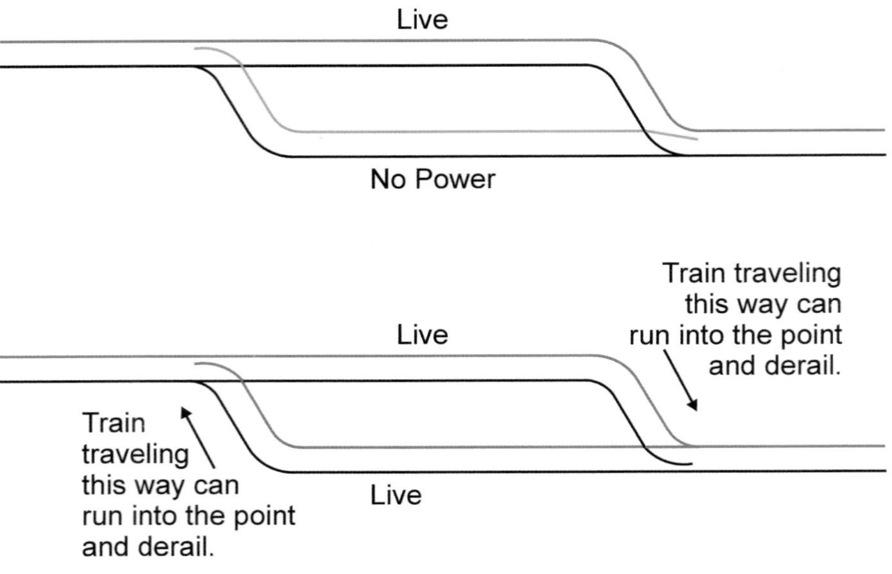

Figure 1 *- Dead frog points with no extra wiring. If both points are set to the same line, that line will be live and the other line will be isolated.*

Figure 2 *- Dead frog points with no extra wiring. If the points are set differently then both lines are live and trains can be driven into points set against them resulting in derailments.*

If the points are set to different lines (figure 2) then both lines are powered. It is now possible to drive a train along either loop until it reaches the point at the far end, which is set against it, resulting in a derailment.

Live frog points require extra wiring with switches linked to the points (figure 3). As a minimum the rails beyond the frog must be gapped at some point so that opposite polarities never get the opportunity to meet. This arrangement works in a similar way to figures 1 and 2 except that when the point at the far end of the loop is set against a train once the locomotive crosses the insulation gap it will stop as both rails will be the same polarity (i.e. both red or black).

So far we have looked at the bare minimum needed to get a loop to function. If you have a DCC controller then that is all that you need to do. Analogue DC layouts can gain extra operational benefits from adding a little extra wiring.

Where a loop is on a single track line it is often used so that trains travelling in opposite directions can pass each other. One train pulls into the loop and then the one travelling in the opposite direction arrives. Both trains can then proceed along the track that the other one is no longer occupying (figure 5).

DCC

For DCC layouts it is normal for the whole layout to be live at all times so we need to add extra power feeds to overcome the isolating effect of the points. To do this we run jumper wires from the top loop to the bottom loop (figure 4). If you are using sectional track points you can purchase special clips from Hornby, which look a bit like staples, which fit on the points and do this job for you. Whichever method you use the result is that however the points are set, a locomotive in the loop will always be powered.

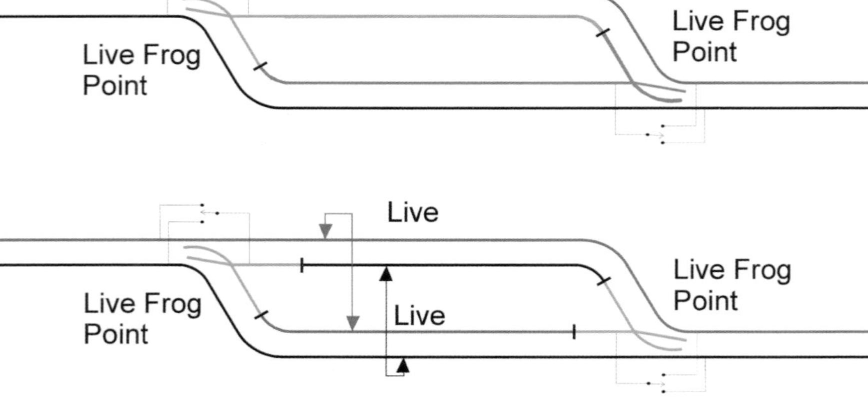

Figure 3 *- Live frog points require extra wiring and switches linked to the points.*

Figure 4 *- For DCC layouts we need to add extra feeds so that both tracks are always live.*

If we add an extra isolated section on each loop we can force a train to stop regardless of the way that the point at the end of the loop is set. The section can be linked to a signal for added authenticity. This allows a locomotive to be held by the signal regardless of how the points are set or what else is going on in the station.

This simple addition allows greater operational flexibility. With the locomotive at the front of the train isolated the station pilot can add or remove vans at the back of the train (figure 7). If the locomotive has been stopped right at the end of the isolated section we can back a pilot locomotive down, couple on to the front of the train locomotive and we have a double-header. By reversing the process we can split a double-header up. This is the sort of functionality you get with DCC at a fraction of the cost.

Things get more complicated when you add sidings to a loop. You need to ensure that they will receive power at the right time. Figure 9 shows an example of this where two sidings and a loco spur have been added to the lower loop track. For the sake of simplicity I have assumed dead frog points – wiring it for live frog ones will add further complexity and is left as an exercise for those who wish to prove that they can do it.

The key addition us the extra feed between the points on the lower loop. This provides power to both the loco spur and the sidings regardless of how the points on the main line are set. If this feed was not there then the loco spur could only be used when the left hand main line point was set to the loop and the sidings could only be used when both the right hand end main line point and the loco spur point were set correctly.

I have added an isolating section on the loco spur so that the station pilot can be held regardless of how the points are set. If you wish to hold a locomotive in the sidings then you will have to set the points against it.

Of course with DCC you can dispense with the isolating sections but you will still need the extra feed and to run extra feeds to the sidings and loco spur.

FIGURE 5 - Trains passing at a loop on a single track line.

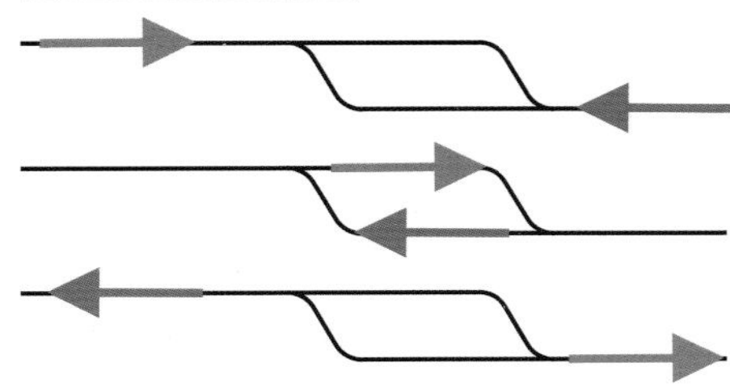

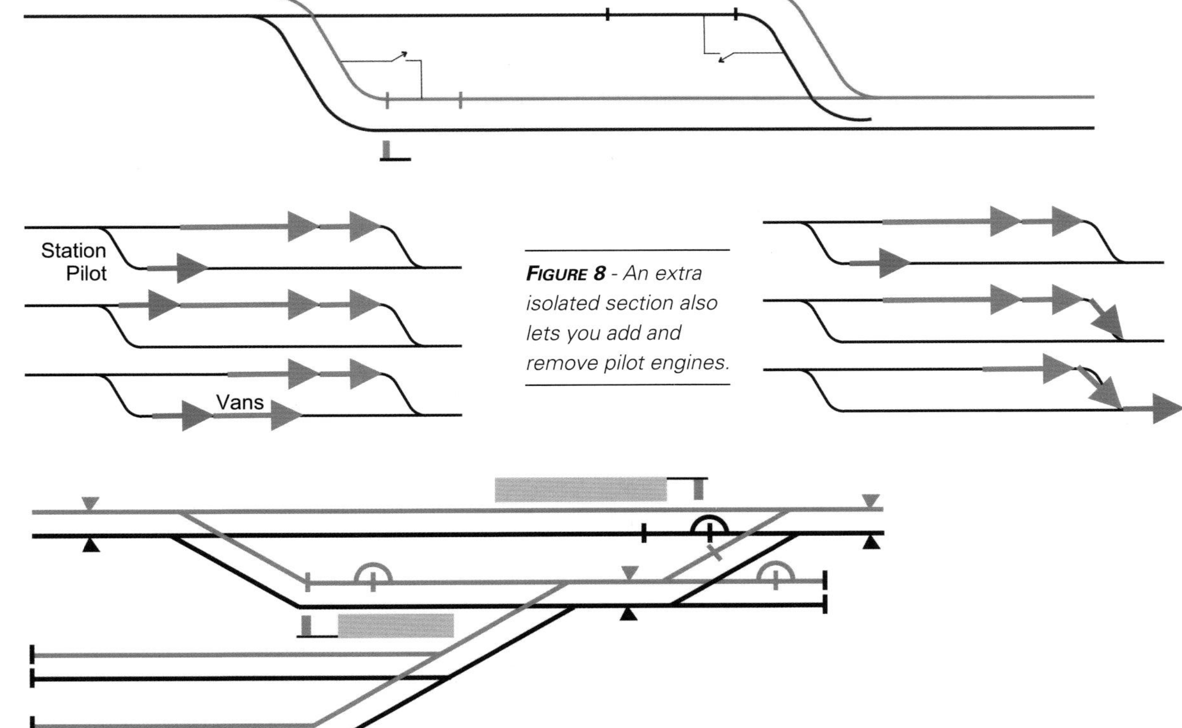

FIGURE 6 - An extra insulating gap on each track allows a train to be held in the loop regardless of how the points are set.

FIGURE 7 - With an extra isolated section on each track a station pilot can add or remove vans at the back of a through train.

FIGURE 8 - An extra isolated section also lets you add and remove pilot engines.

FIGURE 9 - Things get more complicated once you start adding sidings.

CHAPTER 7 Lighting With Bulbs and LEDs

In the days of yore the only way to get light in a model was to use a small light bulb. These suffered from a number of problems: they weren't particularly small, the small ones certainly weren't cheap, they generated a lot of heat and you needed to be able to get at them to replace them when they blew. With the advance of technology the incandescent bulb has now been replaced in many fields by light emitting diodes (LEDs).

LEDs can address all the incandescent bulb's shortcomings from a modelling perspective: they come in a variety of sizes – down to ones that are almost too small to handle, they can be purchased cheaply if you buy in quantity, they generate no heat when lit and, for our purposes, have an unlimited life as long as they are not mistreated. Indeed, for most modelling applications they are quite possibly the perfect light source. Nevertheless the incandescent bulb still finds a place in many models.

Commercial products such as these street lamps often use bulbs rather than LEDs.

When you use a bulb in a model you need to ensure that the heat generated by the bulb will not damage it and that if the bulb needs to be replaced you can do this without completely destroying the model. It is also a good idea to run the bulb at a lower voltage than its rating; this has the double benefit of it not running so hot and having a longer life.

12 Volt rated bulbs should be run on a 6 to 9 Volt supply, either AC or DC. If you wish to use a 12 to 16 Volt supply then the bulbs should be run in pairs, one after the other. This is called in series.

If you wish to run more bulbs from one switch then the bulbs, or pairs of bulbs, should be wired in parallel, as shown in the diagram.

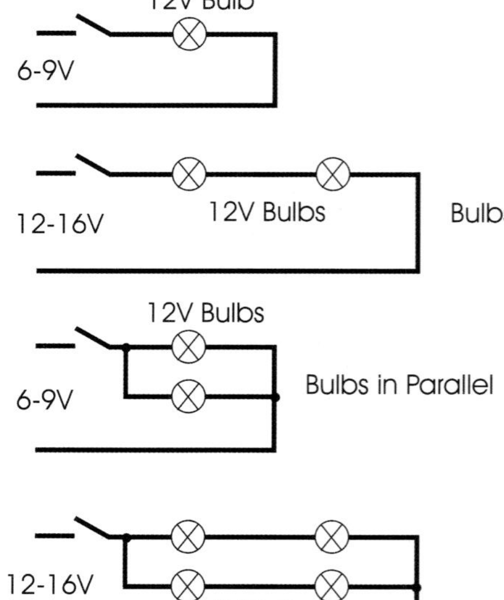

12V bulbs should be run on a 6 to 9V supply, either AC or DC, to prolong their life. If you wish to use a 12 to 16V supply then you should run the bulbs in series.

LEDs come in a wide variety of shapes, sizes and colours. In the early years of their development they were large, red and expensive but now they come in a number of useful sizes and colours. For OO gauge one of the most useful is the 3mm LED (also known as 'T1' style). This is a 3mm diameter unit with a domed head which is ideal for fitting in locomotives and signals. Single colour LEDs come in red, amber, yellow, green, blue and two versions of white. The standard white LED has a blue tinge and is ideal for representing modern high-intensity locomotive headlights, security and florescent lighting, the other type, usually referred to as 'golden-white' has a yellow tinge and is suitable for

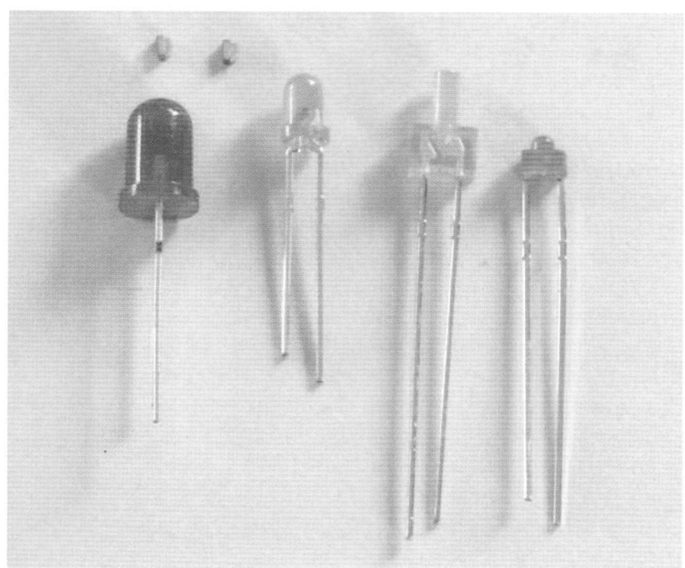

Left to right: A 5mm diameter red LED, 3mm diameter green LED, yellow 2mm lighthouse LED, 1.8mm diameter amber LED and those two specks above the 5mm red LED are surface mount (SMD) white LEDs – now they are really tiny.

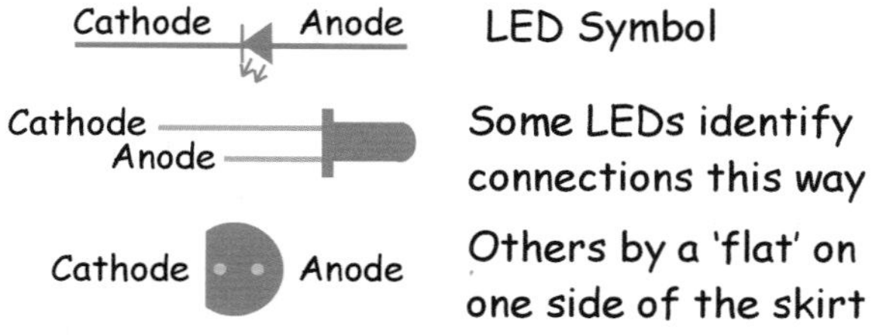

In circuit diagrams the symbol for an LED is a diode with two arrows, representing the light. The drawings show how the connections on a standard LED relate to the symbol.

older headlights and traditional light bulbs. You can also purchase bi-colour LEDs which can be used to show two or more colours. A bi-colour red/green LED can show red, green or yellow whilst a red/white LED has obvious uses for train head and tail lighting.

So what is an LED? Firstly it is most definitely not a lamp, it is a diode. The light that it produces is a useful by-product of its function. This means that whilst you can connect a bulb into a circuit either way around, an LED must be connected the right way around otherwise it will not light. Unlike a bulb an LED has very little resistance to current flow so cannot be used as a current limiting device, indeed it must be protected from excessive currents using a resistor.

In an ideal world a typical LED will operate from a 2V DC supply drawing a current of 20mA, or thereabouts, so to use them on a model railway we need to add a resistor to limit the current that the LED will draw. In fact most LEDs are quite bright, even on a lower current such as 15mA. Left to its own devices it will draw as much current as the power supply will provide and have a bright, but brief, existence. To work out the size of the resistor we need to do a little maths (sorry). We need to take the supply voltage (e.g. 12V), subtract 2 from it (the 2V our LED needs) and then divide the result by 0.015 (the 15mA, or 0.015A that the LED needs to operate).

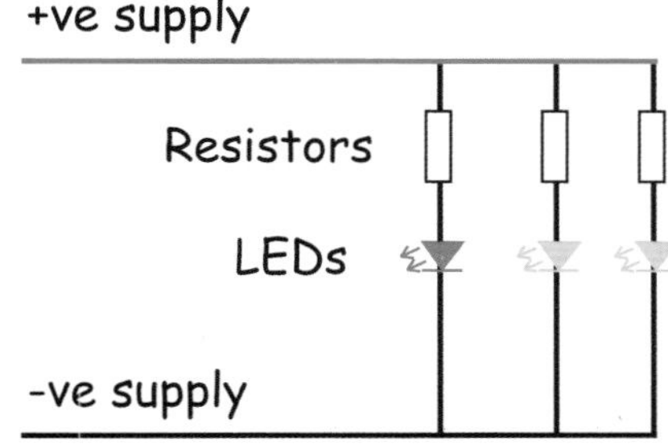

When wiring LEDs you should ensure that each has its own resistor. The positive output from the power supply should be connected to the LED's anode and the negative output to its cathode. The resistor can be connected to whichever side of the LED is convenient.

So for a 12V supply the calculation is:

12V – 2V = 10V
10V / 0.015A = 666 Ohms

Now resistors come in a range of standard values and the nearest to 666 Ohms are 560 Ohms (too low) and 680 Ohms (too high). There is a bit of leeway in choosing a value but, given that most LEDs are quite bright, selecting the higher value is usually gives a perfectly adequate light. As we are limiting the current in the circuit to 15-20mA then a small 0.25 Watt resistor will be perfectly adequate. Don't be tempted to try and run more than one LED off each resistor. Resistors are cheap and it is a false economy to skimp here.

White and blue LEDs tend to need a higher voltage to operate than the other colour versions – typically about 5V. For these you need to change the calculation for the resistor to: Subtract 5 from the supply voltage and then divide by 0.15.

So in this case for a 12V supply the calculation is:
12V – 5V = 7V
7V / 0.015A = 467 Ohms
Nearest standard value = 470 Ohms

Bi-colour LEDs come in two- and three-lead versions. In both cases there are actually two LEDs inside the plastic housing. On a two lead version the LEDs are connected with opposite polarity so that, for a red/green LED applying the voltage one way the red LED would shine, applying it the other way the green LED would shine and on an AC voltage, where the current flows either way, both would shine giving a yellow light. On a three lead version the two LEDs have one common terminal. Connecting a voltage across the red and common terminals would produce a red light, green and common a green light and with both the red and green terminals connected to the voltage at the same time you would get yellow.

The plastic case of an LED is quite large compared to the size of the LED buried inside; with careful filing you can reduce the size of the housing, for example to fit in a signal head, or change its shape to make an indicator for a road vehicle. Lighthouse style LEDs which have a long cylindrical section are particularly useful for producing odd shapes and sizes. A word of warning – if you go too far with the filing and get to the internal parts the LED will cease to work. The internal gubbins can usually be seen through the case – so as long as you check your progress frequently you shouldn't have any problems. Another way to use an LED is as a source for a fibre-optic strand. Simply drill a suitably sized hole in the top of your LED and glue the fibre-optic strand into the hole with some super-glue.

Earlier I said that LEDs like to operate on DC. We have already met the bi-colour two-lead LED that can operate on AC, to give a yellow colour, but what about using standard LEDs on AC? Well you need to add a standard diode, before or after the LED, to protect it from the reverse voltage.

For a LED on an AC supply the calculation for the resistor is:

Multiply the supply voltage by 0.7 then subtract 2
(or 5 for a blue or white LED) and finally divide by 0.015
16V AC Supply, Red LED: 16V * 0.7 = 11.2V
11.2V – 2V = 9.2V
9.2V / 0.015A = 613 Ohms
Nearest standard value = 620 Ohms

Resistor standard values from 100 to 1000 Ohms:
100, 120, 150, 180, 220, 270, 330, 390, 470, 560, 680, 820, 1000

Colour Light Signals

Now we'll look at a practical application of our electrical knowledge, installing a colour light signal. LED based signals are available from a number of manufacturers, in this case I shall be using a 4mm scale example from the Eckon range; similar products are available for N gauge from CR Signals.

A Class 47 is held at a red signal. The signal is an Eckon model..

Colour light signals come in a variety of configurations. Those with three or more bulbs stacked vertically are for multiple-aspect-signalling (MAS) which combines the functions of both home and distant signals enabling higher speeds, closer headways and full or partial automation of the signalling system. Two aspect colour light signals on the other hand are normally used as an alternative to conventional semaphores.

A 2-aspect Signal

The signal that I have chosen is Eckon's ES2H 2-aspect home signal which comes with red and green aspects. A distant version, ES2D, is also available which has green and yellow aspects. The signal comes as a simple kit containing two pre-wired LEDs, a resistor, a metal tube for the post and some plastic mouldings.

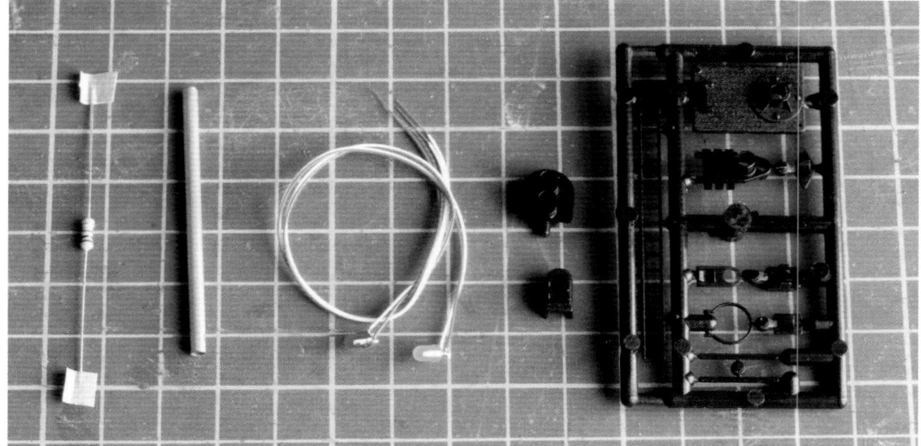

This is what you get in the Eckon signal kit. From left to right: a resistor, the signal post, the two LEDs, the signal head and rear cover and the sprue of plastic parts.

Building the Signal

Push the metal post into the base and then push the platform onto the other end. Push the signal head into place on the platform and then glue the ladder in place. You can now push the two LEDs into position, with the red one at the bottom of the signal and feed the wires down the post. Place the cover on the back of the signal heads, add the safety ring at the top of the ladder, the strengthening struts and any of the additional components as required to complete the assembly.

To disguise the wires running from the signal head to the post it is a good idea to put a touch of dark grey or black paint on them. If fitted the diamond indicator should be painted white and the telephone box light grey. The telephone box needs a black/white diagonal striped panel on the front. I prepared mine on a computer along with the signal's number for the identification panel.

The diamond or D-shaped panels indicate that the signal is track-circuited so that the driver does not need to sound the locomotive's whistle when forced to stop. For more information on the wide array of signs and indicators used on railways over the years, I recommend a look at the Rail Signs website, www.railsigns.co.uk.

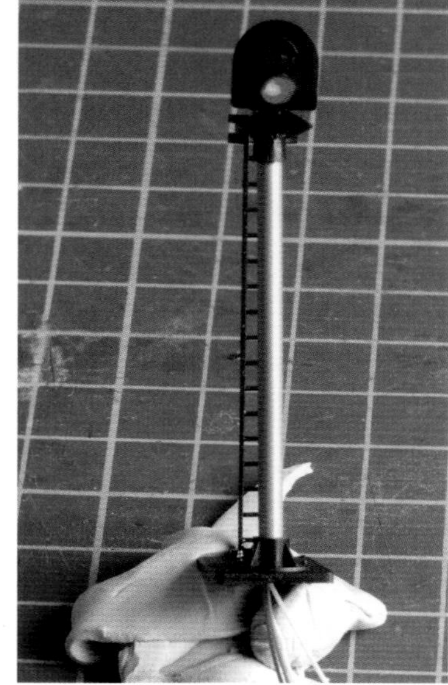

With the basic assembly completed the signal can be tested. The red LED should go at the bottom. I used some BluTack to hold the base in place on the workbench.

Wiring the Signal

The signal should always show either red or green. It should never show both red and green and should only be off if it has failed, in which case the driver would treat it as being red.

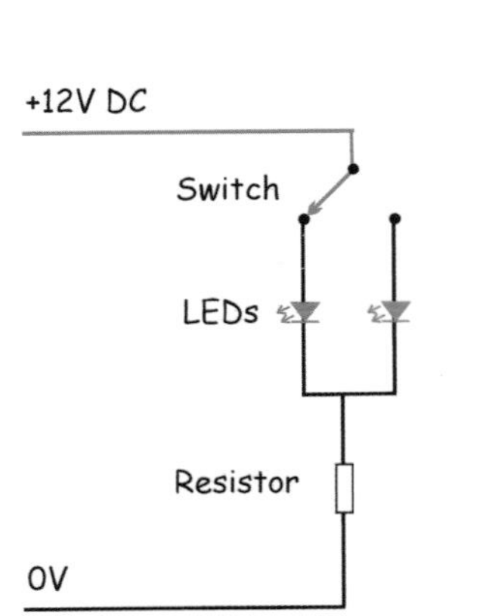

CIRCUIT 1 - *Using a SPDT switch we can make the signal display red or green.*

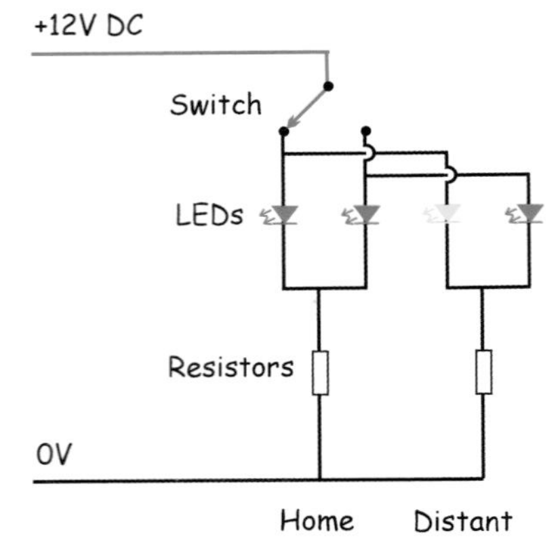

CIRCUIT 2 - *A distant signal, showing green or yellow, can be controlled by the same switch that we use for the home signal.*

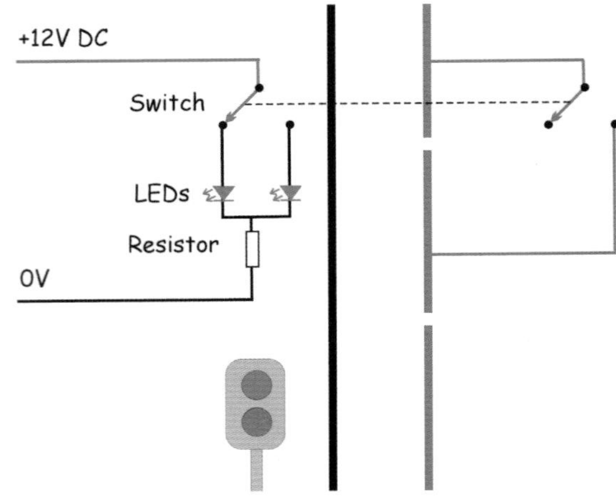

CIRCUIT 3 - *Using a DPDT switch we can isolate a section of track beyond the signal to prevent trains over-running the signal on red.*

We can use a SPDT switch to connect the signal to the power supply, as shown in Circuit 1. If you have a distant signal as well that can be wired in as shown in Circuit 2. When the home signal shows green the distant shows green and when the home signal shows red the distant shows yellow.

If we use a DPDT switch we can stop trains from overrunning the signal. Circuit 3 shows how this is done. We isolate a section of rail just past the signal and only connect it to the rest of the layout when the signal is green. When the signal is red the section of track is electrically isolated and any locomotive driven into it will lose power and stop.

We can refine this circuit by adding a diode as shown in Circuit 4. This allows trains travelling from behind the signal to pass through the isolated section but still stops trains that have passed the red signal. This enables us to use the signal on a line where trains can travel in either direction and to reverse out of the section if we have overrun the signal.

CIRCUIT 4 - *By adding a diode it is possible for trains travelling in the opposite direction to pass through the isolated section unhindered. It also enables trains that have overrun the red signal to reverse out of the isolated section.*

+12V DC
Switch
LEDs
Resistor
OV
Diode
1N4001

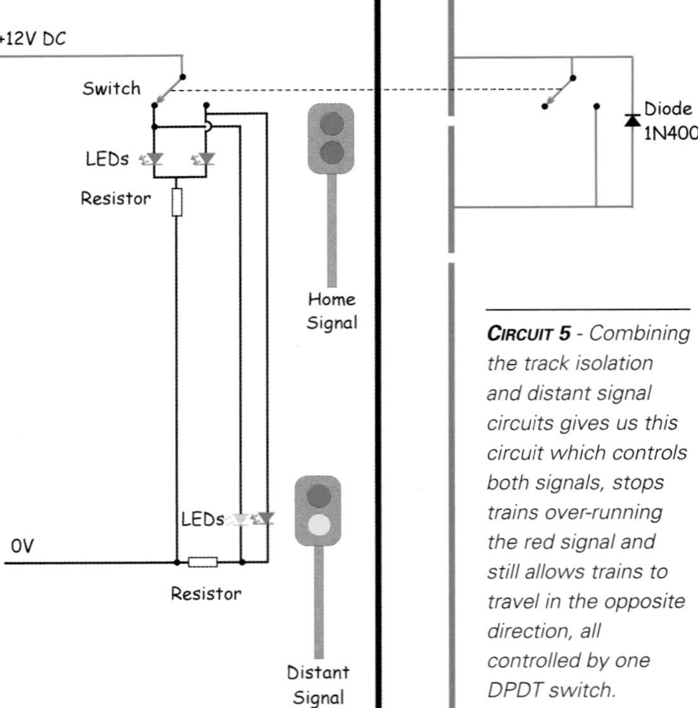

CIRCUIT 5 - *Combining the track isolation and distant signal circuits gives us this circuit which controls both signals, stops trains over-running the red signal and still allows trains to travel in the opposite direction, all controlled by one DPDT switch.*

A 3-aspect Signal

Multiple aspect signalling (MAS) is a more complicated system to implement on a model railway as the indication on each signal is affected by the next signal down the line.

This 3-aspect signal has a route indicating 'feather' illuminated to show that the train will take a diverging route from the main line. The small signal is a position light signal for shunting moves. Both are 'N' scale models produced by CR Signals.

Multiple Aspect Signalling

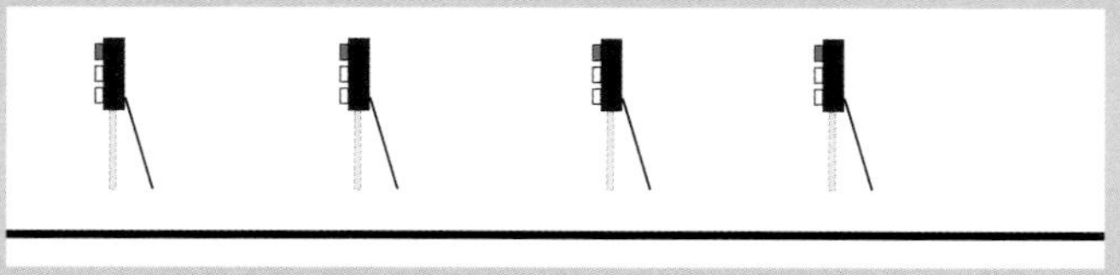

1. *With no trains on the line MAS signals will all show green.*

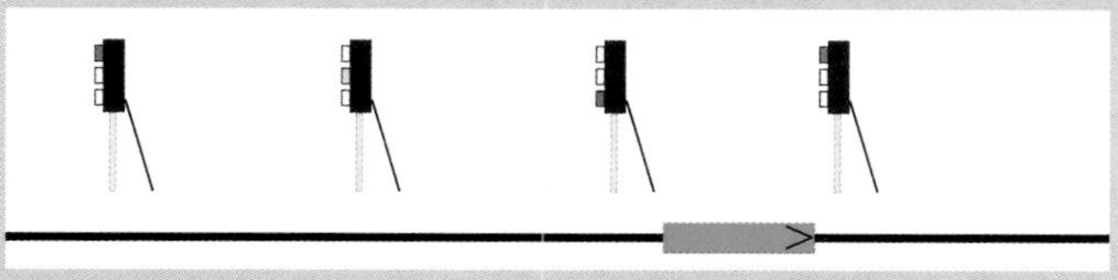

2. *With a train on the line the signal behind the train shows red, and the signal behind that shows yellow. With 4-aspect signals the third signal behind the train would show a double yellow.*

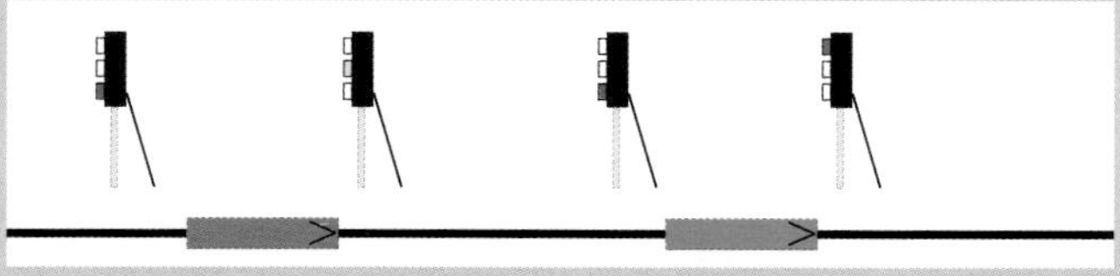

3. *When a second train starts to catch up the driver sees a yellow signal warning him that the next signal is at red. The two signals behind him show red and yellow to protect the rear of his train.*

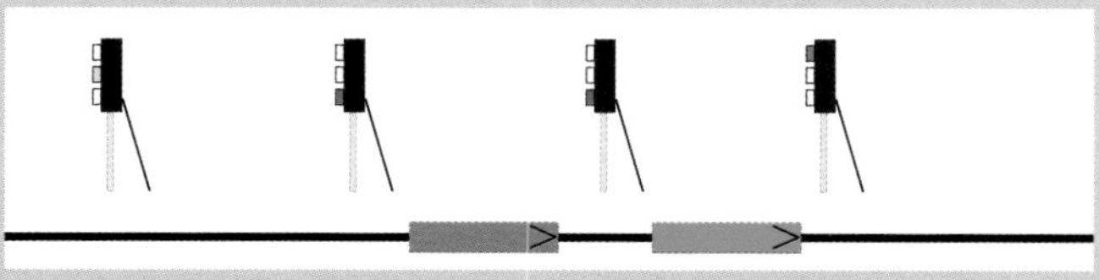

4. *Once the second train has passed the yellow signal protecting the first train, the signal turns red. The red aspect over-rides the yellow one.*

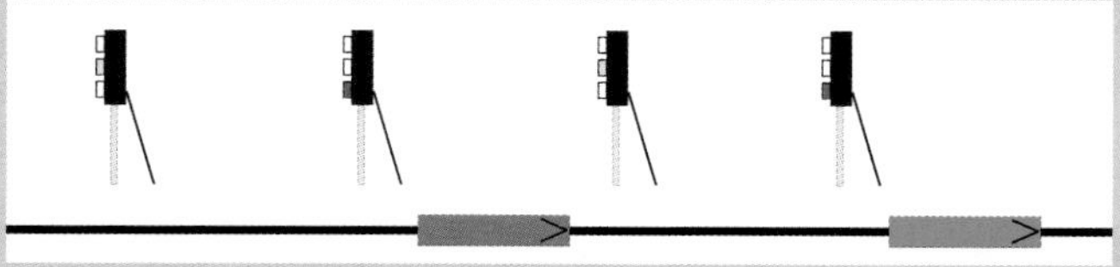

5. *As the first train draws away the red signal in front of the second train changes to yellow, allowing that train to proceed.*

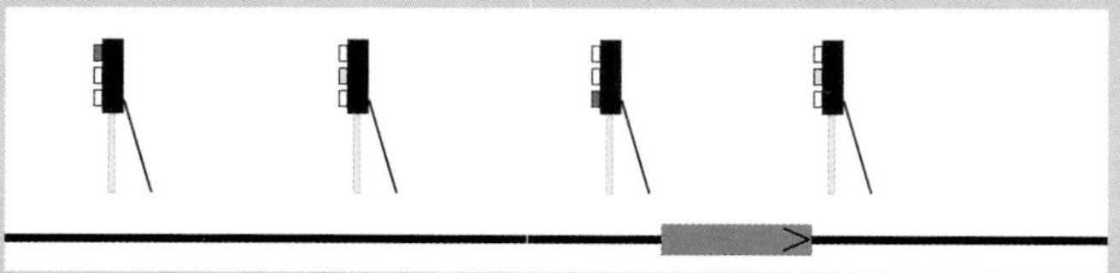

6. *The second train can carry on under yellow signals, one block behind the first train. MAS allows higher speeds and closer headways than the equivalent semaphore signals, with the added benefit that it can happen without any intervention from the signalman.*

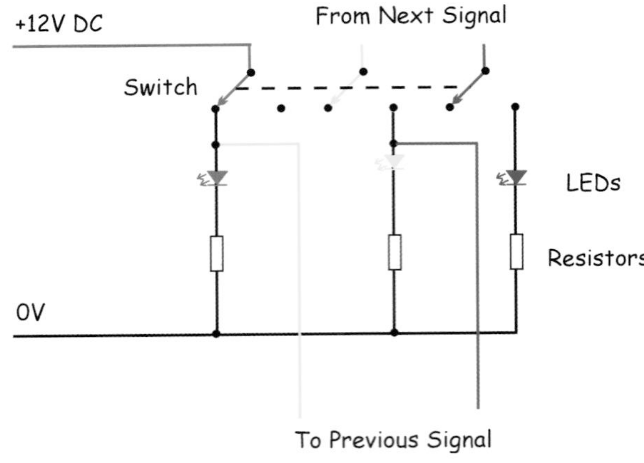

LEFT: Two wires connect each signal with its neighbour. These control the aspect displayed if the signal is not red.

With three or more lights to control on each signal and the state of the next signal down the line to consider, controlling MAS signals on a model railway is harder than 2-aspect ones.

It is possible to purchase electronic modules, such as those from Heathcote Electronics, to automate the process. These incorporate an infra-red train detector to establish when a train passes a signal along with circuitry to read the next signal's aspect and control the LEDs. It is also possible for the signal to be set to red by an external switch which is useful at junctions, for bi-directional running and for the signalman to stop the train. There is also an option to isolate a section of track by the signal to automate train operation.

Manual operation of 3-aspect signals is possible using 3-pole 2-way switches. Whilst these are not commonly available you can purchase 4-pole 2-way push buttons (Rapid Electronics 78-0505 Std 4-pole Changeover Switch), which will also work for 4-aspect signals or provide an isolated track section by a red signal. To operate them all you need to do is set the switch to red for the signal immediately behind the train and set any others to yellow/green. The actual aspect that the other signals display is determined by the circuit.

One method of controlling MAS signals on a model railway is to use electronic units, like this one manufactured by Heathcote Electronics.

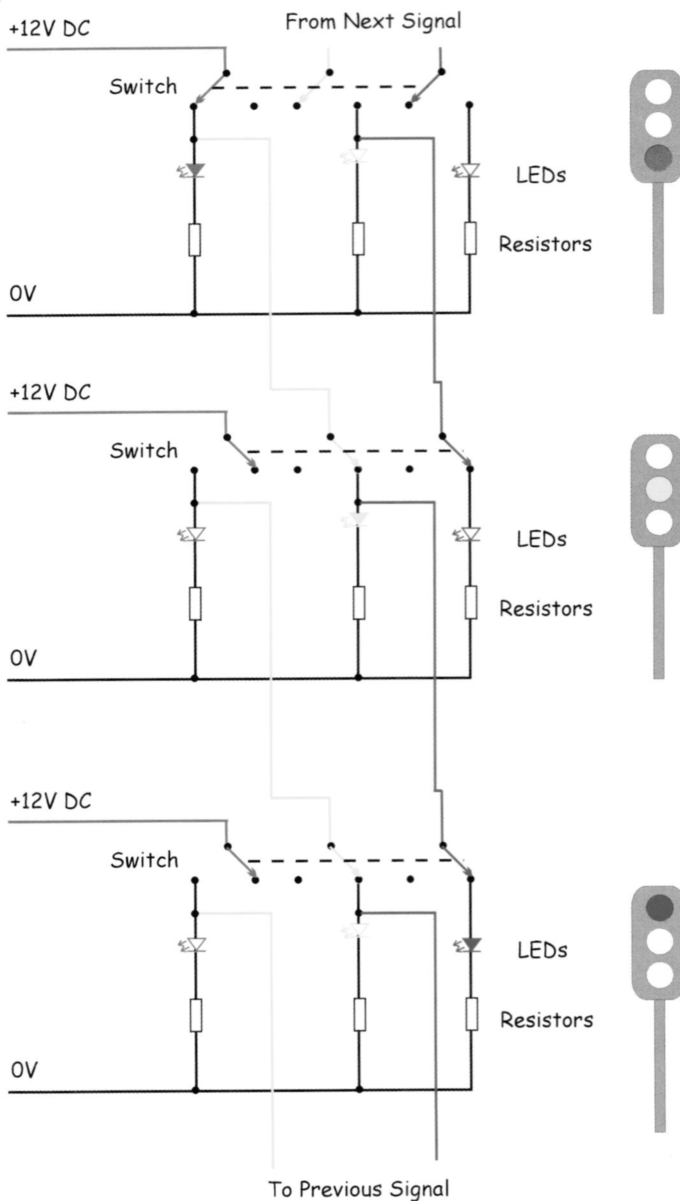

LEFT The 3-aspect MAS circuit showing how the aspects on each signal are controlled.

Fun With Diodes

CHAPTER

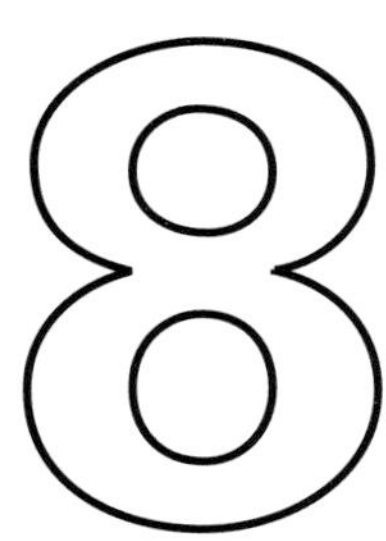

We have looked at light emitting diodes (LEDs), and in this chapter we will look at ordinary diodes. They are semiconductors - a family that includes transistors and integrated circuits – which is a posh way of saying that sometimes they conduct electricity and sometimes they don't. Diodes are effectively a one-way street for electricity – it can flow through them one way but not the other.

So, what can a diode do for us? Quite a lot actually, they can convert AC (alternating current) from a mains transformer into DC (direct current) to run electric motors, protect the ends of sidings, sort out reverse loops, give us directional lighting in locomotives and provide one button route selection on our control panels.

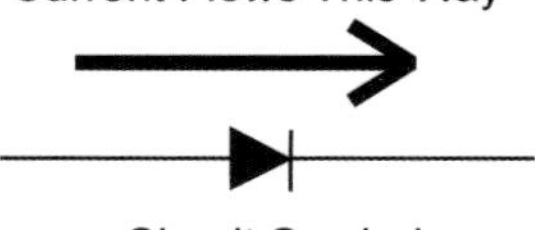

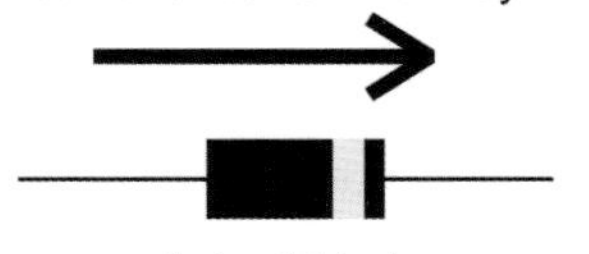

A diode allows electricity to flow only in one direction. This illustration shows the symbol used for diodes in circuit diagrams and what they look like in reality. It is vital to get them the right way around, otherwise your circuit won't work – so always double check.

You Got Protection?

By feeding the end of a siding through a diode you can stop a locomotive from over-running the buffers. Apart from the obvious use on sidings where visibility is limited or non-existent this is useful anywhere to protect your valuable locos from human error. The advantage of using a diode rather than a switch is that you can simply reverse the loco out of the siding.

If you want to get fancy, then by adding an LED (and current limiting resistor) facing the other way then when a loco is driven into the protected section the LED will light to remind you to turn the power off – again, very useful if you can't see the end of the siding. The LED will also light if you forget to reverse the controller before trying to back the loco out of the siding.

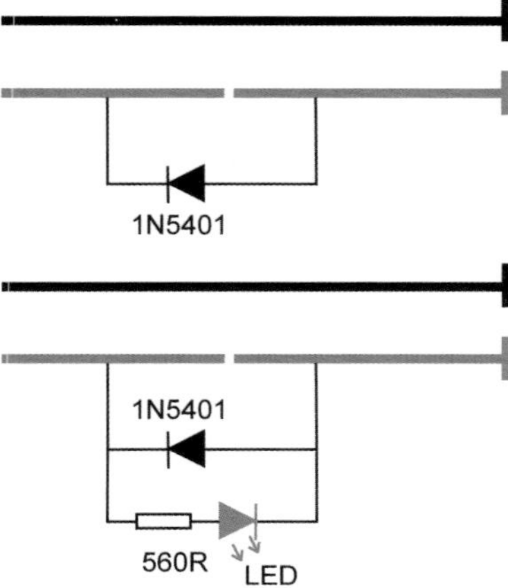

In the upper diagram we have a diode protecting the dead end siding. By adding an LED and current limiting resistor we get a warning light. The LED and resistor only allow a very small current to flow, not enough for the locomotive to move.

This Way Round

Reverse loops are a nuisance on model railways as at some point rails of the opposite polarity need to meet. Using four diodes, or a package of diodes called a bridge rectifier, you can make reverse loops easier.

The main line is connected directly to the controller which also feeds the input of the bridge rectifier. The reversing loop itself is connected to the output of the bridge rectifier.

The bridge rectifier takes the track voltage and directs it so that the positive and negative rails are always on the same side in the loop. This means that trains will always go in the same direction on the loop.

To operate the loop you drive along the main and into the loop entrance. You stop the train in the loop, switch the point so that the train can come out, reverse the controller and drive the train out. No extra switches are required.

The bridge rectifier is also used to convert the AC output from mains transformers to the DC used to run our electric motors – power supplies tend to include a few other components to smooth the output and regulate the voltage, but the bridge rectifier is at the heart of it. I shan't cover power supplies – if you are confident about building one, you shouldn't be reading this!

Lead Kindly Light

Directional head and or tail lights can be made using either bulbs or LEDs. You will need a normal diode and your bulb or LED and resistor. Simply connect the diode and bulb in series (one after the other) and connect to track pickups. The bulb will light in one direction of travel but the brightness will be dependant on the track voltage.

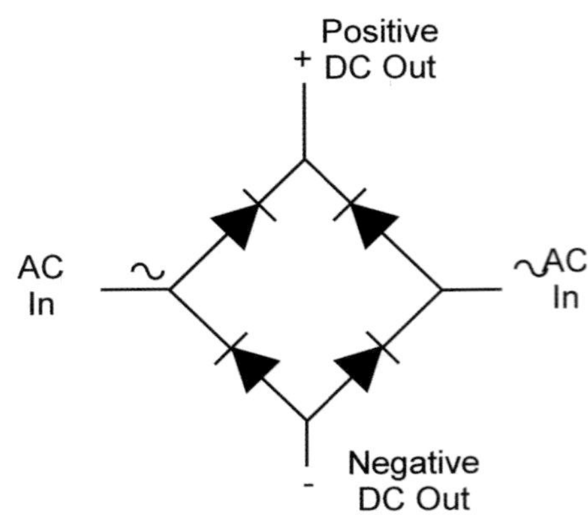

Circuit Symbol

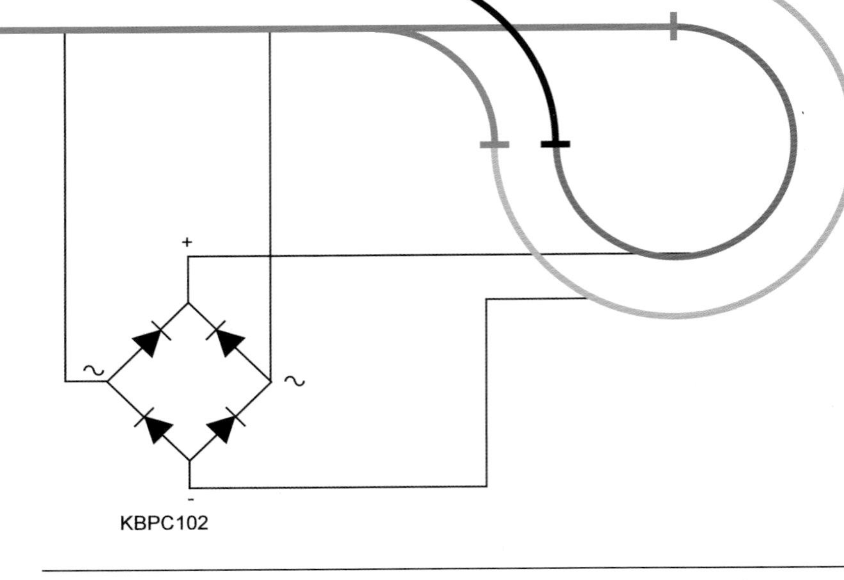

ABOVE AND RIGHT: This is the circuit symbol for a bridge rectifier and what they look like in reality. You can connect the AC inputs either way around but the DC outputs need to be connected correctly. Markings on the rectifier identify which terminal is which.

Actual Bridge Rectifier

ABOVE: Using a bridge rectifier to power a reverse loop saves you from installing any extra switches. This loop is set up for clockwise operation. The main line is shown powered for a train travelling into the loop (remember – the right rail is positive when travelling forward). Once the train is in the loop we can reverse the direction switch on the controller. The red and black rails on the main line will swap over, but the purple and grey rails, which are fed through the bridge rectifier will not and the train can be driven out of the loop.

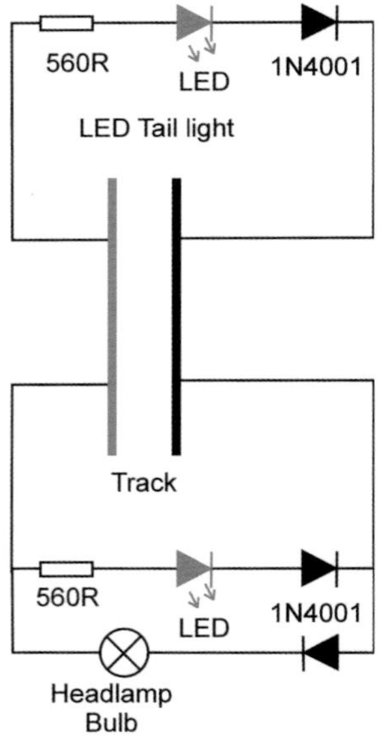

FAR RIGHT: Here are two examples of directional lighting. At the top we have a tail lamp. It will light when the red rail is on the left (train heading down the page) but not when it is on the right (train heading up the page). At the bottom we have head and tail lights connected, each with their own diode. With the red rail on the left (train heading down the page) the tail light is on and the headlight is off. With the red rail on the right (heading up the page) the tail light would be off and the headlight on.

Press For Action

If you have installed solenoid point motors you will know that sometimes you have to push a lot of buttons to set up a route, especially in fiddle yards. By using a capacitor discharge unit (CDU) and some diodes we can make a single button operate a number of point motors.

Imagine a five track fiddle yard. This needs four point motors, each operated by two buttons or one switch. To get to track A you only need to set point 1 to normal (N) but to get to track D you need to set points 1 and 4 to reverse (R) and points 2 and 3 to normal – that's four controls to operate. Now imagine how much easier things would be if you just had to press one button to select a track.

The first thing we need to do is create a table showing which points need to be operated in order to get to each track. For our five track yard the table would look like this:

	Point 1		*Point 2*		*Point 3*		*Point 4*	
	N	**R**	**N**	**R**	**N**	**R**	**N**	**R**
Track A	X							
Track B		X		X				
Track C		X	X			X		
Track D		X	X		X		X	
Track E		X	X		X			X

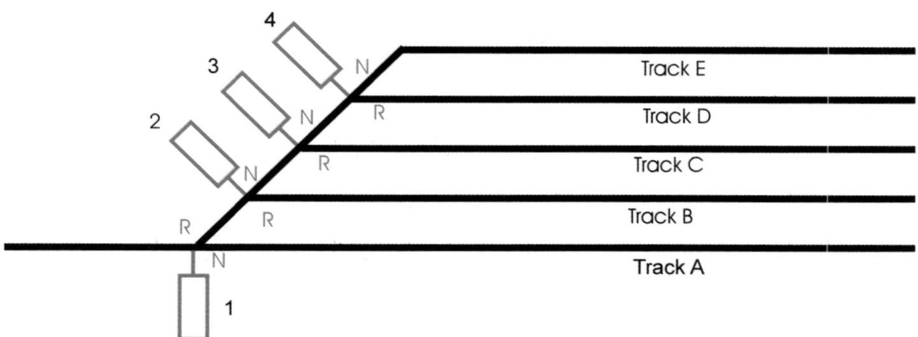

A five track fiddle yard needs four points, each with their own motor and buttons or switch. That is a lot of switches to operate.

The crosses indicate which way each point has to be set in order to access each track.

In some cases we are not interested in how the points are set, for example if we select track B the train will not be travelling over points 3 and 4 so we don't bother to set them.

Where there is only one cross in a column we can connect that point motor terminal straight to the switch but where there are more than one cross we need to use a diode to connect the point motor terminal to the switches. The table can be converted to a circuit diagram by replacing the crosses with wire links or diodes. In the diagram a dot indicates where two wires join.

The best way to construct a diode matrix is to use an electronic stripboard and solder the diodes and wire links in place, however for a simple one, such as a three or four track yard, you can use screw terminal blocks.

A Note On Component Types

Diodes and bridge rectifiers are common components and are relatively cheap.

For most uses a standard 3A rectifier diode such as a 1N5401 is ideal. Where you are using the diode to protect an LED, one with a lower rating, such as a 1A rated 1N4001 can be substituted.

For bridge rectifiers a 3A rated component such as a KBPC102 will be suitable. Whilst a lower rated one will be okay most of the time the extra current capacity will be useful if you get a short circuit.

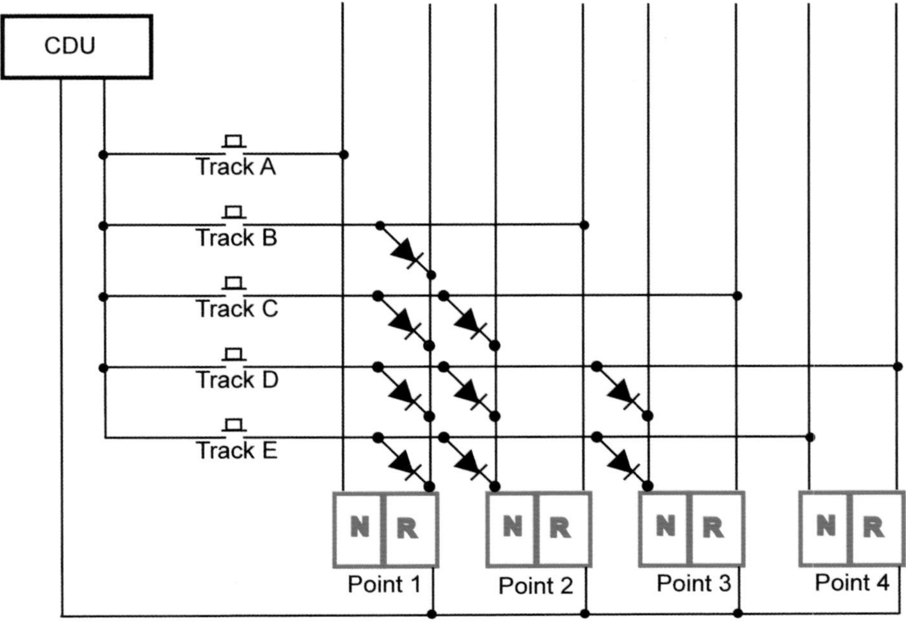

The circuit diagram for our diode matrix is basically the same as the table that we devised. We need the capacitor discharge unit (CDU) as some routes operate more than one point motor.

CHAPTER

Practical Examples

There is no 'right way' to wire a given track formation. The requirements will vary depending on the number of controllers, choice of live or dead frog, manual or electrically operated points and how the layout will be operated. In this chapter I shall take a few sample track plans and show how they could be connected up.

Fiddle Yard Throat

This is one end of the fiddle yard on a continuous run. The double track main line comes in from the right with the fiddle yard lines on the left. The top two lines are for trains running from left to right, the bottom two for trains running from right to left and the centre two are for multiple units that can enter and exit in either direction.

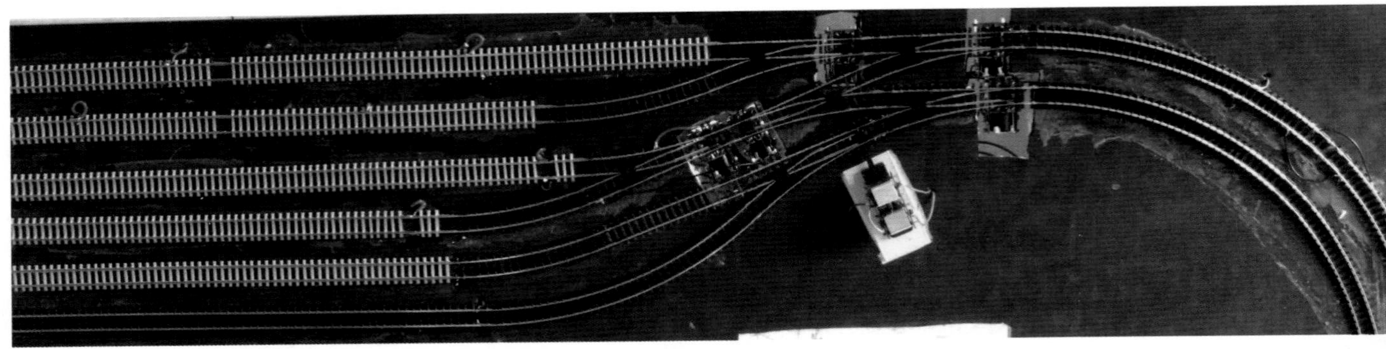

ABOVE: This is one end of the fiddle yard on a continuous run. The double track main line comes in from the right with the fiddle yard lines on the left.

Option 1: Manual Point Operation – Dead Frogs

If the points are dead frog examples operated manually then the absolute minimum wiring required is for insulated rail joiners to be placed at the locations shown in the diagram and the centre sidings to be fed from an SPDT switch that connects them to either the upper or lower main line.

To run a train into one of the centre sidings set the points and throw the switch to connect to the lower main line. To run a train out, set the points and throw the switch to connect to the upper main line.

To run a train into the lower sidings or out of the upper sidings simply set the points.

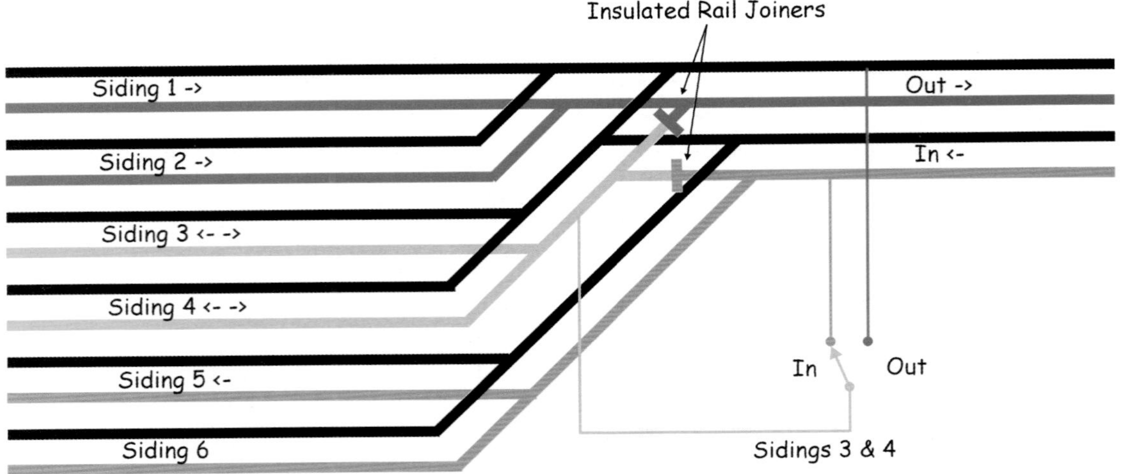

With manually operated dead-frog points a single SPDT switch to control the bi-directional sidings 3 and 4 is all that is needed.

Option 2: Electrical Point Operation – Probe and Stud

Most fiddle yards are situated in inaccessible locations so electrical operation of the points is a common need. The cheapest way to do this is with twin-solenoid point motors and probe and stud operation.

Most of the point motors are connected in the same way with one stud for each coil, however point motors 2, 3 and 4 share 4 studs between their 6 coils. The point operated by PM3 always needs either PM2 or PM4 set to complete the route, PM4 for an inbound train and PM2 for an outbound.

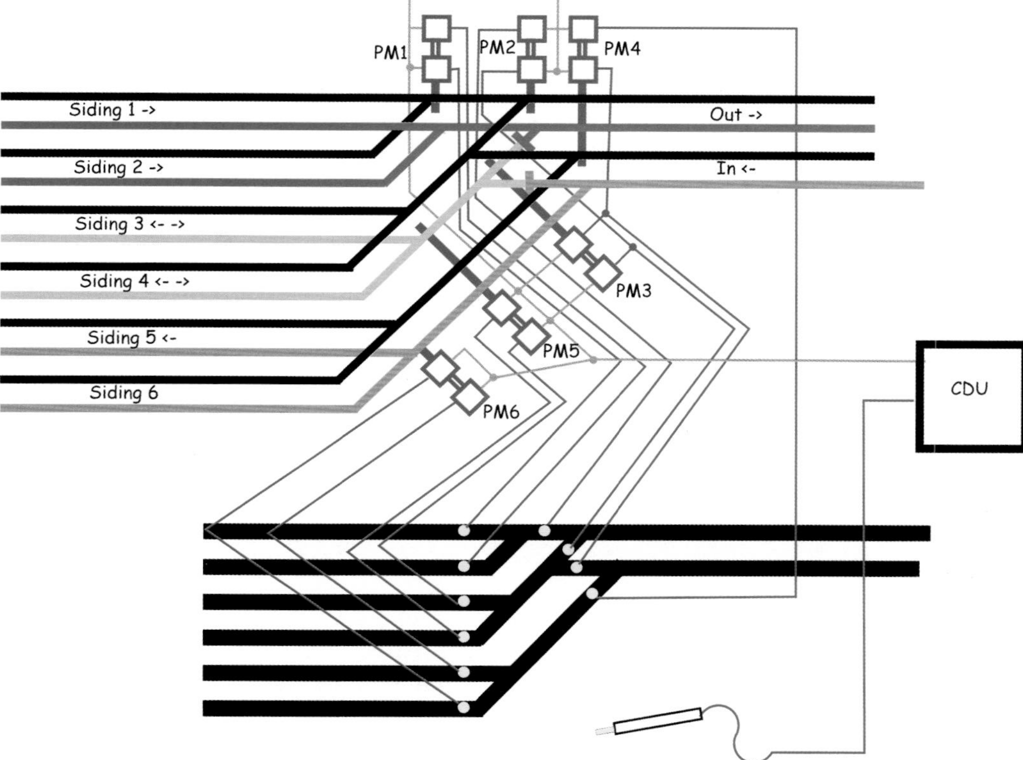

Six point motors require a lot of wires. You can see how things get complicated very quickly as the number of things being controlled increases.

Probe and stud operation of point motors.

To select a route you simply press the hand-held probe onto each of the studs along the route in turn.

This wiring is in addition to that shown for Option 1. You can automate the operation of the switch to select the controller for the centre sidings by using a switch on the point motor that operates point number 3.

Option 3: Electrical Point Operation – Diode Matrix

On a large fiddle yard probe and stud operation is both tedious and prone to error. It is a lot easier if you can select the route as a whole rather than operating each point.

To create a diode matrix we need to establish which points needs to be set for each possible route.

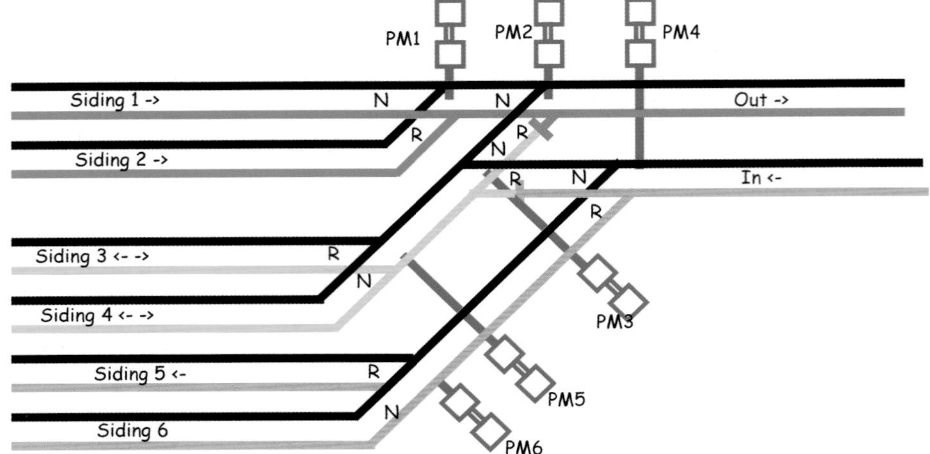

First we need to establish the possible routes, which are:

Siding 1 Outbound
Siding 2 Outbound
Siding 3 Outbound
Siding 4 Outbound
Siding 3 Inbound
Siding 4 Inbound
Siding 5 Inbound
Siding 6 Inbound

Each route will operate two or more points, as follows

Route	PM1	PM2	PM3	PM4	PM5	PM6
1	N	N				
2	R	N				
3		R	N		R	
4		R	N		N	
5			R	N	R	
6			R	N	N	
7				R		R
8				R		N

This gives us a diode matrix that looks like this; note that because only one route operates PM1-N, PM1-R, PM-6N and PM-6R they do not need a diode, just a wire link.

The best way to construct a diode matrix is to use two pieces of copper clad stripboard placed back to back, so that the copper strips run at right angles to each other. Use one board for the routes and the other for the point motors.

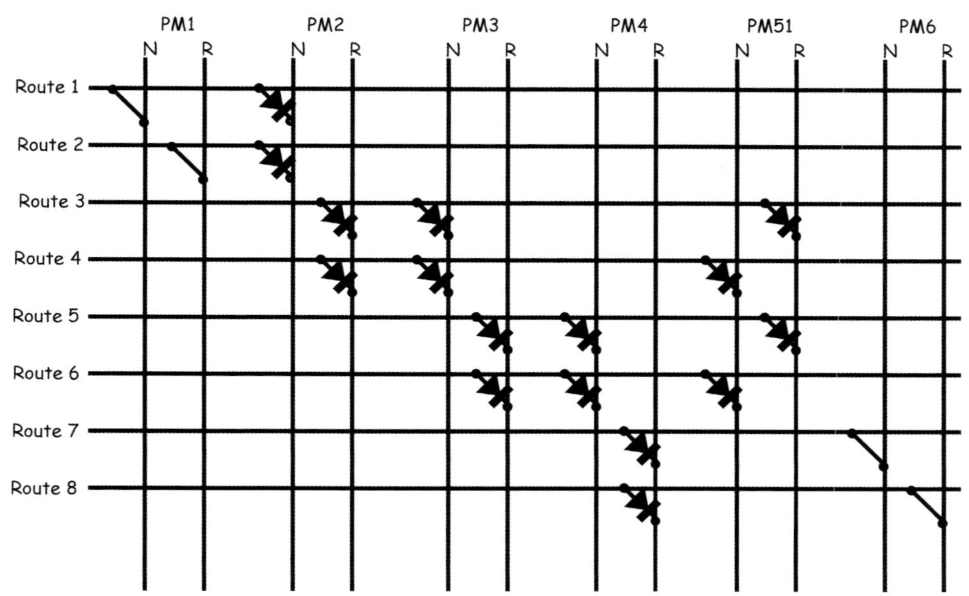

The circuit diagram for the diode matrix is drawn out to look similar to the table of routes that we compiled. The route selection switches are connected to the horizontal wires and the point motors to the vertical wires.

Solder the anode of each diode to the 'route' board and pass the cathode lead through a hole then trim and solder to the 'point motor' board. Once all the diodes and wire links are in place solder connecting wires to the copper tracks and run them to the point motors and switches.

As a route requires the simultaneous operation of two or three point motors a CDU (capacitor discharge unit) will be needed.

The routes can be selected in a number of ways:

Probe and stud – a stud for each route

Individual buttons – a button for each route

Rotary switch – a rotary switch to select the route and a button to activate the point motors

Option 4: Live Frog Points

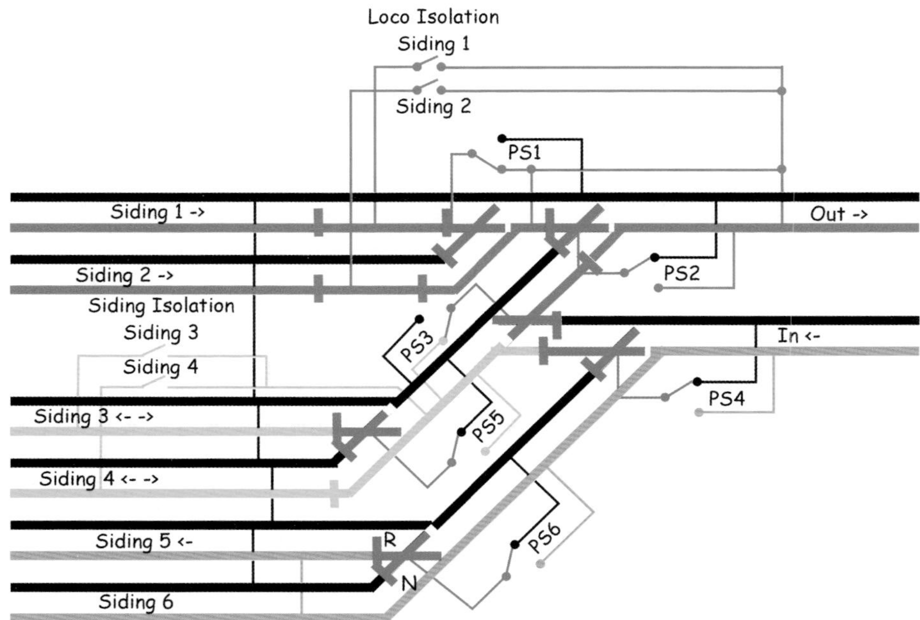

Adding live frog points also introduces extra isolation sections. As the sidings are double-ended, you cannot use the points to isolate them.

Adding live frog points requires switches linked either to the points or point motors. Each point needs its own SPDT switch, marked 'PS' in the diagram. You also need to run a number of jumpers to bridge the gaps caused by the points.

Unlike dead frog points you cannot use live frog points to isolate a double ended siding so it is necessary to add isolation sections. Sidings 1 and 2 have short lengths of track to isolate the locomotive at the head of a train. On siding 2 the isolation section is in the red rail rather than the black rail which is the one that runs to the frog. This is as a result of applying our rule of putting section breaks in the red rail rather than the black rail. Sidings 3 and 4 are isolated along their whole length for multiple units, which may have power pick-ups at either end, or even the centre, of the train. Sidings 5 and 6 do not have isolating sections at this end, they are for trains travelling right to left and would have isolating sections at the far end of the siding as part of the other pointwork.

Option 5: Panel Indication

With hidden fiddle yards it is very useful to have some indication on the control panel of how the points are actually set. This requires switches linked to the points or point motors. If you are using live frog points then the panel indicators need to be independent of the frog switching, so you will need DPDT rather than SPDT switches.

+12V DC
Point Motor Switch
Point Indication LEDs
Resistor
0V

Using one pole of the point motor's switch we can run LEDs on the control panel to show how the point is set.

Option 6: Isolating Sections

It is very useful to be able to isolate the fiddle yard sidings especially with double ended ones where power can be connected at either end leading to unscheduled departures. Whilst we installed these as part of the live frog scheme in Option 4 they are equally useful with dead frog points – enabling you to isolate a train regardless of how the points are set.

For the upper and lower sidings it is only necessary to have part of the siding isolated whereas the bidirectional lines need to be fully isolated since the pick-ups on a multiple unit aren't necessarily on the leading car.

Insulated rail joiners are added at the places shown. The bottom two sidings are isolated at the far end, which is a mirror image of this end. The top two sidings have feeds that go via switches to the upper main line. The centre

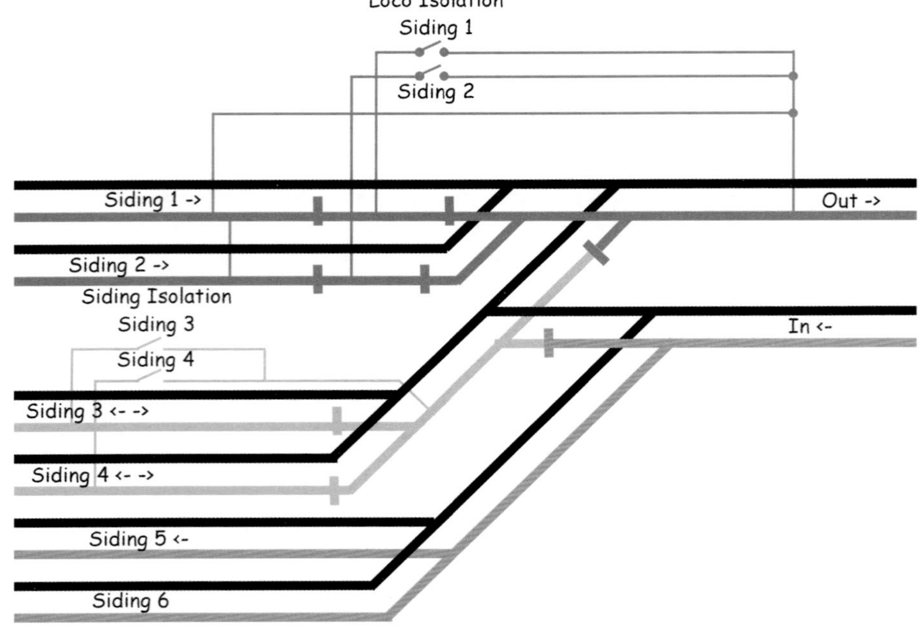

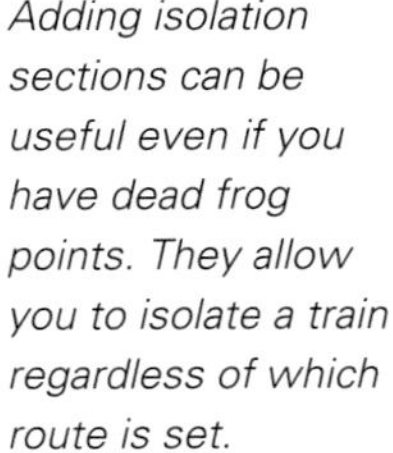
Adding isolation sections can be useful even if you have dead frog points. They allow you to isolate a train regardless of which route is set.

sidings have feeds that go via switches to the output of the switch that selects which controller is connected to them (see options 1 & 2).

Option 7: Track Occupation Indicators

To make life even easier it would be nice to know which sidings are occupied. By installing an occupation detector at the end of each siding we can know if there is a train there. The diagram shows an IRDOT installation. The IRDOT is produced by Heathcote Electronics and detects passing trains using an infra-red beam. The unit can be configured to show that a section is occupied, unoccupied or both.

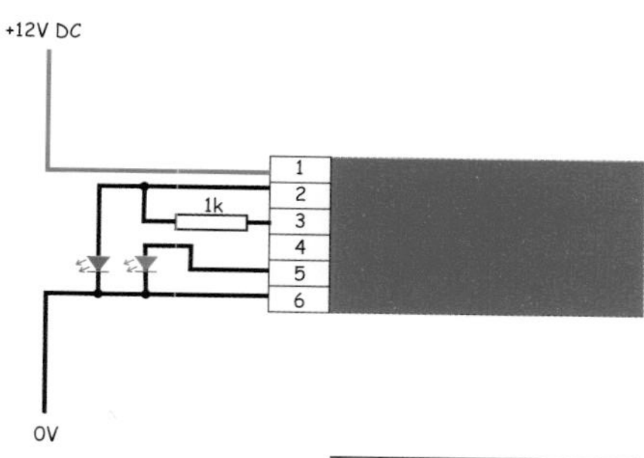

Irdot: Using IRDOT modules from Heathcote Electronics you can detect which tracks are occupied. The diagram shows a red 'occupied' LED and a green 'empty' LED. These could be combined in a single bi-colour LED.

Wiring Complexity

It is interesting to note just how many wires and other components are needed for this relatively simple piece of track.

Option 1: SPDT switch, 3 wires
Option 2: 6 point motors, Probe & studs, 19 wires.
Option 3: CDU, Diode matrix (16 diodes), Rotary switch, Button
Option 4: 6 SPDT point motor switches, 18 wires
Option 5: 6 DPDT point motor switches, 18 wires, 12 LEDs
Option 6: 4 on/off switches, 8 wires,
Option 7: 4 IRDOT, 16 wires, 4 LEDs

Giving a grand total of 6 toggle switches, one rotary switch, one button and 16 LEDs on the control panel, 6 point motors each with a DPDT switch attached, a CDU, 4 train detection units, a diode matrix board and 82 wires connecting them all up. Of course that is only for one end of the fiddle yard, the other end needs just the same amount of wires, switches and sundries. Is it any wonder that the wiring under the average layout looks like a rat's nest?

This may look complicated, but it is only the wiring for the point motors and isolating sections. The terminal block on the left is ready to be connected to point switches for panel indicators when they are installed.

Out and Back Layout

This plan is for an out-and-back layout. Although drawn as an N gauge or OO9 narrow gauge layout, a similar track plan could be used in a larger scale.

Being a small layout the initial wiring scheme shows one controller. The track is divided into electrical sections to allow locomotives to be isolated anywhere on the layout. The hidden return loop behind the top level station is isolated on both rails, not just the red rail, and fed through a DPDT switch to act as a reversing section. In use you would set the switch so that the rail polarities matched at the entrance of

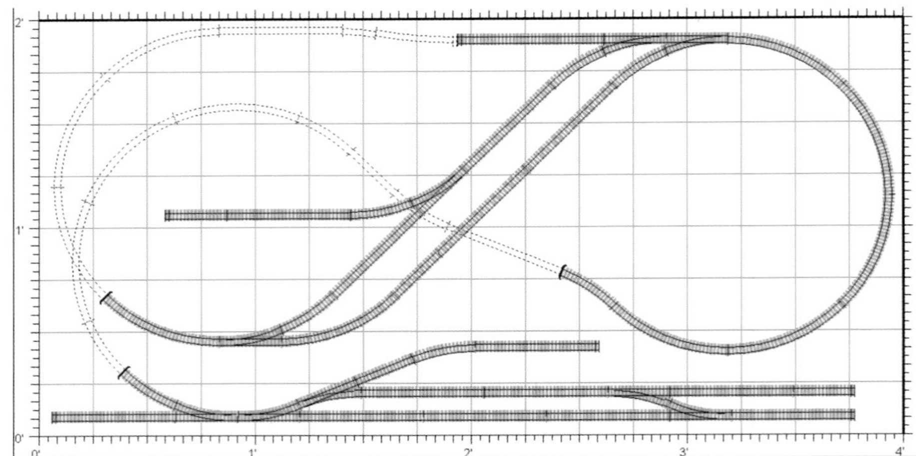

This plan could be built as either an N or an OO9 layout in the space shown. The same track plan could be opened out and used in a larger scale.

the loop, drive the train in, stop it, throw the switch to reverse the polarity, reverse the direction on the controller and then drive the train out again. By using a centre-off DPDT switch you could isolate a train in the loop, hidden off scene.

With two controllers you can have two trains running at once. On a layout like this both trains would need an operator's full attention, so you would need two operators. The second wiring scheme is arranged so that each operator has control of a station. The operator will drive trains that arrive at his station, since it is easier to start a train that you might not be able to see than to stop one accurately. Departing trains are driven by the other operator. As it is likely that for much of the time the layout's owner will be operating on his own, the bulk of the switches are located at the main station.

As this is a sm layout we are likely to have operator, but want to isolat locomotives anywhere on

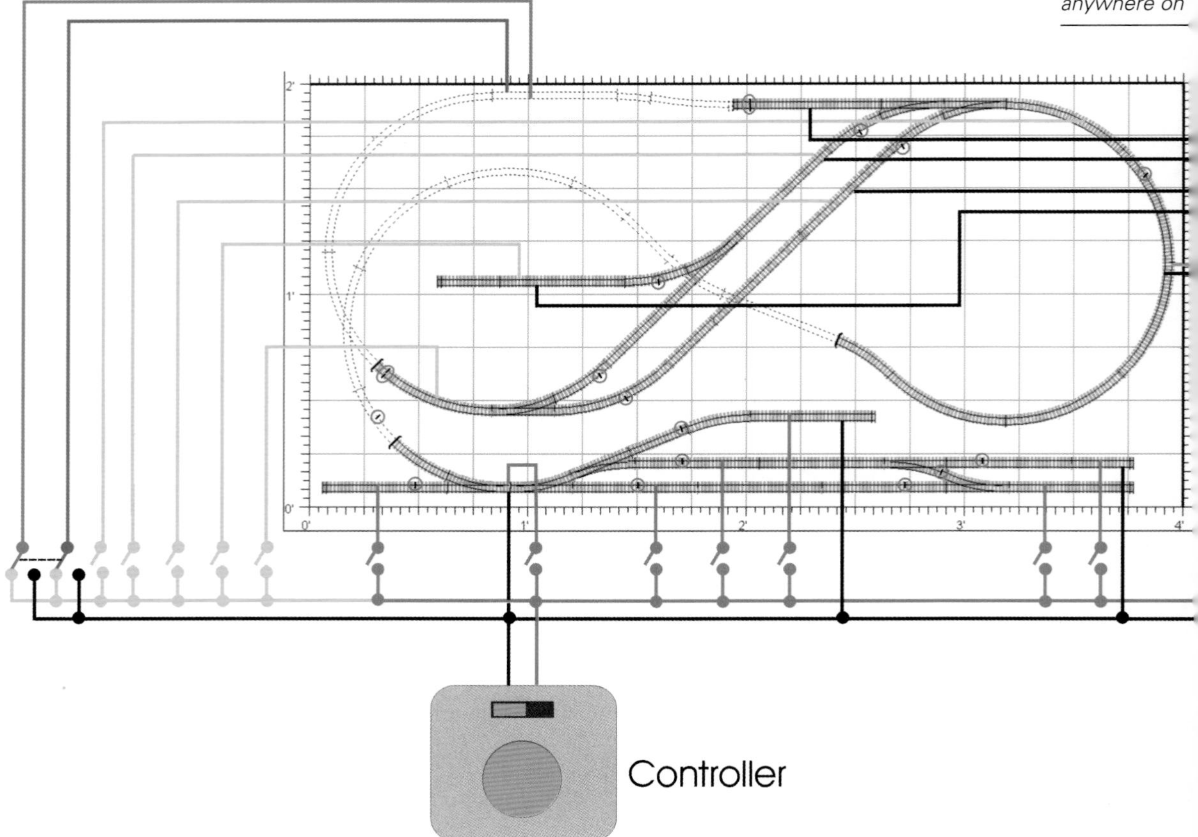

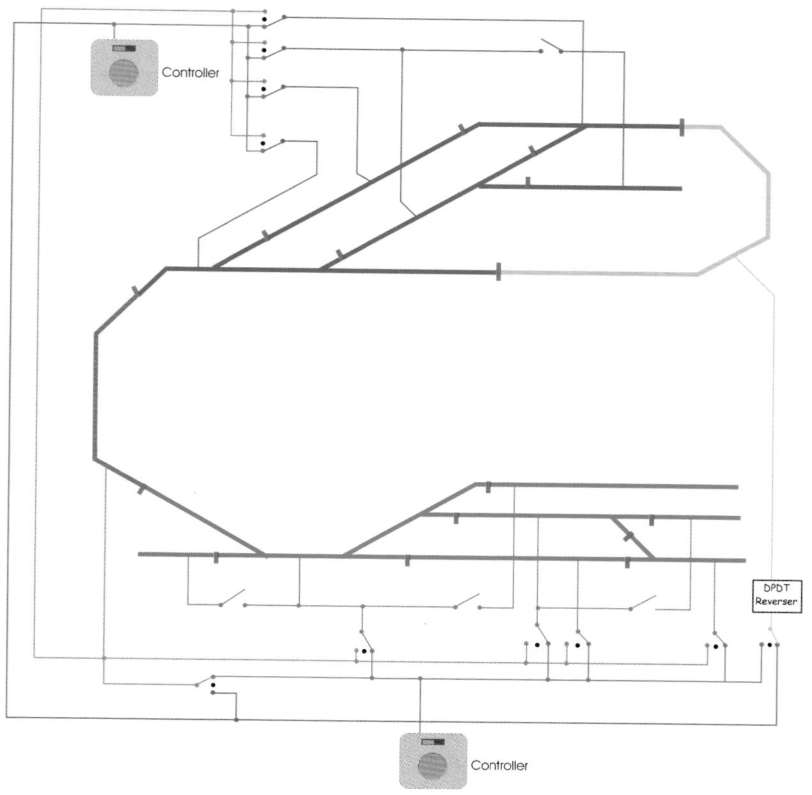

With two controllers it is possible to have two trains running at the same time. This scheme has been designed so that each operator is based at a station and drives the trains that arrive there, departures being controlled by the other operator. For clarity the black rail feeds are not shown.

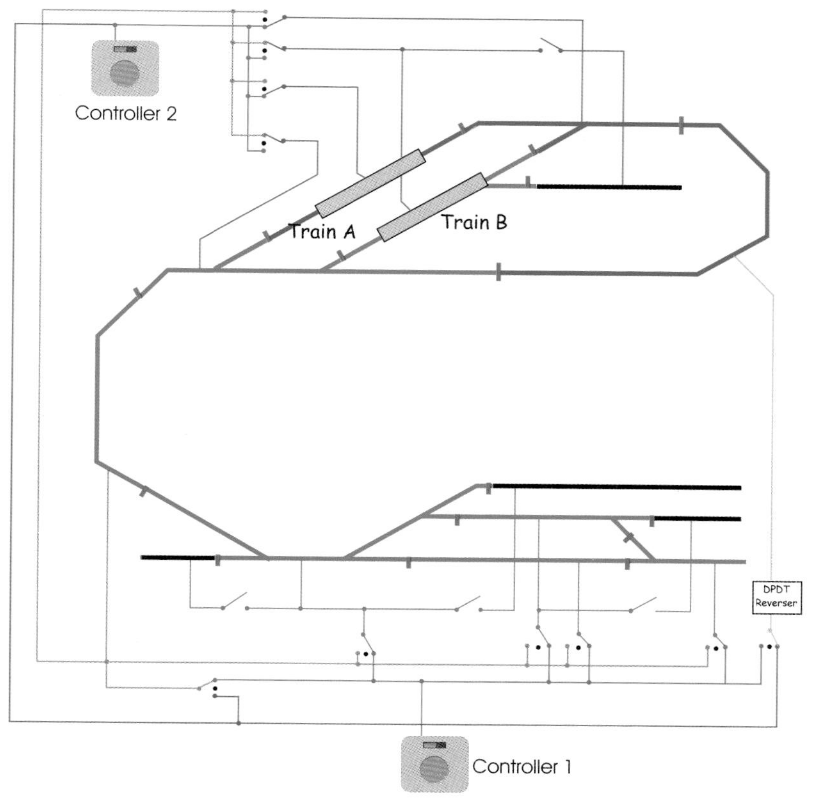

Train A is ready to depart for the hidden loop using Controller 2. Train B will run to the terminus with the terminus operator using controller 1.

Appendix:

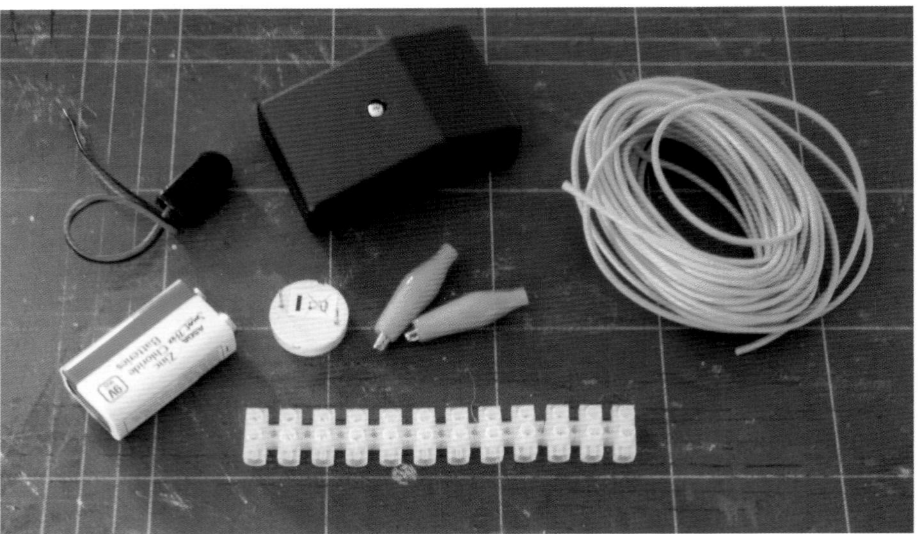

Build A Continuity Tester

Whilst a test meter is an invaluable tool for the model railway builder it does have its limitations. From time to time there is a need to trace wires or establish if a connection has failed. All too often this requires a long reach and it can be difficult to perform the necessary contortions and watch the meter at the same time. This is where a continuity tester comes into its own.

A continuity tester is a simple device that makes a buzz when its two probes are connected together. Given a long pair of leads, one of which is clipped to one end of the wire under test, all you need to do is poke the other end with a probe and listen for the buzz.

You can build your own tester in a few minutes from readily available components. The one shown here used parts from Maplin Electronics but suitable parts are available from many electronic suppliers. The full list is as follows:

5A Terminal Block (3 sections from strip needed)	
PP3 Battery	
2x Self-adhesive pads	
BA42 24/0.2 Wire 10M Yellow	£2.29
NE19 Rigid PP3 Clip	£0.59
KU58 PCB Buzzer	£1.39
2x FK35 Yellow Croc Clip	£0.69 each
LH14 Box PB1 Black	£2.29

Assembly is very simple, with only two soldered joints required and will only take a few minutes.

Step 1: Cut three terminals off the terminal block with a Stanley knife, strip the ends of wires from the PP3 clip and screw them into two adjacent terminals.

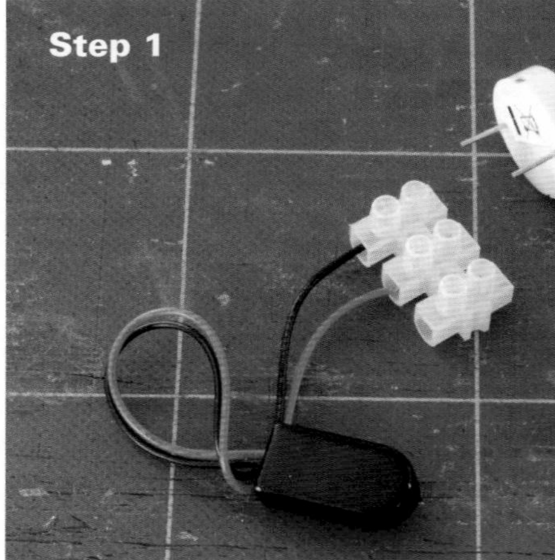

Step 2: Screw the buzzer in to the other side of the block, into the outer two terminals. Cut two

lengths of wire and strip the ends. Fix one wire to the centre terminal and the other one to the end terminal that is not connected to the PP3 clip. If you now push the clip onto the battery and hold the two free ends of the wires together you should get a sound from the buzzer. Don't worry about using a pad to hold the battery in place – it will last for ages.

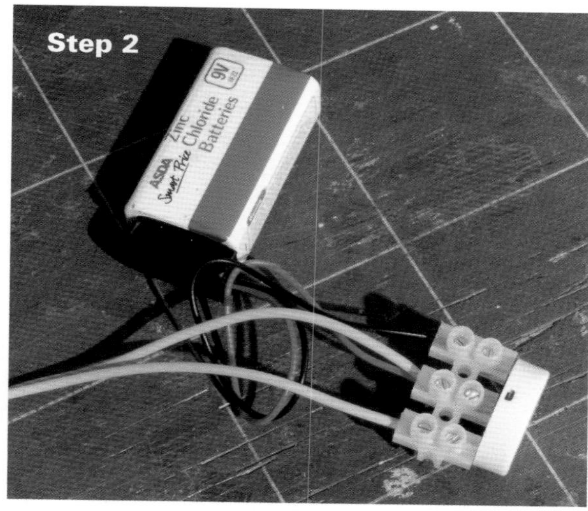

Step 2

Step 3: Drill two holes in the case and pass the wires through. Drill another hole for the noise from the buzzer to escape. Use the two self-adhesive pads to hold the terminal block and battery in place. You can now screw the lid on the box.

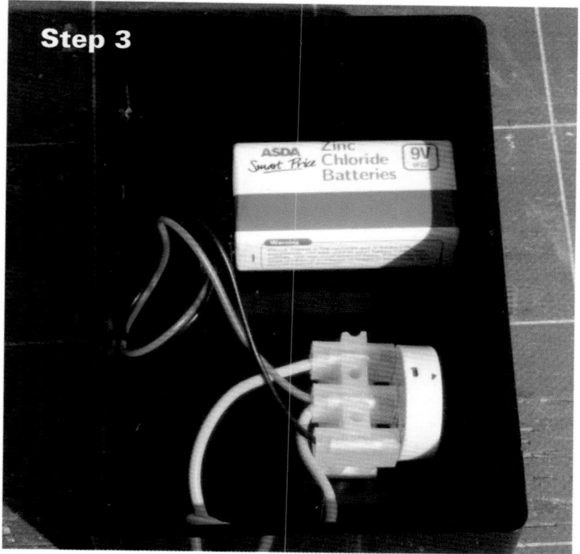

Step 3

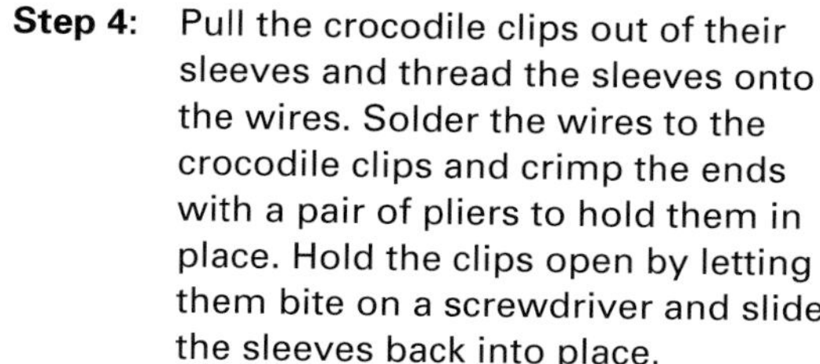

Step 4: Pull the crocodile clips out of their sleeves and thread the sleeves onto the wires. Solder the wires to the crocodile clips and crimp the ends with a pair of pliers to hold them in place. Hold the clips open by letting them bite on a screwdriver and slide the sleeves back into place.

I used two leads about 5'- 6' long to enable the tester to reach from one end of a 9' long layout to the other. I used another pair of crocodile clips and another length of wire to make an extension lead. When not in use the leads are simply wound around the tester's box.

In use one lead is clipped in place, onto a rail, switch terminal or wherever convenient and the other lead is used to poke where you think the other end of the wire comes out. Sometimes it is useful to grasp a short length of stiff wire in the crocodile clip's jaws to use as a probe. If you get a buzz when you poke then you've got the right place, if you don't then either you've got the wrong place or the circuit is broken somewhere.

The tester comes into its own when you have a number of stray wires that have come loose – you can very quickly establish where the other end of each wire goes, and thus where they should be connected. It is also good for tracing mysterious faults in circuits – for example if you think that a switch isn't working properly just connect the tester across the terminals to check.

Once you have built one you will wonder how you coped without it.

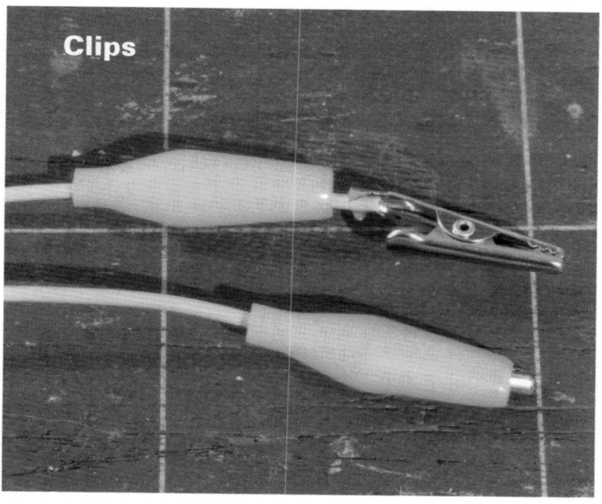
Clips

The continuity tester in use.

Appendix: Suppliers

All Components
PO Box 94, Hereford, HR2 8YN
Tel: 01981 540781
www.allcomponents.co.uk

Brewsters Ltd
112 New George Street
Plymouth
PL1 1RZ
Tel: 01752 665011
www.brewstersbatteries.co.uk

CR Signals
'Birkby'
5 The Crescent
Doncaster Road
Rotherham
S65 1NL
http://www.crsignals.com

Eckon
4mm scale colour light signals
Available from model shops

Express Models
65 Conway Drive, Shepshed,
Loughborough, LE12 9PP
Tel: 01509 829008
www.expressmodels.co.uk

Heathcote Electronics
Electronic control modules.
1 Haydock Close
Cheadle
ST10 1UE
Tel: 01538 756800
www.heathcote-electronics.co.uk

Maplin Electronics
Stores nationwide
Tel: 0870 4296000
www.maplin.co.uk

Rapid Electronics
www.rapidonline.com

Squires
Mail order, some exhibitions and shop – free catalogue on request.
100 London Road,
Bognor Regis,
PO21 1DD.
Tel:01243 842424

Glossary

AC (Alternating Current): Instead of a constant ***voltage*** (see DC) the ***polarity*** continuously varies from positive to negative and back again.

Amp: A measure of electrical ***current***, usually written as A, e.g. 3A is 3 Amps.

Analogue control: The traditional means of controlling the speed of a model railway locomotive by varying the ***voltage*** applied to the track.

CDU (Capacitor Discharge Unit): An electronic device that is designed to overcome some of the twin-solenoid point motor's idiosyncrasies. It charges up from a power supply and then releases a large, quick pulse of power when you operate a point motor. The pulse ensures that your point motors won't get burnt out if a switch gets stuck on and, as a bonus not only does it enable you to operate a number of point motors at once but helps to ensure that even sticky motors throw all the way and don't get stuck half-way.

Common return: A method of wiring up a model railway that can save money on switches and wiring. Basically each controller's 'red' wire is connected to the 'red' rails on the layout via whatever switches you need. The 'black' wire of each controller is connected directly to the 'black' rails on the layout, thus the 'black' wires (the 'returns') are grouped together (in 'common') saving on wiring on the black side of the circuit.

Current: Current is flowing electricity. The higher the current (measured in ***Amps***) the more power it has and the more work that it can do. A modern OO gauge locomotive may use 0.5A or less. A larger, heavier O gauge locomotive may well use over 1A.

DC (Direct Current): The voltage applied is always in the same ***polarity***.

DCC (Digital Command Control): A system where the controller puts a constant ***AC voltage*** on the track and adds a high frequency control signal to it. This signal is picked up by a special circuit, called a decoder, in the locomotive which controls the speed and direction of the motor. This allows you to control many different locomotives on the same piece of track.

Dead frog: With 'dead frog' points a small section of rail at the frog is electrically dead. This solves the problem of short circuits but can lead to locomotives stalling on the dead section of track, especially if you use small tank locomotives or larger locomotives that only pick up current on a few wheels.

Diode: A 'one way street' for electricity. ***Current*** can only flow in one direction through a diode.

Diode matrix: A method of making a single button operate a number of point motors.

Frog: The part where the rails come together at a point.

Insulator: Something that will not conduct electricity. An insulating rail joiner will not allow electricity to flow between the two pieces of rail that it joins.

Isolate: To cut something off from an electrical supply, usually by turning a switch off. A locomotive on an isolated section of track is disconnected from the controller and will not move, regardless of the controller's setting.

LED (Light Emitting Diode): A special form of ***diode*** that lights up when ***current*** flows through it. LEDs do not generate heat, are long-lasting and available in small sizes and so are ideal for putting lights in models.

Live frog: With 'live frog' points a larger section of rail is electrically isolated from the rest of the layout and connected to whichever rail the point is set for.

Polarity: The direction that electrical ***current*** will flow and a ***voltage*** is applied. Electricity flows from the positive output of a controller to the negative or ground connection.

Rectifier: A **diode** used to convert **AC** to **DC**. Usually four ***diodes*** are connected together to make a bridge rectifier.

Short circuit: Where a fault causes the electricity to find a 'short cut' and the two terminals of the power supply are effectively connected directly together. This will cause the power supply to shut down and may result in heavy current causing damage.

Slow motion point motor: A device for working points that is made from a small electric motor that drives an arm from one side of the point to the other.

Twin solenoid point motor: A device for working points made from two solenoids (electromagnets) which pull an arm from one side of the point to the other.

Volts/Voltage: A measure of electricity, usually written as V. Mains voltage in the UK is 240V ***AC***, most model railway locomotives run on 0 to 12V ***DC.*** Whilst mains voltage can kill you, the lower voltages used on model railways are much safer and are unlikely to cause you harm.

Circuit Symbols

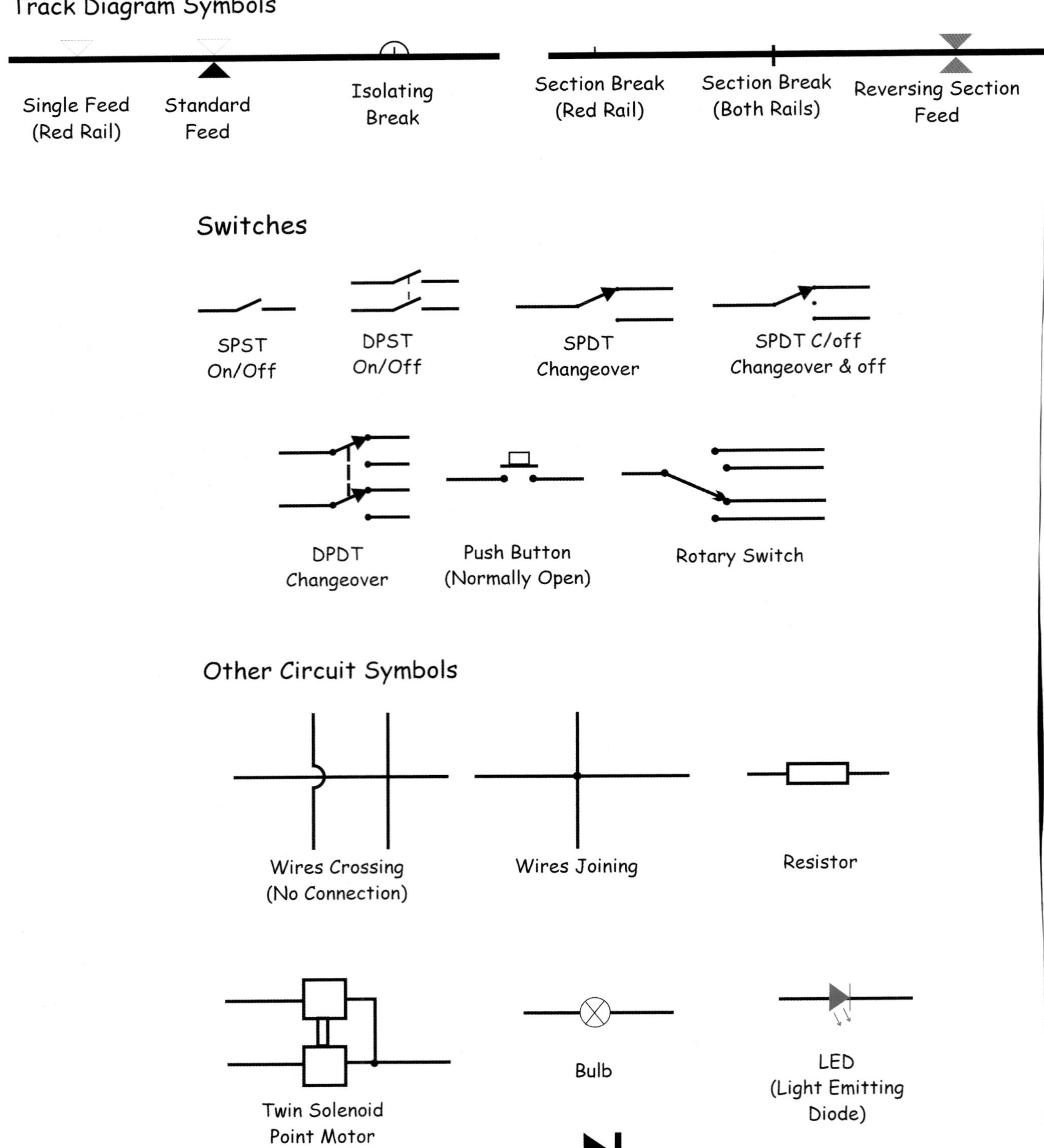

THE SPYCRAFT MANUAL

This is a Carlton Book

First published in 2005 by
Carlton Books
20 Mortimer Street
LONDON
W1T 3JW

ISBN 1 84442 577 0

Executive Editor: Roland Hall
Project Art Director: Darren Jordan
Illustrations: Peter Liddiard, Sudden Impact Media
Production: Lisa French

Printed and bound in Singapore

DISCLAIMER

The inclusion of a subject in this book does not indicate the encouragement of its use or undertaking. Spying is a serious business and the information and techniques portrayed in this book are for illustrative purposes only – none of them should be acted upon. Neither the author nor the publisher accept any responsibility for any loss, injury or damage howsoever caused. Some acts described in this book may be illegal. None of the acts in this book should be undertaken by a person who is not a spy.

AUTHOR'S NOTE

For the purpose of this book I have made several assumptions. Spies, handlers and field agents are all people who are trained and employed by an Intelligence Agency. Agents are those people who have been recruited to work for the spies, handlers or field agents. When referring to spies, handlers, field agents or agents, I do so only in the masculine sense – however, he or him should be read as both masculine and feminine.

PICTURE CREDITS

Brixmis Association: 96r; Hawkeye Systems: 68r; US Department of Defense: 14, 18, 63tr, 71, 92b, 93l, 95, 97l, 99tl, 99tr, 102r, 104l, 107, 108, 109, 122l, 122br, 139.

THE SPYCRAFT MANUAL

BY BARRY DAVIES B.E.M.

CONTENTS

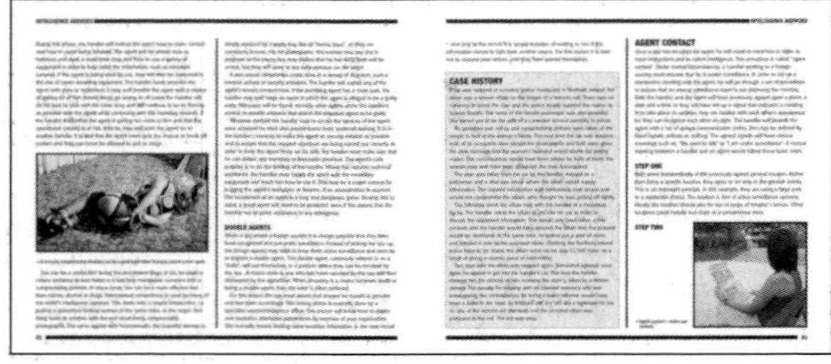

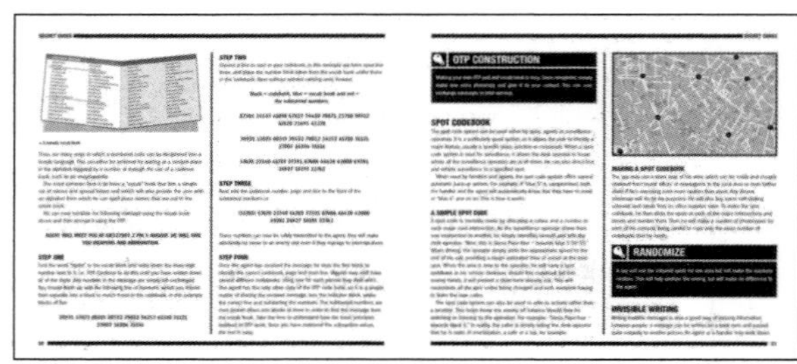

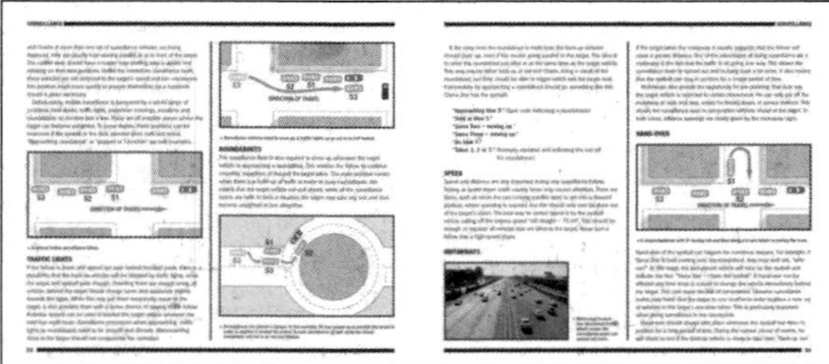

CONTENTS

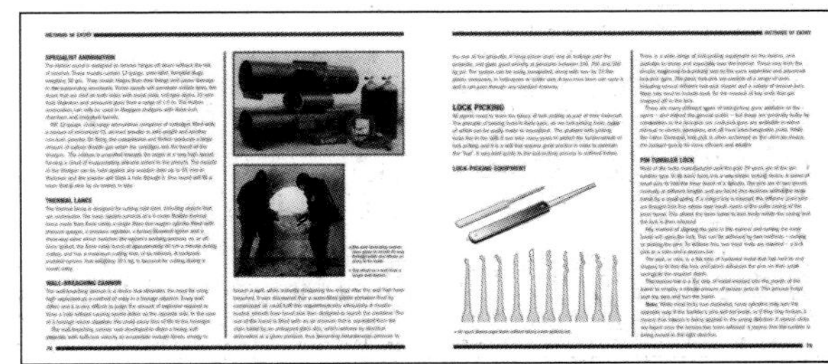

CONTENTS

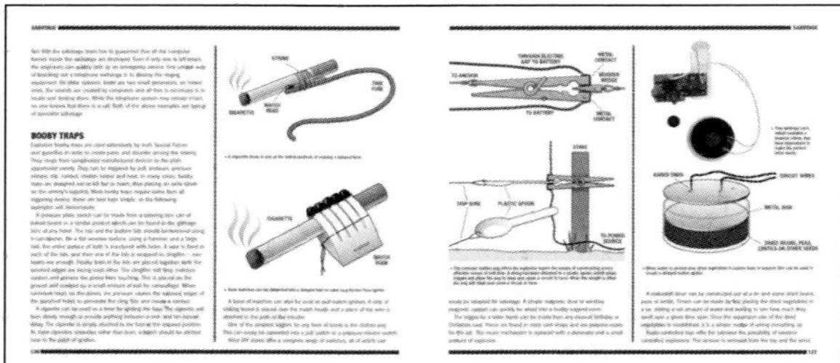

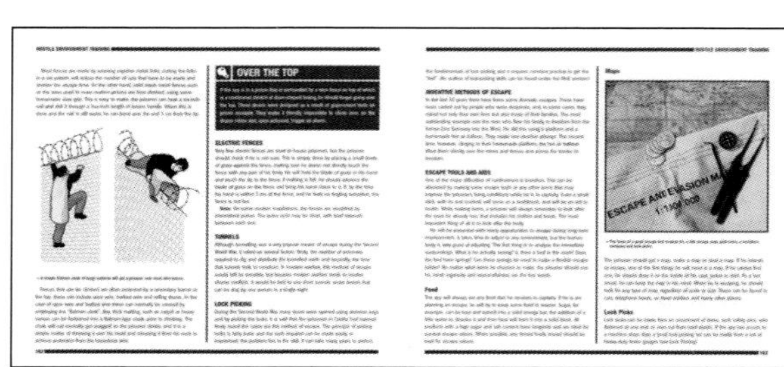

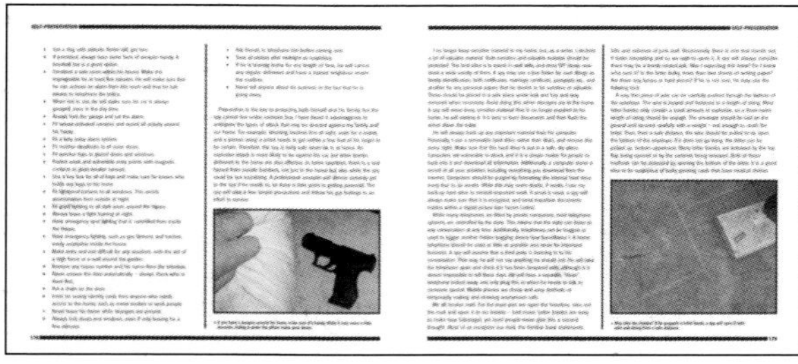

FOREWORD by Richard Tomlinson

To be a professional in any occupation, one must acquire the skills and tools of the trade and in this respect the modern spy is no different. The skills taught to a would-be spy are known as 'tradecraft'. It is a set of rules, or standard operating procedure. These are diverse, and include agent contact, surveillance, sabotage and a multiplicity of other subjects.

In the past, these skills would enable the spy to covertly gather intelligence, but today he finds himself little more than a frontline soldier. Equipped with these tradecraft skills and modern technology, the spy enters the underworld of espionage and counter-terrorism. Here he must operate in a hostile environment, among people of different cultures, faiths and beliefs. It is a world most of us never see, never hear of, but it exists in a layer of society controlled by the most powerful people in government.

A new enemy is at our doors – terrorism. Recruitment for the intelligence services has never been so intense, or so needed. Every year, brave men and women volunteer to be spies, learn their tradecraft skills, and when ready they are sent on operations. Their deeds may be great, but they go unheralded, and failure often results in torture and a slow, painful death.

RICHARD TOMLINSON

“Therefore, I say:
Know your enemy and know yourself;
in a hundred battles, you will never be defeated.
When you are ignorant of the enemy but know yourself,
your chances of winning or losing are equal.
If ignorant both of your enemy and of yourself,
you are sure to be defeated in every battle.”

— *Sun Tzu, The Art of War, c.500 b.c.*

INTRODUCTION

Many years ago, my work as an SAS soldier took me to Northern Ireland. For the most part, my duties there consisted of undercover work and covert operation. With little guidance or support from Security Services, we would identify and infiltrate people we believed to be involved in terrorist activities. Our techniques were honed through constant operations, which demanded skills such as lock-picking, foot and vehicle surveillance and photography to name but a few.

On the odd occasion we came across something really worthwhile, the Security Services in London would inevitability raise a lazy eye. My first contact with an MI5 agent did not create the best of impressions; he was unfit, overweight and, in terms of technical expertise, our own people were light years ahead. Things have changed since those days and today the SAS plays a large part in the day-to-day operation of the Security Services – for the most part doing the "dirty work".

After leaving the SAS, I pursued a career in counter-terrorism, a subject that has now become a goal for most of the western intelligence agencies. So I decided to gather, collate and describe many of the techniques used by the world's leading intelligence agencies and call it *The Spycraft Manual.*

I shall no doubt find myself in hot water for some of the material contained in this book. I am not worried, as I can prove that the all of it is in the public domain and available to anybody.

The basic principle behind this manual is to demonstrate where the intelligence world stands today by describing the techniques and tradecraft skills used by most of the world's leading intelligence agencies. There is a limit to what I can write about, not for reasons of security, but based purely on the sheer magnitude of the subject. As a result, I have opted for a middle-of-the-road explanation that covers the main reasons for why we have spies and what a spy must learn in order to both survive and to be a good spy.

Some subjects, such as surveillance, are easy to categorise. Others, however, are individual and are more difficult to place within a structured framework. To combat this, I have included several topics as "pop-up" subjects that appear where I feel they are relevant. There are also several "case histories" that explain the reality of spying.

The Spycraft Manual is a book that talks about how spies learn their tradecraft and skills and how they employ them in the field. Each individual subject contains masses of fascinating information, and it covers subjects from the seven basic drills of agent contact to satellite surveillance and lock-picking, making it an utterly unique and fascinating peek into the very real present-day world of espionage.

Finally, for better or worse, intelligence agencies will always be with us, and they will always possess the means to delve deep into our innermost secrets. Let us hope that the sanctity of freedom, for which so many secret agents have died, rests consciously on the minds of those who currently control and direct covert operations.

LEGAL IMPLICATIONS

For the most part, the people who carry out daily surveillance operations – such as the police or private detectives – are governed by the basic laws of the country. While this should be true of intelligence services, few countries act within the framework of either national or international law. Even when they have been exposed, many will do all everything their power to annul the situation. To this end I place no emphasis on the law and how it might affect various intelligence agencies around the world.

However, the reader of this book should note that some activities discussed herein are carried out by professional agents and spies and are not legal in any country and they should never be attempted by civilians or other non-spies.

CHAPTER 1

They are the unseen warriors that walk the streets, always under the threat of danger. Since 9/11 their job has become even more precarious, and methods of discovering the enemy more complex.

INTELLIGENCE AGENCIES

Intelligence agencies have existed in one form or another for centuries; their role was always to spy on each other. Much of that stopped in the early 1990s due to the disintegration of communism. By 2001, following the 9/11 attacks on the World Trade Center, a new enemy had been found: "Global Terrorism". In the world of terrorism, knowledge is everything; without it there is very little chance of success.

Although knowledge can be obtained from a number of sources, the primary method is through spying and surveillance. The United States and the rest of the world were looking for the perpetrators of this fiendish crime. They could only be found through collecting and analysing good intelligence.

Collecting intelligence involves human resource agencies (such as the CIA or MI5) and agencies who rely on OOJARIC). In addition, embassies normally have an operating system from which they can establish information on a particular country. There is also the military. Finally, there is open information, obtained largely through the world's media. In some cases, this can be a far quicker means of obtaining information than via government agencies. In addition to the media, there is normally a head of department, an official who follows the direction of their government. For example, the prime minister may pose the following question to his head of security: "Do we know who is responsible for last night's car bomb attack?"

The answer to this question is derived from information that has been gathered, interpreted and analysed into intelligence. The intelligence is then distributed to those who decide what course of action is required.

Where do we start looking for information? First, we look at those who have the capability and intent. Capability: "I know how to make a bomb from just about anything in the kitchen, but I have no intention of doing so, because it is dangerous and illegal." (I have the capability but not the intent.) Intent: "I don't know how to make a bomb but as soon as I am able to I will kill my neighbour." (I do not have the ability but I have the intention to commit harm.) Intelligence agencies are there to gather information about people who have both the capability and the intention.

One of the principal threats currently facing the world is that of bioterrroism. To Defend against such a threat and the vast devastation any biological attack could cause, governments are constantly on the lookout for terrorist organizations who have the capability to manufacture and deliver such weapons. Current biological threats come from the possible manufacture of anthrax, cholera and smallpox by terrorist organizations.

Who collects the information will depend largely on the enemy target and where that enemy is located. In most cases, several agencies will co-operate to achieve the same goal. Almost everyone is traceable. Individuals within the group use credit cards, mobile phones, vehicles, shipping, or may just be spotted walking down the street. Wherever they go, they can be tracked. Even terrorists living in remote areas can be found by the use of spy planes or satellite surveillance.

CIA

The Central Intelligence Agency was a late developer in terms of international espionage. Its predecessor, the Office of Strategic Services (OSS), was not formed until 1942. It officially became known as the CIA in 1947 after the National Security Act was passed and was charged with gathering, correlating, evaluating and disseminating intelligence affecting national security. Reporting to the Senate Select Committee on Intelligence and the House Permanent Select Committee on Intelligence, most of its operational ability and efficiency can be held accountable by the State. At times, this leads to public accusations and criticism of its activities, especially in the case of the Iran-Contra affair and Watergate. Although CIA involvement in both cases was not proved, suspicion still remains as to its responsibility. However, its role in the Bay of Pigs invasion of Cuba (1961) and in the Iraq missing weapons of mass destruction debacle, have proved damaging.

The headquarters of the CIA can be found on 258 acres of highly secured land at Langley, Virginia. Costing more than $46 million to build, its tight cluster of buildings houses the specialists that make up the 20,000 employees based there. Approximately another 20,000 employees are based in various US offices and American diplomatic centres around the world. This number also includes those field staff on active field operations. Staff numbers have fluctuated vastly over the organization's history; following the end of the Cold War, staff numbers were reduced dramatically. However, with the new threat of Al Quaeda and the fall-out from the misleading intelligence which led to the second Gulf War, one would expect that the CIA will increase its recruitment of both field and support personnel.

The CIA today is divided into four specialist sections, or "directorates", all of which are concerned with the gathering and analysis of intelligence. In general, the CIA's sources are either manpower or hardware intensive and both require huge amounts of funding.

The Directorate of Operations is responsible for gathering foreign intelligence by covert means and classical espionage. At least a quarter of the estimated 8,000 overseas staff include case officers responsible for running several thousand agents in other countries. The Directorate of Intelligence is concerned with the production of finished intelligence, whether in the form of quick-reaction briefings or long-term studies. The focus is worldwide, but the directorate is split into regional departments (African and Latin American; south and east Asian; European; near eastern; Slavic and Eurasian) as well as four offices that specialize in different types of analysis: resources, trade and technology; scientific and weapons research; leadership analysis and imagery analysis.

The Directorate of Science and Technology provides a supporting role in terms of collecting and processing intelligence collected by covert technical means. This includes signals intelligence (SIGINT), imagery, satellite data and open source. The directorate is based at a site at Reston in Virginia and also includes the National Photographic Interpretation Center. It is estimated that there are about 26,000 staff employed here, including engineers, physicists, linguists, chemists, computer programmers and imagery analysts.

The final division is the Directorate of Administration. As its name implies, it provides administrative and technical support backup to the other facilities. It is also responsible for training field staff in espionage basics such as lock picking, letter opening, etc. It is reported that about 1,000 personnel are employed within this directorate.

Since 9/11, the role of the CIA has become even more important in gathering intelligence to pre-empt any threat from militant Islamic terrorists such as Al Quaeda. Much criticism has already been levelled at the organization over whether or not warnings of a terrorist attack using aircraft were picked up and disseminated to the appropriate quarters of government. In addition, the CIA has recently been heavily lambasted over the weapons of mass destruction intelligence fiasco in Iraq. The Director of the CIA at the time, George Tenet, has recently resigned – reportedly for reasons unconnected with Iraq. It remains to be seen whether the new director will restructure the organization or whether he will recruit more field staff to answer the growing threat of international terrorism.

MI5/MI6

▲ **Despite numerous intelligence indicators, the 9/11 attacks on the United States of America went ahead unchecked.**

Although military intelligence in England can be traced back to Elizabethan times, a dedicated service was not established until 1909, when MI5 and MI6 were created as internal departments under the control of the Secret Service Bureau. Military Intelligence Department 5, under the control of Captain Vernon Kell, was then responsible for exposing German spies. MI6, under the command of Captain Mansfield Cumming, was in charge of gathering foreign intelligence. The responsibilities of MI5 grew in 1931 when it was charged with assessing all threats to national security and was given the title of the Security Service, although its previous name has remained in popular usage.

During the Second World War, MI6, now known as the Secret Intelligence Service (SIS) recruited and trained members of the Special Operations Executive (SOE), a force that became crucial to wartime intelligence gathering and sabotage behind enemy lines. At the end of the war, many of these operatives were reabsorbed into SIS.

Previously under the command of the military, both services later became divorced from the armed services. MI5 became the responsibility of the Home Secretary and MI6 reported to the Foreign and Commonwealth Secretary. Both were issued with directives that defined their roles.

MI5 today is still responsible for national security and counter-espionage activities, but it does not have the power to arrest suspects. This job falls to Scotland Yard's Special Branch, which is also responsible for the presentation of evidence at court on MI5's behalf. MI6's principal role is to provide intelligence gathered from foreign sources in support of national security, defence and foreign and economic policies.

Although traditionally rivals, both services have had to work together closely, especially when events exposed weaknesses in their operations. Scandals, such as the defection of British agents spying for the Russians (Burgess, MacLean and Philby) and the Profumo affair (1963) in which the Secretary for War of the time was caught sharing a high-class call girl with a Russian agent, created massive embarrassment for the services. Also, incidents such as the hijacking of the Iranian embassy in London in 1980 and the Libyan Peoples' Bureau in 1984, not to mention the "Troubles" in Northern Ireland, have meant that the two services have had to work together closely and share information in order to diffuse foreign threats on home ground.

Major changes took place in both services following the end of the Cold War. Staff numbers were reduced, as were budgets, as it was deemed that the threat from the Soviet Union was no longer so great. Arab terrorism still posed a danger, but the greatest danger came from Northern Ireland, whose terrorists had started to take their campaign onto the mainland. It is thought that many city-centre bombings, on the scale of the Manchester bombing in 1996, were averted as a result of gaining good intelligence.

After the Good Friday Agreement (1998), it seemed that yet another threat had been removed, but it was soon replaced by another, potentially far greater, danger. Al Quaeda had always been a terrorist organization worth watching but, following the atrocities of 9/11, they suddenly became national security threat number one. Al Quaeda were not the only ones in the spotlight. Interest was also renewed in Iraq and its dictator, Saddam Hussein, following speculation that he possessed weapons of mass destruction. Both the security services in Britain and in the US claimed to have evidence to back up the accusation and it was on the strength of this evidence that the two countries and their allies went to war. In fact, as was published in the Butler Report in July 2004, it was clear that much of the so-called "intelligence" disclosed to the public was inaccurate. A lack of agents on the ground, second-hand intelligence and the claims of a few defectors who wished to see the overthrow of the regime, had all contributed to misleading claims about what Saddam actually possessed. Somehow, somewhere, between the intelligence agencies, the Joint Intelligence Committee (JIC) and Whitehall, suppositions became definites and hearsay became evidence. Although the Butler Report cleared anyone of purposely misleading Parliament and the public, it remains an embarrassing episode for the intelligence services, their bosses and perhaps, above all, Tony Blair.

Currently, the staffing level at MI5, based at Millbank in central London, is around 1,900. MI6, recently relocated to its new headquarters at Albert Embankment, is far more secretive about its employment figures, but one

GCHQ

The British Government Communications Headquarters (GCHQ) is a Civil Service department that reports to the Foreign Secretary. The department works closely with the intelligence organizations MI5 and MI6 and its objective is to protect the interests of the nation and keep government information systems safe. It does this through division into two parts: Signals Intelligence (Sigint) and Information Assurance.

GCHQ is responsible for solving codes and ciphers and many of the people working there are experts in cryptology, mathematics, languages, computing and related disciplines.

could safely assume that similar numbers to MI5 are involved, excluding those operatives in the field about whom nothing is known. The threat from terrorism remains real enough and if anything can be learned from the Butler Report it is that more spies are required and more intelligence about Al Quaeda and its allies needs to be gathered. This will probably lead to an escalation in recruitment for both MI5 and MI6.

KGB

KGB stands for Komitet Gosudarstvennoy Bezopasnosti, or The Committee for State Security. The most feared security service in the world was created after the Russian Revolution in 1917. Lenin took command of the old Tsarist secret police, the Okhrana, and reorganized and renamed it the CHEKA (Extraordinary Commission for Combating Counterrevolution and Espionage). The organization would be renamed many times. From 1922–23 it was the GPU (State Political Administration) and from 1923–34 it became the OGPU (United States Political Administration). From there it changed to the NKVD (People's Commissariat for Internal Affairs) and then the MD (Ministry of Internal Affairs) and it only became known as the KGB in 1954.

Throughout its evolution, the organization developed a dreaded reputation, especially among its own people. During Stalin's reign, murderous thugs, who were only too happy to carry out Stalin's often paranoid and bloody missions, headed the organization. For example, during the collectivisation of land, the organization was responsible for the displacement and murder of millions of Russians.

The more familiar, modern-day form of the KGB only came about after Stalin's death in 1953. It became the most important part of the Soviet Union's intelligence service. As well as its own operations, it also oversaw the work of the GRU (Chief Intelligence Directorate of the General Staff of the Red Army), the military intelligence wing. It was still extremely powerful; it was allocated a huge budget and possessed a staff that numbered in estimates from 500,000 to 700,000. Agents were not only involved in foreign espionage but also in domestic spying, with members secreted in every town and factory. Anyone considered to have views that ran counter to the Party line was considered a traitor, was informed upon and was inevitably dealt with by the KGB's SMERSH Division. This was a division within the secret service responsible for meting out punishments and assassinations to those considered to be an internal security threat.

During the Cold War, KGB agents targeted the western powers, especially top officials and military commanders with access to national secrets. Their favourite method involved the entrapment of an individual, usually through sexual temptations and blackmail. Another popular method was to employ listening devices in various foreign embassies. In 1975, the KGB managed to secrete a sophisticated listening device into the American Embassy in Moscow. However, in order to activate it, it had to be bombarded by radioactive waves fired through the embassy windows. It was later reported that the Ambassador, Walter Stoessel, had to be sent home because of radiation poisoning.

The KGB's headquarters could be found at the infamous Lubyanka Square in downtown Moscow. The huge, intimidating building was once feared, but in later years it has been opened up to public inspection, thanks to the intervention of successive presidents from Yuri Andropov (1982–84) (once a KGB chief) onwards.

Since the collapse of the Soviet Union, the KGB has been on a rocky road. In 1991, certain sections of the KGB Spetsnatz forces attempted to storm the Russian parliament building and force a coup against president Mikhail Gorbachev and other senior politicians. However, once there, some of the forces refused to take part and so the coup failed. The ringleaders were arrested and, in October 1991, Gorbachev signed a decree abolishing the KGB. Since then, most of its directorates have continued through separate organizations. However, it is interesting to note that the current president of Russia, Vladimir Putin, is also a former chief of the KGB. Today, Russia's security forces are more concerned with the fight against global and internal terrorism, especially that issuing from Chechnya and other former Soviet states.

MOSSAD

Mossad, the shortened form of its full Israeli name – ha Mossad le-Modin ule-Tafkidim Meyuhadim (The Institute for Intelligence and Special Tasks) – is Israel's powerful and secretive intelligence agency. It was formed by Israel's prime minister, David Ben Gurion, in 1951, with the primary directive: "For our state, which since its creation has been under siege by its enemies, intelligence constitutes the first line of self-defence ... We must learn well how to recognize what is going on around us." The name Mossad was appropriate for an institution responsible for the defence of

Israel as it was also the name of an organization that, during the 1930s and 40s, helped to smuggle thousands of Jewish refugees into Palestine.

Mossad is responsible for gathering intelligence, secret operations connected with national security and counter-terrorism. Because of the conflicts Israel has had with its neighbours, much of its focus is on the Arab nations and, in particular, the activities of terrorist organizations such as Hamas and the PLO. However, it also conducts espionage and intelligence activities throughout the world and is still involved with the undercover movement of Jewish refugees from hostile countries, such as Ethiopia, Iran and Syria. It currently provides the West with information on the movement of known Arab terrorists and has excellent relations with corresponding western intelligence agencies, in particular with the CIA.

The headquarters of Mossad are in Tel Aviv. Details about employee numbers are hard to obtain, but it is estimated that between 1,200 and 1,500 work there. The "Institute" is headed by a director – currently Meir Dagan – who is only responsible to the prime minister. In line with its importance to the State of Israel, Mossad has a huge budget and, in contrast to other foreign intelligence agencies, also has the power to deal with countries with which Israel has no diplomatic relations. Its inner organization, although obscure, has at least eight known departments.

The largest of these is the Collections Department, which is responsible for espionage operations. It possesses offices in other countries – both acknowledged and unacknowledged – which are in charge of directing and recruiting agents. The Political Action and Liaison Department is in charge of communications with the foreign intelligence services of other countries as well as countries with which Israel does not normally engage. It is also responsible for political activities. The Special Operations Division is perhaps the one most often thought of when Mossad is mentioned. It is responsible for extremely covert actions such as assassination, sabotage and paramilitary activities. Also known by its other name, Metsada, one of its duties is to track down individuals who have harmed Jewish people in any country. One of its most publicized operations was the location and kidnapping of the Nazi war criminal Adolf Eichmann in Buenos Aires, Argentina. They managed to smuggle him back to Israel where he was put on trial, found guilty and hanged. Also linked to this department is Mossad's special army unit known as the "Sayaret Matkal", or General Staff Reconnaissance Unit. This secretive force, known colloquially as "The Guys", numbers about 200 men and id responsible for many of the covert actions that take place.

The Research Department handles the analysis of intelligence, providing daily, weekly and monthly reports. It is organized into 15 geographical desks: the US; Canada and western Europe; the former Soviet Union; Africa; Latin America; China; the Mahgreb (Morocco, Algeria and Tunisia); Saudi Arabia; Syria; Jordan; Iran; the United Arab Emirates; Iraq and Libya. There is also a "nuclear desk" concerned with weapons of mass destruction. The Technology Department researches and develops technologies that might be useful to Mossad and the LAP (Lohamah Psichologit) Department handles all propaganda and psychological warfare operations.

It is worth mentioning that many of Israel's top politicians and leaders began their working lives within the ranks of Mossad: Yitzhak Shamir, Menachem Begin and Yitzhak Rabin had all been, at one time or another, part of the Mossad organization.

THE SPY

The dictionary describes a spy as (i) a person employed by a state or institution to obtain secret information from rival countries, organizations or companies; or (ii) a person who keeps watch on others.

However, this simple explanation does not come close to explaining the real complexities that make up the modern spy. Today's spy is far removed from the James Bond image we see on our cinema screens. Gone are the classical military and political intelligence agents that fight against enemy or rival states. The dinner jacket has been replaced by a bullet-proof vest worn underneath shabby clothes. If there is any comparison between fiction and reality, it is in the world of Q, for today's spy is equipped with state-of-the-art electronic wizardry.

Intelligence in the field of counter-terrorism is a different and, in many aspects, a more arduous and dangerous task. The lives of many agents are in continual danger. The rules of the game are cruel, as moral and ethical considerations are simply negated by the bullet. There is no honour between rivals on the streets of Kabul or Baghdad and only the quick survive. A modern spy must blend in, live among the enemy, speak their language and befriend and exploit the enemy at every opportunity. They are required to be streetwise, rough, tough and deadly.

All spies receive some form of basic military training. This involves learning how to fire a variety of weapons, self-defence and resistance to interrogation should they get caught. After the basic training, some spies are trained in the

▲ CIA operators in Afghanistan being briefed in the field.

intervention. For the most part, however, spying is a lonely, shadowy game, fraught with danger. For this reason, the modern spy must learn all the basics of tradecraft. For example, in the United Kingdom, spies go through a procedure known as the Intelligence Officers' New Entry Course (INOEC). This course take place in various parts of the country, including the Fort at MI6's training establishment in Portsmouth and the SAS base at Credenhill, Hereford.

arts of surveillance, others become technical officers, but by far the most dangerous job is that of the field officer. One vital role for this type of spy is to recruit local agents, people he can use to his advantage, people who will happily kill for him. Finding such people is the key to success in any intelligence operation. First and foremost he must identify the right person, someone who is in a position or has the skills to carry out his dirty work. Once he has established such a person he must go about recruiting them, discovering their weakness and exploiting it. In many instances, a field agent will be responsible for recruiting and running several agents at the same time, none of whom will know of the others' existence.

In the West, spies are trained and controlled by massive organizations such as the CIA or MI5. These provide the spy with technical support and, when required, hard back-up with a call on the full weight of military

WHAT MAKES A GOOD SPY?

One of the first skills a spy must have is good observation. No matter where he is or what he is doing, his mind should be systematically recording places, events and people, with great recall accuracy. The military have a lesson on this subject. They place a number of objects in an area some metres away from trainees. They are given a short period of time in which to observe all the objects before they are taken away. They are not allowed to write them down for several hours.

The spy will learn to remember objects in a room he has entered for the first time or car number plates. He will register the number of windows in a house he has just passed. The trick is to keep as much information in his brain for as long as possible and perfect the skill with constant practice.

The spy uses logic to understand things. How did they do that? How can

I do this? What if I go in totally the opposite direction, not just physically but mentally? Is there another way to solve this situation? He tries lateral thinking.

He adjusts his attitude to the situation and thinks before he reacts. What do people expect of him? What is his role model? It is no good pretending to be a bum if he is dressed like a prince. The weak have always been taken advantage of – if the situation allows, he takes control himself. He takes an interest in people, this takes the focus off himself. Most people are only too happy to boast about their social position, wealth, family or occupation, so he takes advantage of this. "That sounds interesting, it must be a wonderful job," will open up a conversation that could deliver lots of useful information. He plays on people's emotions: "I have just broken up with my girlfriend, she went off with another woman." His comment will get him both sympathy and inquisition into his ex-girlfriend's sexual habits. Another good opener in recruiting a possible agent is: "I have just won the lottery – not all of it, but a good sum."

The spy listens to his sixth sense and analyses any gut feelings he may get. There are many basic instructions in the human brain that warn us of danger – he learns to recognize them and take appropriate action. He may walk down a street and spot the same person he saw only an hour ago in a different part of the city – is this just a coincidence?

He only ever takes calculated risks and is never a gambler. With a calculated risk he can spot the drawbacks and adjust his plans accordingly. He analyses his actions and bases his actions on solid information. If he takes a gamble, he only needs to fail once. Here is how a spy thinks:

- A spy is always aggressive in a dangerous situation, because he can guarantee that the enemy will be. He'll let them know he is not to be messed with.
- He knows his own strengths and weaknesses.
- He knows his own territory and its inhabitants.
- It is better to be known than to be a stranger to the area and its inhabitants. The spy has a cover story to protect him.
- He knows when to get out and always has an escape route planned.
- When the situation goes pear-shaped and he gets caught – he never gives up.

THE COVER STORY

The one thing that must stand up in the world of spying is the spy's cover story. They must be who they say they are and, when working in a foreign country, be able to prove their identity. By far the best way of obtaining a cover story is to make it as near to the truth as possible; details such as his age and place of origin, his education, and his likes and dislikes, for example. By doing so, he does not fall into a trap when an enemy Intelligence Agency starts an in-depth background check into your life.

Many spies enter a foreign country as part of the embassy staff or as part of a diplomatic mission. In some countries, the role of the Defence Attaché is little short of a spymaster. His position will not allow him to partake in direct actions, but he will act more as an umbrella for a network of spies and agents working on behalf of his country. Spies are recruited by a government from time to time simply because they have the right qualification. They could, for example, be a businessman who has just won an order into a foreign country. This grants him an automatic cover story and a legitimate reason for travelling. However, both of the above examples are restricted, firstly by protocol and secondly by a lack of espionage training. The real answer is to train a potential spy in the arts of tradecraft and provide him with a believable cover story.

COVER STORY EXAMPLE

An English spy was sent to work in the border country of South Armagh in Northern Ireland. His accent was English, as was his manner, but he managed to operate and collect information from the local farmers for six months. How did he manage it?

He adopted the role of a salesman selling impactors for an American company that had an overseas office in Belfast. The impactor, which fitted to the back of most standard farm tractors, was designed to break up old concrete. It was a solid cover story; he even arranged for a demonstration of the impactor at a local agricultural show, all of which added credence to his entry into a known terrorist area. His explanation was simple; the company had afforded him six months in which to establish the impactor, after which his job would be in jeopardy. For their part, the American company were keen to have someone try to sell their implement, although everyone knew it was far too expensive.

The spy did his homework, first by obtaining good road maps and aerial photographs of the area. Secondly, he researched how and where the IRA had been active and also did the same for the local British army. By doing this he could establish a route into the area he wished to visit without being stopped either by the IRA or by the British army. The latter would not pose a major problem but, in the eyes of the locals, it was best to stay clear of any association. He made all of his visits during daylight hours so that he could avoid being stopped by an IRA roadblock.

Although his movements around the area looked casual and random, they were meticulously planned. He managed to visit most of the farms and smallholdings in the area, taking in a local pub at lunchtime. At first, his reception by the locals was mixed. Some accepted him immediately while others eyed him with suspicion. The most common question that arose was "What are you doing here? You know this is a dangerous area?" This was a perfect question because it allowed the spy to open up the conversation with regards to the IRA. "That's all newspaper stuff. I have not seen any of the problems." At this point the local farmer would fall into a conversation recalling all the deeds of the local IRA. If the conversation went on for more than five minutes the spy would casually ask the farmer if he would like a drink. "I have a bottle in the car." Few refused.

Within two months he had built up a list of friendly farmers and restricted his lunchtime drinking to one particular public house. Having assessed all the people he had met, the spy set about homing in on several, the first being the daughter of the publican. She was a girl of about 24 years old, good looking and full-bodied. Since her father had died when she was very young, she helped her mother run the bar. Friday and Saturday nights saw her receiving a lot of attention from the local young men who attended the pub from both sides of the border. Because of this she had not ventured far from home and had seen little of the world. As far as she was concerned, the spy, who was some 35 years old, had appeared in the pub like a breath of fresh air. While the spy had noticed the attention whenever he entered the pub, he played on it in a friendly, but low key, way.

One lunchtime, the spy discovered early in the conversation, that her mother was away for several days. The spy turned on the charm and the girl fell for it. Closing time was 3 pm, but the girl indicated that he could stay if he wanted – he did. In the four hours until the bar opened for the evening, the spy made love to the girl three times – she was hooked. At 7 pm the bar opened; the spy had one pint and left. As he drove back to his safe house in Armagh city, he recalled all the names the girl had mentioned.

The liaison endured secretly for three months. Each time they were alone, the spy would ask his seemingly casual questions, all of which had been carefully rehearsed, with the miniature microphone faithfully recording every word the girl said. The information she gave was predominantly about the young men she had known since they became of drinking age. They had used the pub and had tried to impress her with their stories of heroism by pretending to be members of the IRA. For the most part this was just bravado, but she knew that one or two of them spoke the truth. "Be careful of him when he comes in," she would tell the spy. "He's a real nasty piece of work."

One day the spy simply never came back and after a time he was forgotten. He had managed to infiltrate a dangerous area by using a substantial and plausible cover story. The spy had taken time to get to know the area and the inhabitants before asking any questions. With the use of alcohol he had gained information from the farmers, with charm he had gleaned valuable information from the pub owner's daughter. By never exposing himself at night, he had managed to avoid running into direct confrontation with an IRA roadblock.

RECRUITING

Spies work for the intelligence services of their respective countries. They see themselves as either case officers or field officers, both of which are commonly referred to as "handlers". They rarely go into a foreign country and do the dirty work themselves. When a spy is operating in a foreign country, the best way to gather information is to recruit local agents. The basic plan is to get these agents to steal anything for you while never disclosing the spy's true identity. Once an agent is recruited properly, the spy can use them for just about anything: soliciting vital information, sabotage, deception, covert operations, assassination and sex. While this might sound a little outlandish, you must keep in mind that the recruitment machinery of most intelligence agencies is built on lies, deception and, above all, using people.

Most recruited agents are classified as either "primary" or "access". A primary agent will have direct access to what it is the spy requires, while an access agent is a go-between. When the operation is in the planning stages, a certain amount of money will be allocated to the handler to recruit agents and, in order to recruit several agents, the spy will need extra funding. The money may come from the intelligence agency budget or be self-generating from the operation, i.e. the sale of weapons or drugs. Money can buy most things – friendship, favours, sex and drugs – although the latter may well be directly supplied by the intelligence agency. However, the best tool a handler can have is the ability to tell totally believable lies.

POTENTIAL AGENTS

◂ **Recruiting the right agent is very important. This engineer will have intimate knowledge of the project.**

The first task of the handler is to spot his intended agent. That means finding people who have access to the information he requires. He may initially select several people and then narrow down his list accordingly. He will look for the lonely secretary or the disgruntled. The potential target may be a computer programmer or a code-breaker, but it would be better to recruit an analyst, as they have access to more information. Soft potential targets include:

- People with a careless security attitude or a grudge.
- Defectors who have fled their own country.
- Detainees or prisoners who will work for a reduced sentence.
- Foreign agents who have been caught and "turned". These are known as "double agents".
- People who can be threatened or blackmailed.
- Those who might be tempted by financial reward.

Once the handler has spotted someone in a position that best serves his interests, he must find a way to make them co-operate. First he must decide how he is going to make the initial contact. When doing so he must be careful to put some form of security and safety measures in place before approaching the new agent.

Having chosen his prospective agent, the handler must then evaluate him, test him and finally train him to do the required job.

The evaluation process is used to determine an agent's reliability and his capability to produce the required information. This process starts off with the initial contact between the handler and the agent. The handler will get to know the agent and will be trying to discover any weaknesses that will help. By this time the handler will have perfected his cover story and will be in full flow as to why he is in the country, where he lives and what work he does. He will also act a little superior, as if his job is extremely important. As the relationship becomes more refined, and after a degree of trust has been established, the handler will start providing little favours to the agent. If the handler has done his homework, he will know roughly how much the potential agent earns, from which he can deduce both his living conditions and his lifestyle needs. These rewards will then be increased, but always in a safe and logical way so that the agent does not become suspicious. When the moment comes to ask the agent to risk obtaining information for the handler, the handler will not depend solely on monetary rewards; a second and third option, such as blackmail, will be in place. At this stage in the recruitment process, the agent suddenly becomes aware of the trap he has fallen into; he has betrayed his country, his employer, his friends and his family. This is where the handler's cover story can come in useful, as it will allow him to add some lies to ease the agent's conscience. If the prospective agent categorically refuses to co-operate and indicates that he will go to the authorities, the handler must consider killing the agent.

Once the handler has hooked the agent, he will start the testing phase, effectively checking that the agent is capable of delivering the required information. If this proves successful, then the agent's training will begin.

During this phase, the handler will instruct the agent how to make contact and how to avoid being followed. The agent will be shown how to construct and mark a dead-letter drop and how to use a variety of equipment in order to help solicit the information, such as miniature cameras. If the agent is being used for sex, they will then be instructed in the use of covert recording equipment. The handler rarely provides the agent with guns or explosives; it may well provide the agent with a means of getting rid of him should things go wrong. In all cases the handler will do his best to stick with his cover story and will continue to be as friendly as possible with the agent while continuing with the monetary rewards. If the handler thinks that the agent is getting too close to him and that the operational security is at risk, then he may well pass the agent on to another handler. It is vital that the agent never gets the chance to break off contact and they can never be allowed to quit or resign.

▲ A sexually compromising situation can be a good lever when trying to recruit a new agent.

Sex can be a useful tool during the recruitment stage. It can be used to coerce someone to turn traitor or it can help manipulate someone into a compromising position. In many cases, sex can be a more effective tool than money, alcohol or drugs. Heterosexual compromise is used by many of the world's intelligence agencies. This starts with a simple introduction, i.e. putting a glamorous-looking woman in the same room as the target. One thing leads to another, with the end result being compromising photographs. The same applies with homosexuals; the beautiful woman is simply replaced by a pretty boy. Not all "honey traps", as they are commonly known, rely on photographs; the woman may say she is pregnant or the young boy may declare that he has AIDS. Both will be untrue, but they will serve to put extra pressure on the target.

A non-sexual compromise could come in a variety of disguises, such a criminal actions or security violations. The handler will exploit any of the agent's known compromises. If the promising agent has a clean past, the handler may well stage an event in which the agent is alleged to be a guilty party. Witnesses will be found, normally other agents under the handler's control, to provide evidence that proves the proposed agent to be guilty.

Whatever method the handler uses to co-opt the services of the agent, once achieved he must also provide some basic tradecraft training. It is in the handler's interests to make the agent as security-minded as possible and to ensure that the required objectives are being carried out correctly. In order to keep the agent firmly on his side, the handler must make sure that he can deliver any monetary or favourable promises. The agent's sole purpose is to do the bidding of the handler. Where this requires technical assistance, the handler must supply the agent with the necessary equipment and teach him how to use it. This may be a covert camera for bugging the agent's workplace or firearms, if an assassination is required. The recruitment of an agent is a long and dangerous game. Bearing this in mind, a good agent will need to be protected, even if this means that the handler has to prove assistance in any emergency.

DOUBLE AGENTS

When a spy enters a foreign country it is always possible that they have been recognized and put under surveillance. Instead of picking the spy up, the foreign agency may wish to keep them under surveillance and even try to implant a double agent. This double agent, commonly referred to as a "mole", will put themselves in a position where they can be recruited by the spy. A classic mole is one who has been recruited by the spy and then discovered by the opposition. When discovery is a choice between death or being a double agent, then the latter is often preferred.

For this reason the spy must ensure that anyone he recruits is genuine and test them accordingly. This testing phase is normally done by a specialist counterintelligence officer. This person will know how to detect and neutralize attempted penetrations by enemies of your organization. This normally means feeding some sensitive information to the new recruit

– and only to the recruit. It is simply a matter of waiting to see if this information comes to light from another source. For this reason it is best not to overuse new recruits until they have proved themselves.

CASE HISTORY

A car was stopped at a routine police checkpoint in Northern Ireland; the driver was a known villain on the fringes of a terrorist cell. There was no evidence to arrest the man and the police simply reported the matter to Special Branch. The name of the female passenger was also provided. She turned out to be the wife of a convicted terrorist currently in prison.

An operation was set up and compromising pictures were taken of the couple in bed at the woman's home. The next time the car was stopped, both of its occupants were shown the photographs and both were given the clear message that the woman's husband would shortly be getting copies. The consequences would have been severe for both of them; the woman may well have been disfigured, the man kneecapped.

The man was taken from the car by the handler dressed as a policeman and a deal was struck where the villain would supply information. The required information was deliberately kept simple and would not compromise the villain, who thought he was getting off lightly.

The following week the villain met with the handler at a motorway lay-by. The handler asked the villain to get into his car in order to discuss the requested information. This would only have taken a few seconds and the handler would have assured the villain that the pictures would be destroyed. At the same time, he pulled out a wad of notes and handed it over to the surprised villain. Thinking the Northern Ireland police force to be stupid, the villain went on his way £1,000 richer as a result of giving a useless piece of information.

Two days later the villain was stopped again. Somewhat agitated, once again he agreed to get into the handler's car. This time the handler showed him the pictures of him receiving the money, taken by a hidden camera. The penalty for sleeping with an interned terrorist's wife was kneecapping, the consequences for being a police informer would have been a bullet in the head. As it turned out, the SAS did a legitimate hit job on one of the terrorist cell members and the recruited villain was promoted in the cell. The rest was easy.

AGENT CONTACT

Once a spy has recruited his agent, he will need to meet him in order to issue instructions and to collect intelligence. This procedure is called "agent contact". Under normal circumstances, a handler working in a foreign country must assume that he is under surveillance. In order to set up a clandestine meeting with the agent, he will go through a set of procedures to ensure that an enemy surveillance team is not observing the meeting. Both the handler and the agent will have previously agreed upon a place, a date and a time or they will have set up a signal that indicates a meeting is to take place. In addition, they are familiar with each other's appearance, i.e. they can recognize each other on sight. The handler will provide the agent with a set of unique communication codes; this may be defined by hand signals, actions or clothing. The agreed signals will have various meanings such as, "We need to talk" or "I am under surveillance". A normal meeting between a handler and an agent would follow these basic steps.

STEP ONE

Both arrive independently at the previously agreed general location. Rather than fixing a specific location, they agree to be only in the general vicinity. This is an important principle. In this example, they are using a large park in a residential district. The location is free of video surveillance cameras. Ideally, the location should also be out of range of telephoto lenses. Other locations could include bus stops or a convenience store.

STEP TWO

▸ **Agent contact – make eye contact.**

Both the handler and the agent make discreet eye contact at some distance from each other. The handler, being the senior of the two, may use a prearranged signal to tell the agent that he has spotted him, such as moving a newspaper from one hand to the other or lighting a cigarette. The signal must be a movement that does not attract the unwanted attention of any enemy surveillance operators. It is important for both players at this stage carry out their surveillance with just one or two people; later they will literally surround their target with very large numbers.

STEP THREE

Once the recognition signal has been established, the handler will simply walk off, leaving the agent to follow at a distance. This ensures that the handler is clean and that he has not grown a tail. Surveillance teams on foot work on what is called a "floating-box principle". This means that they would form a very loose formation around the subject they are following. All main entry and exit points to a particular location will also be covered.

▲ Agent contact – check to see if I am followed.

STEP FOUR

When the agent has satisfied himself that the handler is clean, he will make a signal to him. This will usually be the carrying out of some everyday task, such as re-tying his shoelaces. Now the roles are reversed, this time the handler follows the agent to establish that he is also "clean".

▲ Agent contact – signal all clear, now check me.

STEP FIVE

▸ Agent contact – the meet.

When the handler is satisfied that neither he nor the agent are under surveillance, he will give the signal to meet. On the other hand, if either the handler or the agent suspects that a surveillance team is in the vicinity, they will simply abort the operation and walk away. Once they meet, they will discuss any issues and agree upon the date, the time and the location of their next clandestine meeting. This will also include several back-up plans in case that meeting is thwarted by surveillance.

ACT INSTINCTIVELY

It is vitally important to trust your instincts, because if something appears to be suspicious it is better to be safe than sorry. Many people are surprised to learn that it is not difficult to detect a surveillance team. If the agent requests a meeting with his handler, the latter must be careful that he is not being set up. Such a request by the agent is known as a "blind date".

PASSING MESSAGES

Messages can be passed in any number of ways. They can be done visually, in order to avoid contact association between the handler and the agent, or they can be covertly delivered. Over the years, both handlers and agents have devised numerous ways of passing messages. I have outlined a number of different techniques below:

HOLLOW COIN

▸ Paying for goods or services is a "natural" way to pass a message on, especially when it is hidden in a hollow coin.

Every country in the world has a currency system in place in order for the population to carry out their daily business, such as buying food, eating in cafes or paying for everyday goods. This is a natural transaction and one that is exploited by spies. Say that the handler needs to meet with his agent. He walks down the street and buys a newspaper, or stops for a coffee. The very action of buying a newspaper or a coffee requires that money change hands. If the newsagent or waiter is the contact, what better way to pass a message?

SOURCING MATERIAL

You can get your own hollow coin by purchasing one from a store which sells magic tricks.

A DEAD-LETTER BOX (DLB)

A dead-letter box is commonly referred to as a "DLB". It is a precise place where a message, or any other material, can be covertly left by one person and be collected by another. The aim of the DLB is to transfer a message without either parties making contact, thus avoiding being observed by others. The DLB can be located in almost any place providing that the placement and the pick-up can be carried out naturally. Placing a container in the ground, under a park bench or in a trash can have all been used. The secret of a good DLB is ingenuity.

DLB PROCEDURE

While each country has its own methods for teaching DLB procedures, the one devised and perfected by the KGB is the best example of how it should be done. Providing both the sender and receiver have proficient skills in counter-surveillance techniques, conforming to the KGB method will guarantee safe delivery.

THE DLB LOCATION

The spy will find a good location where he is are temporarily unseen by any surveillance team. He chooses his spot either to fill or to insert a DLB position or a container. He will always choose a location that is populated, such as a park or public transport, and avoid isolated places. He will then find places close to the DLB, but far enough away to avoid suspicion, where he can leave a signal that either the DLB is ready for filling, that there is material in the box that the material has been picked up. These signals should be foolproof and unspotted by any surveillance team.

Several DLB places should be known and agreed to by both the handler and the agent. Likewise, a timing system should be in place for each DLB drop. The time spent in the area should be limited and the pick-up should never take more than 15 minutes. To increase security for a DLB, the handler and agent should have a number of fake DLB locations. These should be worked into the handler's or the agent's normal daily routine. All the handler and the agent have to do is to walk past these fake DLBs on a regular basis.

STEP ONE: READY-TO-FILL SIGNAL

Once the delivery device is made, the spy cn pass information to his handler. Assuming that a predetermined area has been agreed on, the first step is for the agent to signal that he is "ready to fill" the DLB. This might take the form of a chalk mark or a piece of chewing gum stuck on a park bench. The idea is to produce a signal that can be seen clearly but which is virtually imperceptible to the general public's eye.

◂ Ready to fill signal.

STEP TWO: READY-TO-PICK-UP SIGNAL

Once the handler sees the ready-to-fill signal, he will make a ready-to-pick-up signal. As with the agents "ready-to-fill" signal, this will normally involve something simple, such as lighting a cigarette or making a chalk mark. On seeing this, the agent will place or fill the DLB. Once this task has been done, the agent will then remove his ready-to-fill signal. By doing so, he is simply informing the handler that the material is in the DLB.

◂ Ready to pick up signal.

◂ This DLB is nothing more than the body of a plastic pen covered with similar covering to the bush. Perfect concealment

STEP THREE: ALL-CLEAR SIGNAL

Only when the handler has seen the agent remove the ready-to-fill signal will he approach the DLB and collect the message. He will remove his own ready-to-pick-up signal the moment he has recovered the message. This tells the agent that he has recovered the message and that the DLB is now empty.

At this stage both the handler and the agent will leave the area. In the event that the handler has not shown up within the prearranged time, the agent will simply remove his ready-to-fill signal.

SECRETS OF DLB PLACEMENT

A spy will always remember that the aim of the DLB is to transfer information without the knowledge of any other person than the contact. The spy keeps these rules in mind:

- He will always assume both himself and his contact are under surveillance
- He will create a DLB that fits in with his normal daily routine.
- He will make DLB placement and retrieval accessible and swift.
- He will be creative in his choice of container or hiding place.
- If he or his contact are apprehended, he will make sure the DLB cannot be discovered.

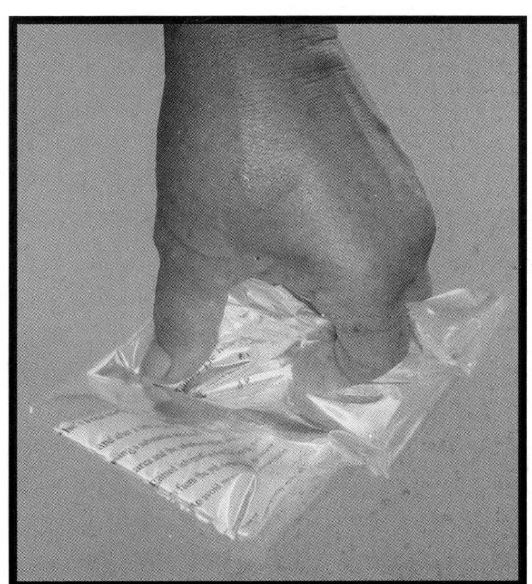

Although a message can be hidden underwater, the water should not be too murky and deep. Hiding the DLB is only half the problem – it has to be recovered quickly too.

USING A DLB

DLBs have purposely been made in the form of a hollow spike that has a screw top to make it waterproof. The message is simply put inside and then, at the right location, forced into the earth by standing on it. It is possible to construct a DLB from any form of tubing, but a better way is to use an old cigar case. This is almost perfect for the job, as it already has a waterproof screw top. Because the case is only made of light aluminium and can easily be crushed, the spy may disguise it as a twig instead of pushing it into the ground. He finds a stick of roughly the same thickness and removes the bark; he then uses this to cover the cigar tube. He then walks through the park holding it in his trouser pocket, making sure that the pocket has a hole in it and dropping his DLB at the required location.

Gluing a magnet inside a film container makes a quick and easy DLB. It can be attached to the metal underside of a table, chair or other household or office furniture.

CHAPTER 2

The art of writing and passing on secret messages is vital in a world where information means power.

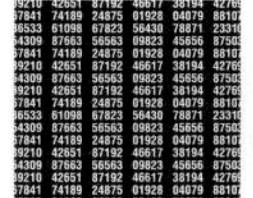

SECRET CODES

There is evidence to suggest that coded messages were used as far back as Roman times. Codes and cryptology methods have been developed enormously since then, principally for use in military operations. For the most part, spies and agents were the first to use such codes and little has changed today.

While messages can be passed covertly between the handler and the agent, there is always the possibility that the opposition might detect the exchange and intercept the message. To this end, all messages should be coded in one form or another. Many ingenious devices have been used over the years to enable governments, the military and spies to pass messages. One of the more widely known devices was the World War II German Enigma machine. Both Britain and America dispatched teams of agents in order to capture an Enigma unit so that they could learn its secrets and use any information they obtained to their advantage.

Despite its complexity, the Enigma machine's weakness lay in the fact that its code could be deciphered, even though this took an enormous effort. The main reason for this was simple; the coding and decoding procedure was a systematic and structured process. This meant that, no matter how complicated the system was, it could still be broken. In order for a coding system to be truly unbreakable, it must work in an unstructured way, in other words, randomly. The development of the One-Time Pad (OTP) went a long way to achieving this goal.

HOW TO USE ONE-TIME PADS (OTP)

A one-time pad, or OTP as it is generally known, is used for secret communications by just about all of the world's major intelligence agencies. Perfected in 1917 during the First World War, an OTP consists of random keys (number blocks) with the whole making a pad. These numbers are used only once, hence the name. OTP is the only cipher system that cannot be cracked. At the height of the Cold War, not a single OTP sent by the KGB was cracked by the American or British intelligence services.

SAMPLE OTP

PAD 5 - PAGE 17

01	25271	39210	42651	87192	46617	38194	42769	91808	31347	53927
02	69221	67841	74189	24875	01928	04079	88107	39658	80219	52768
03	87301	36533	61098	67823	56430	78871	23310	90312	47820	22495
04	43278	54309	87663	56563	09823	45656	87503	44596	23320	24319
05	39221	67841	74189	24875	01928	04079	88107	39658	80219	52768
06	65271	39210	42651	87192	46617	38194	42769	91808	31347	53927
07	93278	54309	87663	56563	09823	45656	87503	44596	23320	24319

The above is a sample page from a one-time pad. The numbers are generated by random selection; the pad is numbered, as is the page and the line. There are only ever two copies of the OTP, one with the intelligence agency and the other with the field agent. The intelligence agency's copy is normally kept by the cipher operator, who works in a high security building, thus ensuring the safety of the copy. Very few people have access to the "pad", neither do they know which agent is using which pad. Only the ciphered message is passed up for intelligence analysis. The field agent will have the second copy. If he is compromised then he will destroy his pad in a special wallet that burns the pad in seconds. Even when the enemy has managed to get their hands on an agent's pad, there are simple checks that can be put in place to confirm authenticity. If the intelligence agency has the slightest suspicion that their agent has been compromised, they will automatically destroy their pad.

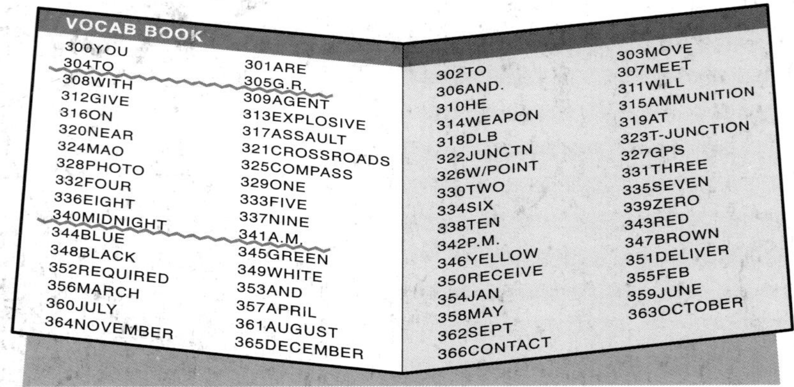

▲ **A sample vocab book**

There are many ways in which a numbered code can be deciphered into a simple language. This can either be achieved by starting at a random place in the alphabet triggered by a number or through the use of a common book, such as an encyclopaedia.

The most common form is to have a "vocab" book that lists a simple set of names and special letters and which will also provide the user with an alphabet from which he can spell place names that are not in the vocab book.

We can now translate the following massage using the vocab book above and then encrypt it using the OTP:

AGENT WILL MEET YOU AT GR327903 2 PM 5 AUGUST. HE WILL GIVE YOU WEAPONS AND AMMUNITION.

STEP ONE

Find the word "agent" in the vocab book and write down the three-digit number next to it, i.e. 309. Continue to do this until you have written down all of the digits. Any numbers in the message are simply left unchanged. You should finish up with the following line of numbers, which you should then separate into a block to match those in the codebook, in this example blocks of five:

30931 13073 00319 30532 79032 34253 61310 31131 23003 14306 31516

STEP TWO

Choose a line to start in your codebook, in this example we have used line three, and place the number block taken from the vocab book under those in the codebook. Next subtract without carrying units forward.

Black = codebook, blue = vocab book and red = the subtracted numbers.

87301 36533 61098 67823 56430 78871 23310 90312 47820 22495 43278

30931 13073 00319 30532 79032 34253 61310 31131 23003 14306 31516

57470 23560 61789 37391 87408 44628 62000 69281 24827 18191 12762

STEP THREE

Next add the codebook number, page and line to the front of the subtracted numbers i.e.

(51703) 57470 23560 61789 37391 87408 44628 62000 69281 24827 18191 12762

These numbers can now be safely transmitted to the agent; they will make absolutely no sense to an enemy unit even if they manage to intercept them.

STEP FOUR

Once the agent has received the message he uses the first block to identify the correct codebook, page and start line. (Agents may well have several different codebooks, using one for each person they deal with). The agent has the only other copy of the OTP code book, so it is a simple matter of placing the received message, less the indicator block, under the correct line and subtracting the numbers. The subtracted numbers are then broken down into blocks of three in order to find the message from the vocab book. Take the time to understand how the basic principles involved in OTP work. Once you have mastered the subtraction values, the rest is easy.

OTP CONSTRUCTION

Making your own OTP pad and vocab book is easy. Once completed, simply make one extra photocopy and give it to your contact. You can now exchange messages in total secrecy.

SPOT CODEBOOK

The spot code system can be used either by spies, agents or surveillance operators. It is a particularly good system as it allows the user to identify a major feature, usually a specific place, junction or crossroads. When a spot code system is used for surveillance, it allows the desk operator to know where all the surveillance operators are at all times. He can also direct foot and vehicle surveillance to a specified spot.

When used by handlers and agents, the spot code system offers several automatic back-up options. For example, if "blue 5" is compromised, both the handler and the agent will automatically know that they have to meet at "blue 6" and so on. This is how it works:

A SIMPLE SPOT CODE

A spot code is normally made by allocating a colour and a number to each major road intersection. As the surveillance operator drives from one intersection to another, he simply identifies himself and tells the desk operator. "Nine, this is Sierra Papa four – towards blue 5'30–35." When driving, the operator simply adds the approximate speed to the end of his call, providing a rough estimated time of arrival at the next spot. When the area is new to the operator, he will carry a spot codebook in his vehicle. However, should this codebook fall into enemy hands, it will present a short-term security risk. This will necessitate all the spot codes being changed and with everyone having to learn the new codes.

The spot code system can also be used to refer to actions rather than a location. This helps throw the enemy off balance should they be watching or listening to the operation. For example: "Sierra Papa four – towards black 6." In reality, the caller is simply telling the desk operator that he is static in one location, a cafe or a bar, for example.

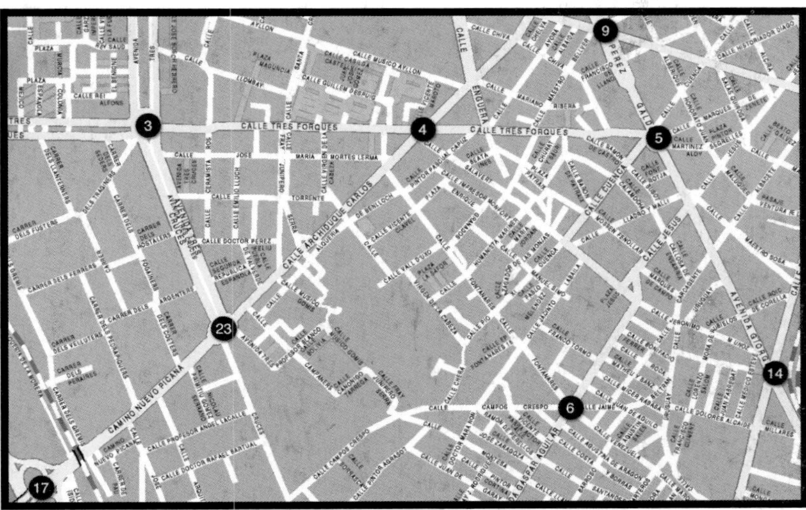

MAKING A SPOT CODEBOOK

The spy may use a street map of his area, which can be easily and cheaply obtained from tourist offices or newsagents in the local area or even farther afield if he's exercising even more caution than usual. Any decent streetmap will do for his purposes. He will also buy some self-sticking coloured spot labels from an office supplies store. To make the spot codebook, he then sticks the spots at each of the major intersections and streets and number them. Then he will make a number of photocopies for each of his contacts, being careful to copy only the exact number of codebooks that he needs.

RANDOMIZE

A spy will use the coloured spots for one area but will make the numbers random. This will help confuse the enemy, but will make no difference to the agent.

INVISIBLE WRITING

Writing invisible messages is also a good way of passing information between people; a message can be written on a bank note and passed quite naturally to another person. An agent or a handler may walk down the street and discard an empty packet of cigarettes, a natural process, but the inner paper layer may well contain an invisible message. Despite having been around for centuries, the art of invisible writing is still widely used by many intelligence agencies today.

One of the problems with traditional invisible ink is that the author cannot see what they are writing. As a result, the message has to be short and very precisely written. Even when they were writing with an ultraviolet pen, the authors could not see what they were writing and the message could only be seen when the ink was highlighted with a special ultraviolet light.

Then, some years ago, the British intelligence service discovered, purely by accident, that a Pentel Rollerball makes a brilliant tool for invisible writing. The rollerball, commercially available in most parts of the world, writes normally on a piece of paper. The writing is then pressed against the piece of paper that will carry the secret message. The original ink dries almost immediately, so to the eye the message paper looks blank. However, when it is swabbed with a developing fluid, the message miraculously appears. It therefore allows the author to write a detailed and well-spaced letter in real time and transfer it to a blank piece of paper by what is known as "offset" printing. The transferred message will only become visible when it is developed.

MAKING INVISIBLE INK

▲ Any carbon-based clear liquid such as lemon juice or milk makes excellent invisible ink.

Any clear (not visible to the eye when dry), carbon-based liquid can be used to make invisible ink, milk and lemon juice being the most common. It is best to use normal writing or computer paper, as glossy or absorbent paper distorts the writing. Using an old-fashioned metal nib pen, although a toothpick would suffice, the spy will dip this into the milk or lemon juice and simply write his letter. The wetness provides some idea of he has written, but once the liquid is dry then the writing will disappear.

The best way to read the message is by using a domestic iron. The spy will run the hot iron over the paper. Because the liquid is carbon-based, it will turn brown and thus develop his message. Agents have used various forms of heat, such as gently moving the paper over a candle flame, in order to reveal the hidden message.

OTHER METHODS OF ENCODING AND DECODING MESSAGES

CODE WORD

The handler can make a list of code words that he can pass on to the agent; the list may be ten code words long and contain words where only one letter of the alphabet appears (no repeats) i.e. Blackstone. Blackstone may appear as number 4 on the list. The message may be hidden in a DLB or passed as a secret message. By a totally different signal, the handler will also indicate the list number, in this case number 4.

STEP ONE

The handler will write out the alphabet, next he will write down the code word followed by the rest of the alphabet omitting the letters in the codeword.

Plain text: A B C D E F G H I J K L M N O P Q R S T U V W X Y Z
Code: B L A C K S T O N E D F G H I J M P Q R U V W X Y Z

STEP TWO

The handler will construct his message by taking the code letter below the normal alphabet letter. For example: I will meet you in the park. This will be translated as –

N WNFF GKKR YIU NH ROK JBPD – and then passed on to the agent.

STEP THREE

The agent, having received the numbers, checks the list for the number. The list may have been memorized to increase security further. The agent then writes out the alphabet, with the code word and the remaining alphabet written underneath. Using the encoded letters he will be able to decode the message.

ENCODING

If the message were to fall into enemy hands, regular blocks could help them decode the message. For example, the single letter N must either be an "I" or an "A". This can be avoided simply by dividing the encoded message into a four-letter block as shown below.

NWNF FGKK RYIU NHRO KJBPD

In the following message the code letter is PYROGENIC.

OGRJ OGOR JMMG RSDX

INGENIOUS CODES

Some of the codes that have developed over the centuries have been truly ingenious and, while these are rarely used today, it is worth looking at them. Although the best way of transcribing a message is to use the alphabet, the alphabetic and figure form can transcribe into symbols or sound blocks. While the best example of the latter is Morse code, many intelligence agencies have experimented with microwave and other sound devices.

MORSE CODE

Morse Code is just a simple substitution code based on dashes and dots. The dash is normally three times as long as the dot. The best way to define the difference is to repeat the words to yourself: "dot daaassh". Morse code can be sent in many forms, including radio, light flashes or acoustic sounds such as tapping on a water pipe.

A .-	I ..	Q --.-	Y -.--	
B -...	J .---	R .-.	Z --..	
C -.-.	K -.-	S ...		
D -..	L .-..	T -	0 -----	5 .....
E .	M --	U ..-	1 .----	6 -....
F ..-.	N -.	V ...-	2 ..---	7 --...
G --.	O ---	W .--	3 ...--	8 ---..
H	P .--.	X -..-	4 ....-	9 ----.

SYMBOL CODE

Many codes have taken the form of symbols. In biblical times, it was believed that the sign of the fish drawn in the sand was a sign of a believer in Jesus Christ. Symbolic writing can be complicated and can take years to decipher, as is the case with Egyptian hieroglyphics. A more down-to-earth symbolic code is "Pigpen". This uses a grid system designed in such a way as to allow two letters of the alphabet into each segment of the grid. The shape of the grid containing the letter forms the code.

STEP ONE

A grid is drawn in which all sectors are different. Then the alphabet is filled in; first in a logical order, i.e. AB in the top left-hand corner, following which they can be placed at random. If this is done, then both parties must know the sequence.

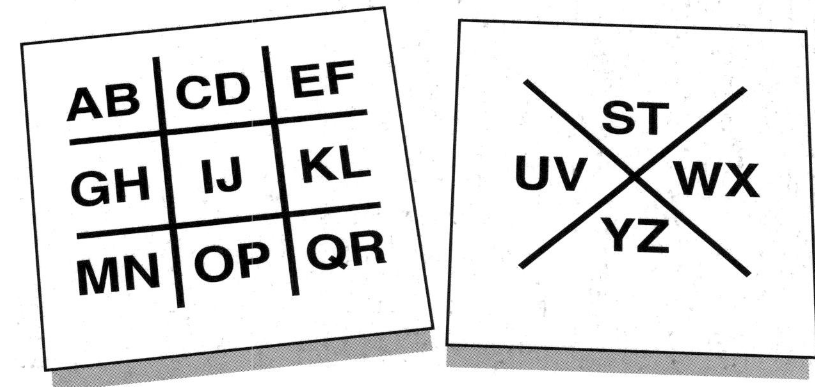

STEP TWO

The code is written using symbols, note that the second letter in each sector is denoted by a dot. The encoded message will look something like this. As with any encoded message, word block is best broken up into regular blocks to avoid the enemy decoding the message, should it fall into their hands.

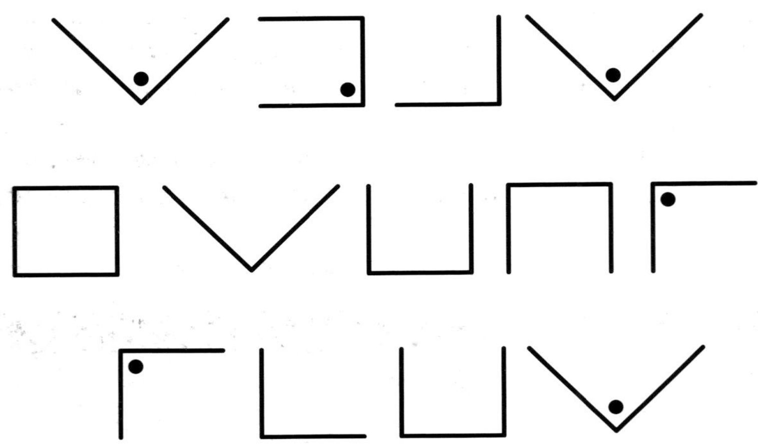

ENCODING AND DECODER RINGS

This a very simple substitution cipher, but one that can be used over and over while changing the code each time. Basically it uses two wheels, one that is about 1 cm smaller than the other. These wheels can be made of any material that can be written on. Around the outer edge of each wheel is the alphabet and the numbers 0 through to 9. The clock-face method is most commonly used to ensure that the writing is evenly spaced, so that the outer and inner markings are directly in line with each other. The idea is that the smaller disk can rotate inside the larger.

RING CONSTRUCTION

Two alphabetical and figure disks can be created using Microsoft Word. They are then printed out and stuck on to cardboard to ensure a more secure platform. Then they are pinned together in the middle so that the inner wheel rotates.

▲ Some simple cipher wheels.

STEP ONE

To encode a message, the spy simply turns the inner disk to wherever he wishes to start. He can rotate the inner disk until the A is now aligned with P. Using the outer disk as his plain text he writes down the aligned letter on the inner disk to form his code. The inner and outer circles need to be carefully aligned to read off.

STEP TWO

It is a simple matter of passing the code to the handler or agent together with the original start place on the outer disk; in this instance P. The matter can be made more complicated by having a more complicated start code, P7–V4–S6. To decode the message, he first places the inner disk at P and reads off the first seven letters. The inner disk will then be moved to V for the next four letters and to S for the remaining six. Decoded message should be kep in blocks.

COMPUTERS

There is nothing new about computer encryption. It uses the same cryptography methods that have been used for centuries. Few people, other than government intelligence agencies, had any need for cryptography prior to the digital age. That has all changed today. Businesses and individuals all generate information which, for one reason or another, they wish to remain secret. The difference in normal human forms of cryptology and those developed for computers is simply one of security, i.e. it is easy for a computer to crack a human code, but not vice versa. Most computer encryption systems belong to one of two categories – symmetric-key encryption and public-key encryption.

Symmetric-key encryption is a secret code based on one individual computer. In order for one computer to send the encrypted message to another computer, the second computer must first know the same secret code. The secret code is the key to unlocking the information.

Example: In a simple form, a text-encoded message is sent to another computer telling the user that the secret code is 3. The encrypted process automatically changes the alphabetical information letters to 3 places down i.e. A becomes D and B becomes E etc.

This is a very simple explanation of how computer encryption works, but it should be stated that today's encryption systems are highly advanced.

Public-key encryption uses both a private key and a public key. Whereas only your computer knows the private key, any other computer that wants secure communications can access your computer's public key. In order to decode the incoming message, the receiving computer must have and use both the public and the private keys.

PASSWORD PROTECTION

Secret data can be sent by computer by using the "Options" button found in the "Tools" file of Microsoft Word. The spy will be asked for a password in the "Security" box. (On a Mac, the procedure is via "Protect Document" in "Tools"). The password has to be reconfirmed but the document is then secure as the recipient cannot open it without knowing what the original password is.

A spy will change his password regularly.

HIDING A TEXT FILE IN A DIGITAL PICTURE

One way of sending secret messages is to hide confidential data in inconspicuous graphic files. This file is then sent to a contact over the Internet or on a disk. With the appropriate software and code word, the text can be taken out of the picture. One such system uses the well-known steganography technology that is also used for digitally watermarking pictures. Bitmap graphics consist of pixels that can be modified to store your text. If the altered picture – containing the text file – is then seen by someone else, it will simply look like a normal image. It works by removing or altering some of the bits that make up the picture pixels and replacing them with the text. To the human eye these changes cannot be seen as only insignificant information is removed and this is done across the whole spectrum of the digital image.

One of the best shareware programmes for hiding text inside pictures is called StegenICE and a free download can be found at the following address:

http://madmax.deny.de/siteJS/indexJS.htm

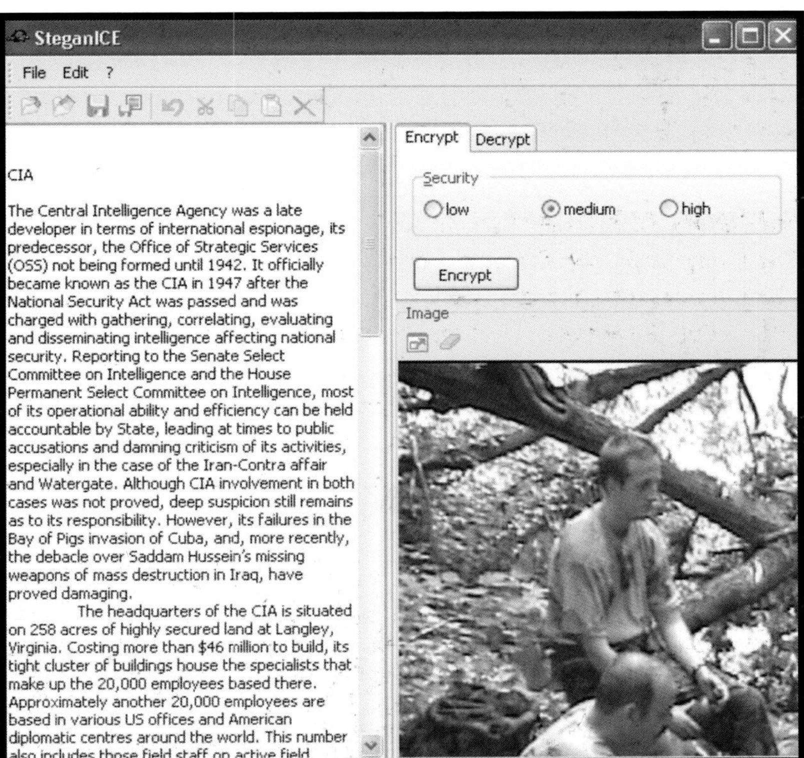

▲ Hiding text in a picture is a modern, hi-tech way to conceal a message.

CHAPTER 3

We are all being watched, listened to, and recorded – all of the time.

SURVEILLANCE

There are many forms of surveillance but, for the most part, people believe that they can go about their everyday lives expecting a certain amount of privacy – this is not true. Every single person in Europe is under some form of surveillance every day. They will not deliberately be observed or overheard, but records of their movements and actions will be recorded. Close Circuit Television (CCTV) cameras currently monitor city centres, major stores, petrol stations and motorways. Credit card transactions can be traced. Your emails can be read, as can every stroke of the keyboard. And then there is Echelon…

ECHELON

Echelon is the name given to the massive worldwide surveillance system that is capable of capturing and scanning every telephone call, fax and email sent anywhere in the world. Using sophisticated satellite systems, earth stations, radar and communication networks, as well as an array of ships and planes, the system is capable of monitoring both military and civilian communications. It was originally developed during the Cold War by the English-speaking countries to eavesdrop on communications between the Soviet Union and its allies. Now that need is no longer pressing, it is being used instead to monitor terrorist communications, as well as the activities of organized crime groups, alongside more traditional espionage methods.

Although details about the system are still shrouded in secrecy, some facts are known. The main proponents are the US and the UK, but they are backed up by Canada, Australia and New Zealand. Each country is responsible for monitoring a certain part of the Earth. For example, the US listens in over most of Latin America, Asia, Asiatic Russia and northern China. Britain monitors Europe, Africa and Russia west of the Urals. Canada sweeps the northern parts of the former USSR and the Arctic regions. Australia is responsible for Indochina, Indonesia and southern China and New Zealand handles the western Pacific.

In practice, the way Echelon works is simple. All the members of the alliance use satellites, ground receiving stations and electronic intercepts that enable them to pick up all communications traffic sent by satellite, cellular, microwave and fibre-optic means. The communications captured by these methods are then sent to a series of supercomputers that are programmed to recognize predetermined phrases, addresses, words or known voice patterns. Anything deemed to be of interest is then sent to the relevant intelligence agency for analysis.

In the US, the agency responsible for Echelon is the National Security Agency (NSA), based at Fort Meade, near Washington. It is estimated that both its staff and resources exceed those of the combined CIA and FBI. Canada's Echelon program is handled by the Communications Security Establishment, an offshoot of the National Security Agency, and is based in Ottawa. In Britain, General Communications Headquarters (GCHQ) located at Cheltenham, is concerned with Echelon. You have to remember that the locations of smaller stations are spread across the globe in strategic positions.

After the Cold War and before 9/11, the US primarily used Echelon as a means of intercepting messages from South and Central America in an effort to thwart drugs barons. Other organized crime gangs and terrorists, such as the Russian Mafia and Hamas, were also a target. However, following 9/11, it must now be assumed that Echelon is on the alert for any messages that might warn of an attack by Al Quaeda.

Although such usage of a surveillance system can only be a positive thing, Echelon has also had its fair share of detractors. Certain accusations have been made that Echelon has been used for commercial gain by the countries involved, enabling them to undercut competitors and to double deal to their own national economic advantage. Debates have even been raised in non-participating countries and within the EU. Nevertheless, the intelligence gains provided by the system in the new climate of global terrorism are likely to drown out any protests in the future.

WHAT IS SURVEILLANCE?

Surveillance is a technique used to obtain information, to make connections, to produce new leads and to collate evidence. Surveillance can be carried out by one of the following methods.

- Human, visual and audio.
- Electronic, video and audio.
- Aerial and satellite surveillance.

Surveillance may be carried out in order to obtain evidence of a crime or to identify persons who have been indicated in subversive actions. Surveillance methods help to establish a person's location and may well lead to an association with other criminals. The location of stolen or contraband goods can be exposed, leading to an admissible case in court. However, the main way that surveillance is used is to gather military intelligence. Governments have long since learned that information gathered on the potential lethality and capabilities of another nation can help them prepare for defence or attack. One good example is acoustic intelligence. This is derived from monitoring the sounds made by enemy surface vessels and submarines. These sounds can be analyzed to provide a unique signature for each vessel currently at sea. Knowing the location of enemy nuclear submarines or battle fleets provides advance warning of any attack.

One major problem with military intelligence is the amount of information they collect. Having information is one thing, interpreting its full and true value is quite another. The enormity of this quandary was highlighted by the 9/11 Al Quaeda attacks on the United States. The information that an assault was about to take place was available from several sources: the interpretation and immediate action lagged too far behind. Echelon should have detected some traffic. Or do the perpetrators of the atrocity have a method of sending messages that cannot be detected? Whatever the reason, it proves that electronic surveillance, no matter how sophisticated, is only effective if it has the back-up of good analysis and the correct distribution of intelligence.

In reality, surveillance is simply monitoring the activity of a person or persons, a place or an object. In order to do this successfully, intelligence agents need to consider several factors about the target. For example, if the target is a person then he will most probably move around, either on foot or by vehicle. If the target is in a house in the country, a static observation position (OP) would be set up. Note that following people and surveillance is undertaken by spies and it is usually illegal. Civilians and members of the public should not do it. The various methods of surveillance consist of one or a combination of the following:

- Static surveillance.
- Foot surveillance.
- Mobile surveillance.
- Technical surveillance.

SURVEILLANCE OPERATOR

A surveillance operator.

A good surveillance operator is known as a "grey" person. That is to say that they mingle with people, but that no one ever takes any notice of them. Their personality appears nondescript. They have no outstanding physical features and their dress is innocuous. They are deliberately trained to be Mr and Mrs Nobody, so insignificant that no one ever gives them a second glance.

Yet this is only an outward appearance, as the surveillance operator requires many skills. They must be patient, as surveillance operations can go on for months, sometimes even years. They must be adaptable, as many targets can act erratically. If the target is a professional spy, they will deliberately check to see if they are being followed and will take evasive actions in order to throw off any unseen surveillance operation being carried out against them.

Surveillance operators must have confidence not only in their own abilities but also in those of their team members. They must have a good memory, good hearing and excellent eyesight. Most of all, though, surveillance operators must blend into the background and become almost invisible. If the target takes a bus, one of the team must follow. The target will observe anyone who entered the bus at the same stop and be aware that they may be surveillance operators. In this situation, the surveillance operator becomes an actor, conversing with the passenger next to him as if they have known each other for years. The target may even approach the surveillance operator and deliberately confront him as to why they are being followed. In this instance, the operator must deliver a response that satisfies the target's inquisition.

The surveillance operator must also learn advanced driving skills and be able to operate any number of different vehicles. Most surveillance operators in the United Kingdom undertake a high-speed driving course with the police. This involves handling a vehicle at speed. They must also have a good knowledge of the area in which they are working. This is particularly helpful when a target has become temporally "unsighted". Above all, they must possess and develop a "sixth sense" – something that comes with good training and experience.

Some surveillance operators specialize in technical surveillance. They must learn how to use and operate a whole myriad of technical equipment, such as cameras and listening devices. In many cases this means covertly breaking into someone's property and inserting an audio-visual device. To do this successfully surveillance operators are required to learn method of entry skills, such as lock picking. Other operations may require them to crawl beneath a vehicle during the hours of darkness and insert a tracking device.

It is important for the surveillance operator to understand who or what the target is. If the target is a person, he needs to ask himself whether that person is aware that they may be under surveillance. If the target is a foreign spy, then he will have been trained in counter-surveillance methods. Even if the target is a common criminal, he may, due to the nature of his activities, become suspicious of being followed. In many cases, a surveillance target may not be aware that he is being watched or followed, or he may have been getting away with his activities for so long that he has become complacent. Knowing these factors helps the surveillance team decide on the number of people required and what approach they should take. Likewise, where the target is a static location, such as a building, it is important for the surveillance operators to evaluate what resources are needed.

MASTER OF DISGUISE

◂ Disguise should be subtle.

There may be times when a spy or agent is required to become a master of disguise. He may suspect that he is under surveillance and wish to throw his pursuers off in order to make an important meeting, for example. Or he simply may want to go somewhere to observe someone or something and not be recognized. Whatever the reason, there are two basic methods: the immediate quick change and the deliberate disguise.

A quick change requires some thorough and prior preparation. For instance, it is possible to change his stature, dress or appearance or a combination of all three. Stature can be addressed by stooping, limping, effecting a height change or body bulk size. Changing his dress requires conversion or having an alternative item of clothing with him. Likewise his appearance can be changed in a few minutes if he is prepared. The basic rule is to start off as Mr Average and change into Mr Nondescript.

The spy will remember that it is easier to dress down than it is to dress up – by the same token it is easier to look older than it is to try to look younger. All these tricks can be done on the move, but they are best performed while temporarily out of sight, such as in a crowded pub toilet. Changing his ethnic appearance is a good ploy to use at night or during foul weather. The spy will make use of the following tricks:

- Placing a stone in his sock to create a realistic limp.
- Making himself look taller by adding rigid foam pads to his shoes.
- Wearing a cap. When he removes it, he looks shorter.
- Placing half a folded newspaper on each shoulder to make his waist look thinner.
- Putting cotton wool in his mouth to swell out his cheeks.
- Putting on or removing glasses.
- Burning a cork and blackening his face where he normally shaves – to imitate stubble.
- Using soot, burnt paper, talcum powder or cigarette ash to change his hair colour.
- Carrying a dark brown shoeshine sponge, so that he can totally cover his face, neck and hands.
- Carrying items in his pockets, such as a carry bag, fold-up walking stick, cigarettes, baseball cap or a plastic raincoat.

A deliberate disguise is a more planned affair, but the same basic tactics apply. If the reason for disguise is for the spy to go somewhere and not look out of place, he will undertake a recce of the area to pick up ideas. The spy will never be inclined to dress to bring attention upon themselves. If the area is busy with tourists, or students for example, he will dress accordingly.

SURVEILLANCE VOICE PROCEDURE

Vehicle surveillance operators must learn some basic codes and a jargon that, while being slick and brief, is clear enough for all personnel to understand. There are several reasons for doing this; firstly it helps identify who is doing what and where a particular surveillance vehicle is in relation to the others. Secondly, it helps to minimize the amount of voice traffic over the radio.

One such code, popular with surveillance teams, is the phonetic alphabet. It can be used to identify targets, vehicles, operators and places. Numbers are added to enlarge and identify various units, for example, vehicle SP4 would be spoken as "Sierra Papa Four" and be part of a Special Patrol surveillance team.

WHO'S LISTENING?

While covert radio conversations are secure and cannot be listened to by any third party, the fact that a vehicle is transmitting something can be detected. In many cities, especially where the district is controlled by terrorist organizations, it would be practical to assume that they have a monitoring capability. This is usually found in the form of "watchers", young men or women who stand on the street corners with a handheld device that indicates that a vehicle is transmitting on a secure frequency. Of course, this helps the enemy identify possible surveillance vehicles.

THE PHONETIC ALPHABET

- A Alpha
- B Bravo
- C Charlie
- D Delta
- E Echo
- F Foxtrot
- G Golf
- H Hotel
- I India
- J Juliet
- K Kilo
- L Lima
- M Mike
- N November
- O Oscar
- P Papa
- Q Quebec
- R Romeo
- S Sierra
- T Tango
- U Uniform
- V Victor
- W Whisky
- X X-ray
- Y Yankee
- Z Zulu

Surveillance operators also use other terminologies to indicate a number of actions the target vehicle is likely to carry out. This terminology also helps the surveillance team keep the target vehicle within sight and thus avoid a lost contact. While they vary from country to country, here are a few examples of vehicle surveillance terminology with an explanation as to what each means.

TYPICAL TERMINOLOGY USED BY VEHICLE SURVEILLANCE TEAMS

"Back-up, can you?"	Eyeball request to back-up vehicle to ascertain whether a handover is appropriate. Response is either "Yes, yes", "No, no" or "Back-up can at next junction".
"Back-up"	The second vehicle in the convoy.
"Cancel"	Ignore the instruction or information just given.
"Come through."	Given after "hang back" to bring the convoy through.
"Committed."	The target vehicle is committed to travelling on the motorway.
"Contact, contact."	The eyeball has been regained by one of the vehicles in the convoy, following the search procedure. The pick-up vehicle will also give a location.
"Convoy check."	Request from eyeball to determine position of vehicles in convoy, to which all vehicles automatically respond in turn. Motorcyclists should respond without specifying their precise position, after Tail-End Charlie has reported. When all correct, eyeball calls "convoy complete".
"Down to you."	The final transmission made by eyeball before handing over surveillance to another vehicle.
"Eyeball regained."	The target vehicle is once more under surveillance.
Eyeball.	The vehicle or officer that has primary visual contact with the target and that is directing the operation for the time being.
"Footman out."	A vehicle in the convoy has put an officer out on foot.
"Going round."	The target vehicle is commencing a second or subsequent circuit of the roundabout.
"Hang back."	Transmission from eyeball, indicating that the convoy should hold back as the target is slowing down or has stopped.
"Held."	The target has made a temporary stop. This will normally be followed by an explanation for the stop, i.e. traffic lights, pedestrian crossing, traffic congestion etc.
"Left, left, left."	The target vehicle has turned left. In some cases, such as on a motorway, the junction number may be added, i.e. "left, left, left 57".
"Manoeuvering."	Warning issued by eyeball, indicating that target is, for example, manoeuvering on the forecourt of a garage, business premises, car park etc.
Nearside, offside.	Indicates that the nearside/offside traffic indicator is active on the target vehicle.
"No change."	The situation remains unaltered.
"No deviation."	The target vehicle is continuing straight ahead, as at a crossroads. It is said to reassure the team that there has been no change of direction.
"Not one, not two."	The target vehicle negotiating a roundabout has passed first, second exits etc.
"Off, off, off."	Transmission by the eyeball, indicating that the target is now on the move.
"Original, original."	The target has resumed after a stop, in the same direction of travel as before.
"Out, out, out."	Transmission by the eyeball, indicating that the target is alighting from a vehicle or that he is leaving a premises.
"Reciprocal, reciprocal."	The target vehicle has done a U-turn and is now returning along the same route.
"Right, right, right."	The target vehicle has turned right.
"Roundabout, roundabout."	The target is approaching a traffic roundabout where he has a multiple choice of exits.

"Roger, so far?"	An intermittent request by the transmitting officer asking recipients whether they have understood a lengthy period of dialogue.
Shadow car.	The vehicle being used to support the footman.
"Stand down."	Cancellation of whole operation.
"Standby, standby."	Instruction issued by eyeball, alerting convoy to possible movement of target.
"Stop, stop, stop."	Target vehicle has stopped in circumstances other than a "held" situation; the target vehicle is slowing down and may be about to stop or conditions require caution.
Tail-end Charlie.	The vehicle at the rear of the convoy.
"Taken first/second."	The target vehicle has taken the first, the second exit etc.
Target.	The person who is the target of the observation.
"Temporary loss of eyeball."	A temporary visual loss of the target vehicle has occurred.
Total loss.	The eyeball has not been regained after the temporary loss. A total loss will normally be followed by a pre-planned search procedure.
"We are bulked."	Only the target can be held.
"Who has?"	Used to confirm the surveillance vehicle with the current eyeball on the target.
"Who's backing?"	Request from eyeball vehicle to confirm there is a back-up vehicle ready to take over.

MEANINGS

Certain units do not include "Contact, contact" in voice procedure as this is reserved purely to indicate physical contact.

Assuming that there is a basic three-vehicle surveillance team, Sierra One, Two and Three, with Sierra One having eyeball and with the team using a simple spot-code system, a typical conversation might go as follows:

"All stations this is Sierra One – I have eyeball – towards green 25. Who's backing?"
"Sierra Three – backing." (Indicating that they are behind Sierra One.)
"Sierra Two – Roger that." (Sierra Two confirming situation awareness.)
"Sierra One – target still straight 50/60." (Indicating that the target is continuing at a straight speed of 50–60 mph.)
"Sierra Two – Roger that." (Confirmation.)
"Sierra Three – Roger that." (Confirmation.)
"Left, left, left – Sierra Two can you?" (The target vehicle has turned left and Sierra One is asking Sierra Two if they can take the eyeball position.)
"That's a roger." (Sierra Two confirms that they will take up the eyeball.)
"Sierra Three – backing." (Confirming that Sierra Three has moved into the backing position.)

That the voice procedure becomes clipped as the unit progresses into the follow. Familiarity and good co-operation between surveillance operators all help to minimize the airtime, but will still provide everyone with a verbal picture of what is happening.

TARGET RECCE

Once the target has been identified, an in-depth surveillance operation may well ensue. However, as with most things military, the planning phase must first take place where a number of procedures are set out. One of the first objectives is to gather detailed information on the target's known place of residence or place of employ, depending on the type of operation to be undertaken. This information comes from a wide range of sources and is normally the start of the suspect target's personal file. Assume that a known spy has been seen talking to an unknown. That unknown would have been followed back to a house. Simple enquires will reveal the person's name and address. This is the start point from which some of the following material will be gathered.

- Aerial photographs.
- A detailed planning layout of the building.
- Any police or criminal records.
- Any driving convictions.
- Place of employment.
- Target's vehicle make and registration.

▲ A quick target recce shows that this house is well protected with an alarm system, high walls and barbed wire fencing.

Today, aerial photographs can be downloaded over the Internet. These provide enough detail to be able to plan a covert operation against the target's dwelling. Planning applications showing detailed internal rooms are also freely available from the local town hall. Likewise, intelligence officers can easily obtain police records and convictions. However, one of the best ways into a person's life is to do a full "target recce", a military term for really close on-site reconnaissance.

Surveillance units carry out a target recce in order to collect as much information about the target's house as possible. Prior planning will include studying maps, aerial photographs, local information and all known facts. A route to and from the target must be assessed, as well as any time limitations in which to carry out the task, and the intelligence officers need to collect the correct equipment required for doing the job. This ensures that the officers do not run into the target or enter the premises while the target is at home.

Pictures will be taken of the building indicating front, back and side elevations. The building material will also be noted, as will any entry or exit points. The position of external services, telephone and electricity will also be filmed and recorded, as will be position of the rubbish bin. All this initial information will aid any technical team that is required to enter the building and fit any audio-visual monitoring devices. Finally, several preliminary sites will be noted in order to set up a static OP that can observe the target building around the clock.

GARBOLOGY

Garbology simply means taking the trash or garbage from a household or business and examining it. It can prove a very good source of information, providing many details about a target. The idea is to collect garbage discreetly and to examine it at leisure, recording all of the items. The main advantage of garbology is that it is non-obtrusive and it almost always goes unnoticed. **Note**: Spies and secret agents do it but it is illegal in some countries, and non-spies should never undertake garbology.

GARBOLOGY TECHNIQUES

Once a spy's target is housed, the spy will make a note of the garbage disposal system. These may vary from town to town and from country to country, but in almost all cases, the garbage is picked up by a waste-disposal company. The spy watches for and makes a note of the garbage truck's date and time of arrival at the target premises. He checks to see if the garbage container is for individual use or for many houses. In many countries, the individual must take their garbage to a shared container. If so, he must establish whether the target takes out his garbage at certain times.

He will watch and observe the best time to collect the target's garbage. The hours of darkness are best, but if a pick-up has to be made during daylight hours, he will dress accordingly, in the manner of a down-and-out, carrying a plastic bag, for example. A spy will always wear a pair of thick rubber gloves when doing this.

He will lay out the garbage contents on a large plastic sheet and discard all useless items such a food waste. He will always keep a written note as to the type of food being consumed, i.e. fast food, expensive food etc., and check each individual item and make notes on each. For example, he may:

- Count the number of cigarettes butts and identify the brand.
- Count the number of alcohol bottles or cans and identify the make.
- Set aside all correspondence, papers such as telephone bills and bank statements, for detailed examination later.
- Photograph any items that may be of interest, such as discarded clothing, magazines, computer disks or empty non-food packaging.
- Carry out an in-depth examination of all correspondence and paper products.
- Write down his observations and conclusions for each separate garbage pick-up. He will carry out at least four separate pick-ups within the period of a month in order to make a minimum assessment.
- Report any important discoveries that he thinks may be of immediate interest and use to the current operation.

RUBBISH TIP

A spy will learn the date for refuse collection at his target's home and will always remove garbage without his target's knowledge.

▲ The contents of this refuse sack indicate that someone in the home is a heavy smoker, likes beer and has a cat. The documents show details of credit cards, together with a copy signature, bank account, travel arrangements etc.

The outcome from a good garbology probe over several weeks can be very revealing. The information gathered will be properly documented with a list of attributes added to the target's file. Here are some of the things the spy might expect to find out about the target:

- His correct name and address.
- His personal finances, including the name of his bank and his account number.
- His credit card usage.
- His signature. (Taken from discarded credit card receipts.)
- The telephone numbers he may dial, especially frequently-used numbers.
- His email address.
- His work or employment address.
- The amount of cigarettes he smokes.
- The amount of alcohol he consumes.
- Toiletries that he uses.
- A rough idea of his weekly expenditure.

The list of clear and precise information that can be obtained through garbology is endless, but it needs to be done in a methodical way and there are some important things to consider. One factor a spy must take into account is the number of people being catered for at the target's premises. If the target lives alone this is not a problem. One way for a spy to determine household numbers is to carry out a clothes line assessment.

CLOTHES LINE ASSESSMENT

▲ The clothes line may indicate who is living in the house.

When he is in a position to observe a target's house, the spy will look at the clothes line. Almost all households, including flats, hang out some washing during the week, sometimes on the same day every week. Observing the clothes line over a period of a month can provide the following information: the number of people living at the address, their approximate age and their sex.

PROTECT AGAINST SURVEILLANCE

Anything that can prove the agent's identity will be burned in a metal bucket or container, including all unsolicited mail and bank statements. He will only put discarded food in the bin and take bottles to the bottle bank or other recycling centre. If he thinks he is being watched, he will discreetly place his garbage bag in someone else's bin. He will never throw away any bank statements which have address correction slips attached, as a person can request for a new card to be sent to a different address, and they may already have the spy's signature from discarded credit card receipts or other materials they may have gathered.

STATIC SURVEILLANCE OUTLINE

A static surveillance position is normally known as an "observation position" (OP), which can either be in an urban or a rural area. They are set up to observe a fixed location or object for a predetermined amount of time. Their objective is to obtain information through the use of human visual and technical recording devices.

Setting up an urban surveillance is quite difficult and depends largely on the selection of a safe location in which to install the OP. Where possible, the urban OP should have the best vantage point from which to observe the target building. This will include both the entry and exit points of the building, something that is crucial to establish both the movements of the target and any visitors that he may have.

RURAL OP

An OP is a covert site from where surveillance activities can be carried out and intelligence gathered. Field agents are experts in setting up OPs and remaining in them for long stretches at a time. In rural areas, this is often done in the most hostile of conditions. The secret of a good rural OP is to make sure that it blends in with the natural surroundings.

Wherever an OP is located, the rules for its construction remain the same. A site must not be vulnerable to discovery and must afford a good view of the target position. A concealed entrance and exit are also needed. High ground, although good for visibility, is an obvious spot and one that any suspicious target will search.

Once the site has been chosen, the OP should be constructed under cover of night. If this is not possible, then some natural daytime cover should be invented, road works or farm labouring, for example. The structure can be made out of any material – waterproof sheeting, ponchos, camouflage nets and natural or locally available materials are all useful, as long as the end product blends in with everything around it and cannot be easily seen. OPs tend to be built in a rectangular shape, where the observers lie in pairs.

▲ Military surveillance operations can last months.

In addition to food, water, clothing and sleeping bags, operational gear is also stored inside the OP: weapons, radio equipment, binoculars, night sights, cameras and telescopes. This can make conditions cramped and uncomfortable, a situation often made worse by adverse weather conditions. No sign of the men's presence can be left, since it might mean that the OP is discovered by a suspicious target. Therefore, even normally private functions, such as urinating and defecating must be done in the OP. Smoking, cooking and the wearing of deodorant or aftershave are not appropriate in an OP. Once the hide has been established, a self-disciplined routine is essential; sloppiness may lead to the target discovering the spy's presence.

MEXE SHELTER – THE ULTIMATE OP

Although now obsolete, the MEXE shelter was used by two Territorial Army units – 21 SAS and 23 SAS – and, for its day, was the ultimate rural OP. They were deployed in the forward observation or "hide role" in Germany during the days of the Cold War. The shelter was designed to accommodate a patrol of four fully equipped men, for a period of several weeks. The MEXE shelter was installed deep underground, in a hole that the four soldiers had to prepare. Once the MEXE shelter had been erected in the hole, the soil and turf were placed over the top to provide both protection and camouflage.

The main components comprised of a steel frame, which had a load-bearing limit able to support a vehicle crossing the ground above. Once the frame was assembled it was covered with a skin manufactured from special composite fabric that was both waterproof and NBC (Nuclear, Biological and Chemical) agent-proof. The latter property also prevented scent permeating through to the surface of the ground, thus preventing tracker dogs from detecting the presence of the occupants. A prefabricated hatch allowed the soldier to enter and exit the shelter.

In the event that the former Soviet Union ever invaded West Germany, the intention was for the SAS unit to remain underground until the Russian troops had passed them by. The MEXE shelter was equipped with both a periscope and covert radio communications, allowing reports to be sent of troop movements and strengths. At a given signal, the SAS would emerge from their hides and attack the Russians in the rear. Amazingly enough, many of these shelters were forgotten and they remain buried all over Germany to this day.

URBAN OP

The Urban OP is situated in a populated area, which means it is in some type of building. The ideal location is normally a room overlooking the target house; observation equipment is installed in such a way as to monitor the target, while remaining undetected from the outside. The room, or adjoining rooms, are prepared to accommodate the surveillance operators on duty. Likewise, the entrance to the OP from the street is from the rear if possible. Most major cites are crammed with civilians, some of whom are curious, while others wish to be friendly. As a result, a logical explanation is usually prepared to explain the occupation of the OP when it is surrounded by other residents. Here are a few points which are looked for when a spy sets up an urban OP:

◂ Urban operations require significantly different locations.

- Location must have good visual access over the target location.
- Good radio communications to the control desk and the foot and mobile units are vital.
- Correct surveillance equipment, cameras, telescopes etc, need to be installed.
- Entry to and from the OP should be covert in nature.
- The OP needs to be large enough to accommodate at least two operators.
- The OP needs to have cooking and toilet facilities.
- Unobtrusive changeover routines need to be set up.

In essence, a good urban OP is a room from which the spy can observe the target and record his movements without being detected. In some cases, although it is rare, the intelligence agency may put an OP in an occupied house. If the position is the best one available, then a thorough check will be made on the occupants before they are approached. Even then, these occupants are given a cover story, i.e. the operators are from the "drugs squad" and have a suspect under surveillance.

FOOT SURVEILLANCE TECHNIQUES

In general, targets are not followed once, but many times. In doing so, the surveillance operators build up a pattern of the target's general behaviour. If this is the case, surveillance will be termed as "loose" and the operators will remain at a safe distance to avoid being compromised. Surveillance on the target can be done in short stages until a number of known "triggers" can be identified i.e. at 5:05 pm from Monday to Friday they leave their place of employment. Loose surveillance is normally carried out against a target who is living in a fixed location for a given period of time.

If the target has recently arrived in the country, or has suddenly come to the attention of the intelligence services, then the initial surveillance will be "close". This means having the target visual at all times during the surveillance. This form of surveillance requires the very best operators and their aim is to establish some basic information about the target, such as housing, his employment and his associates. Once these basics are known, loose surveillance techniques can then be employed.

Both foot and mobile surveillance operations have three distinct phases: the trigger, or pick-up, the follow and the housing. Any operation will be based on the fact that you need a starting place, normally a location where you know the target to be, or where he will be going. The surveillance will involve following the identified target and, finally, placing them in a known abode, the target house, for example.

CASE HISTORY

A known suspect who ran a barber's shop was using his premises to transmit information between terrorist cells. The barber's shop was on the second floor and so an elevated position was required to obtain good visual through the windows. After an initial recce, it was decided to place the OP in a small space behind the clock tower in the town hall across the street. The space was six feet long by four feet wide with a flat wooden surface. At either side of the clock were wooden ventilation slats, wide enough for the lens of a camera and a powerful telescope to fit between. Both of these looked down through the barber's window, providing a good view into the occupancy of the barber's chair.

The operation was mounted by an insertion team who scaled the outside wall and gained access to the roof. From here they entered the OP via a small inspection hatch in the outer roof. Equipment and food were hauled up from the ground using a rope with a karabiner attached.

The cameras and telescope were set up during the first night and communications were confirmed with the desk operator. One of the two operators would observe the target and take photographs while the other slept. The sleeping arrangement was a single sleeping bag on the hard floor. All food was cold (chicken and sandwiches) and the toilet arrangements were a plastic bag with no privacy. Photographic film and a written report were lowered to a back-up team who arrived at the base of the building every other night during the hours of darkness. The two surveillance operators remained in the OP for 12 days, producing evidence of association that eventually led to the demise of a four-man terrorist cell. Additionally, some days into the surveillance, a young 16-year-old schoolgirl was seen to be waiting around the doorway that led up to the barber's shop. Her activities were monitored and, while there was no association with any terrorist activities, she was arrested for soliciting.

TRIGGER OR PICK-UP

If the target has not been located there can be no follow. It is vital, therefore, to have a good trigger. The type of trigger used can be static (best), mobile or technical. If the target's house or place of employment is under constant observation by a static OP then this can be used to provide the trigger. The time that the operation commences will be deduced from the static OP's events log. Surveillance units will be in position in good time and wait for the "standby" trigger from the static OP when they detect signs of target movement.

▲ **Here, the target can be seen getting in his car – the perfect opportunity to "trigger" the start of mobile surveillance.**

Where the target is in a difficult location, such as a large car park, the trigger may well come from vehicle surveillance operators covering either the target vehicle or the exits. Such instances can easily lead to a lost contact. This can be avoided by knowing the target's route and by positioning a second trigger vehicle at a critical location.

Both static and mobile triggers can be enhanced by the use of technical surveillance devices (*see* Tracking). These can be covertly fitted to the target vehicle either on a temporary or on a permanent basis. Most modern devices are generally at rest if a vehicle has been stationary for more than 15 minutes and are then activated by the door opening and the key being turned in the ignition. The technical tracking device sends a very accurate position signal on demand from the desk operator; this can either be constant or at predetermined time intervals. The signal is displayed on a computer screen that has a street map overlay. The target's vehicle position can also be monitored with the use of small mobile phones used by the foot or vehicle surveillance operators. Other technical triggers, such as hidden microphones and cameras close to the target's premises, can also be used, but these are not as reliable as tracking systems, as these continue to be of use during the follow.

Once the trigger has been activated, in the case of a foot follow, the trigger will simply state the target is "foxtrot", or "mobile" with vehicle surveillance. The surveillance will commence until the team leader has decided that the target is "housed", at which time the operation is called off.

SINGLE PERSON SURVEILLANCE

It is difficult for one person to conduct good foot surveillance, as by its very nature it means keeping the target visual at all times, but, as the saying goes, "If you can see him he can see you." No matter how good the individual, if he is following someone who has been trained in counter-surveillance techniques, the chances are he will be compromised. However, there are opportune times, such as when a suspect target is inadvertently recognized by an off-duty surveillance operator. As odd at it might sound, in many large cities, off-duty surveillance operators have entered a restaurant, stepped on to a bus or have been driving along in traffic, when they have recognized a known target. At this juncture, the target is usually unaware of the chance sighting and is happily going about his business – for the surveillance operator it is an ideal opportunity. While the follow may only be brief, there is a chance that it could provide some interesting information.

◂ **Single person surveillance in thinly populated areas is extremely difficult to maintain for any length of time.**

The key to successful single-person surveillance is not to remain too close. The spy will choose a good vantage position, such as a corner on a street junction, which allows him to observe four streets at the same time. For a surveillance operator acting alone, or when close surveillance is employed, there are a few basic rules.

- If opportune target is acquired – he will call for back-up.
- When in a congested area, he will close up on the target.
- In less congested areas, he will hang back and stay loose.
- He may take out a shopping bag and look into the shop windows.
- He will assess the target's walk speed, impetus and activity i.e. are they shopping, going for a social drink, etc?
- He will observe target's alertness and note any counter-surveillance activity.

DETECTING COUNTER-SURVEILLANCE

It is important for the surveillance operators to recognize signs of counter-surveillance. This helps identify whether the target is actively engaged in unlawful activities or whether he is simply displaying normal social behaviour. A known target who is about to meet his handler or agent will almost certainly carry out some counter-surveillance techniques. When doing so, the target will watch to see who reacts unnaturally or who is taken by surprise. He will observe any person who suddenly changes direction or seems to be giving a signal to another person. These are just a few of the signs the operator should look for:

- Stopping, turning and looking at anyone to their rear.
- Making a sudden change of direction or reversing their course.
- Walking slowly and then speeding up suddenly.
- Turning a corner and stopping to see who comes round it.
- Going into a building, such as a pub, and immediately exiting via another door.
- Checking constantly in the reflection of a shop window.
- Waiting to the last minute to step on to a bus or an underground train.
- Getting off at the next stop, waiting and catching the next bus or train.
- Deliberately dropping something to see if anyone picks it up.
- Changing their appearance or clothing.

FOOT SURVEILLANCE TEAM

Note: following someone is not legal and non-spies should not do it.

The basic surveillance foot team consists of a three-person unit. The unit's main objective is to keep at least two sets of eyeballs on the target at all times. An initial procedure for keeping a target under observation is as follows:

- On target trigger, the first operator remains behind the target.
- The second operator hangs back to keep the first operator in view.
- The third operator will walk on the opposite side of the street, almost parallel with the target.

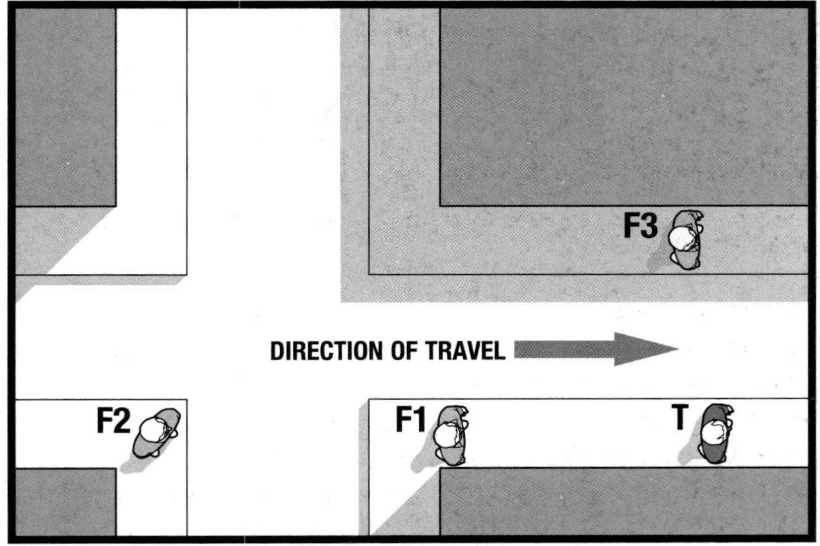

▲ **The three-man surveillance team basic follow.**

- On a linear follow, one and two may change places as and when necessary. If the target changes to the other side of the street, number three takes up the immediate follow, with number two moving across the street as back-up. Number one will remain parallel to the target.

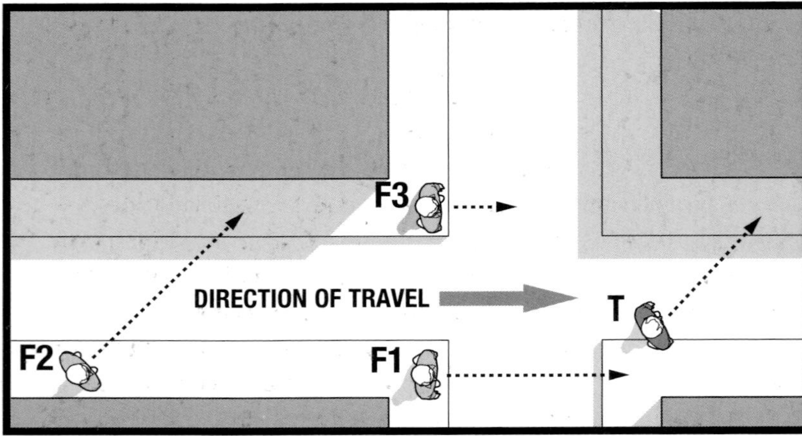

▲ The simple changeover of positions when the target crosses the road.

- On target turning left or right, number one operator will go straight across the road and take up parallel position. Number two can choose to take up the lead while number three crosses the road to become back-up.

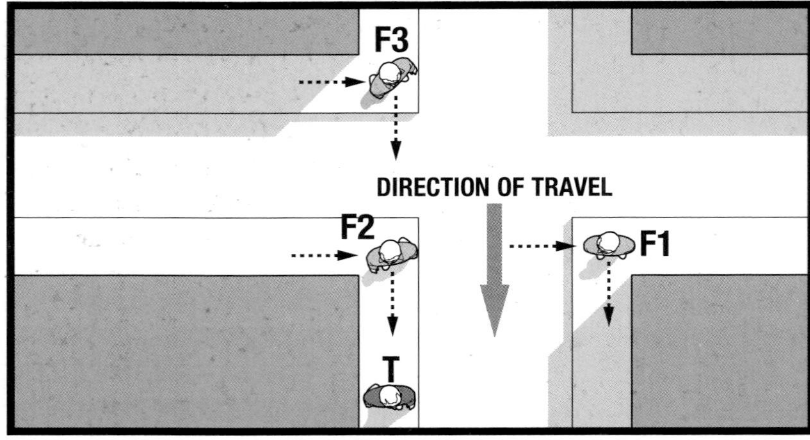

▲ The simple changeover of positions when the target changes direction.

- If the target is deemed to be of particular importance, then several foot surveillance teams will be deployed at the same time. It is possible during the follow for a target to adopt a mode of transport. For this reason, most surveillance is a combination of both foot and mobile.

◀ If the target stops to make a call it may be a good opportunity to gather information.

- If the target enters a telephone booth, number one will walk past and take up a location in front of the target. Number two will enter the adjacent booth, if there is one, enter money and make a real call, back to the office, for example. He will discreetly try to observe any actions the target makes and listen to his conversation if possible. He will never enter a phone box while carrying a mobile phone, as this is a dead giveaway.
- If the target drops an item, it should be collected. However, this could also be a ploy on behalf of the target to see if he is being followed.
- The team will always make a note of any person the target gives anything to. While the purchase of a newspaper may seem innocent it is also a way of passing a message.

The introduction of tracking systems (*see* Tracking) now offers the surveillance team a much greater degree of control – over the target, surveillance operators and vehicles. The whole follow can be tracked and recorded by the desk officer, who can monitor the whole operation at a glance. This allows surveillance operators to be more relaxed and decreases the chances of being spotted by the target. However, tracking devices cannot deliver important facts, such as the target's actions.

RECORDING INFORMATION

It is not enough simply to follow the target around to see where he goes. A detailed report must be kept. One of the primary reasons for people becoming spies or agents is monetary reward. Foot surveillance provides the opportunity to see how much money a person is spending each month. How much does he spend in the supermarket, the pub or on new items, such as televisions and other electrical goods? The monthly total can be easily checked against the target's normal earnings. Several targets have been caught out in this way. Here are some pointers to watch out for:

- Does the target lead a lavish lifestyle compared to his known income?
- What type of credit card is the target using? Does he use the same cashpoint on a regular basis?
- Does the target have any sexual preferences? Does he visit gay bars or prostitutes, etc?
- How much alcohol does the target consume?
- Does the target compromise himself, e.g. has he been seen with a rent boy?
- Is the target a user of drugs?
- Where does the target visit frequently?
- Are there any unusual deviations in an otherwise normal route to and from a location?
- Does the target employ counter-surveillance tactics?

The answers to these questions and many more provide the surveillance team and other with vital information. If the target is a gay, drug-taking type who likes to throw his money around, the intelligence agency may well find him a lover. Visits to the same location, on a regular basis, may indicate a DLB. If the information is extremely good it may be used to confront the agent and turn them into a double agent.

MOBILE SURVEILLANCE OUTLINE

Mobile surveillance involves the use of vehicles, boats or aircraft to follow a target who is also mobile in some mode of transport. This type of surveillance requires skilful driving, good observation, set procedures and excellent communications. It also takes a lot of discipline on the part of the driver, as surveillance more than often turns into a chase rather than a discreet follow.

The same basic principles that apply to foot surveillance also apply to vehicle surveillance. However, the practice of vehicle surveillance is more difficult because of the complications created by traffic congestion, restrictions imposed by traffic laws and the increased possibility of the operation being discovered. Just as is the case with foot surveillance, an individual operating in a single vehicle will be limited in his capability, whereas a team of vehicles acting together will enhance the prospects of a successful operation.

The surveillance vehicle should accommodate either two or three people, thus making a foot follow possible in the event of a target going foxtrot. Having at least two people in the vehicle will also allow the driver to concentrate on his driving while the passenger remains alert to the surroundings. A driver can use numerous techniques to reduce the risk of detection, such as switching off one of the headlights during a night-time follow. This will confuse the target if he is watching in his rear-view mirror. To make the target's car more easily recognizable, a distinctive feature may be attributed to it, such as smashing the tail-light. To make this look natural, it is always done when the vehicle is parked in a busy street or in a car park. It may also tip the target off to the surveillance operation.

When the target vehicle is temporarily parked, one of the surveillance operators will go on foot while the other remains with the vehicle. If the target vehicle is parked for any length of time, the surveillance vehicles will intermittently move their position. Those remaining in the car will also sit in the passenger seat to make it appear as though they are waiting for someone.

A good area knowledge will enable the spy not to have to constantly study the map, which means taking his eyes off the target. However, the introduction of onboard GPS tracking devices has alleviated this problem to some degree. Before any surveillance operation can begin, though, certain questions must be asked.

- Is mobile surveillance the best way of achieving the goal?
- Is the operational area well known?
- Is the operational area urban or rural, i.e. will foot surveillance be required?
- Is the target's awareness level known?
- Is the target's vehicle known?
- What is the pick-up point or trigger?

The answer to these questions is normally self-evident. If the target is likely to travel large distances, it may be better to employ a helicopter than to deploy six mobile surveillance vehicles. Likewise, the target may use a form of transport that can out-run or out-manoeuvre the surveillance vehicles, a motorbike, for example.

Knowing the trigger for the target vehicle is also vital. In the normal course of events, all team vehicles will familiarise themselves with the streets around the trigger. A briefing is given before the operation begins, at which point all surveillance vehicles will be given their call signs, assigned start points and time in position (known as the "plot up"). Once on the ground, one vehicle may decide to do a drive past or may decide to put an operator on foot in order to confirm the target's location, i.e. are the house lights on? Is the target's vehicle parked outside? The pattern of the vehicles will be set in such a way that they will trigger a follow, irrespective of which direction the target vehicle drives. As is the case with foot surveillance, the actual trigger will come from either a static OP, a foot operator or one of the surveillance vehicles. Communications are tested and all vehicles confirm "in position".

SURVEILLANCE VEHICLES

Surveillance vehicles come in all shapes and sizes. Each is designed to cover a different aspect of surveillance; they include static vehicles, mobile and airborne. The static vehicles are normally vans, but they can be cars or even lorries. Their main function is to monitor a target by parking up close to the target's dwelling or place of employment. Some are manned while others are left unmanned, but all are capable of listening, videoing or triggering the start of a surveillance follow.

MOBILE SURVEILLANCE VEHICLE

A vehicle selected for surveillance work must be mechanically sound, fitted for use in all weather conditions and suitable for the area in which the surveillance is to take place. The vehicle will be a soft, nondescript colour such as grey, and will not have any distinguishing marks, such as front-mirror-hanging dice or rear-window adverts. The surveillance vehicle pool will be large enough to allow the vehicles to be rotated on a regular basis.

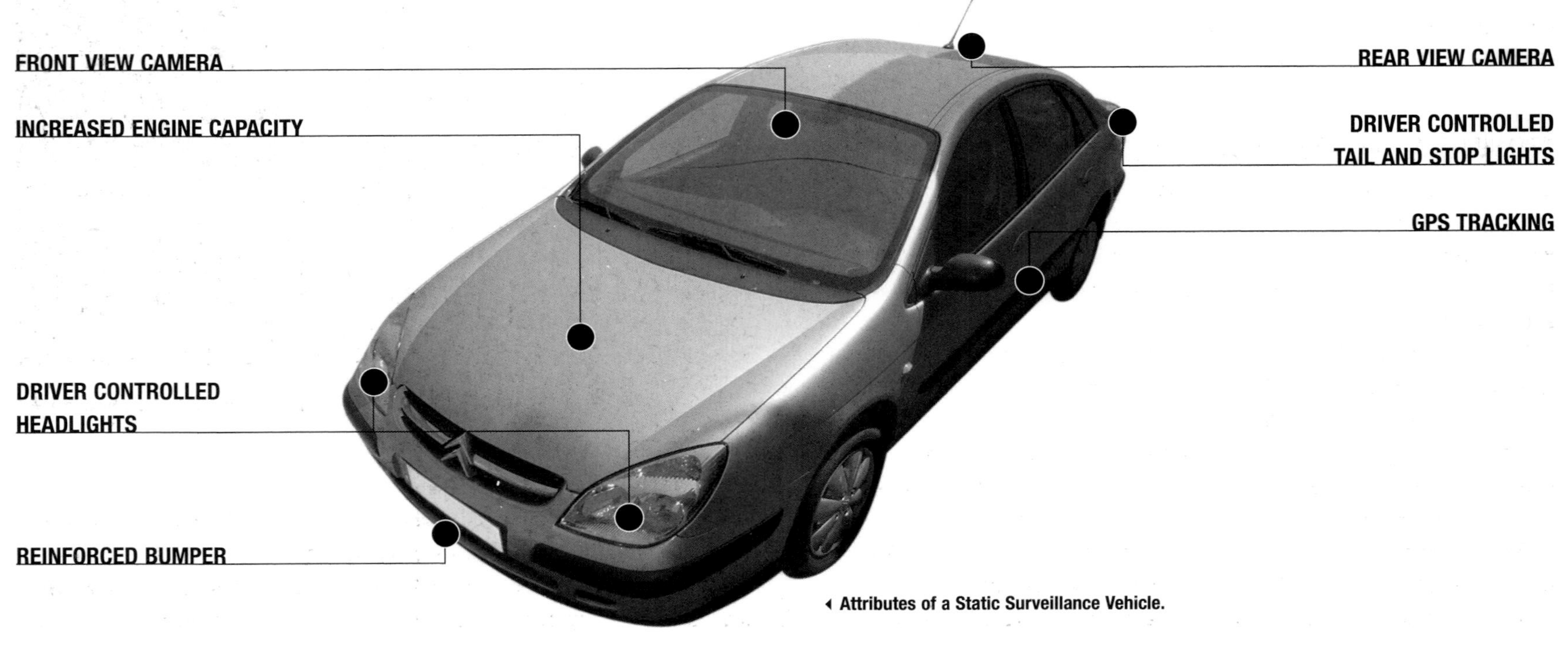

Attributes of a Static Surveillance Vehicle.

Most surveillance vehicles incorporate many features as standard, such as the use of cut-off switches to activate or deactivate the headlights or brake lights. These are of particular importance when the vehicle is being used for a night-time drop-off or pick-up. In such instances, the driver will deactivate the brake light so as to give no indication that he is slowing down.

Covert radio systems are fitted as standard and are normally invisible to the untrained eye. The radio unit will be hidden within the car while the aerial will be formed into an induction loop and hidden under the roof lining. A presser switch will also be hidden under the carpet, normally near to the driver's or the passenger's hand or foot. Both driver and passengers will have a small hearing aid that picks up the incoming signal from the induction loop. A hidden microphone will transmit when they press the hidden hand or foot switch. Cameras, both fixed and video, can be added to the surveillance car, as can GPS navigation and other tracking devices.

The apparent make and type of the vehicle can be deceptive. The rear boot may indicate a model with a 1300 cc engine, while in reality the car will have been modified to take a much larger capacity engine. Other modifications could include a powerful battery and improved radiator system to avoid overheating in long traffic delays. Internal temperature control is a necessity, as the surveillance occupants may be sitting in their car for long periods of time in unfavourable weather conditions.

MOBILE SURVEILLANCE TECHNIQUES

Once intelligence officers have plotted up and it has been established that everyone is in position, it is simply a matter of waiting for the trigger that will action the surveillance. The pick-up phase will depend on the location and the number of possible routes the target can take, an example is shown right.

Once the target indicates that he is about to move, the trigger gives the "standby". All vehicles will follow the procedure to acknowledge this by calling off their call sign in alphabetical order, e.g. Sierra One – Roger; Sierra Two – Roger, and so on. The drivers will then turn on their ignitions, while everyone listens to the trigger commentary. This will be a step-by-step talk through.

"Target leaving house, locking door, heading for target vehicle, vehicle door open, ignition – target is mobile – Sierra Three, can you?"

This indicates that the target has left his house, has got into his car and has driven off. The trigger will have established that the best-placed surveillance vehicle to eyeball the target is Sierra Three and, by simply posing a question, indicates to everyone which car is immediately behind the target. This is a difficult part of surveillance and it is vital that everyone knows what is happening and who is where. At this stage, it is vital that all surveillance vehicles fall into place, adopting their correct positions. However, it is also important that no one overreacts until the trigger has confirmed that the target is mobile – he may well leave the house and walk down the street. In such incidents, the trigger would simply end his message with the words "target is foxtrot". At this stage, if deemed necessary, foot surveillance would be employed.

Even the best plot-up positions can go wrong. Other road users can pull out in front at a critical moment, for example, but the surveillance operator must remain calm and report the fact that the target is "unsighted". A good plot-up plan will cover all possible "choke points", leaving little to chance. However, in the event that the target is unsighted by everyone, the eyeball is up for grabs.

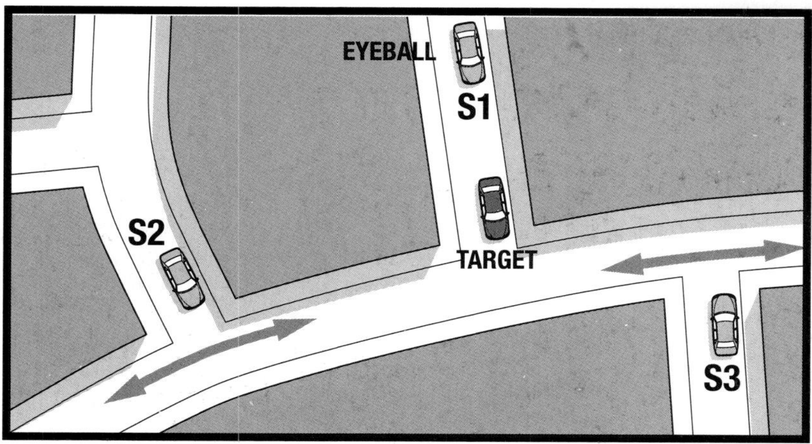

▲ **The idea behind a perfect "plot-up" is to make sure you can eyeball the target leaving and cover it in any eventuality.**

SURVEILLANCE FLEET

Assuming that one vehicle has taken up the eyeball, the others should fall into place, one immediately behind and one hanging back. While the eyeball can be immediately behind the target, it is often better to have at least a one-car separation; the same applies to the back-up vehicle and tail end Charlie. If more than one set of surveillance vehicles are being deployed, they are usually kept running parallel to or in front of the target. The control desk will have a master map plotting who is where and advising on their best positions. Unlike the immediate surveillance team, these vehicles are not restricted to the target's speed and can manoeuvre into position much more quickly to prepare themselves for a handover, should it prove necessary.

Unfortunately, mobile surveillance is hampered by a whole range of problems: road works, traffic lights, pedestrian crossings, accidents and roundabouts, to mention just a few. These are all possible places where the target can become unsighted. To some degree, these problems can be overcome if the eyeball or the desk operator gives sufficient notice. "Approaching roundabout" or "stopped at T-junction" are two examples.

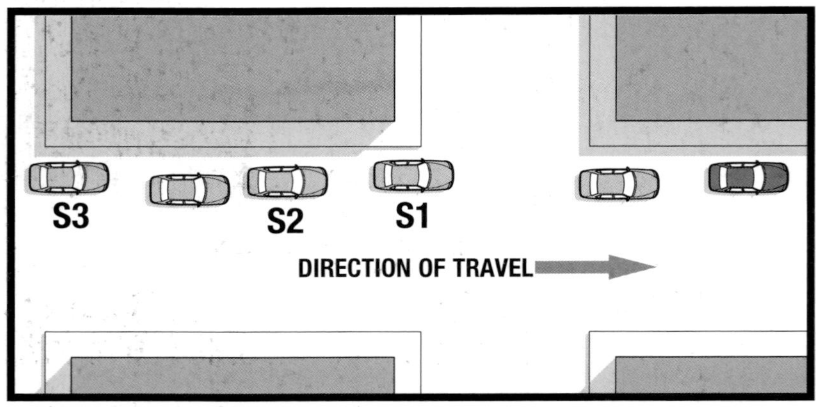

▲ A normal mobile surveillance follow.

TRAFFIC LIGHTS

If the follow is linear and spread out over several hundred yards, there is a possibility that the back-up vehicles will be stopped by traffic lights, while the target and eyeball pass through. Providing there are several lanes, all vehicles behind the target should change lanes and accelerate slightly towards the lights. While this may put them temporarily closer to the target, it also provides them with a better chance of staying in the follow. A similar system can be used to bracket the target vehicle wherever the road has multi-lanes. Surveillance procedures when approaching traffic lights or roundabouts need to be smooth and discreet. Manoeuvering close to the target should not compromise the operation.

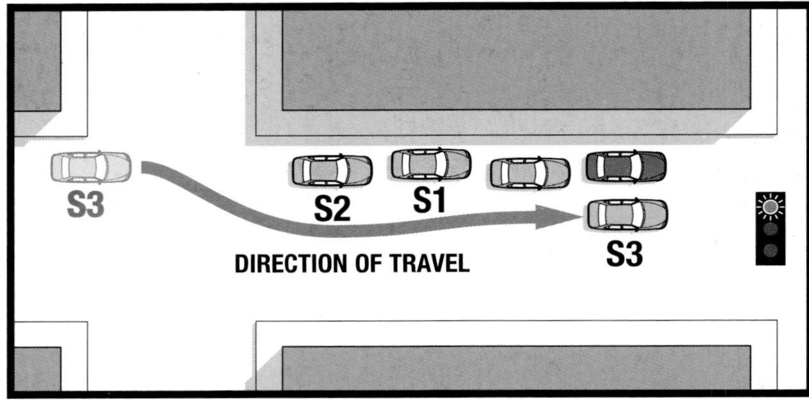

▲ Surveillance vehicles need to move up at traffic lights, so as not to be left behind.

ROUNDABOUTS

The surveillance fleet is also required to close up whenever the target vehicle is approaching a roundabout. This enables the follow to continue smoothly, regardless of the exit the target takes. The main problem comes when there is a build-up of traffic at major or busy roundabouts; this means that the target vehicle can pull ahead, while all the surveillance teams are held. In such a situation, the target may take any exit and thus become unsighted or lost altogether.

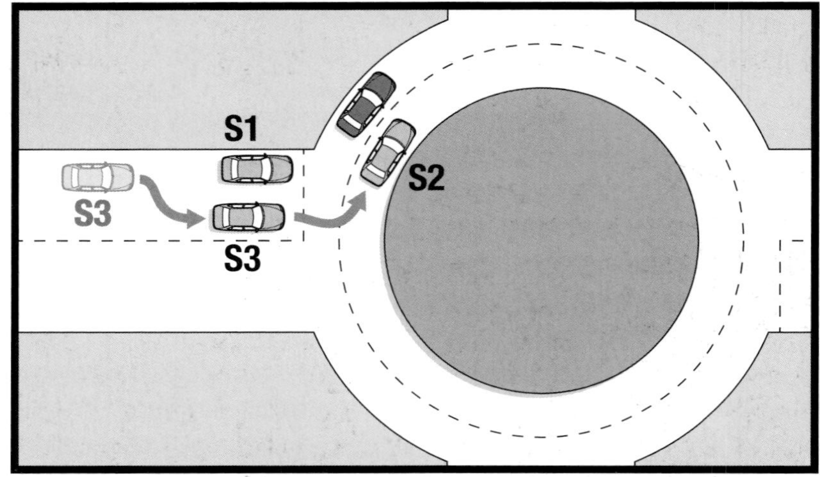

▲ Roundabouts are always a danger. In this example, S2 has moved up to parallel the target in order to shadow it around the island. In such an instance S2 will circle the island completely and fall in as tail-end Charlie.

If the entry onto the roundabout is multi-lane, the back-up vehicles should close up, even if this means going parallel to the target. The idea is to enter the roundabout just after or at the same time as the target vehicle. This may require either back-up or tail-end Charlie doing a circuit of the roundabout, but they should be able to trigger which exit the target took. Commentary for approaching a roundabout should go something like this (Sierra One has the eyeball).

"Approaching blue 5." (Spot code indicating a roundabout.)
"Held at blue 5."
"Sierra Two – moving up."
"Sierra Three – moving up."
"On blue 5."
"Taken 1, 2 or 3." (Normally repeated and indicating the exit off the roundabout.)

SPEED

Speed and distance are very important during any surveillance follow. Driving at speed down small country lanes only causes attention. There are times, such as when the cars running parallel need to get into a forward position, where speeding is required, but this should only ever be done out of the target's vision. The best way to control speed is by the eyeball vehicle calling off the target's speed "still straight – 35/40". This should be enough to regulate all vehicles that are blind to the target. A spy will never turn a follow into a high-speed chase.

MOTORWAYS

◂ Motorways feature one-directional traffic, which means the surveillance team can spread out more.

If the target takes the motorway, it usually suggests that the follow will cover a greater distance. One of the advantages of doing surveillance on a motorway is the fact that the traffic is all going one way. This allows the surveillance team to spread out and to hang back a lot more. It also means that the eyeball can stay in position for a longer period of time.

Motorways also provide the opportunity for pre-planning; that is to say, the target vehicle is restricted to certain movements. He can only get off the motorway at exits and stop, unless he breaks down, at service stations. This allows the surveillance team to pre-position vehicles ahead of the target. In both cases, advance warnings are clearly given by the motorway signs.

HAND-OVER

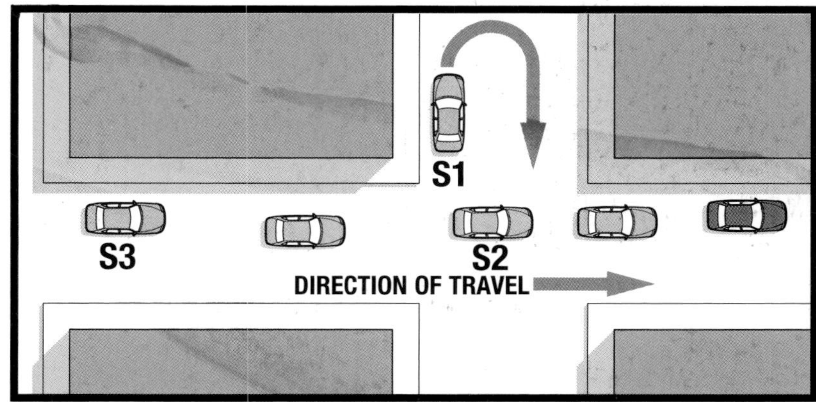

▴ A simple handover with S1 turning left and then doing a U-turn before re-joining the team.

Hand-over of the eyeball can happen for numerous reasons. For example, if Sierra One is held coming onto the roundabout, they may well ask, "who can?" At this stage, the best-placed vehicle will take up the eyeball and indicate the fact: "Sierra Two – I have the eyeball." A hand-over can be effected any time there is a need to change the vehicle immediately behind the target. This cuts down the risk of compromise. Likewise surveillance teams may hand over the target to one another in order to place a new set of vehicles in the target's rear-view mirror. This is particularly important when doing surveillance in the countryside.

Hand-over should always take place whenever the eyeball has been in position for a long period of time. During the normal course of events, he will check to see if the back-up vehicle is ready to take over; "Back-up can you?" If the response is affirmative, the eyeball will indicate when. At the same time, back-up will move up closer, but will make sure that he is discreet about his movement. There are many good and logical places where the eyeball can be handed over: junctions, lay-bys and garage forecourts being prime examples. Once a hand-over has been executed, all vehicles will acknowledge their new positions, i.e. back-up becomes eyeball, tail-end Charlie becomes back-up and the original eyeball becomes tail-end Charlie.

TARGET STOPPING

▲ The target stops for food. This normally require a fresh plot-up ready for when the target leaves.

At some stage during the follow, the target vehicle will stop. This could be for any number of reasons: to fill up with petrol, to take a break, or simply because he has reached his destination. Whatever the reason, it is up to the eyeball to make the call, "Stop, stop, near side." The warning should be given in time to stop all cars in the rear, while the eyeball continues on past the target vehicle.

This may be a temporary halt, which will be indicated by the nature of the stop, i.e. if the target drives into a garage forecourt, or drives into a supermarket car park, it is most likely temporary. In the case of the latter, it will be up to the team leader to indicate if some of the operators should follow on foot. Details such as this will have been discussed during the initial briefing for the operation. While stopping at a garage most vehicles can be held until the target is known to be on the move once more.

However, if the target moves into a larger area, such as a supermarket, which will require foot surveillance, new plot-up positions will be assigned, together with a new trigger. This allows for a clean start whenever the target decides to move on once more.

NIGHT DRIVING

◂ Night surveillance is really difficult, especially when the traffic is heavy. In this scenario a tracking device is often used to "ping" the target.

Night surveillance is difficult, especially in poor weather conditions. This means that the eyeball is required to get closer to the target vehicle and that frequent hand-overs have to take place. If he is checking his map or GPS, he will make sure that he does it with a small flexi-light and not with the car interior lights. Often the interior light is removed altogether, especially if the operation is likely to require a lot of footwork and getting in and out of the car. The target will be able to spot these intermittent illuminations in his rear-view mirror. The spy will also make sure that all the surveillance vehicles have working head, side and tail-lights, as a broken one is nothing more than a marker to the target.

If the back-up vehicle or tail-end Charlie fall too far back, they may request the eyeball to "touch red". This is a request for eyeball to hit his brake lights for a few seconds, so that the others can re-establish position.

MOTORBIKE

Motorbikes are particularly well suited to mobile surveillance in heavy traffic. Their size, speed and manoeuvrability are far greater than a car. However, a motorbike is distinctive amid traffic and the rider needs to be highly trained. A motorbike is particularly good at searching ahead if the eyeball has been held up and has lost contact with the target. The bike can remain in contact with the target until the surveillance team can re-establish the eyeball. In many cases, the motorbike rider will act independently from the rest of the surveillance team, listening in to the follow conversation, while using his own initiative with regards to positioning. Motorbikes can perform several other functions during any mobile surveillance, such as picking up foot operators who have been left behind during a temporary stop.

Using a motorbike in heavy traffic enables the rest of the team to keep up.

CAT'S EYES

The reflection of cat's eyes in the grass is perfectly normal to see. It makes a great "pick-up" signal.

CASE STUDY: CAT'S EYES

A template for making cat's eyes. The overall length of the cat's eyes is usually about 30 cm long and 10 cm across the cat's face.

This is made from a small sheet of plywood, a small tin of matt black paint and two cat's eyes. The latter are usually made from glass beads, backed with silver foil. The outline of a cat's head on top of a spike is drawn on an A4 sheet of paper. If a spy needs a pickup down a dark country lane this is a great device for leaving a pickup or dropoff notice to another agent.

Note: Do not attempt to dig out cat's eyes from the centre of the road – it is dangerous and illegal.

A target recce may be carried out as part of a surveillance operation. Once the operator has finished, he will require a pick-up. In the city, this can be arranged by simply stating a street or a location such as a pub. In the countryside, however, such places are hard to specify. If a surveillance operator wishes to be picked up at an unspecified location, he will simply use a set of "cat's eyes", so-called because of the cat's eyes we see on the roads at night.

The operator requesting a pick-up will merely inform the desk operator that he requires a pick-up between spot code yellow 3 and red 14. He may do this at a prearranged time, but more likely, he will call for the pick-up only when he is ready. The stretch of road between yellow 3 and red 14 may be several miles long, and this is where the cat's eyes come in. The agent simply plants his cat's eyes in the grass at the side of the road, making sure that the head is visible to oncoming traffic. The pick-up car then travels along the route between the spot codes until the driver sees the cat's eyes reflecting in the grass – at the signal, he deactivates the brake lights and stops with the rear nearside passenger door open.

The agent, who by this time is lying hidden nearby, jumps to his feet, picks up the cat's eyes and gets into the car, which then drives away. The whole operation takes just seconds. Any other vehicle driving down the road may well see the reflection from the cat's eyes and automatically assume that it is a cat in the grass. If the driver of the pick-up vehicle has a car in his rear-view mirror he will just go round the area until he is clean and approach the pick-up site again.

AIRBORNE SURVEILLANCE

▲ **Using a helicopter for surveillance allows the vehicles to stay well back.**

The use of helicopters in surveillance is a great asset as it allows the follow vehicles to hang back and avoid being detected by the target. While a helicopter may be easy to spot, most can sit off the target at a distance of several miles and still keep track on the vehicle through the use of powerful cameras, most of which have day-night capability.

Helicopter surveillance has become popular with the police as it provides an overt observation platform for many different operations, such as traffic control and police pursuit. Helicopters also have the advantage of speed and unrestricted progress while in the air, making them ideal for:

- Surveillance.
- Aerial photography.
- Aerial reconnaissance.
- Electronic tracking.
- Communications relay.
- The insertion and extraction of agents.
- Rapid back-up.

In addition to helicopters and light aircraft, unmanned drones for military surveillance have been used for many years. New, smaller models have now been perfected for civilian surveillance use, some of them no larger than an insect (*see* Technical Surveillance).

SURVEILLANCE CHECKLISTS

- Definition of operation objectives.
- Research of all available information on the target.
- Procurement of photographs and physical descriptions.
- Establish licence numbers and make of vehicles used by target.
- Listing of target's known associates.
- Establishment of whether the target is likely to be armed.
- Obtain a detailed sketch of the target's premises or an aerial photograph.
- Definition of points of entry and exit.
- Getting hold of a detailed street map of the target's premises and the surrounding area.
- Establish codes for the target, his associates, locations and any alternate plans, etc.

AGENTS' MANNING REQUIREMENTS

- Outline the number of surveillance operators required.
- List types of surveillance required, i.e. OP, static or mobile.
- Calculation of the minimum number of vehicles required.
- Identification of specific operators for individual tasks.
- Consideration of male/female surveillance teams and any ethnic requirement.

AGENTS' EQUIPMENT

- Checking and testing of all radio equipment (both for the vehicle and personal use). Include spare batteries.
- Issuing of adequate funds (including change) for telephone calls, parking, meals, etc.
- Requesting of all forms of technical equipment required, cameras, binoculars, etc.
- Consideration of carrying a change of clothing or disguise.
- Development of a recovery procedure in the event of a breakdown or an accident.
- Field testing all communications with base station.
- Installment of repeaters in areas of poor communications if required.

AGENTS' OPERATIONAL BRIEFING

- Reiteration of the problems arising from compromise to the surveillance operators.
- Emphasis of the need for safe and discreet driving.
- Examination of operational objectives and consideration of the benefits of surveillance.
- Distribution of all available data, such as photographs and telephone numbers.
- Designation of radio channels and proper radio procedures.
- Ensuring all drivers fuel their vehicles prior to any operations.
- Testing and distribution of any required specialist equipment.
- Going through procedure if counter-intelligence is detected.
- Planning a familiarization run of the target's premises and the surrounding area.

There will always be a post-operational debrief which allows all those who took part in the operation to have their say. Things to be discussed will include the route taken, any deliberate stops made by the target, any photographs or video footage that have been taken. Mobile surveillance has a habit of going wrong and the debrief must deal with any points of possible compromise, as well as discussing any solutions that could be taken.

OVERVIEW OF TECHNICAL SURVEILLANCE

The vast amount of technical surveillance equipment available to a surveillance unit is almost too great to catalogue. The advances in camera miniaturization and wireless communications are unprecedented. Much of the research into military and government surveillance equipment has, after a few years, produced equipment for the civilian market. There was a time when specialized equipment such as this could only be found in a few shops. Today, it is freely available over the Internet.

Surveillance cameras are everywhere.

Overt surveillance is everywhere: CCTV has spread through the major cities of the world like a rampant colony of insects. The cameras watch the traffic, the trains, the planes and they watch you!

IT technology monitors the workplace. Your telephone calls are recorded and your pass is registered as you enter or leave a building. In some government buildings you are actually "tagged" as you enter and are monitored as you move around. Technology can watch, monitor, record and assess your every movement. Add the specialist capabilities of a government surveillance unit and you would think that no one could hide – but some do. Osama Bin Laden for one, together with many other terrorists.

While the armoury of electronic devices is numerous, they are and will always remain, technical devices, capable of doing only what is required of them. It may be possible to construct a camera no larger than a pinhead that can send good quality pictures around the world, but there are plenty of other things to be taken into consideration. First, the intelligence agencies must locate their target, and that is not as easy as it might sound. Secondly, they must get close enough to be able to install a technical device covertly and, finally, they must maintain it, i.e. they must change its batteries or fix it if it fails to work. When the target is hidden in a cave, deep underground and guarded by devoted followers, it presents the intelligence agencies with a difficult task.

We have all experienced the reduction in size of most electronic goods, but in the surveillance industry this has been far more extreme. Whereas in the 1950s intelligence agency technicians struggled to reduce the size of a camera, today's digital versions can be pinhead-size. Nano-technology is rapidly replacing miniaturization as we know it. The cameras and transmitters of tomorrow will be almost invisible to the human eye.

CASE HISTORY

When a large quantity of weapons and explosives were found in a very delicate and politically hot location, it was decided that the best approach was to carry out a technical attack. This would be backed up by two static, rural OPs and a hit force stationed in the nearby police station.

As the weapons and explosive were hidden in a small attic, it was decided to insert a small technical device on the trap door, the only possible entry point. A magnetic break-trigger was drilled into the wood that surrounded the hatchway, and the device remained totally undetectable. The trigger was connected, via a small transmitter, to the local police station, which was monitored by the hit team.

After two weeks of no activity, a team were sent into the building to carry out a battery change. To the amazement of the surveillance team, over half of the weapons and explosives had been removed. Upon testing, the device was found to be faulty.

In order to prevent the removed weapons and explosives from being used, the remaining stock was removed by the surveillance team. They took them to another locality several miles away and hid them. Acting upon a tip-off, the remaining weapons and explosives were then discovered. This discovery was made public through the media.

The reason for this was logical. The terrorists knew that the second half of their stock had gone missing, and had surfaced in another location unknown to them. This told the terrorists that the intelligence agency knew all about the original hide and, therefore, they might know about the half that had already been removed. This bluff by the surveillance operators prevented either the explosives or the weapons from ever being used.

ADVANCE BUGGING

Strange as it might sound, one of the best ways to insert a technical device is to anticipate where the target will turn up in the future. For example: at the height of the Cold War the CIA would spy on the USSR and the KGB would spy on the United States. In order to do this, spies had to enter the country under a cover story and find accommodation, buy or rent a car and arrange all the normal social niceties that allowed them to fit in. After a while the number of incoming spies started to increase and certain patterns started to emerge. The spies arriving in the United States had all been fully briefed and were able to hire a car and to drive it legitimately. They would also have been well versed in the street layout of most major cities. Next they found somewhere to live, close to the embassy, in an area popular with the Russian community – they had any number of choices.

After some time, the CIA realized that the Russians favoured one particular car hire company; it was cheap and offered good cars. Likewise, the Soviet Embassy recommended a couple of good estate agents who would organize a long lease at reasonable rates. Both the car rental company and the estate agents were perfectly legal and had no connection with the CIA – other than renting out the cars unknowingly and offering short leases on houses.

The CIA would hire a car for a week, take it to their technical department and make sure that every possible device that could be fitted was. They also had time to fit the devices in such a way that they would never be found. The same would happen to the houses they leased. Cameras and listening devices would be fitted covertly in every room. At this stage, they would be deactivated, thus avoiding any counter-measure sweep used by the Russians. Once the new occupants had settled in, the systems would be activated and the CIA would be free to monitor at their discretion. While this technique might sound complicated and, perhaps, a little hit and miss, it was both very cost-effective and produced some excellent results.

COUNTER-MEASURES TO TECHNICAL SURVEILLANCE

Anybody could be under surveillance, so it is important to be able to spot the telltale signs. Those who believe that they are under surveillance, or those simply suspicious of the fact, may choose to purchase, and use, specialist equipment to confirm the situation. Always remember, anything you do, write or say can be monitored by a myriad of technical devices.

A spy working in a foreign country, always assumes that they are under surveillance. Anyone can be bugged for any amount of reasons. Companies bug each other for commercial gain and for inside trading information. People going through a divorce often use detectives to find out damaging information on their spouses. Insurance companies spy on people they believe to be making a bogus claim – the list is endless. To that end, there is a general list of counter-measures that both the general public and spies should look out for. A handler who is about to arrange a meeting with a recruited agent, a head of business that is about to announce a multi-million pound order should realistically suspect that some form of technical surveillance will be, or already has been, focused on him. Here are some indicators of technical surveillance:

- If someone has detected mobile or static surveillance in the past, but has become convinced that they are no longer being watched. The enemy may have already planted – and be using – technical surveillance instead.
- All is not right in a home. The furniture seems to have moved around – just a tiny bit – or personal effects are not where they were.
- A home or office has been burgled, but nothing of significance has been stolen. That could mean a professional team has entered the premises and implanted a number of technical devices. There may be loose plasterwork or plaster crumbs. The spy will check all electrical fittings including the phone. He will check the walls and ceiling for any telltale signs or bulges and open and check any fixed items, such a fire alarms, plug sockets, light fittings and wall clocks.
- The door locks are not working as smoothly as they have done for years. A good indicator that someone has been using lock-picks to gain entry. The spy will install a dead bolt type locking system, heavy enough to stop the average locksmith. He will check external doorframe for indentations. This could mean that a hydraulic jack has been used to spread the doorframe and release the locks and bolts from their housing (*see* lock picking).
- The phone may make odd noises: it rings and there is no one there or there is a tone when the phone is on the hook. All these indicate a telephone tap.
- The television, car radio or AM/FM radio develops strange interference. This could mean that the unit has been tampered with and that a hidden wireless microphone has been implanted. It might well be picking up static from a device near to the television or radio.
- Sales persons offering you free gifts, such as a pen, a cuddly toy or a clock radio may have installed hidden audio-visual devices with a wireless transmitter.
- A spy will take notice of any van-type vehicle that has suddenly started to appear in his street. These are usually disguised as utility or trade vehicles. He will check the vehicle with a walk-past. If he cannot see clearly into the whole vehicle, he will suspect that it is a technical surveillance vehicle. He may use a stethoscope pressed against the windowpane to try to detect any microwave "buzzing" and check for any vehicles in line of sight of the window.
- A spy will never allow anyone to enter his premises without good reason. Telephone or electrical engineers, do not just "turn up". He will check the identity of anyone he is not sure of and watch them while they are working if he is suspicious.

Telltale signs – such as bits of fallen plaster – especially just below a vent or electrical fitting, are a sign of possible tampering.

If a spy thinks that his home or premises has been violated, he will call his own technical people and have them do a sweep.

CASE HISTORY

Four Square Laundry was an operation set up by a force known as the Military Reconnaissance Force (MRF), an undercover unit that functioned in Northern Ireland in the early 1970s. One of their tasks was to operate a mobile laundry service that collected from house to house. They were assured of good custom, as their prices were far lower than those of their nearest rivals. However, prior to washing, all the clothes would pass through a machine that would test them for traces of explosives. When a contaminated item was found, all that they had to do was to read the address label. This was a good indicator that bombs were being assembled at that address or someone associated with it. Unfortunately, several members of the MRF who had been former members of the IRA, converted to work for the British and then changed their allegiance back to the IRA. This led to a Four Square van being shot up. The male driver was killed but the woman managed to escape. Both were British undercover agents.

AUDIO-VISUAL SURVEILLANCE

One method of surveillance allows the target to be observed both audibly and visually (with photographs and videos). Most modern devices can record both sound and pictures concurrently. The audio element provides voice patterns from which the target can be identified. The video element reveals an individual's hand and body gestures and facial expressions. Audio-visual is by far the greatest tool in the modern-day surveillance arsenal.

A combination of audio-visual devices can be hidden just about anywhere, even on an unsuspecting person. Homes, offices, vehicles and even public transport are easy targets for a technical department of any good intelligence agency. Hiding a "bug" in light fittings, smoke detectors, toys, clocks, garden rocks, front doors or in the bedroom ceiling are all easily achieved. The secret to fitting a good audio-visual surveillance device is to be inventive. The spy will always consider how long the device will be in place and work out battery consumption. Where the hiding place offers sufficient space, a series of batteries will be fitted to avoid having to return to the target's home to fit replacement batteries. He will always check that the area around the hidden device is clean of any debris or dirty finger prints.

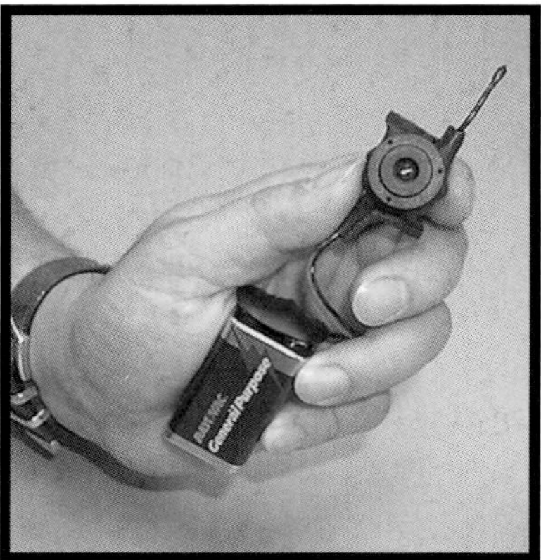

Audio-visual technical devices can be hidden almost anywhere.

This ship that sits above the fireplace had a wireless covertly fitted audio-visual device. There was enough room for extra batteries and a motion sensor. The camera only activated when someone was in the room.

A camera hidden in a smoke alarm.

A wireless audio-visual device fitted in a child's toy.

A wireless camera hidden in a mobile phone.

MICRO-AERIAL VEHICLES (MAV)

Since early the 1990s, there has been a lot of research into making small aerial vehicles which can take photographs and record video. These are basically unmanned drones, very much like the model aeroplanes made by amateur enthusiasts. That, however, is where the similarity ends. MAVs are both silent and capable of producing excellent real-time images as well as geo-referenced (on-board GPS) stills. Some are fitted with communication capabilities that allow pictures to be sent back while the vehicle is still in flight. They are perfect for short range, real-time situational awareness and reconnaissance information. MAVs range in size from 30 cm wide to 3 cm wide, making them almost invisible.

A Predator plane.

COMPUTER SURVEILLANCE

There is hardly a home or an office these days that does not contain a computer, most of which are linked to the Internet. For this reason, intelligence agencies regard computers as a vital element of surveillance. Computer surveillance, commonly known as "hacking" or "reading", is the ability to access a target's computer and to investigate any information that may be of a suspicious or incriminating nature.

Both PC and laptop computers can be modified in a number of ways. It is possible, for example, to fit a separate word processing system in a laptop, which, for the most part, will never be discovered. The designated user activates the system and, once finished, he simply hits a combination of keys to return the laptop to its normal state. This allows him to write and store messages outside of the laptop's normal functions, thus preventing any messages from being found if the laptop is lost or stolen.

Another system, known as SRAC (Short Range Agent Communication), allows messages written on a computer to be downloaded onto a small SRAC transmitter. This device, slightly larger than a cigarette packet, continually sends out a low power interrogation signal. When the receiving agent is close enough – about 100 m away – the SRAC transmitter makes contact automatically and "burst" transmits any waiting message.

TRACKING

Tracking devices, which may vary in type, size and ability, have become both increasingly popular and extremely accurate. The small tracking device, such as the one used in the Bond film *Goldfinger*, is now very much a reality. Even though the technology of tracking devices has improved, they should only be seen as an aid to surveillance rather than an independent stand-alone system.

SATELLITE

Satellites have been used for the purpose of intelligence gathering since the late 1950s. There are three types of imagery satellites: photographic, electro-optical and synthetic aperture radar (SAR). The first satellites used conventional photography, i.e. they had a camera installed that looked down and took a picture of the earth. The film, once finished, would be scanned and processed into an electronic signal or ejected in a capsule and dropped back to earth. This method stopped in the mid-1980s. By comparison, electro-optical imaging satellites take pictures of a specified target; this is then transmitted to a ground station back on the earth's surface. The camera works in very much the same way as a normal digital camera, thus allowing for straightforward transmission of the image.

Both of the above methods have one failing – cloud cover can obscure the target area. The SAR system overcomes this by using microwaves that are fired down towards the target area. Microwaves have the ability to penetrate cloud cover and the SAR satellite simply creates a picture by analysing the returning microwave reflection. Once computed, the image is sent digitally back down to earth.

Satellite images have improved dramatically over the years and definition these days is now down to just a few centimetres. The advances in satellite images for the purpose of intelligence include 3D modelling, which is done by blending images from a variety of sources. This clarity enables intelligence agencies to have a clear idea of what is happening in any part of the world at any time. This includes spotting potential spies doing a "walk through" of a city or an area before they are actually assigned to a job. In addition, the commercial interest in satellite imagery has improved greatly; high-grade images are now widely available over the Internet.

The disadvantage of satellites is their high cost and their relatively short lifespan. To help combat this, NASA is developing a new type of unmanned spy plane. These will operate some 30 km above the earth's surface and will be sustained by solar power. The aim is to try to get the new spy planes to fly in a controlled orbit at very low speeds. This combination should produce excellent imagery and should reduce the current reliance on satellites.

GPS/GSM

There have been great advances in this form of tracking. The arrival of the Global Positioning System (GPS) and the widespread use of mobile telephones provide an excellent platform for tracking. GPS's accuracy is increasing and will continue to do so as the European "Galileo" system comes into operation in 2008. When this happens, the accuracy of a ground position will be down to mere centimetres. Likewise, the advances in mobile phone technology continue to race ahead and excellent coverage is now available over most of the world's populated surface.

Current GPS/GSM tracking devices have shrunk to the size of a cigarette packet and they continue to become smaller. Their signal can be transmitted over the GSM network from anywhere to anywhere and even when a GSM signal in not available, the tracking device is capable of storing its positions until a signal can be regained. These signals transpose onto a computer map that indicates the movement of a tracking device in real time. Tracking devices can be installed in vehicles, on people or can be attached to movable objects.

THE GLOBAL POSITIONING SYSTEM (GPS)

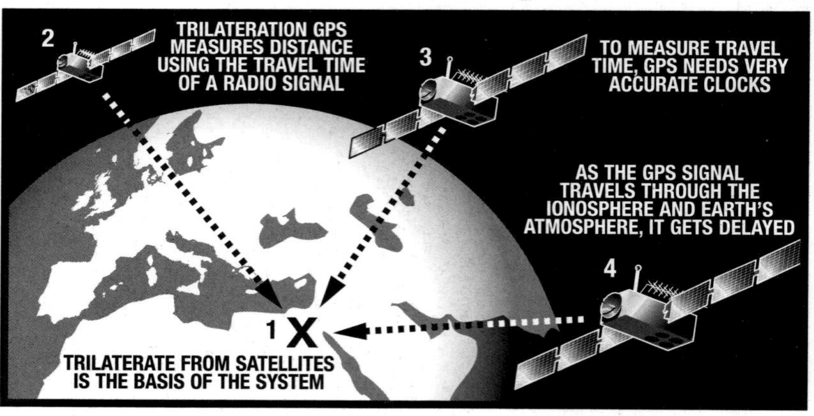

▲ The introduction of GPS has revolutionized surveillance.

The United States Department of Defence launched its satellite-based navigation system in the 1970s. It is made up of a network of 27 satellites (only 24 are actually used with the other three being kept in reserve) and was originally intended for military applications. Cruise missiles and smart bombs are guided to their target by GPS. In the 1980s, the US government made the system available for civilian use, making it easier for commercial aircraft and ships to operate. Although the US government can switch the system off, it normally operates anywhere in the world, 24 hours a day and in all weather conditions. The GPS system (for civilian use) operates on a frequency of 1575.42 MHz in the UHF band and is free.

These satellites circle the earth in a very precise orbit and transmit signal information to earth. GPS receivers acquire this information and use it to calculate the user's exact location. A GPS receiver must acquire at least four satellite signals in order to calculate latitude, longitude and altitude. The more signals a receiver can "lock on" to, the higher the accuracy. As the receiver moves over the earth's surface, the position is updated. In doing so, the GPS unit can provide details on the object's speed, bearing, track, journey distance and distance to destination. Most modern GPS receivers, such as those in the TACCS system, can produce an accuracy of up to 1 m.

TACTICAL COMMAND AND CONTROL SYSTEM (TACCS)

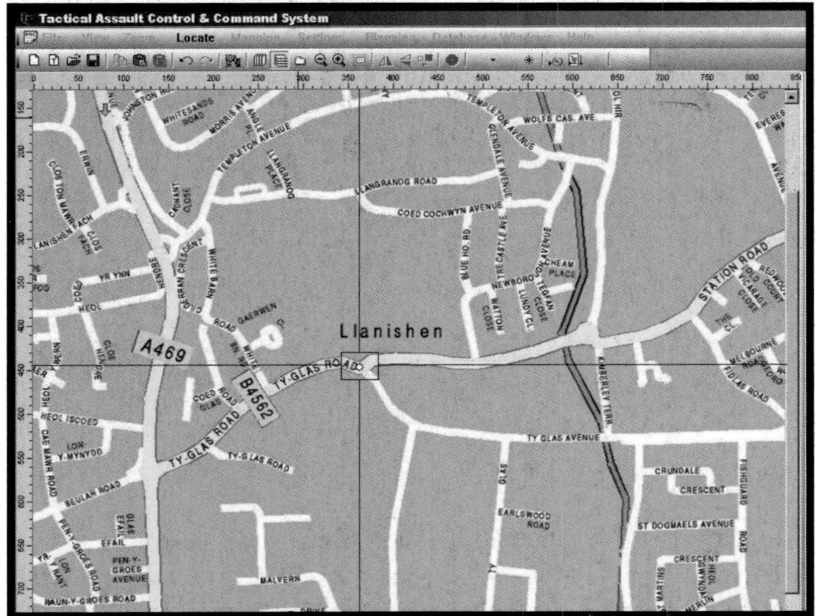

▲ TACCS is capable of tracking anything, either friend or foe.

The introduction of GPS/GSM tracking devices has revolutionized both foot and mobile surveillance. One such system is the Tactical Command and Control System (TACCS), which is produced in the United Kingdom. This form of surveillance is still very much in its infancy, but its capabilities have already made an impact. An additional bonus for many countries is its cost, which, when compared to drones and other satellite surveillance methods, is minuscule.

The TACCS software is Windows-based. It is extremely easy to use, yet it incorporates state-of-the-art, sophisticated functionality. The system is a stand-alone, secure-encrypted and self-contained GPS/GSM tracking and monitoring system. It also offers the user real-time planning and extensive database provision. The user is capable of tracking people, objects and vehicles, belonging either to the enemy or to their own forces. The TACCS system is a spatial decision support system that integrates GIS, GPS and GSM together with multimedia technologies. The TACCS package of software and hardware is designed to ease operational control anywhere in the world.

TACCS software is designed to aid independent unit commanders by supporting real-time information. This allows for the efficient use of unit

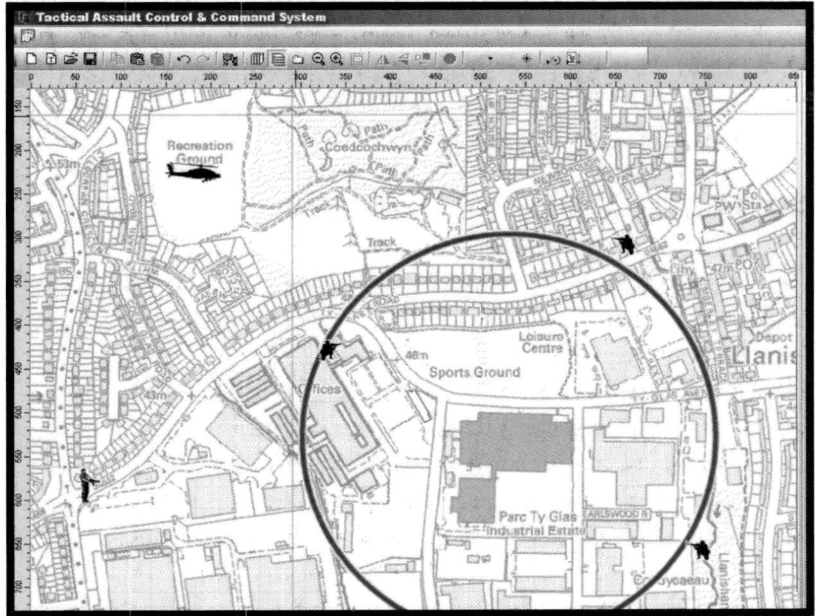

▲ The TACCS planning application allows real-time tracking with interactive multimedia participation.

personnel whilst providing a record of events for surveillance, assault operations, debriefing, report writing and future training.

The planning profile of the TACCS system allows the user to geo-reference any map, aerial and satellite photographs or scanned drawing within a few minutes. Icons representing people, vehicles or objects are then placed on the screen using a simple drag and drop sidebar library. This element of the software is particularly useful for planning and executing assault operations or for establishing contingency plans. The system also stores data, such as previously recorded surveillance sessions, personnel profiles and predefined contingency plans. The TACCS system can be used by a variety of military or civil commands to carry out a number of operations:

- Undercover surveillance
- VIP monitoring
- Anti-drugs units
- Counter-terrorism teams
- Covert military operations

Due to the high number of satellite signals received, TACCS can locate personnel, vehicles or objects with great accuracy. Certain devices can be programmed directly from the software to provide a series of specific tasks such as geo-fencing. This allows terrorists or known drug dealers to be fenced electronically – should they enter or leave a geo-fenced area an alarm is triggered. Each device can send its position update automatically or by request from the software. In the case of an emergency, the surveillance mobile device can be programmed to transmit an emergency message, together with co-ordinates, back to the software and/or other surveillance personnel who are working on the network.

The planning feature allows the operator to insert a highly accurate ground vision of the area, be it the seating layout of a commercial aircraft, the platform of an oilrig or a building rendered in 3D. The comprehensive assault screen is unlimited in its ability to provide a detailed picture of who is where and what is happening in real time.

The planning window allows the user to "grab" a section of any geo-referenced map and use this for detailed planning. The user can then build up an interactive model of the immediate incident area. Field operators, such as assault team commanders, can then be monitored by the commander as they move around the map. This ability provides the unit commander with precise real-time control right up to the point when an assault is made.

TACCS SURVEILLANCE MOBILE

The TACCS mobile is ideal for the surveillance operator as it looks natural and does away with traditional body-worn radio.

The TACCS Mobile is a revolutionary communication/navigation instrument. It looks and operates in a similar way to any mobile phone and is, therefore, ideally suited to surveillance work as it offers both a natural and secure way of communicating with other operators or the base station. Communication can be carried out using voice, text or SMS. The mobile is equipped with a GPS navigator and street maps can be inserted for any location in the world. A pre-programmed panic button, when pressed, sends an SMS to the control centre providing information on the user's location. Lost or kidnapped people can be found as a result of this feature and, for the user, it could mean the difference between life and death.

TACCS AUTO/MAGNETIC

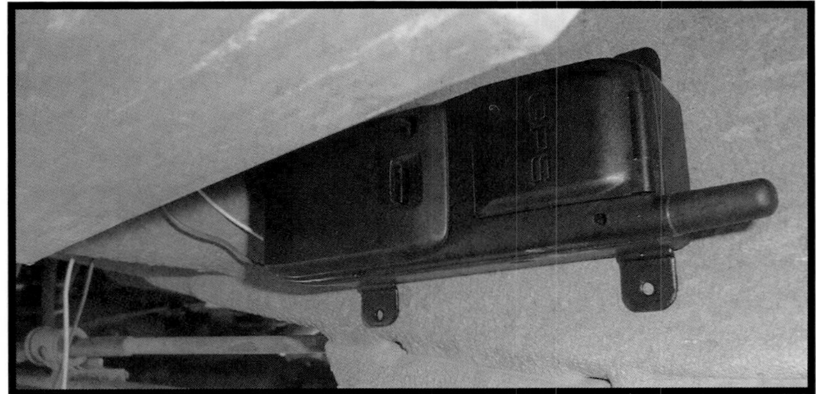

▲ The TACCS tracking device can be magnetically fitted in seconds. Given a few minutes the device can be wired into the vehicle's electrical system.

The TACCS Auto/Magnetic can be fixed in a vehicle the spy intends to track either by another TACCS device or from the TACCS control centre. Once fixed, the TACCS Auto can be tracked anywhere in the world where there is a GSM coverage. The unit can be hardwired and permanently fitted using a back plate and the relevant cabling. This is normally done for the user's own vehicles. When the TACCS Auto/Magnetic is used on target vehicles, there are two options – the "quick fix" and the "magnetic conversion".

The quick fix involves the two wires protruding from the unit, the ends of which have bulldog grips. The unit is hidden under the car in a position where it will not be easily found. The bulldog grips are then attached to the nearest positive and negative terminals. An external aerial can be fitted in order to get the best GPS signal. This procedure takes about four minutes to perform, but it removes the problem of battery power. Once the type of target vehicle is known to the field operators, they will acquire a similar model and carry out tests to determine the best location to place the unit, to attach the power cables and to fit any remote aerial. This cuts down the amount of time that will be required to fit the unit onto the target vehicle. It also adds to the accuracy of the GPS signal.

In an emergency, and for rapid deployment, the fixed back plate can be exchanged for a heavy-duty magnetic plate. The unit is then simply placed under the target vehicle. However, the unit then has to rely on battery power. This will last any time from between six to 24 hours, depending on the amount of tracking signals requested. The unit has an emergency cut-off at 20 per cent of battery power, enabling the desk or field operators to locate the target vehicle at a specified time – normally during the hours of darkness. Once again the field operator will find a similar type and make of vehicle in order to establish the best position to place the TACCS Auto/Magnetic. The characteristics of the unit make it perfect for covert surveillance.

TACCS ASSAULT

The TACCS Assault is a body-worn unit used mainly by field operators who carry out "dirty" jobs. It requires no installation; it is simply switched on in order for it to operate. As with other TACCS units, it sends back a position on request in order for the commander to control or assist during "hard-hit" raids. The TACCS Assault unit has a large panic button, operated in emergencies such as "man-down". The unit also incorporates a very sensitive microphone that enables the commander to listen to the surrounding conversation. In this mode the unit can be planted and used to covertly listen to a target's conversation.

TECHNICAL OBSERVATION EQUIPMENT

There is little point in locating and constructing a good OP if the spy does not have the correct equipment with which to observe the target. The surveillance operators must make a list of their technical requirements prior to entering the OP and these must enable viewing over a 24-hour period and in all weather conditions. This list may include monoculars, binoculars, telescopes, periscopes, night-vision devices, thermal imaging devices and acoustic devices. Many of these devices can produce still photography, video or audio playback. A major consideration when selecting equipment should be the range to target, the magnification requirements and current audio volume (traffic noise) between the OP and the target. The technical equipment used might include:

- Binoculars and telescopes
- Conventional and digital cameras
- Analogue and digital video cameras
- Night-vision equipment
- Pinhole and microcircuit cameras
- Wireless and remote image transmission technology

OBSERVATION

The equipment is only an aid when it comes to surveillance; the "mark one" eyeball is still the best observation device around.

BINOCULARS AND TELESCOPES

Binoculars and telescopes have been with us for centuries and they are still one of the best surveillance aids available today. The spy will generally have a small pair of binoculars to hand, either on his person or in the surveillance vehicle. Binoculars are quick to acquire a moving target; on the other hand, telescopes, which are often mounted, are much slower.

Modern telescopes are extremely powerful and capable of immense magnification. They are generally used in the OP, whether it is in a rural or an urban location. The secret to selecting the correct telescope is to assess the range to the target and to define the definition required. While it is often too easy to select a very powerful telescope, this can pose several problems. The first is one of stabilization – if the telescope is too powerful, the target image will appear "shaky" and the spy will not be able to read target detail correctly.

▲ Modern telescopes are highly advanced, and they remain the backbone of surveillance.

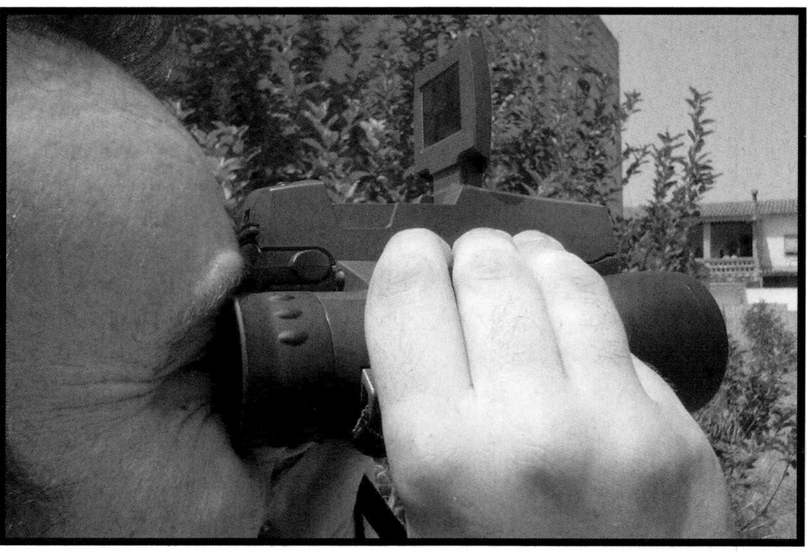

▲ Binoculars with built-in video and still camera.

CONVENTIONAL AND DIGITAL CAMERAS

Until the 1950s, cameras were the epitome of surveillance. The only other reasonable source of technical information came from a telephone tap. There is much truth in the saying "a picture is worth a thousand words", as a camera can capture a single moment in time. In surveillance terms, that may be the moment when the target's identity is established or when you discover his association with another. Whatever the case, it provides a lasting image for others to examine.

The first "spy" camera was little more than a normal camera reduced in size; it required film, which in turn required processing. From such simple beginnings, subsequent years have seen some wonderful and ingenious adaptations. Surveillance or "spy" cameras were to be found hidden in books or vehicles, they were sometimes used in Ops, with a telephoto lens attached. These "conventional" cameras produced outstanding quality in their definition clarity. They could also be adapted for use in total darkness by using infrared. Ingenious enough, but then came the digital age.

INFRA-RED (IR)

It is possible for a spy to convert a normal SLR camera into an infra-red camera. The process is fairly easy and, in the absence of any other night-vision camera, is worth doing. It requires two items – a gelatine filter and a high-speed infra-red film.

A rough template of the flash lens can be marked out using the face of the camera flash. The sheet of gelatine filter is (held by the edges and) placed on the template and cut around, leaving a generous overlap. It is then carefully fixed onto the lens flash with masking tape, making sure there are no gaps for light to shine through.

A roll of high-speed infa-red film is carefully loaded into the back of the camera in total darkness, and the camera is now ready to take photographs – also in total darkness.

It important that the spy pre-focuses his camera, as he will obviously not be able to see anything in the dark. If the spy is intending to take photographs of documents, for example, he will prepare beforehand a measuring stick, which he will use to guage the distance between the camera and the documents in the darkness.

◂ It's simple to convert a camera into an infra-red camera capable of taking pictures in total darkness.

DEVELOPING IR PHOTOGRAPHS

Although it has diminished with the advancement of digital cameras, developing photographs is still a required tradecraft skill. While this should be done under ideal conditions, the spy often has to improvise. The following is a basic method for developing infra-red film. Some basic photographic chemical and equipment is needed. Many photographic shops sell basic kits that contain just about everything you need, including a set of instructions. There are two stages in producing a photograph from a roll of film: firstly, developing the film and, secondly, developing the picture from the film.

DEVELOPING THE FILM

To do this requires a developing tank. This is a small, black plastic tank with a reel inside. The top is unscrewed and the reel removed. The spy will then lay the parts out so he can identify them in the dark. The top and bottom of the reel move in different directions for about 5 cm. There is also an inner edge, into which the film is threaded.

The developer preparation is done by adding warm water – around 28ºC – to the quantity specified on the label. Enough water is needed to cover the film when it is in the tank. The stop solution and fixing agent is prepared as described on their instruction labels.

The following process must take place in total darkness. The film is removed from the camera and some 30cm pulled free. This is fed into the reel. The start point should be located here. Once the film is partly in position, the two parts of the reel will feed in the rest of the film.

The reel is placed in the tank, the top is screwed on and developer added. A paddle stick is provided with the tank that fits through a hole in the top and clips into the reel. The film is agitated using the paddle stick for six minutes and 45 seconds before the developer is emptied out. The stop solution is inserted and agitated for one-and-a-half minutes before emptying out the solution. The fixing agent is then poured in and agitated for five minutes. The fixing agent is then poured out.

The film will now be developed. The top is unscrewed and the open tank placed under a running tap for several minutes in order to remove any chemicals. Once this has been done, the reel should be taken out and the developed film slowly removed. Clothes pegs can be used to weight the roll open and hang it in a clean warm place to dry. The careful use of a hairdryer will speed up the process.

While the film is drying, three flat trays are prepared, filled with 5 cm of developer, stop and fixer. As the negatives are small, an enlarger will be required in order to print out a picture that can be viewed easily.

Once the film is dry, it can be cut into manageable strips of four to six exposures. A strip is placed in the enlarger and manoeuvred until the desired exposure is visible on the enlarger board. The height and the focus should be adjusted to the desired size the enlarger should be switched off and a sheet of contact paper placed on the board. It should be exposed for five seconds by switching on the enlarger lamp. The contact paper should then be removed and placed in the developer dish. It should be agitated by hand until the picture is visible and sharp. It should then be removed from the developer and placed for one minute in the stop solution. Finally, it should be placed in the fixing agent for five minutes before removing it, washing it in clean water and hanging it up to dry. It will be necessary to experiment with both exposure and developer timings in order to achieve the best results. **Note:** it is easy to see why digital cameras are so popular.

DIGITAL

▲ **This digital SLR has a very high megapixel output (6.1 million).**

While the first digital cameras produced poor-quality pictures, it did not take long for them to catch up with their more conventional counterparts. Digital cameras today are, in terms of quality, capable of taking near-perfect photographs, the results of which can be viewed instantly. Most are capable of running rapid sequences or full video, albeit at a lower resolution. While these features are a major asset to any surveillance operator, their true capabilities come from the fact that they are digital. This means that, when it comes to taking or transmitting images, a digital camera can be controlled electronically. A digital camera can be disguised as a rock and placed in your front garden. It can take pictures day or night on command or by sensor activation. These pictures can then be downloaded by RF, over the Internet or via the GSM network. Most digital cameras used for surveillance are available commercially. If there is an adaptation, it is simply in their usage, that is to say they are disguised in one form or another.

NIGHT-VISION SYSTEMS

Night-vision systems range from miniature "pocketscopes" to large, tripod-mounted models. The present range of third-generation image intensifiers, which can operate with virtually no available light, can be adapted to suit various phases of surveillance; individual weapon sights (IWS), night observation devices (NODs) and night-vision goggles (NVGs). All should be available during the various stages of surveillance depending on the requirements for the moment; NVG for a target recce, a NOD observation or IWS, if a night assault phase is required.

Thermal imagers can also be supplied for surveillance and target acquisition during night and day. A number of different models, varying in size from hand-held types to tripod-mounted devices coaxially mounted

◂ **Night-vision weapon sight.**

with laser rangefinders, are available. When the target is obscured by weather, smoke, dust or any other form of masking, thermal imagers have the distinct advantage over image intensifiers, as they work on heat detection. Depending on the type and model, night-vision devices can work over distances up to several thousand metres.

◂ Due to a change in fighting tactics, night vision has become an everyday item with Special Forces and intelligence agents.

HOW NIGHT VISION WORKS

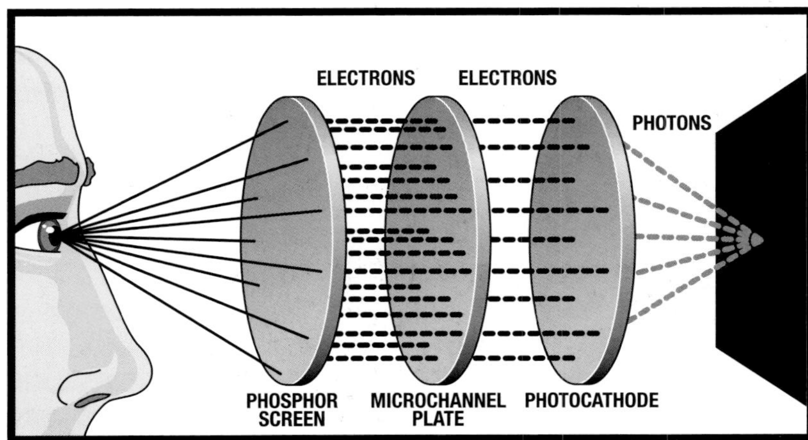

▴ How an image intensifier works.

There are two forms of night vision: image intensifier (light amplification) and thermal imaging (infrared). Image intensifiers take small amounts of light (starlight and moonlight) and convert the light photons into electrons. These electrons are then multiplied inside the image intensifier tube before being converted back into photons. This provides the viewer with a clear night vision image that would be impossible for the human eye. The process of most image intensifiers causes the viewed image to appear green, a distinctive characteristic of night vision.

The first operational night vision device appeared in the mid-1960s and was used extensively in the Vietnam War. These could be hand-held or used on a weapon. They have progressed by generation, the latest being Generation 3. The photocathode in Gen 3 enables vastly increased viewing distance under near total darkness. Because an image intensifier emits no beam, it is known as "passive" night vision.

Thermal imaging has been around since the 1940s, but it was overtaken by the introduction of image intensifiers – until the shortcomings of the latter became obvious. In certain operations, a thermal imager is very much superior to an image intensifier, as it can locate human or structural images that would be obscured to image intensifiers by smoke, cloud, mist or snow, to name just a few. Because they need to emit a beam of infra-red light, they are known as "proactive" night vision.

LISTENING DEVICES

As is the case with audio-visual devices, there are an unbelievable amount of listening devices available for surveillance. They range from straightforward bugging devices hidden in a building or in a vehicle to microwave or laser beams that are aimed at a window. No matter which device is used, the most important aspect with any system is to anticipate where the best reception can be achieved and balance this with placing the correct device in the best possible position.

The best position for a listening device depends on the target's social habits. That is to say, does he spend a lot of time in the home, in the office or driving his car? While he may spend several hours a day in his car, is he alone? Drivers don't generally talk to themselves while driving. The original target recce will provide an insight as to the best place to fit a listening device. For example, if the family gathers in the kitchen, this would be an obvious location. Alternatively, if the target spends eight hours a day sitting at an office desk, this may also prove a good opportunity to use a listening device. In the final event, a full range of listening devices may be deployed in order to monitor most of the target's conversation.

CHAPTER 4

Overtly or covertly, gaining entry to a building is one of the essential skills for a spy. Gaining information from public or not-so-public sources forms the basis of much spycraft.

METHODS OF ENTRY

All of the information and techniques explained in this section are in the public domain. They outline the skills of secret agents and Special Forces operating in foreign countries. None of the literature in this section will tell you how to construct a bomb or how to make real explosives. Similarly, the section on lock picking is merely an outline and the skills required to perfect the art take years to master.

Methods of entry cover a wide variety of spycraft skills, which fall into two categories – covert (gaining access) and overt (making access). If a spy wishes to plant a bug in the target's house, he will most probably wish to enter the premises and leave covertly. In contrast, a raid on a suspected terrorist bomb-making factory would almost certainly be initiated by the use of force that will inevitably result in a loud noise at the point of entry.

In its basic form, infiltration is simply gaining access to a structure, whether it is a building, an aircraft, a ship or a vehicle. To gain access, a spy may have to climb up, abseil down or carry out direct penetration, i.e. he may need to go through a wall. Much of the equipment required for MoE is termed "low tech", and, for the most part, has been developed through necessity or constant civilian usage. Counter-terrorist techniques have turned the humble builder's ladder into a rapid means of access, while much of the cutting equipment used has been developed from items similar to those used on a day-to-day basis by the rescue services.

Other more specialist MoE skills use a mixture of military and civilian techniques; these include lock picking and the use of explosives. Covert entry can be made by picking the locks, or by silently cutting through steel bars or doors. Overt entry, on the other hand, is normally carried out using the fastest methods – through the use of explosives or wall-breaching cannons. Although this type of work is highly specialized, it is important that a spy has a general working knowledge of such skills.

When access to a house or building is required, the agents will normally carry out a target recce (see Surveillance section). This entails a simple observation of the premises to establish the correct address, the main points of entry and to ascertain the time when the property is occupied. Once this basic information has been collated, a method of entry will then be formulated. Depending on the security devices protecting the house, a plan will be made either to break in – and make it look as though a burglary has taken place – or to effect a covert entry.

Surprising as it may seem, it is often better for a spy to break in during daylight hours, especially if he intends it to look like a robbery. At 10 am in the morning, the man of the house is likely to be at work, the children are probably at school and the wife could well be out shopping or at work. In contrast, a house is almost always occupied from six in the evening and throughout the night.

ALARMS

▲ **The picture on the left shows a normal house, while the one on the right has been "cleaned" to show how its occupants have protected from possible attack.**

All but a few alarms are controlled by a four-digit code that is punched into a box conveniently situated somewhere close to the main point of entry. This allows the property owner a short period of time to enter the house and to deactivate the alarm. Alarm systems are designed to activate under certain conditions; for the most part when one of the internal sensors has detected somebody's presence or when a door or window contact has been broken. This activates the alarm and the box on the outside of the building is set off. In some cases the alarm may phone the local police (they will only accept VIPs), or even the house owner's mobile phone.

There are several ways a spy can bypass an alarm system. For example, the spy may get a ladder and insert expanding foam into the outside alarm box, remembering to break the light if one is attached. Or he may try to identify the alarm system manufacturer and then obtain the engineer's shutdown code.

While both of these methods are effective, the modern agent will often have a small plate-like device at his disposal (the name of which is classified) that he simply places over the keys on the control box and which will display the correct code instantly. The device measures the pressure of the push buttons, as each is minutely different. The pad is sensitive enough to measure the difference (and will also determine the order) in which the four code keys are pressed. The device works on 70 per cent of known keypads.

The best way a spy has of carrying out daylight entry is by walking up to the front door and knocking loudly (he will not rely on the doorbell as it may be broken), in order to establish whether anyone is at home. If someone answers the door, the spy can simply switch to a back-up plan and say that he is collecting for charity, for example. If no one is at home, he may wish to enter the premises directly, by forcing the door with a wrecking bar or, if the property is hidden from view, using a hydraulic spreader. Or he may go to the rear of the house and try there. He will try not to break glass as it has a nasty habit of making a distinctive sound that could arouse the suspicion of any neighbours.

Once entry has been effected, the spy will consider the amount of time that it will take to plant bugs and to search the place. If he has forced his way into the property, he will make it look like a burglary; if he has entered covertly, he will make sure not to disturb anything. If the house is not under observation from a static OP, he will probably have a sentry posted outside to provide a warning if anyone should return to the property.

MoE CONSIDERATIONS

- A spy will check around the property and take all possible points of entry into consideration. Almost two-thirds of all burglaries take place through unlocked windows and doors.
- He will check under the mat, flowerpot, the nearest garden stone or gnome, and peer through the letterbox for a length of string as it is surprising where people hide keys.
- Street lights often illuminate the front or rear of a property. The spy may use an air rifle to take them out a couple of nights before he intends to enter. He will knock out several in the same street to avoid suspicion.
- The doors are one of the most common means of entry. They are also the most protected, however. The front door normally controls any alarm system, so the spy must either deactivate the alarm externally or enter through this door and then deactivate the alarm. Entering at any other point will instantly trigger the alarm.
- Given their accessibility, windows are the most vulnerable point of entry. However, the spy will always bear in mind the fact that glass makes a sharp, distinctive noise when it is broken.
- Sliding glass doors provide an easy point of entry as their locks are notoriously poor; some 50 per cent of them refuse to lock after a couple of years' usage.
- The spy will make a note of any fences that surround the property. If they are high, he will locate the entry and exit points in the event that he needs to make a quick getaway.
- The spy will not bother with roof hatches unless the property is a large industrial unit or similar type of building.
- Cellars or basement apartments are an ideal point of entry and, while many are self-contained, there is generally a way up into the main house. Basements will give the spy the time he needs to pick locks or to force an entry undetected.
- Garages and tool sheds may not be the main target of attack, but they are generally easy to enter. They will also provide a great deal of equipment – from ladders to cordless drills – that can be used to effect entry in an emergency.

Note: Breaking and entering is illegal and should not be undertaken by civilians.

ASSAULT LADDERS

Assault ladders cater for any eventuality: gaining access to buildings to assaulting aircraft.

There are an extensive range of assault ladders available, most of which were originally developed to cope with terrorist siege situations. These include single section, multi-sectional and extending types in single-width, double-width and triple-stile designs. The best ladders are those that are manufactured from structural grade aluminium alloy with deeply serrated rung sections and heavy-duty rectangular sections. They are fitted as standard with non-slip rubber feet, noise-reducing buffers on all exposed faces, and are finished in black polyester powder coating with etch primer. The reason for having double- and triple-width ladders is to enable several personnel to climb side by side. This allows one of them to open an upper door or window, and enables the others to make an immediate entry. The end result is a lightweight, multi-purpose climbing frame that is adaptable to most requirements.

- Single-section ladders are available in single widths, double widths and triple-stile designs up to four metres in length. They offer silent climbing and are ideally suited for gaining rapid access to public transport vehicles, ships and aircraft or to be used for scaling walls. Wall hooks and sniper platforms can be fitted to all sizes.
- Multi-sectional ladders are mainly manufactured in double-width or triple-stile configurations. The sections of these ladders range in length from one metre up to four metres and can be quickly assembled to give finished lengths of up to eight metres. They can be transported easily in vans or estate cars and provide team capability for two to four personnel, depending on both the length of the ladder and the conditions. They are fitted as standard with heavy-duty channel connectors complete with nylon slides and locking pins. Sniper platforms are also available.
- Wire coil ascent and descent ladders are available in lengths up to 30 metres. As is the case with fixed ladders, they are manufactured from structural grade aluminium alloy and high-tensile wire. They have non-slip rubber feet, noise-reducing buffers on all exposed faces and are finished in black polyester powder coating with etch primer. The ladder is rolled into a coil for transport. Coil ladders are normally put in place via an extendable hook which can be used on a building or for gaining access to a ship.

Vehicle ladder platforms deliver a large number of personnel on target at varying heights.

VEHICLE LADDER AND PLATFORM SYSTEMS

The most common delivery system used by most anti-terrorist teams today is a vehicle ladder and platform system. The system provides the assault team with both delivery and access to buildings, trains, coaches and aircraft. While a covert assault may require the use of normal assault ladders, both the IA and a rapid assault are best carried out by the employment of a vehicle-mounted, multi-role, personnel delivery system. There are various systems being currently developed. Some are designed to fit permanently onto armoured vehicles, while other systems are carried within a standard pick-up and can be assembled in minutes. In both cases, the assembled ladders can be configured to suit a wide range of user needs, capable of deploying fully equipped personnel to a variety of levels. For example, the system can be adjusted to deliver a ten-man assault team directly to the doors of a Boeing 747. The same system can be adjusted in a few minutes to enable an assault on a building window some seven metres above ground level. The system can also be used for assaulting ships if they are in dock.

The members of the assault team are carried on load-carrying platforms that are secured to the sides, top and front hood of the vehicle. In addition to this, ladders can be formed into access bridges if and when a void needs to be crossed. It is also possible to fit a 360-degree turntable with an extended ladder, similar to those used by fire-fighters, which enables multi-role functions at difficult angles.

ABSEILING

Abseiling is used for descending a rock face or the side of a building. It can also be used from a helicopter. Abseiling equipment consists of the following: an abseil harness, designed to be used as either as a full-body harness – permitting a person to be suspended for protracted periods of time e.g. outside a window – or as a simple sit harness for straightforward descending. A normal abseil rope is made of 11 mm-diameter, non-stretch, black polyester rope. This is available in differing pre-cut lengths of 50, 100, 150 and 200 metres. Various descenders are used, the most common of which is a horned, figure-of-eight abseil descender on which the lower ring is set at 90 degrees to the upper one. This eliminates any tendency to twist during a descent. The "stop" descender works on the "fail-safe" principle, meaning that the rope can only move through it if the handler applies pressure to the handle. Any release of pressure on the handle causes the descent to be halted immediately. Karabiners, fitted with locking screwgates that have a breaking strain of 3,000 kg, join the separate abseiling units. Rope bags are used during covert work to ease the smooth deployment of a rope during a descent.

◂ **Abseiling down the face of a building remains one of the most popular methods of entry. As seen here, specially constructed wire ladders can also be used to gain access to buildings.**

SPIDERMAN SUCKERS

Spiderman suckers allow a spy to climb up vertical walls with a great degree of safety. The four vacuum pads will adhere to any surface, be it concrete, sandstone, plaster, wood, glass or metal. Each pad is computer controlled, which means that the vacuum effect of each pad can be constantly measured and adjusted. A visual and acoustic warning signal informs the user about the load-carrying capacity of each pad and a fail-safe method ensures that only one pad can be removed at any time.

The unit is operated using compressed air supplied by an air cylinder that is worn on the operator's back. The air cylinder allows approximately two hours of climbing time. The total unit weight is about 25 kg, and offers a carrying capacity of around one metric tonne. Training to use the device takes about one hour and, with practice, the operator can learn to climb overhangs.

"Spiderman" suckers allow an agent to climb any vertical surface.

RAPID-ENTRY EQUIPMENT

Once a spy has climbed or abseiled into position, they will require a means of gaining entry. Rapid-entry equipment ranges from silent hydraulic cutters and spreaders to sledge hammers, crowbars and axes. These tools are commonly referred to as a "Barclaycard", meaning an entry tool that works particularly well for gaining quick access into a building. Most hydraulic tools use lightweight pumps that can be easily carried by a single spy. The following is a selection of the equipment available:

- A **Manual Door Ram** is a hand-held ram designed to force inward-opening doors. The ram is swung against the lock area and imparts a weight load of approximately three tons. It is effective against all but reinforced steel doors and weighs 16 kg.
- A **Door ripper** is a lightweight tool designed to force outward-opening doors. The blade of the tool is driven between the door and the frame in the lock area. A ratchet mechanism helps overcome resistance by allowing the blade to be worked behind the door thus providing increased force.
- A **Hydraulic Door Ram** is designed to force reinforced inward-opening doors. It is supplied with three sets of claws to suit all standard widths of door from 760 mm to 920 mm. The main ram is positioned over the lock area while the secondary ram forces the jaws into the frame. A valve then activates the main ram to force the door open exerting a maximum force of five tons. An 11-ton version is also available.
- The **Hooligan bar** is an American-designed rapid-entry tool. Essentially, it is a one metre metal bar with various attachments. Two or three blows with the bar will take out most of the window; the hooks are then used to pull out the debris or can be used as leverage on sash-type windows.
- **Spreaders** are used to either lift a door off its hinges or to lift or move a heavy object.
- **Jaws and disk cutters** are used to cut or penetrate any form of metal. Some hydraulic models can cut metal bars that are up to 35 mm thick.

Standard tools such as sledge hammers and bolt cutters are used to remove basic doors and locks.

SPECIALIST AMMUNITION

The Hatton round is designed to remove hinges off doors without the risk of ricochet. These rounds contain 12-gauge, semi-solid, frangible slugs weighing 50 gm. They smash hinges from their fixings and cause damage to the surrounding woodwork. These rounds will penetrate vehicle tyres, fire doors that are clad on both sides with metal plate, cell-type doors, 12 mm thick Makralon and armoured glass from a range of 1.5 m. The Hatton ammunition can only be used in Magnum shotguns with three-inch chambers and unchoked barrels.

RIP, 12-gauge, close-range ammunition comprises of cartridges filled with a mixture of micronized CS, an inert powder to add weight and another non-toxic powder. On firing, the compression and friction produces a large amount of carbon dioxide gas when the cartridges exit the barrel of the shotgun. The mixture is propelled towards the target at a very high speed, forming a cloud of incapacitating airborne irritant in the process. The muzzle of the shotgun can be held against any wooden door up to 65 mm in thickness and the powder will blast a hole through it. One round will fill a room that is nine by six metres in size.

THERMAL LANCE

The thermal lance is designed for cutting mild steel, including objects that are underwater. The basic system consists of a 4 metre flexible thermal lance made from Kerie cable, a single three-litre oxygen cylinder fitted with pressure gauges, a pressure regulator, a battery-powered igniter and a three-way valve which switches the system's working pressure on or off. Once ignited, the Kerie cable burns at approximately 60 cm a minute during cutting, and has a maximum cutting time of six minutes. A backpack portable system, that weighing 10.5 kg, is favoured for cutting during a covert entry.

WALL-BREACHING CANNON

The wall-breaching cannon is a device that eliminates the need for using high explosives as a method of entry in a hostage situation. Every wall differs and it is very difficult to judge the amount of explosive required to blow a hole without causing severe debris on the opposite side. In the case of a hostage rescue situation, this could cause loss of life to the hostages.

The wall-breaching cannon was developed to direct a heavy, soft projectile with sufficient velocity to accumulate enough kinetic energy to breach a wall, while instantly dissipating the energy after the wall had been breached. It was discovered that a water-filled plastic container fired by compressed air could fulfil this requirement very adequately. A muzzle-loaded, smooth bore barrel was then designed to launch the container. The rear of the barrel is fitted with an air reservoir that is separated from the main barrel by an entrapped glass disc, which ruptures by electrical detonation at a given pressure, thus presenting instantaneous pressure to

▲ The wall-breaching cannon uses water to smash its way through walls and allows an entry to be made.

◄ The effect on a wall from a single wall breach.

the rear of the projectile. A loose piston stops any air leakage past the projectile, and gives good velocity at pressures between 100, 200 and 300 kg psi. The system can be easily transported in helicopters or estate cars.

LOCK PICKING

All agents need to learn the basics of lock picking as part of their tradecraft. The principle of picking locks is fairly basic, as are lock-picking tools, many of which can be easily made or improvised by a spy. The problem with picking locks lies in the skill. It can take many years to perfect the fundamentals of lock picking, and it is a skill that requires great practice in order to maintain the "feel". A very brief guide to how a spy goes about the lock-picking process is outlined below. **Note**: picking locks in order to gain unauthorized entry into a person's property is illegal and not recommended.

LOCK-PICKING EQUIPMENT

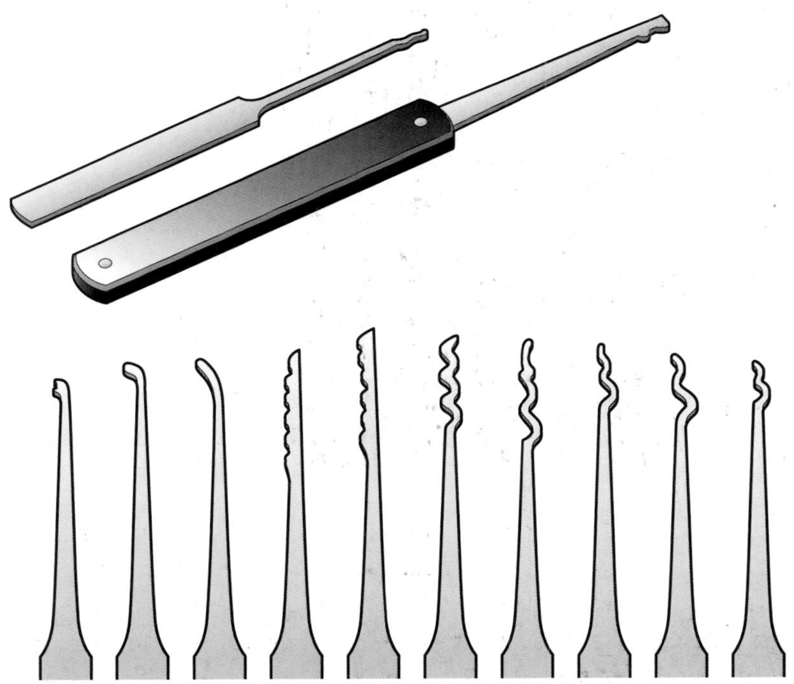

▲ No agent should leave home without taking a lock-picking set.

There is a wide range of lock-picking equipment on the market, and available in stores and especially over the internet. These vary from the simple, traditional lock-picking sets to the more expensive and advanced lock-pick guns. The basic lock-pick set consists of a range of tools including several different lock-pick shapes and a variety of tension bars. Most sets tend to include tools for the removal of key ends that get snapped off in the lock.

There are many different types of lock-picking guns available to the agent – and indeed the general public – but these are generally bulky by comparison to the lock-pick set. Lock-pick guns are available in either manual or electric operation, and all have interchangeable picks. While the Cobra Electronic lock pick is often acclaimed as the ultimate device, the Lockaid gun, in this author's opinion, is more efficient and reliable.

PIN TUMBLER LOCK

Most of the locks manufactured over the past 20 years are of the pin tumbler type. In its basic form, it is a very simple locking device. A series of small pins fit into the inner barrel of a cylinder. The pins are in two pieces, normally at different lengths and are forced into recesses within the inner barrel by a small spring. If a correct key is inserted, the different sized pins are brought into line where their break meets in the outer casing of the inner barrel. This allows the inner barrel to turn freely within the casing and the lock is then released.

Any method of aligning the pins in this manner and turning the inner barrel will open the lock. This can be achieved by two methods – racking or picking the pins. To achieve this, two basic tools are required – a lock pick or a rake and a tension bar.

The pick, or rake, is a flat strip of hardened metal that has had its end shaped to fit into the lock and which advances the pins on their small springs to the required depth.

The tension bar is a flat strip of metal inserted into the mouth of the barrel to employ a minute amount of tension onto it. This process helps seat the pins and turn the barrel.

Note: While most locks turn clockwise, some cylinders may turn the opposite way. If the tumbler's pins will not break, or if they stay broken, it means that tension is being applied in the wrong direction. If several clicks are heard once the tension has been released, it means that the tumbler is being turned in the right direction.

RAKING AND PICKING

There are many different types and designs of lock-picking tools and they can all be used by a spy for different functions. Two are probably sufficient for a spy. Raking is the quickest method of opening a lock. It is fast and straightforward providing that the pin sizes do not change suddenly, such as the combination illustrated below. Before the spy starts he will make sure that the lock is clean and free from any grit or dirt by blowing hard into the lock before attempting to open. Raking involves inserting the pick to the rear of the pins and swiftly snapping the pick outwards, running the tip over the pins in the process.

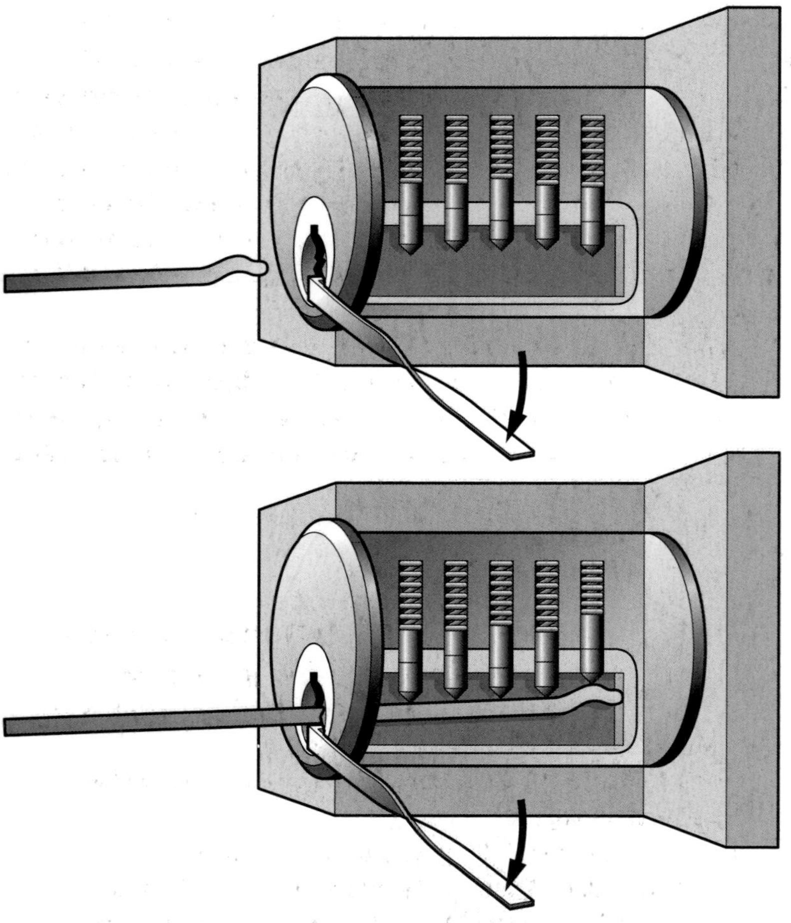

▲ The spy starts raking the lock by placing the pick at the end of the pins. He withdraws the pick, running it over the pins, while maintaining a little pressure on the tension bar.

Prior to doing this, he will insert a tension bar into the bottom of the keyway and apply a slight pressure on the lock's inner barrel. The tension is applied in the unlock direction. The amount of tension exerted should just be enough to turn the barrel once the pins are seated, but not so strong as to bind the pins against the barrel. It is this single "feel" that is the basis of all good lock picking. If the tension is too heavy, the top pins will bind and the shearline will not allow the breaking point to meet. If it is too weak, the pins will simply fall back into the locked position.

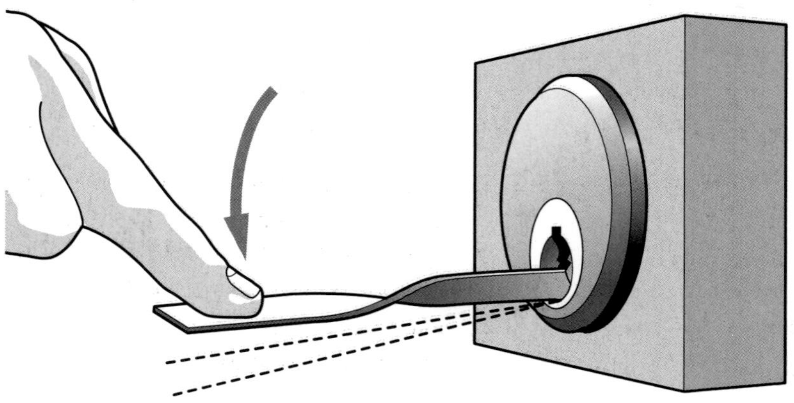

▲ The tension bar simply replaces the key body as a means of turning the tumbler.

When raking, he will have to repeat the operation several times. If the barrel does not turn by the fourth time, he will hold the tension with the tool. He will place his ear to the lock and slowly release the tension. If the pitting sound of the pins falling back to rest is heard, then he has applied too much pressure. If he hears nothing, then he needs to apply more pressure on the tension bar.

The ease with which a lock can be opened will depend on three things: firstly, the length and position of the pins, secondly, the type of tools you use, and thirdly, the make of the lock. Cheap locks will be easier to open than expensive ones. Cheaper locks are generally poorly constructed, allowing for a much greater clearance between the barrel and the body, thus making it far easier to assemble during manufacture. Cheap locks can also have poor barrel alignment and oversized pin holes – both of which make them very easy to pick.

The spy will isten to the pins "popping" and count the number of "pops" for problems pins.

Lock picking is very similar to raking, but it requires a lot more skill, as the pins need to be seated individually. Starting at the back of the lock, the spy feels for the rearmost pin and gently pushes it up. The barrel should move a fraction. Working towards the end of the lock, he will seat each pin in turn until the barrel is released. A combination of one swift rake followed by picking is sometimes the easy answer to cracking the lock.

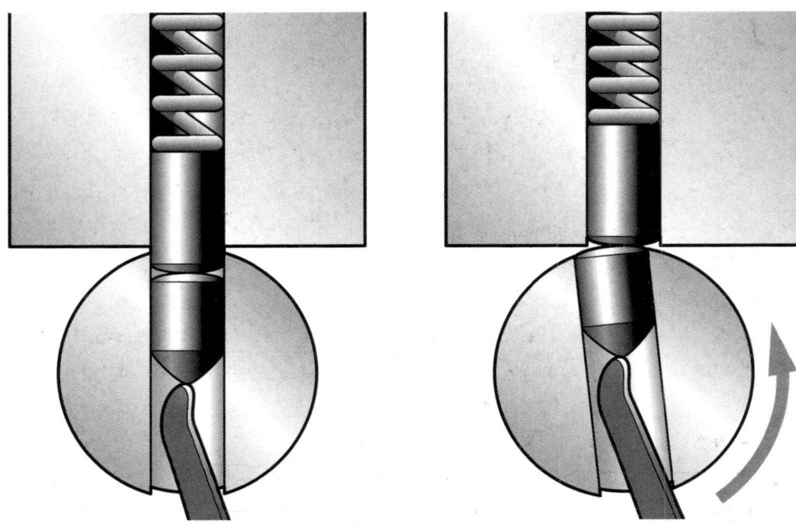

The picks act as the teeth on the key. The pick is pushed into the lock under the pins and used to lift them. Once all the pins reach the shear line the tumbler will turn.

One of the reasons some pins bind or stick is that the top is often mushroom-shaped, causing the top to topple and bind on the shearline. Careful picking will overcome this. One particular make of lock, called Medeco, splits the pins at an angle, making it a very difficult lock to pick.

In an emergency, it is possible to bypass the pins by drilling a line through the lock. The spy will direct the drill towards the top centre of the lock where the tumbler meets the body. He will use a centre punch to provide the drill with a good start guide. A spy will drill straight through for at least three centimetres and will push a screwdriver into the keyhole to turn the lock.

A good agent will develop the feel for lock picking by doing a daily exercise. He will wash his hands and then rub in hand cream. He will massage both hands and fingers for about five minutes and then let them relax. He will find a smooth surface, such as a sheet of glass, (an old picture frame is perfect), and place a few grains of sugar on the surface of it. He will close his eyes and gently use his fingers to locate the grains of sugar. When has done this, he will play with each one of them very gently. He will try to differentiate the size and shape of each grain. This exercise not only helps the spy's feel, but it also helps his mind to visualize what he is feeling. Visualization is the key to understanding the techniques of lock picking.

Note: A spy will sometimes sharpen one end of a pick to a needlepoint. If this point is forced all the way to the rear of a padlock – until it hits the rear plate – the sharpened pick will grip the metal. The spy will try to force the plate either up or down as this will sometimes release the lock without the need for raking or picking.

CLANDESTINE LOCK PICKING TIPS

- The spy will define the lock type and its make during target recce phase. He will purchase a similar lock and practise. If he has the time and the tools, he will cut the lock open and examine its inner mechanics in detail.
- Some locks take time to pick, so a spy will take short breaks to rest his fingers.
- He will avoid scratching the outer face of the lock.
- He will return the lock to its natural state once finished. Leaving the pins in a "floating" position will inhibit the key being placed in the lock.

- Certain keyways are cut at an angle. A spy will make sure he picks to compensate and follow the angle.
- Well-made locks are extremely hard to pick; they are very tight and require a little more tension.
- A "springy" pin is not aligned.
- If the lock is open but the door is not there will probably be internal dead bolts. The spy will probably then use hydraulic spreaders in the door jam, but this is likely to leave large, telltale marks.
- Most locks can be opened, but not all of them are easy. Some people have a natural ability for lock picking, while others struggle.

A LOCK-PICKING SET

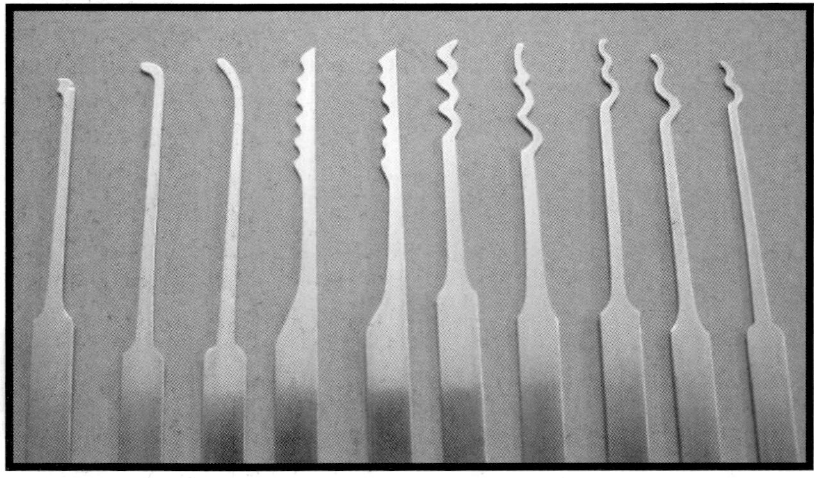

▲ Lock-picking sets must be made from the correct type of metal.

Pick-locks are made from several strips of high-tensile metal and a spy would probably source the material from a model store. Alternatively, a set of heavy-duty feeler gauges that are used by the motor industry could be used. A spy will scan or photocopy a template and print out a copy onto paper. Next, he will carefully cut out the shapes. He will place each individual template onto a separate strip of metal or on one of the leaves of the feeler gauge. For the spy, it is now a matter of grinding down the metal until the desired shape has been achieved. This would be done by placing the metal in a vice and grinding it with a coarse grinder to get a rough outline, before using a fine grinder to finish off. Finally, the spy will remove the paper template to reveal his pick.

The spy will place the tension bar in a vice and heat it with a blowtorch. Once the metal is hot, he will use a pair of pliers to twist the top 15 mm of the bar to a 90-degree turn. He will then bend this over at 90 degrees to form an upright section. To start with he will only need to make three basic tools.

EMERGENCY PICKS

Any type of thin metal can be used by a spy for makeshift picks and tension bars in an emergency. The best two items to use are heavy-duty paper clips or safety pins. These can easily be straightened or bent in order to make all the tools the spy may need to open a lock. However, they are limited to such items as lockers, drawers and filing cabinets, as heavy-duty locks will require a more substantial set of tools to pick.

There are several new types of lock picks available. One is called the fibre pick. This looks and acts very much like a toothbrush, but is used to brush the lock pins instead of teeth. Fibre picks come in a variety of different fibre sizes and strengths, and it is just a matter of selecting the right fibre pick for the purpose. The spy will try several different-sized fibre picks until he finds the one that operates the lock. He will then record the fibre pick number. After a little practice, the operator soon gets to know which fibre pick is right for a certain type of lock. The fibre pick is an excellent tool to use for a clandestine entry, as, unlike hard metal picks, it does not harm the pins and leaves no scratches.

OPENING A VEHICLE DOOR

While there are many ingenious devices available to the agent for opening vehicle doors, this can be achieved by improvisation. One simple way a spy will use to open a vehicle door is to use a strip of plastic banding tape. The spy will take about half a metre in length, and fold this in half, creasing the folded end.

He will use a flat piece of metal to prise the vehicle door open at the top corner (the corner of the door that is furthest away from the wing mirror). This should provide him with enough space to slip in the creased end of the plastic tape. He will push it about 10–12 centimetres, and, using a sawing action, pull the tape down until it is resting close to the internal door release catch. Once in position, he will push one end of the tape inwards while holding the other end firm; this causes the tape to form a bow near the crease. He will work the tape back and forth until the bow is over the release catch. He then pulls the two ends of the tape tight and lifts at the same time. This should unlock the door.

Note: although this is a method used by spies it should not be used by civilians. It is a criminal offence for civilians to break into other people's cars.

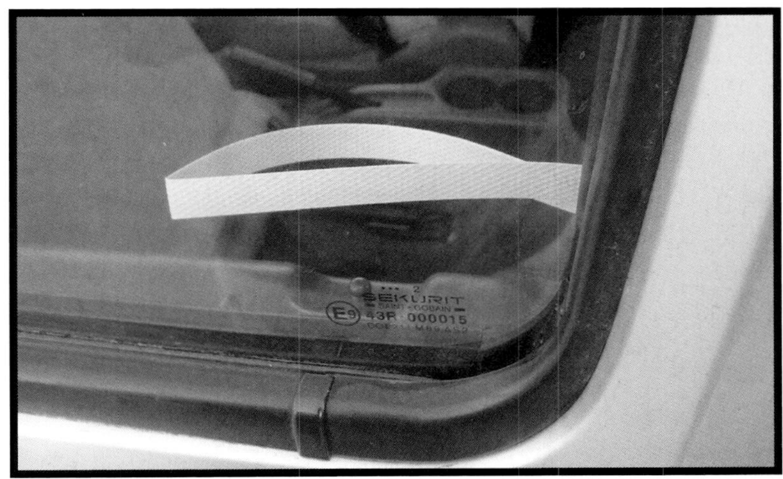

▲ **All that is necessary to open most car doors is a small strip of plastic tape.**

DEMOLITIONS AND EXPLOSIVES

Most agents will have a basic understanding of demolition techniques. However, this type of work is normally left to experts, such as the British SAS or the American DELTA force personnel. While demolitions often form part of the MoE strategy, they can also be used in assassination and sabotage missions. In their base form, most explosives are safe to handle, easy to use, lightweight and have considerable destructive power. From the terrorist's point of view, explosives offer an easy means of causing devastation and, as such, are widely used, mainly in the form of car bombs.

DEMOLITIONS TRAINING

Few people would argue with the fact that the British SAS demolitions wing offers a remarkable course, covering all facets of demolitions and explosives. The practical work progresses slowly from the basic rules of handling explosives to the making of home-made explosives and advanced sabotage. The latter covers in-depth details on destroying places such as oil refineries, railway stations and telephone exchanges. The aim of the SAS demolition course is to teach the pupil how to use the minimum amount of explosive to cause the maximum amount of damage. This requires the use of complex formulas for cutting steel and for the placement of the explosive. The range of explosives now available to the saboteur has increased immensely; technology has led to the development of advanced explosives together with a wide selection of wireless detonating devices.

Modern high explosives are fairly safe to handle; they can be dropped, jumped on and even set on fire, although burning a very large amount is likely to produce enough heat to cause detonation (although we strongly recommend against testing this theory.) Handling modern plastic explosive is a little like playing with plasticine and it too can be moulded into different shapes.

To activate high explosive, a detonator is required; this device comes in two types – electrical and non-electrical. A detonator is a small aluminium tube about 250 mm long and half-filled with a substance known as PETN. The non-electrical detonator is open and ready to receive a length of safety fuse, while the electrical detonator has two wires protruding from it. When a detonator is pushed into plastic explosive and the fuse is lit (or the wires are connected to a battery), the detonator is activated. The speed of a detonator is around 6,000 metres per second; this jump-starts the explosive, which, in the case of PE-4, explodes at around 7,300 metres per second – creating enough energy to cut steel. High explosive only becomes dangerous when both a detonator and an initiation device are added.

MILITARY EXPLOSIVES

The Americans use an explosive compound known as C-4 that is a common variety of military explosive. In its original state it looks very much like uncooked bread dough. As with many plastic compounds, the basic ingredient is cyclonite (cyclotrimethylene trinitramine), which makes up around 90 per cent of the C-4. It also contains a polyisobutylene binder (5.5 per cent) and the plasticizer, the amount and type of which varies with manufacturer.

American military personnel learning the intricate skill of modern explosives. These agents can be seen preparing improvised bombs for use by African rebels.

As with many other modern explosives, C-4 was developed during the Second World War when the original RDX was mixed with mineral oil and lecithin. C-4 is the latest in a line of C (Composition) explosives, all of which were developed after the war.

With the right equipment, bomb construction can be safe and simple for agents.

Variations of C-4 are used widely around the world. The French news agency, AFP, reported that the explosive used in the Bali bombing was of a type manufactured in Israel. As most modern explosives contain a tracer compound, any residue from an exploded bomb in which commercial explosive has been used will enable you to trace the manufacturer.

SEMTEX

Semtex is a Czech-manufactured, RDX-based, plastic explosive. It contains a higher percentage of RDX than the British PE-4 plastic explosive. It comprises 88 per cent RDX and 12 per cent binder/plasticizer. This means that it has a detonating velocity higher than that of the PE-4's 8,500 mps. In the past Semtex was odourless, which made it difficult to detect using the normal type of explosive detection systems. In recent years, however, the manufacturers have introduced a trace element, making it easier to detect and enabling it to be traced forensically.

The explosive first entered the terrorist chain during the 1970s when Semtex H was used at a training school for terrorists in the Crimea by both the Czech intelligence service and the KGB. Elements of the IRA also encountered it during that period in the Lebanon's Beka'a Valley. Thereafter, the Provisional IRA obtained considerable quantities of Semtex H from Libya.

However, successful operations by Irish security forces, who discovered some one-and-a-half tons, subsequently reduced the terrorists' stocks. Since then, the IRA have primarily used Semtex H in the manufacture of munitions – such as mines, mortar bombs and rocket-propelled grenades – while using home-made explosives – such as ANFO (Ammonium Nitrate Fuel Oil) and Re-crystallized Ammonium Nitrate (RAN) – for bombs.

NEW EXPLOSIVE

A new family of explosives has been developed. The Americans for example, have produced Astrolite A-1-5 that is the world's most powerful non-nuclear explosive. It is extremely safe to handle and offers a versatility not available from conventional hydrocarbon explosives. Astrolite was discovered during research into rocket propellant during the 1960s, when ammonium nitrate was mixed with anhydrous hydrazine. This produces Astrolite G, but, when a fine aluminium powder is added, it forms Astrolite A-1-5. It is reported that this liquid high explosive can be safely sprayed from aircraft, and, upon contact, soaks into topsoil to a depth of a few centimetres. With a life of only four days, it is reputedly undetectable, except by chemical agent sensors, and can subsequently be detonated remotely by personnel who are equipped with the necessary initiation device.

It is also believed that the Chinese have developed a new form of high explosive. Two British radical Muslims carried out a suicide bomb attack on a club in Tel Aviv, resulting in the deaths of three people and leaving 50 others injured. One of the suicide bombers managed to escape, but not before he left behind an amount of explosive. Upon investigation, the Israeli analysts concluded that the explosive came from a leading Chinese explosives manufacturer. The explosive was constructed of a new compound, which was both odourless and lightweight. It is believed that this new explosive is also able to pass through airport X-ray machines without being detected.

GENERAL SAFETY RULES

In general, modern explosives are very safe to handle, but certain safeguards should always be in place. For example, charges should be moulded around knotted detonating cord (three knots equal a detonator) as this provides a much better safety margin. It also allows the agent to make up and place a number of charges, and to connect them to a ring-main without the use of a detonator. The detonator is only applied at the last moment when the initiation set is attached.

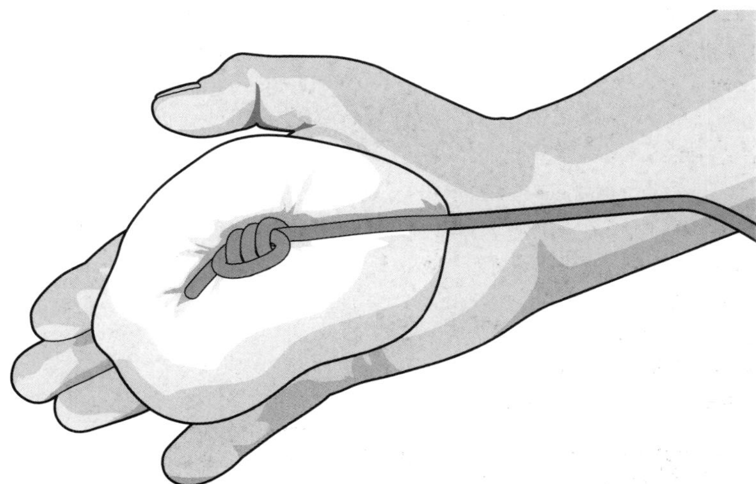

▲ One safety measure is to use knotted detonation cord instead of a detonator.

Explosives

- No smoking when using explosives.
- Training stores should not be mixed with live explosives.
- Live detonators should not be in close proximity to explosives.
- Explosive should not be tamped with metal instruments.
- The minimum amount of personnel on-site when connecting detonators to explosives.

Detonating Cord Safety Rules

- Sharp curves should be avoided when constructing long runs.
- Detonating cords should only cross at junctions.
- Long suspended sections should be avoided.
- A 15 cm tail should always be left.
- The minimum distance between each charge and the main line should be 50 cm.
- The angle of charge should be at least 90 degrees to the main line.
- Waterproof tail ends should be used if the charges are in place for any length of time.

Detonators

- Detonators should be kept away from the explosive until the initiation is required.
- Detonators should be kept away from heat sources.
- The wires from electrical detonators can be short circuited by twisting them together.
- Initiation set can be prepared prior to marrying it with explosives.
- Knotted detonating cord (three knots) can be used in make-up charges.

Conventional explosive is a solid carbon-based or liquid substance which, when stimulated at the correct speed (through the use of a detonator), converts almost entirely to gases of both intense pressure and temperature.

Explosives are divided into two forms, low and high. Low explosive is ignited by a flame and the resulting explosion is a rapid burn that forms combustion. Low explosives contain their own oxygen, so the burning is extremely quick and produces stable gases of high temperature and high pressure. While low explosive provides gases that have a pushing or lifting effect, they are not normally capable of cutting steel. One example of a low explosive is gunpowder.

High explosive generally has a detonating speed in excess of 8,000 metres per second, making the base substance very stable. This substance must be detonated. Detonation involves the almost-instantaneous decomposition of the compounds that make up the explosive. This process is started by an initial shock and the effect is twofold. A small detonator is fired to produce a shock wave that travels outwards from the point of initiation through the explosive and into the target. This shock wave imparts an energy that is strong enough to cut steel. This is followed by the gases, which achieve intense temperatures and the pressure to provide the push. The power of an explosive is expressed by the rate at which it detonates – it is called detonating velocity.

One important aspect of both high and low explosives is the tamping effect. Tamping simply involves containing the gases and allowing them to build to the point where they must break out. The better the tamping the better the effect. A normal firework, for example, explodes with a loud bang only because of the cardboard housing which forms the tamping. Empty the contents of a firework into a loose heap and the compound will simply burn.

▲ The secret of a good explosives expert is knowing where to place the charges.

When detonation occurs, the gases will escape via the least line of resistance away from the direction of initiation. Various materials can be used for tamping – water, clay or sandbags are all good examples.

An agent or a Special Forces team may be required to attack any number of different targets – railway lines, oil refineries or, as in recent years, a drugs warehouse. Every target presents different problems, and circumstances will often govern the chosen method of attack. If time is required for a getaway, concealment of the charges is critical, and this may take precedence over the best place in which to position them. For this reason, complicated formulas have been worked out in order to obtain the best results.

Despite the number of different formulas for cutting steel, concrete and wooden targets, the one overriding factor when it comes to all explosives is the formula "P" for plenty. It is a phrase that is widely used during the SAS demolition course. An SAS soldier will have to learn many technical formulae in order to apply the right amount of explosive to a particular type of explosive target. The "P" for plenty factor is used to err on the safe side.

Another basic component used in explosives is the main circuit of a demolitions set-up, which links all the charges. Most targets that require the use of explosive need to be cut in many different locations at the same time and in order to achieve this, a ring of detonating cord is passed from the initiator around every charge and back again to the initiator. This is called the "ring main". The shock waves then travel both ways; if one end should fail, the other will detonate the charges.

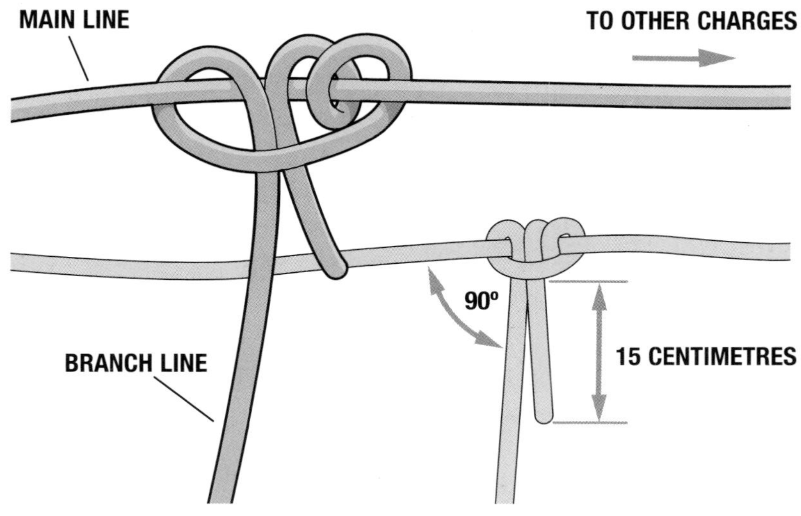

▲ Targets that require several charges can all be connected by a ring main. This allows all the charges to go off at the same time.

Most formula explosives need to be placed in a certain shape and placed flush to the target. With steel beams, it is a simple matter of covering every surface of the "I" beam. When it comes to cutting round metal, the explosive charge may be halved and shaped into a saddle or a diamond, to create a shear effect.

While all precise explosive charges are formed into a shape, the actual "shaped charge" itself normally refers to an inverted cone-shaped explosive charge. The principle behind the charge is based on the inversion of shock waves once the explosive has been initiated; this forms the explosive force into a pinpoint cutting charge which, due to its standoff, can penetrate thick steel. A shaped charge can be found in most anti-tank missiles, but it is also used during demolitions for depth penetration.

FRAME CHARGE/FLEXIBLE CUTTING CHARGE

MoE will often involve cutting through a reinforced door, a window or a wall. To do this, an explosive frame charge is required. Originally developed on a wooden frame to which a metal-cased explosive was attached, the simple aim was to blow a hole through a wall. The size of the frame depended on the area that was to be blown, and the amount of explosive used depended on the thickness of the wall. The early frame charge has since been developed by Royal Ordnance into a cutting explosive known as "Blade". This is a linear-shaped charge made from DEMIEX 200 – an EDX-based plastic explosive that detonates in excess of 7,500 metres per second. Internally, copper produces a shaped charge jet that, on initiation by an L2AI/LIA1 detonator, cuts with fine precision. Blade is fitted with a self-adhesive strip so that it can be attached to the target. The charge is covered by a sheath of close-cell foam. Blade comes in five different weights and thicknesses, each of which can be cut with a knife and tailored to a design of cutting charge. Blade can be incorporated into a conventional explosive ring-main with charges linked together with detonating cord for simultaneous detonation.

▲ Some targets require specialist explosive such as a frame charge which is designed to blast a hole in a wall.

EXAMPLE

A military operation is planned against an enemy city, the first wave of which will be an air strike in order to eliminate the enemy's radar and communications. It would be advantageous if the city lights were off when the raid took place. To accomplish this, the agent is given the task of demolishing an electric power station. The first thing he has to establish is the type of generation equipment used; in this case, there are three inline gas generators, two of which are operational with one in reserve. The most effective way to destroy all three is to attack them in exactly the same place, in this case the weakest point that is common to each individual generator.

While the destruction of a large facility such as a generating station may seem demanding, it can be achieved by just one agent, although for security purposes several would be better. The answer is to produce three identical saddle or diamond charges depending on the size of the parts the agent needs to destroy.

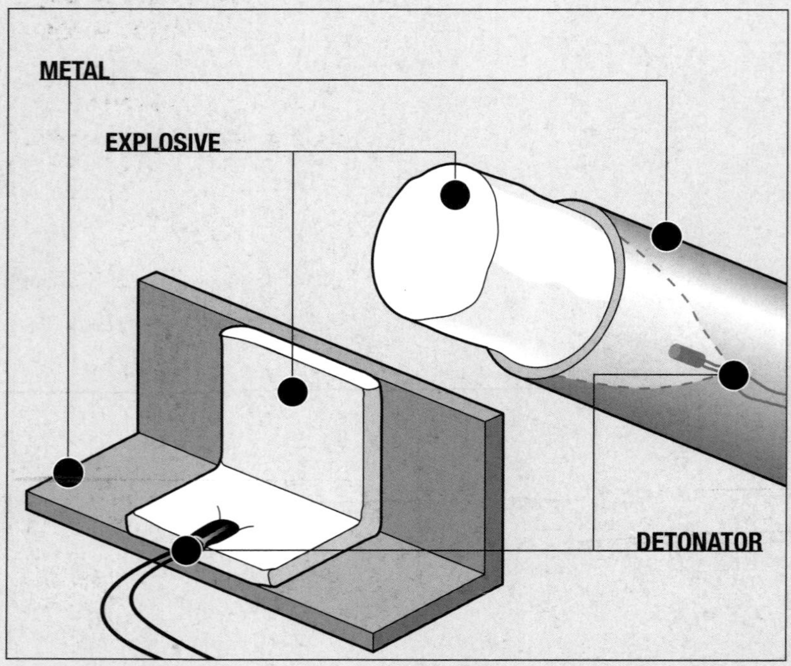

▲ The saddle charge is formulated and shaped to cut round steel bars. Where flat metal is to be cut the explosive is calculated and placed as shown.

DIAMOND CHARGE

The diamond charge can be placed, for example, on half-exposed round steel targets such as the cast housing for the generator drive shaft. The charge is diamond-shaped, with the long axis equal to the circumference of the target, i.e. the shaft, while the short axis is equal to half the circumference. The thickness of the charge depends on the shaft material – for high carbon steel, for example, it should be 2 cm thick. The best way to make a diamond charge is by using sheet explosive.

Calculation:

The generating shaft is 15 cm in diameter.

Therefore the long axis is 47.6 cm. Rounding up to the next highest figure, the long axis of the charge will be 48 cm. The short axis of the charge will be 25 cm. You will note the "P" for plenty rule is applied by rounding up the figures to a whole number. Initiation will take place from simultaneous points of the short axis.

Providing that the agent manages to attach all three charges and can effect simultaneous detonation, the generators should be put out of action. While the diamond charge may not actually destory them completely, the buckle effect on the running shafts will destroy both the generator and the drive motor and the drive casing on the reserve machine will take at least a week to repair.

$$\frac{22}{7} \times \frac{6}{1} = \frac{132}{7} = 18\frac{6}{7}$$

▲ The complexity of explosives formulas ensures the agent only uses the minimum amount of explosives to achieve maximum effectiveness.

IMPROVISED EXPLOSIVES

Fortunately for an agent, military explosive can be purchased from many countries and its commercial equivalent can be found in any quarry around the world. In most countries, there are laws to control explosives. However, these are enforced more through safety than for any other reason. In addition, high explosive is extremely simple to make, with many DIY stores and supermarkets stocking the basic ingredients.

Even when no explosive is available, combustible material, such as gasoline, is always accessible and one gallon of gasoline has the blast power of seven pounds of high explosive when detonated. The use of fertilizer and diesel oil could make up the bulk of a bomb which, in order to achieve the required detonation speed, could then be initiated by commercial explosive. The secret to making any explosive is having a basic understanding of chemicals and chemistry.

When attached to a friendly guerrilla or revolutionary unit, agents and Special Forces units are sometimes required to carry out demolitions work without the use of military explosives. Training friendly forces in another country often involves teaching them the basics of improvised explosives. A good example of this was when American agents trained Al Quaeda soldiers during the Russian invasion of Afghanistan.

Although it is possible to construct a detonator, as a rule, improvised high explosive mixes require a commercial detonator in order to make them work. To this end, most terrorist organisations use a “booster” for the improvised mix. Without the booster, there is a very good chance that the home-made explosives will not detonate due to the crude method of its construction.

CACHE

When working in a foreign country, it is not always possible for the intelligence agency to provide the agent with the correct equipment. To overcome this problem, spies, agents and covert operators are often guided to an existing cache in order to retrieve supplies such as ammunition, weapons or explosives. Caches were widely used by the OSS and the SOE during the Second World War, thus allowing agents to carry out prolonged operations. Modern caches are housed in purpose-built, watertight containers, which can be hidden for years. They are generally deployed during times of peace or when the opportunity arises. During the first Gulf War, hundreds of caches were planted in Iraq, both by the United States and the British. These secret locations are then carefully recorded. Traditionally, however, cache reports are notoriously poor and even if they are well documented, the cache usually evades the seeker.

Note: explosives are dangerous and should only be used and created by experts. In most instances the use of explosives by members of the public is illegal.

CHAPTER

5

By land, sea and air, the modern espionage agent must be placed among the enemy in order to complete their mission.

INFILTRATION

Missions that involve simple car, plane or train travel to a close-by country are few and far between in the current political climate. More common these days is an infiltration operation by an individual or team of agents. Access to many politically volatile countries via "safe" infiltration means is much more limited than a few years ago. What is the implication? Today's spy is going to have a huge amount of work to perform to even get into a territory, before they may start the search for operatives there. Information and technology are the keys to the door.

Planning any clandestine operation requires expertise, experience and a complete understanding of the operational task. For the agent or the Special Forces unit this is generally expressed as the "mission". Before any mission can start, however, there needs to be planning phase; this will involve acquiring knowledge of the terrain, the prevailing weather conditions, the disposition of enemy troops and, finally, the implementation of infiltration and ex-filtration methods. These will depend very much on the "mission" statement and may involve penetration into enemy territory, by land, sea or air.

Infiltration involves the positioning of personnel and supplies into a denied area, making maximum use of deception while they are there to avoid detection as they enter the operational area. The best way of achieving this is usually by air, although this may not always be possible if the enemy employs radar, or if the target area is over jungle terrain, where there may be nowhere to land or drop parachutists. The alternative is to insert personnel by land or sea, but insertion by this method will invariably mean confronting formidable defences, such as coastal patrols, border patrols or minefields. In instances where an enemy has good border and internal security, the means of entry for an agent is restricted. However, modern stealth techniques are advancing rapidly.

The infiltration of an agent or a Special Forces unit normally requires the use of ships, submarines or aircraft, and the intelligence agencies will often work in conjunction with the appropriate military service when it comes to clandestine operations; the different modes of transport used for these operations are normally manned by members of the Special Forces units who have been trained specifically for such work.

FACTORS INFLUENCING INFILTRATION MEANS

- The type of mission to be undertaken is the first thing that is taken into consideration when it comes to selecting the means of infiltration.
- The enemy dispositions may restrict certain means of infiltration. A heavily defended border would make entry by vehicle impossible, for example.
- Unfavourable weather conditions can seriously affect air or sea operations.
- The topography of the land needs be considered. Land infiltration through mountainous or heavily forested areas will make movement very slow. In addition, high mountains force aircraft to operate at heights where they become susceptible to enemy radar.
- Hydrographical factors, such as tide-data, the depth of offshore water and the location of reefs and sandbars can all influence the selection of water as a means of infiltration.
- The number of personnel being infiltrated may be a limiting factor, as will the distance if part of the way is to be made on foot.
- The equipment required in order to carry out the operation successfully may also determine the infiltration method selected.

SPECIAL FLIGHTS

▲ The mighty C130, for many years the backbone of western armies.

The British have two Special Forces flights within the RAF, which form a part of 7 and 47 Squadrons respectively. Aircrew within both flights are trained for special operations – namely low-level deep penetration into enemy airspace and the delivery and extraction of Special Forces personnel. The Special Forces Flight of 7 Squadron is based at RAF Odiham in Hampshire. It is currently equipped with the UK-designated HC.2, a variant of the Boeing Vertol Chinook twin-rotor heavy-lift helicopter that can be fitted with four (two forward and two aft) M134 pintle-mounted mini-guns. Within the next two years, however, the flight will be re-equipped with the HC.3. This will be the first special operations-dedicated aircraft to be purchased by the British armed forces. The same aircraft is currently being operated as the MH-47E by the US Army's 160th Aviation Battalion, who are better known as Task Force 160. It features a glass cockpit, terrain-following, forward-looking infra-red (FLIR), built-in fast-roping brackets, and four .50 calibre Gecal mini-guns.

The Special Forces Flight of 47 Squadron is located at RAF Lyneham in Wiltshire. It is equipped with the C-130K variant (designated C.3 in the UK) of the Hercules transport plane, fitted with an in-flight refuelling probe, electronic counter-measure systems and chaff and flare dispensers. Both the latter are designed to provide a measure of defence against enemy air defence systems. The aircraft are currently being equipped with dedicated night-vision goggles (NVG), that are compatible with cockpit lighting. It is reported that four of the C-130J Hercules on order for the RAF will be for dedicated Special Forces use and that they will be upgraded to the same specification as the MC-130E Combat Shadow which is currently utilized by the special operations squadrons of the US Air Force. This aircraft has terrain-following radar and FLIR systems, an integrated avionics package for long-range, low-level covert ops – which enable precision insertion and re-supply of Special Forces – and NVG-compatible cockpit lighting.

Finally, M Flight of the Fleet Air Arm's 848 Squadron, equipped with the Commando Mk.4 variant of the Westland Sea King helicopter, provides support for the maritime counter-terrorist role.

Over the years the CIA has set up many proprietary companies to provide air support for its agents. During the Vietnam War, they used Air America to support operations throughout the whole of southeast Asia. Most of the pilots were ex-military and they flew a whole range of fixed-wing aircraft and helicopters. Their missions ranged from re-supply to drug running and reconnaissance; much of their work was highly dangerous. Other airlines used by the CIA include SETCO, Evergreen, Hondu Carib and Arow Air.

▲ The 160th Aviation Group supports American agents and Special Forces.

Both Delta and SEAL team 6 are supported by the 160th Aviation Group. While American agents and Special Forces have call on the USAF Special Operations Aviation Command, in reality, most of the clandestine work is carried out by the 160th. Established in 1981, the 160th Aviation Battalion, or Task Force 160, is generally known as the "Night Stalkers", mainly due to their extremely professional night-flying capabilities. In 1990, they were officially designated as the 160th Special Operations Aviation Regiment. It uses a variety of helicopters and fixed-wing aircraft, such as the HH-60G "Pave Hawk", the AH-6G "Little Bird" and the advanced RAH-66 Comanche. There are three battalions, two of which are based in Fort Campbell, Kentucky, and one at Hunter Army Airfield, Georgia. They all specialize in armed attack, insertion, extraction and all three are generally dedicated to the Special Forces.

STEALTH TECHNOLOGY

▲ Stealth technology is now a major aspiration of many Western armies.

Stealth is the simple act of trying to hide or evade detection. It is not so much a technology as a concept that incorporates a broad series of technologies and design features. Stealth technology is a prime goal for most military organizations, including the intelligence agencies. Stealth enables you to sneak up on the enemy undetected. Militarily, this catches the enemy unawares, giving you the advantage of surprise while seriously impeding both the enemy's resistance and defences. In the past, this would have been achieved through camouflage and concealment, but modern stealth technologies mean that in many instances the enemy cannot respond at all, because they simply cannot see you.

The demonstrations of stealth aircraft used during the Gulf War of 1991 illustrated their effectiveness. Since that time, however, current aircraft stealth technology has been seriously weakened by the introduction of particle filter methods for detecting stealth-built aircraft. Despite this, stealth aircraft and sea vessels continue to be built, most relying on shape, and the use of non-metallic materials called "composites". Radar-absorbing paint is also used, especially on the edges of metal surfaces, while other technologies also help reduce the signature.

Stealth clothing has been a desirable asset on the battlefield for a long time, especially for Special Forces infiltrating behind enemy lines. This has been achieved to some degree. One British firm in Cardiff discovered that shredded foil, similar to that used for insulation, could be used to blank out any thermal or infrared signature. This provided perfect night-time camouflage for both soldiers and tanks. However, the insulation material caused the body to overheat and the suits had to be fitted with a cooling system. Despite these drawbacks, the race is on to produce a real day-night stealth system that is suitable for both men and machines.

BORDER CROSSING

▲ Border crossing can provide many obstacles from mines to dogs and machine gun towers.

Because of the line-of-sight principle, both sea and air defences are highly successful when it comes to detecting approaching ships and aircraft. Insertion by either of these methods will require a final covert method in order to cross the border into enemy-held territory. An alternative is to cross the border by foot or by vehicle. Depending on the country, this avenue may also prove difficult, though.

One of the most formidable borders in the world is the one that divides North Korea from the South. This consists of a whole range of defences that include high walls, tripwires, minefields, barbed wire, ditches and armed patrols. It is not an easy place to cross. In 1978, information filtered through to the South Korean intelligence agency that the North were busy digging a tunnel under the border in preparation for an invasion. The North Koreans built the tunnel by digging and dynamite-blasting for more than 1,500 metres, slipping beneath the Military Demarcation Line in the process. The tunnel reaches some 437 metres into South Korea, at an average depth of 73 metres. Once its presence was discovered, the North stopped digging and the tunnel was sealed off with concrete. Although this was the only tunnel discovered, it is thought that several others existed.

Elsewhere in the world, the Israelis are currently building a massive wall in order to stop the Palestinian suicide bombers from entering their territory. The first 110 km of it is already finished and the total 350-km fence will be completed by the end of the year. The wall is extremely high and will be backed up by a combination of fences, walls, ditches, patrol roads and electronic surveillance devices.

◂ While basic in concept the new Israeli wall, designed to keep out Palestinian suicide bombers, is proving very effective.

Most modern borders are guarded by high-tech defences such as seismic sensors that silently detect movement. Other systems involve a series of poles between which several layers of invisible beams are emitted. Breaking these beams sends off a silent warning. These devices work well in principle, but they do have a number of limiting factors. Few of them can differentiate between animals and people and they can also be vulnerable to attack.

OVERCOMING SENSORS

Any sensing system, whether it is an electric fence or a seismic device, can be overcome by creating an error of reasoning. The easiest way to approach this is to have a long piece of rope with a large metal object tied to the end. This is thrown at the electric fence or onto the area where known seismic probes are buried. The result will be an investigation by the border patrol. Some borders are monitored by camera, so make sure that you operate from a concealed position. Once the patrol has come and gone, repeat the process. If this is done during a storm, or during a period of high wind activity, the border guards will eventually turn off that sector or ignore the alarms, putting it down to faulty equipment.

LAND

Land is the least desirable means of infiltration and is usually limited to short movements by individuals or small detachments. However, it is the best alternative if an infiltration team is confronted with difficult terrain and poor weather conditions, as land infiltration has its greatest chance of success when the enemy's border defences are inadequate, or if the combat zone is fluid. Insertion by land is carried out either on foot or by using a vehicle. While the final entry point may require the agent to move on foot, the distance from the start point to the actual operational areas will normally require the use of a vehicle. The most widely used modes of four-wheel transport are the Light Strike Vehicle (LSV) and the basic military jeep, such as a HMMWV (High-Mobility Multipurpose Wheeled Vehicle) or a Land Rover.

ADVANTAGES OF LAND

- It is simple and requires minimal support.
- You have flexibility if you are compromised by the enemy.
- You have the ability to change routes as operational needs dictate.
- You can remain comparatively covert if you travel at night.

DISADVANTAGES OF LAND

- It is slow compared to infiltration by air.
- You are subjected to long-term exposure to the enemy.
- There is a limit to the amount of supplies and equipment that can be carried.

Light Strike Vehicles

▲ The light strike vehicle (LSV) looks the part but its performance leaves much to be desired

LSVs were used by both the American and British Special Forces during the Gulf War, although neither of the two British variants were considered to be as reliable as the Land Rover 110. The Longline LSV has a VW 1.91 flat-four, water-cooled petrol engine, while the Wessex Saker has a Perkins Prima 80T 1.993, four-cylinder, water-cooled, turbocharged diesel.

Although there are four-man LSVs, most are designed to carry two or three soldiers, with stowage for the crew's kit in panniers and racks along the sides of the vehicle. Despite their "beach buggy" appearance, the vehicles are not cheap and additional items – such as Kevlar armour and ignition retardant fuel tanks – come as extra. After initial trials during their warm-up training in the Gulf, the SAS decided to drop the LSVs from the mobile fighting columns.

HMMWV (Humvee)

▲ America's new multi-purpose all-terrain vehicle, the "Humvee", has already seen action.

The Humvee – real designation Highly Mobile Multi-purpose Wheeled Vehicle – is a high-mobility, multi-purpose military vehicle produced by AM General Motors. The introduction of the Humvee in 1985 provided a single-platform, multi-mission truck that has become the mainstay of the US military. It is the basis for over 65 types of combat vehicle, from delivering ammunition to supporting special operations units and is acclaimed as the world's most versatile, dependable and mobile tactical wheeled vehicle. AM General has produced more than 175,000 Humvee's for the US and more than 50 for other friendly international forces.

Land Rover

▲ A Land Rover being used by the British SAS. This picture was taken deep inside Iraq weeks before the allies attacked. They roamed at will, looking for the elusive Scud missiles, or any other opportune target.

For many years, the British SAS used a specially painted Land Rover known as the "Pink Panther". In the Gulf War, the SAS used the existing Land Rover 110, modified with extra stowage and weapons mounts, including smoke-dischargers mounted on both the front and rear bumpers. These vehicles were sturdy enough to withstand several months of hard operations behind enemy lines. Land Rover now produces a Special Operations Vehicle based on the 110 used by the SAS, retaining many of their special features and modifications. The result is a long-wheelbase, all-terrain weapons platform that is capable of supporting a wide variety of weapons, such as the Milan Mark 19 grenade launcher, and .50 heavy machine gun.

Range Rover

▲ An early Range Rover being driven by a British Brixmis team operating in the former East Germany. These intelligence teams did much to keep tabs on the Russians during the Cold War.

Range Rovers were first used by the SAS following the formation of the anti-terrorist team in November 1972. The government sanctioned the purchase of six Range Rovers and a team of SAS soldiers were sent to the factory to collect them directly from the assembly line. The characteristics of the Range Rover, which at the time was only one year old, were ideally suited to the role – the drop-down tailgate allowed for easy loading and the vehicle itself could be used in an Immediate Action (IA). Twenty-five years later, the Range Rover is still used by the SAS, having been adapted as a main assault delivery vehicle. Platforms and ladders attached to the Range Rovers can carry the assault personnel directly to the required height of an aircraft door or building window.

The Range Rover was also used by Brixmis. This organization started at the end of the Second World War, when Germany was divided into two major zones, the East and the West. Brixmis stood for the British

Commanders'-in-Chief Mission to the Soviet Forces in Germany. The organization was set up on 16 September 1946 under the Robertson-Malinin Agreement between the Chiefs of Staff of the British and Soviet forces in occupied Germany. The idea was to have a mutual exchange of liaison missions that would monitor the troop activities in both German zones, i.e. the Russian mission would monitor military activity in West Germany, while the Brixmis mission would monitor similar activities in East Germany. Brixmis provided most of the intelligence on Soviet and Warsaw Pact military equipment, including some outstanding photography. The Brixmis agreement remained in force until the eve of Germany's reunification on 2 October 1990.

The function of Brixmis was to shadow all troop movements, especially those of the Russians inside East Germany. In order to do this, specially adapted vehicles were used. These had four-wheel drive with strengthened suspension, plus half a tonne of armoured plating under their belly. Fuel-tank capacity was increased and the internal windows were blacked out so that the occupants could take photographs without being observed. The Range Rover was selected by Brixmis in the 1970s as it provided a good observation platform through the sunroof. This was particularly good for the RAF section, who could observe Soviet airfield activity some distance away.

Daimler Benz GS-182 Snowmobile

▲ Snowmobile used to cross the Arctic tundra. This vehicle is ideal for infiltration under such conditions.

Clandestine operations often take place in Arctic conditions where the only means of transport is skis or a snowmobile. The GS-128 has become the industry standard for many Special Forces units operating in Arctic climates. This high-speed military snowmobile is capable of negotiating the roughest terrain at speeds of over 100 kmh. The GS-182 uses a CH002 burning system that can be switched to a high-output electric motor for quiet running. The snowmobile normally carries two people – one man steering, the other armed.

SEA

Infiltration by water includes the use of surface and subsurface craft. Up to the point where the personnel disembark from the parent craft it is a secure and economical means and, if the operator's target area is close to the coast, then it is an infiltration method that should be considered. Many countries have a long and open coastline that is difficult to defend against small clandestine teams. While radar and sonar may pick up large surface and subsurface shipping, smaller vessels can slip by undetected. Small rubber craft can carry both a four-man unit and their equipment right up to the beach; they can be launched from submarines, boats and helicopters and can be powered either by engine or paddle. Their one disadvantage is lack of speed if the infiltration unit is discovered on the beach.

▲ The first hostile area for many infiltration teams is the shoreline. This must be secured before a clandestine landing is performed.

Divers offer a better alternative, as they are hidden up to the point where they emerge from the water. If discovered, they can simply return to the protection of the water. However, divers require specialist training. Their main advantage is their ability to attack coastal targets, such as shipping harbours. As is the case with small rubber craft, they can be delivered by submarine, ship, helicopter or by parachute.

Surface swimmers can also be delivered in the same way, and, for the most part, will remain undetected. They require no specialist training and are hidden until they reach the coastline. One method tried by the British Special Forces was to use surfboards to assist their approach. These were delivered by submarine some four miles off the coast of Norway. The swimmers simply lay on the boards, with their packs secured between their legs at the rear. They achieved good speeds and did not suffer from tired limbs, as would have been the case if they had swum.

ADVANTAGES OF SEA

- Operations can be long range.
- The weather has little or no effect up to point of disembarkation.
- Evacuation is possible with a "no-go" operation.
- Operational briefings can continue en route.
- Large quantities of supplies can be delivered.

DISADVANTAGES OF WATER

- The visibility of the mother craft.
- Vulnerability to enemy shore defences during landing.

Canoe

During the Second World War, the canoe became one of the mainstays of infiltrating agents and Special Forces during covert operations. The "Klepper" two-man collapsible canoe is still used by both the SAS and the SBS, although its use has declined somewhat. This German-designed canoe, which proved to be much lighter than the previously used Cockle II, came into service in the 1950s and remained until the mid-1980s. Despite its primitive design, the frame is made from hardwood Mountain Ash and Finnish Birch, the deck is covered with self-drying cotton woven with hemp and the hull material has a core of polyester cord surrounded by rubber. It is ideal for clandestine insertions onto hostile coastlines. It can also be carried ashore and camouflaged by its crew. The canoe's skin is loose fitting until "airsponsons" that run under each gunwale are inflated. It measures 5.2 metres long, 89 cm wide and 61 cm deep and will pack into a bag 69 cm x 58 cm x 20 cm.

Extensively used during the Second World War, the canoe has fallen from grace mainly due to its slow speed and poor load carrying

Assault Boats

There are several small boats available for clandestine operations. Many countries use a mixture of medium inflatable boats (MIBs), rigid inflatable boats (RIBs) and fast interceptor craft (FICs). Of these, the most remarkable is the Halmatic Very Slim Vessel (VSV). In addition to normal boats, Special Forces also operate a range of small landing craft air-cushion vessels (LCAC). Both the Americans and the British use a similar 12-metre-long hovercraft capable of speeds up to 30 knots across water and land. They can carry up to 16 fully equipped personnel or two tonnes of stores.

▲ Assault boats can be used for river or open sea operation. Their construction, once flimsy, has been greatly increased. This picture shows an armoured rubber assault boat.

The Rigid Raider assault craft, which replaced the older inflatable Gemini, is much speedier when it comes to disembarking the men on board. Fitted with four lifting points, the craft can be transported by helicopter and is powered by one or two 140 HP Johnson outboard motors with a top speed of 37 knots. It is capable of carrying nine fully equipped men with a coxswain. The Rigid Raider claims to be virtually unsinkable. Both British SBS and SAS have recently taken delivery of 16 new RTK Rigid Raiders that have been specially adapted for them and are constructed from Kevlar that gives them a hull weight of less than 300 kg. This means that a four-man patrol can carry the craft, even when it is fitted with twin 40 hp motors.

The Americans use the Rigid Raiding craft (RRC) that is some eight metres long and capable of carrying a section of eight marines with full kit. The new Mk 3 RRC has a 240 BHP inboard diesel engine giving it a speed of more than 30 knots when fully laden to a range of 120 nautical miles.

One of the most impressive high-speed delivery platforms is the Halmatic VSV. This vessel is wave piercing and offers high speeds in rough weather conditions. It has a very low radar signature and no heat spots, making it hard to detect. Additionally, its linear acceleration causes no discernible hump speed. It has the ability to carry high payloads with very little loss of speed over a considerable range. It is air-portable by both fixed-wing and helicopter. The Halmatic VSV comes in two sizes, at 16- or 22-metre lengths. The latter is capable of carrying up to 26 passengers, including equipment. Due to its stealth capabilities, the Halmatic is widely used for seaborne covert insertion by many countries.

▲ High speed, wave piercing boats such as the British Halmatic or this American TK used extensively to insert agents.

Marine Assault Access System (Moby)

▲ The MOBY system helps agents gain access from the sea surface.

The marine assault access system has been designed to provide access from the water to elevated marine structures and vessels. The system, which raises a flexible ladder and grapple, is particularly suitable in operations where silence and stealth are of paramount importance. The device is compact, extremely portable and has proven operational advantages that are unsurpassed by any other existing equipment. One diver can deploy the device to the target with ease, and its compact design allows mobilization within seconds, together with easy manoeuvrability during operation. The system is used by both the SAS and the SBS when quick access is required and when the use of traditional ladders or grappling hooks is not feasible.

Divers

Divers are used to perform many roles, such as sabotage on shipping, covert entry to offshore facilities and underwater searches prior to VIP visits, to name but a few. Normal SCUBA equipment is unsuitable for military operations, as bubbles indicate the diver's position. Modern systems include the electronically controlled Divex closed-circuit, mixed-gas, rebreather stealth system. This compact unit is both easy to operate and maintain, giving the diver up to four hours of submersion, depending on the underwater activity. The Divex system is ideal for covert operations as it leaves no traceable bubbles, either below or above the surface.

▲ **Divers can be inserted by air, or delivered to the area by submarine or boat. This flexibility makes them extremely useful as they remain unseen until they reach the shoreline.**

Divers can carry a wide variety of equipment, as can be seen by a new underwater digital camera which was designed for the Navy SEALs. This digital camera can be used up to a depth of 50 metres and can take either IR or normal spectrum pictures. The camera, which can be switched between single frame and video mode, connects to a specially modified diving mask that allows HUD-style viewing. The camera also has a standard 10x telephoto option, a wide-angle option and can be fitted with a fibre-optic flexi-lens. The memory can store up to 30 minutes of video or 500 still images, thus making it an invaluable asset for reconnaissance purposes. Other diver systems include the deployment of underwater GPS navigation and communications.

UNDERWATER COMMUNICATIONS

It is difficult for divers to communicate underwater without the use of an umbilical line. However, a new system has emerged that makes such a task easier. The diver speaks into a mask, or a mouthpiece-mounted microphone (various microphone-earphone configurations are possible to fit a range of masks, breathing systems and even re-breathers). The voice signal is converted into an ultrasonic-equivalent signal within the diver unit, amplified and is then applied to the transducer. The transducer resonates to produce a sound signal of optimum wavelength that can be carried long distances through water.

Transducers of a similar wavelength (approximately 31 KHz) mounted on the other diver units or lowered into the water on a cable from the surface supervisor, receive and transmit such signals. The received signals then undergo the reverse process to yield the original speech signal in the diver's earphone or in the supervisor's headset and speaker.

Through-water communications are still in their infancy and are affected by many factors. Some of the energy is absorbed and converted to heat (attenuation) and some of the energy is scattered by fish, seaweed and bubbles (diffraction). In addition, the surface and the seabed will affect the sound intensity by reflecting the sound back into the water, causing interference. Temperature variations in the water may refract the signal. The sound intensity of through-water communications will, therefore, be affected by both the speed of sound in water – 1,480 metres per second – and variations in water temperature.

Special Forces divers also practise parachuting into water for both clandestine entry and counter-terrorist operations. A water jump differs from a land-based parachute drop in as much as the parachutist must disconnect from the parachute prior to hitting the water. This allows him to swim free of the parachute should it cover him on landing. Agents can also be inserted by parachuting into the water before swimming to the operational area.

Convertible High Speed Surface/Submarine Vessel

▲ Submersibles offer a perfect way of getting a team close to a ship or oil rig installation undetected. It has the ability to travel on or below the water surface.

This is a fast offshore boat that has deflatable-re-inflatable hull tubes and waterproofed, pressurized operating systems. While on the surface, it serves as an offshore rigid hull that can be converted into mini-submarine mode in less than 20 seconds, even while underway. The boat is powered by outboard motors on the surface and by electric propulsion when it is underwater. It is capable of carrying up to six combat divers plus their equipment and standard fuel bags. The surface range of the vessel is 100 nautical miles at a speed of over 30 knots; underwater, it has a range of ten kilometres and a speed of around two to three knots. It can dive to a depth of 100 metres. The underwater performance can be greatly improved by substituting standard lead acid batteries with silver zinc units. The boats can be deployed from a road trailer towed by a large car, a submarine, a patrol craft or by helicopter, all of which will greatly extend the combat diver's range and operational capabilities.

These sub-skimmer craft are uniquely versatile, making them indispensable for reconnaissance, surveillance, agent handling in hostile territorial waters and waterborne clandestine missions of many kinds where divers are involved. It offers an ideal method of approach for such scenarios as oil rig and ship-at-sea assault operations, delivering divers covertly to the target.

Submarines

▲ As can be seen here, submarines have been used for many clandestine infiltration operations.

Small submarines are used by many countries, mostly for the purpose of gathering information and for carrying out clandestine operations. North Korea developed a small submarine with the express purpose of inserting groups of Special Forces into South Korea. On one occasion the South Korean Navy captured a North Korean 70-ton Yugo-class submarine that had become entangled in fishing nets off the port of Sokcho. The same region saw another incident when, in September 1996, another North Korean mini-submarine ran aground in Kangnung. A firefight ensued and most of the 24 crew and Special Forces were killed or drowned.

The Americans developed the Mark-XII ASDV, an advanced swimmer-delivery submersible that carries combat swimmers and their cargo inside a fully flooded compartment. The vessels are launched from larger host submarines. The Mark-XII is fitted with a range of advanced sensors, including sonar, IR, UV and thermal imaging. Navigation is provided by the MUGR, a miniature, underwater GPS Receiver. The Mark-XII is used by all Navy SEAL teams, the British SBS and the French GIGN. The Russians use the Sirena-UM manned torpedo, as well as small submarines. In October 1981, the Swedish Royal Navy detected Soviet submarine activity near their navy base at Karlskrona. Similar activities resulted in depth charges being dropped, in order to force the vessels to the surface. Investigations by divers and from sonar devices discovered the tracks of several small submarines apparently working from a mother ship. Comparable activities were also discovered off the coast of Scotland.

AIR

Insertion by air is particularly good, as it allows the operators to be lifted directly into enemy territory; it also provides a rapid means of extraction. Most air operations require a landing site (LS), where troops are infiltrated by helicopter and are actually placed on the ground, or a landing zone (LZ) for dropping personnel by parachute. In instances where a helicopter can infiltrate an enemy area but not actually land – such as in a jungle or built-up areas – personnel would normally reach the ground by rope. A similar system can be used for "hot extraction" from a hostile area. While these are the main methods for clandestine operations, many others have also been tried.

Helicopters, although noisy, have the capability to deliver agents directly to a given point thus avoiding borders. They can either land or hover while troops descend by rope or ladder.

ADVANTAGES OF AIR

- The speed of delivery.
- The accuracy of delivery.
- Short exposure to enemy.
- The ability to perform simultaneous missions.

DISADVANTAGES OF AIR

- Vulnerability to enemy air defences.
- Reliance on favourable weather conditions.
- The risk of possible injury to personnel and damage to equipment.
- The possible compromise of DZ or LZ.

Fast Rope Insertion/Extraction System (FRIES)

FRIES is a fast rope insertion and extraction system. This enables personnel to be lowered into places where the helicopter can not land.

▲ Some systems can deliver or snatch up to 10 personnel.

FRIES is a rope, manufactured from high-tensile, multifilament nylon, that incorporates eight nylon rope loops in the last few metres. This rope is suspended from a helicopter and the soldiers can attach themselves to it. The system is designed to be non-rotating, enabling problem-free deployment. It also has a high extension capability, can absorb dynamic loads and ensures a smooth descent when troops need to be "snatched" out quickly.

FRIES enables agents and Special Forces personnel to be deployed into, and retrieved from, dangerous situations by simply clipping themselves and their equipment to the loops with quick-release karabiners. The system increases the deployment speed of airborne forces and reduces the risk of helicopter and personnel vulnerability. A Blackhawk helicopter, using a two-rope system, is capable of delivering a group of 12 men in a little over ten seconds once it is in the correct hover position.

Individual Flying Platforms

During the 1960s, the American military researched the effectiveness of jetpacks. Although they achieved a working model, it was not deemed to be efficient as the amount of fuel required to fly it was incompatible with the amount of time a soldier would be required to fly it. There has been some renewed interest in individual flying frames in recent years, but, at the time of writing, no working model is available other than the powered paraglider.

The Para Hawk is a propeller-powered platform that uses a parachute as a means of flying. Although the idea was first developed in the United States, it was then taken up by a retired SAS pilot, who started designing his own aircraft near to the SAS headquarters in Hereford. The first models were ready during the mid-1980s and the SAS carried out field trials on the Microlight aircraft, as it was then known. The aircraft consisted of a three-wheeled trike and a Ram-Air parachute. The trike had a rear-mounted engine, the propeller of which was housed in a protective cage. The pilot was strapped into an open seat in front of the engine where his right foot would control the accelerator. Revving the engine would speed the trike forward, forcing the ram-air parachute that was attached to the trike to act as a wing. The Microlight required little room for take-off and landing, added to which a pilot could be taught to fly it in less than a day. Despite the fact that it was almost impossible to stall the Microlight, SAS trials were discontinued after several messy landings. Newer forms of backpack-mounted Para Hawks manufactured in the United States are much improved and their evaluation is still ongoing.

▲ This is one of the original Para Hawks used by the British SAS. It was found in a small airfield in Namibia, close to the CIA's abandoned intelligence centre.

Parachuting

▲ Parachuting provides a good method of infiltration.

Most Special Forces are taught basic parachuting skills. A normal course involves making four low-altitude 60 metre (200 ft) static line jumps, seven normal 240 metre (800 ft) jumps and two water jumps. Standard British parachutes are the PX1 Mk 4, the PX Mk 5 and the PR7 reserve, all of which have an equipment suspension strap and an integral jettison device. Once on the ground, the parachutist can jettison the canopy and clear the Drop Zone (DZ) immediately. All parachutes, whether they are American, Russian or British, are very similar in style. However, modern parachutes open very quickly, thus allowing for a lower altitude jump.

HAHO (High Altitude High Opening)

HAHO is a method of air insertion where the parachutist exits the aircraft at a height of up to 9,000 metres (30,000 ft) and opens his parachute immediately. Using a RAM Air parachute, the parachutist can then glide for several miles; this allows the parachutist to infiltrate the enemy area undetected, across borders or major enemy concentrations. GPS can be used in-flight to track the individual's position in relation to the earth's surface and assess drift to the LZ area. In the early 1980s, the British SAS dropped a team of free-faller parachutists off the south coast of England using the HAHO principle; all of them made it into France.

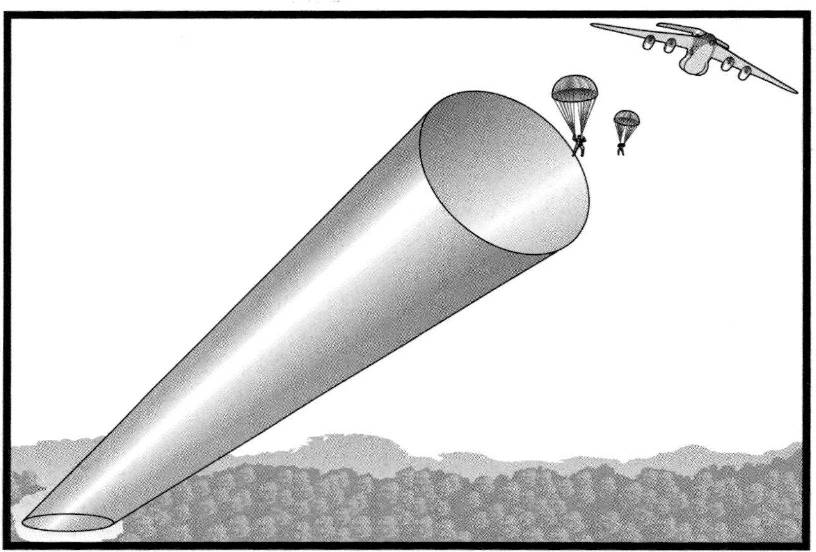

▲ HAHO means the parachute is deployed very high. The height allows them to drift up to 30 kilometres, an idea way of crossing borders undetected.

HALO (High Altitude Low Opening)

In a HALO drop, the parachutes do not open until approximately 750 metres (2,500 ft) above the ground. This requires the parachutist to free-fall for most of the way – a method of infiltration that is fast, silent, accurate and tends to land the team in the same spot. The speed of descent in free-fall is fast, but may vary slightly with each individual and the position he holds. For example, in a normal "delta" position, he will descend at a rate of 200 km per hour (120 MPH), but in a "tracking" position this may well increase to 280 km per hour (175 MPH).

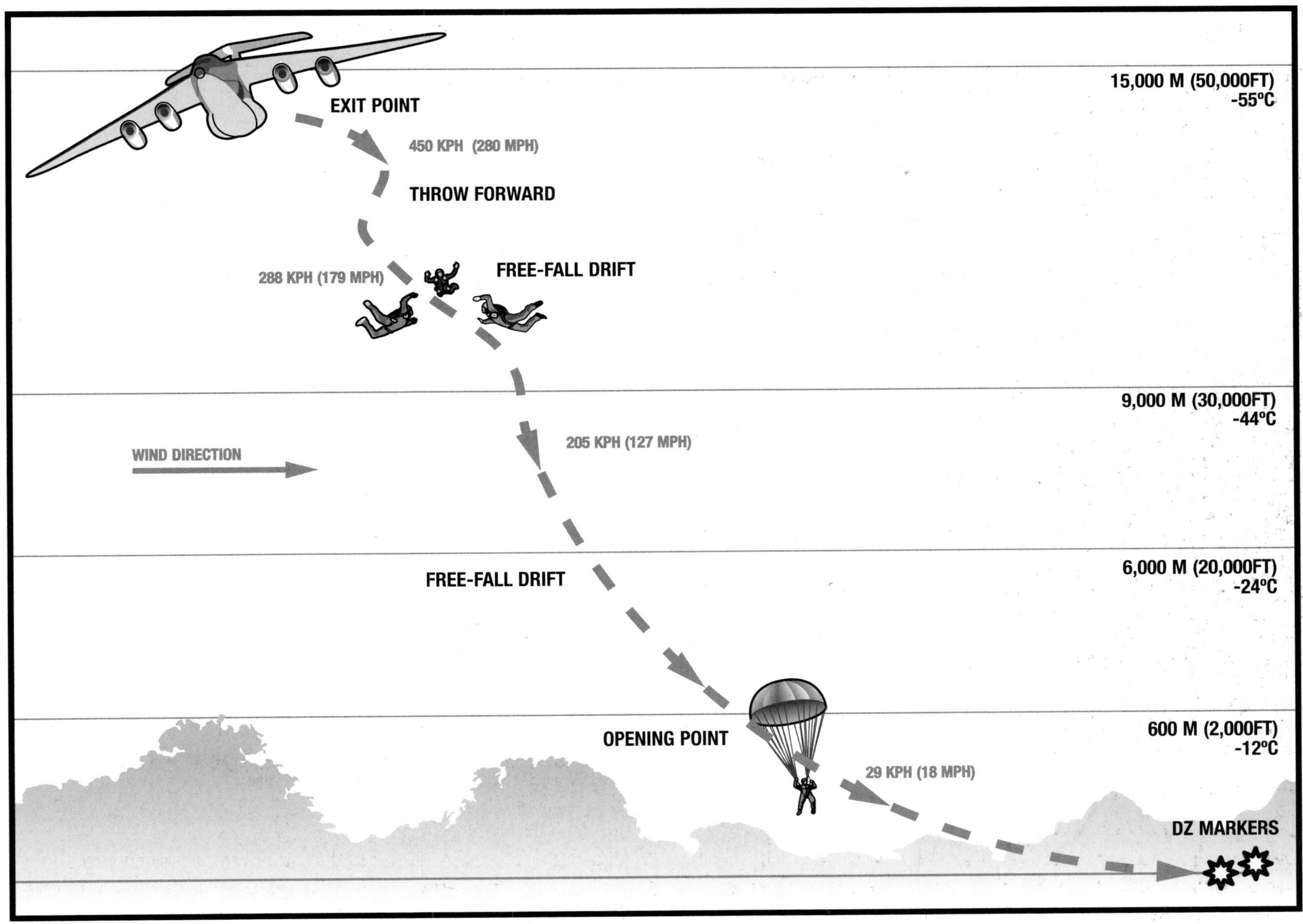

▲ HALO is mainly used for putting agents or Special Forces into a specific area. They fall to a height of around 600 metres which leaves them enough time to manoeuvre the chute into the DZ.

CHAPTER 6

'Black Ops' are used by governments the world over. They give them the power to stabilize or destabilize a country. They may be used to remove another governing power or to make way for an invasion.

CLANDESTINE OPERATIONS

A clandestine operation is any form of operation undertaken by one government against another foreign power. These operations are normally conducted in enemy-held, enemy-controlled or politically sensitive territory. Operations that are both covert and that entail a final assault mode are known as "black ops". These are normally carried out by military personnel seconded to an intelligence agency, and are approved with the purpose of stabilizing or destabilizing the current ruling power, or to prepare the ground for an invasion.

The means by which this is done may include: supporting an opposition group, assassination, sabotage, deception or psychological warfare. Most of these would be carried out by indigenous forces who are organized, trained, equipped, supported, and directed to varying degrees by both agents and Special Forces personnel. The overall aims are to weaken the opposing government by seizing material assets, damaging or destroying installations and changing the political environment. This aim is achieved by psychological operations that are backed up by subversion, deception and direct action – including incursion, ambushes, sabotage, assassination and the small-scale raids.

▲ A member of the American Special Forces working with the Northern Alliance in Afghanistan.

As has been seen many times throughout history, it is sometimes advantageous to openly show support for the overthrow of a particular government. However, this normally leads to full-scale war, which is extremely costly in terms of both material and manpower. For this reason, clandestine operations remain the instrument of choice for the policy makers as it remains the best way to avoid all-out war. The type of operation that is undertaken will be determined by the country involved and that country's current political situation.

On a political level, no government will ever admit to carrying out clandestine operation, and most will adopt the "holier-than-thou" approach. Despite this facade, the intelligence agencies of many countries have murdered, raped, lied, cheated and pillaged in order to achieve their objectives. They have conducted brainwashing experiments, spread disinformation, carried out massive human-rights violations, established brothels, bribed or assassinated political leaders and supported guerrilla groups in order to topple governments. If the threat is seen to be a "clear and present danger", then the appropriate action will be sanctioned.

All of the major intelligence agencies have a department that caters for clandestine operations. In Great Britain, for example, members of the SAS, both present and retired, are employed to carry out the security services' "dirty work", both at home and abroad. In the United States, members of the 1st Special Forces Operational Detachment (DELTA) are used. In 2002, President Bush signed an intelligence order authorizing the CIA and units such as Delta to overthrow, capture or indeed kill the leader of a foreign country. Since the 9/11 attack, assassination is very much back in vogue. As we saw in the Moscow theatre assault of 2002, the Russians use the Alpha teams with great success, while the Israelis have Mossad and other subordinate groups.

RUSSIAN ALPHA

▲ **A member of the Russian Alpha team firing a V-94 large-bore anti-material sniper rifle. As seen here, the rifle can be equipped with a new POS-13x60 telescopic sight.**

The new Russian Federation also has a number of small units it can use for clandestine operations. One is the Special Assignment Centre of the Counter-Terrorist Department of the Federal Security Service. The Centre includes two special assignment units, Alpha and Vympel, and numbers between 1,500 and 2,000 men. The Foreign Intelligence Service has its own special forces. The unit was formed in 1998 and is called Zaslon. Different reports estimate that its numerical strength is between 300 and 500 servicemen.

Alpha is an elite KGB unit whose main functions are counter-terrorism, VIP protection and Special Forces operations – roles that bear more than a slight resemblance to those of the British SAS and with a structure that is almost identical. Little was known about Alpha prior to the coup against President Gorbachev in 1991. During the course of the coup, they reversed the direction of it by standing alongside Yeltsin rather than attacking him in the White House of the Russian parliament, as they had been requested to do by the coup directors. As a consequence of their actions, they gained a very high level of access and the unit itself is no longer under the direction of the KGB. A unit known as "Bravo" works under a similar direction, but its exact role has not been identified.

There are many unconfirmed stories about the Alpha unit, almost all of which have a violent ending. One early story relates how they tricked hijackers into believing that they had left the Soviet sphere of influence and that if they landed they would be landing in a neutral country. They had not. As the aircraft came to a halt, it was rushed by members of Alpha. So fearsome was their reputation, most of the hijackers preferred to commit suicide rather than surrender.

This hard-line approach has also been effective in other areas. One example is Beirut. While the American and British were spending their time on elaborate deals – such as the arms-for-hostages debacle – Alpha allegedly used a much more direct line of reasoning. When, in October 1985, three Russian diplomats were taken hostage by Sunni Muslims, Alpha was dispatched to deal with the situation. Before they reached Beirut, one of the men, Arkady Katkov, had been shot dead and his body had been dumped on waste ground. It did not take the local KGB agents long to identify the perpetrators and, once they had done so, they then spent time tracking down the perpetrators' relatives. Alpha proceeded to arrest some of these as counter-hostages and, just to show that they could be just as menacing, they cut off several body parts and sent them to the kidnappers with a stern warning that other bits would follow if the kidnapped Russians were not released immediately. The tactic worked and since that time no other Russian has been taken hostage by any of the warring factions in the Middle East.

Alpha continues to be a highly secret organization with very little information as to its operation forthcoming. One operation involving Alpha took place on the evening of the October 23, 2002, in a Moscow Theatre. Some 50 Chechen guerrillas had seized the theatre and taken more than 600 hostages. The Alpha assault involved the use of a new type of gas, and although the outcome was successful and the terrorists were neutralized, more than 200 hostages died.

More recently, on September 3, 2004, in Beslan, southern Russia, Chechen rebels, aided by Arab sympathizers, struck again. This time they took over a school, taking more than 1,500 children and staff hostage. Days later and after several hours of confusion, an explosion took place in the school gym that caused the roof to collapse. At that point the Alpha units were sent in. After 12 hours of gunfire, during which half-naked children could be seen running from the building, all resistance was ended. The death toll was put at more than 150 staff and children with 646 (227 of them children) hospitalized. Twenty militants were killed, including ten Arabs who had assisted the Chechens.

Officials claimed the high death toll was due to the rebels setting off an explosive device in the gym. A Russian bomb expert said the gym had been rigged with explosives packed in plastic bottles strung up around the room on a cord and stuffed with metal objects. These had been detonated when members of the Alpha team had tried to enter the gym.

AMERICAN DELTA FORCE

▲ Two members of Delta who helped rescue CIA operatives who were trapped in a prison riot during the Afghan war.

American clandestine operations are normally handled by Delta Force. This unit was started by Colonel "Charlie" Beckwith, an American Special Forces officer who had served with the British SAS for several years. Beckwith's idea was to raise a unit capable of deep-penetration raids, such as prisoner-of-war rescues, hostage rescue and intelligence gathering for larger operations. By early 1978 the unit numbered some 70 men, enough, Beckwith thought, to start counter-terrorist training. This included CQB shooting, assault techniques, MOE and medical training and those who were not parachute-qualified were sent to jump school. A special "House of Horrors", equivalent to the British "killing house" was constructed in order to simulate rescue hostage scenarios. A defunct 727 aircraft was made available, allowing Delta to work on anti-hijack procedures.

On 5 November 1979 the American Embassy in Iran was seized and Delta was ordered to respond. Intelligence for the operation was plentiful, with the CIA and the media both producing satellite images and film footage of the embassy in an effort to highlight the problems involved if any rescue were attempted. Delta took full advantage of all this and prepared itself accordingly; eventually they came up with a workable plan. The rescue attempt failed. The fault, however, lay with the American military administration and not with Delta. Direction and authority for Delta missions has since been tightened, as one American general put it: "It's no good having the best sword in the world if the user cannot wield it correctly." Things have since improved and Delta has gone on to show its capabilities in many roles, including both the Gulf and Afghan Wars.

In addition to Delta Force, the Americans also use a unit known as SEAL team 6. Formed in October 1980, the unit totals some 150–170 men, now based in Dam Neck, Virginia. They have been fully integrated with Delta since 1980, but still retain the capability to operate as an individual unit. This unit almost always accompanies Delta on special operations.

INCREMENT – SAS

The Increment are a selected group of SAS and SBS personnel who are loaned to the intelligence agencies (MI5/MI6) to carry out clandestine operations. Most members of the Increment have spent time with the SAS Counter-Revolutionary Warfare Unit (CRW). This unit can trace its origins back to the Keeni Meeni operations against the Mau Mau terrorists in Kenya in 1953 and special activities organized in Aden. The SAS formed its own CRW

Cell, with the special purpose of developing techniques to counter terrorism. From its inception, CRW was a vision in how the modern-day SAS soldier was to develop. The SAS already have some of the best surveillance skills available, and their extensive military skills are fine-tuned by internal courses. These include the use of improvised explosives and sabotage techniques, advanced shooting skills and training to support guerrilla warfare. Highly developed insertion techniques can be accomplished, using anything from high-altitude parachuting from commercial aircraft to being launched from the tube of a submarine. Today, the duties of the SAS CRW units span the world. They infiltrate enemy territory, gather intelligence, carry out ambushes, undertake demolition work and sabotage and act as bodyguards for VIPs. Some of this work is purely military while the rest is tasked through the Increment.

▲ **Operatives deep within Iraq. Their clandestine operations helped locate many of Saddam Hussein's henchmen.**

OVERSEEING POWERS

It is often difficult to say who actually authorizes a clandestine operation. In theory, the final decision should rest with the country's leader, with the factual support coming from a government body, such as the British Joint Intelligence Committee (JIC). The JIC is the main office for intelligence and they direct and provide the tasking for the Secret Intelligence Service (SIS) – which includes MI5, MI6 and GCHQ. These three are responsible for domestic, foreign and signals intelligence respectively. As most clandestine operations take place overseas, they fall under the control of MI6, who, in turn, will task the appropriate agent or the Special Forces (the Increment) to carry out the operation.

The American equivalent is the CIA, which, since the collapse of communism, has carried out some major restructuring. Clandestine operations are normally tasked by the Directorate of Operations (DIC) along with the Counter-Intelligence Centre (CIC) and their human intelligence (HUMINT) requirement tasking centre. The Clandestine Information Technical Office supports these type of operations and analyses the intelligence.

PLANNING A CLANDESTINE OPERATION

Once authority for an operation has been received, the next phase is the planning. While the objective defines the mission, there are other subordinate aspects to take into account. These are command and control, and the security of the unit. A clandestine unit's plan will take the following factors into consideration:

- All clandestine operations will be based on the best and most up-to-date information available.
- The best method of infiltration and exfiltration will be chosen to ensure arrival in the operation area is undetected. If there is any doubt deceptive measures will be considered.
- Agents make use of the smallest unit possible to accomplish the mission – decreasing the possibility of detection.
- Agents use all forms of stealth technology to remain undetected. They will remember the basics of camouflage, concealment and light and sound discipline.
- Agents utilise the cover of darkness and night observation devices (*see* Surveillance Section). They know that the enemy will also have detection devices.
- Once the intelligence has been analysed and a plan has been developed, rehearsals will be carried out. These are very important, especially when it comes to the on-target phase – the moment when the unit is close to the enemy. Rehearsals also highlight any problems in planning and

clarify points for the team. Contingency plans will also be rehearsed.

- Agents make sure that all communication devices are working. and they make plans for "lost comms".
- Agents will hold an inspection and purge all team members of any incriminating evidence. They remove clothing labels and any items that may lead to identification.
- Agents should isolate photographs and name every member of the team in the event that they are be captured. This will be handed over personally to the (S2) or desk intelligence officer.

SAS IN OMAN

A typical example of a good clandestine operation is illustrated by the actions of the British SAS in the Middle Eastern state of Oman. In 1969, the oil-rich state was constantly under threat from internal communist activists who controlled most of the southern mountains. The old Sultan, Sayid bin Taimur, had hung onto power as his feudal country fell into rebellion, and refused the advice and offers of assistance from his British advisors. Although not a military man, the old Sultan had decided to send his only son Qaboos to the Royal Military Academy at Sandhurst, where he became commissioned into a British Regiment. His return home was not a joyous one. The young Sultan could see the plight of his country and argued for change. His father's answer was to restrict his son's movements and to accuse him of becoming too "westernised".

The situation in Oman deteriorated until 23 July 1970, when the Sultan Qaboos opposed his father, aided by the young Sheikh Baraik Bin Hamood. During the coup, the old Sultan shot himself in the foot and was hastily bundled into an aircraft and flown to England. Qaboos took control, but the situation was far from stable. To ensure Qaboos' safety, four SAS soldiers, trained by CRW wing, were dispatched to protect him. Within weeks, part of the British Army Training Team (BATT) were operating in the country, tasked with raising a local army and defeating the communist-backed guerrillas.

On the recommendations of Lieutenant-Colonel Johnny Watts, commanding officer of 22 SAS, a five-point strategy was put into operation.

- To establish an intelligence operation.
- To set up an information network (Phy Ops).
- To provide medical aid.
- To provide economic aid.
- To raise an army from the local people who would fight for the new Sultan.

The latter of these was considered to be the most important as it involved committing some 60 SAS soldiers. Unbeknown to the British public, the SAS remained in Oman for five years, fighting a bloody, covert war, which cost the lives of many – including 15 SAS soldiers.

EXECUTIVE ACTION (ASSASSINATION)

Author's Note: It is difficult to write about assassination, mainly due to people's perception of the subject. Many people and organizations claim that all life is sacred and, in an ideal world, it would be. We do not live in an ideal world, though. We live in a world where terrorists kill and mutilate without thought, where thousands die as a result of drugs and where children starve or are forced into prostitution – this is not an ideal world, this is reality. What if the American government had an opportunity to assassinate the terrorists who piloted the aircraft on 9/11 two days before it happened? Would their deaths have been justified? The second problem lies in the definition of assassination. Is the clandestine sniper team, whose task it is to assassinate the head of a terrorist organization, so different from the pilot of a bomber who kills hundreds of people? The first will return home under a cloak of secrecy; the second, on the other hand, will return home to a hero's welcome.

Whatever your individual standpoint, assassinations will continue to occur, just as they have in the past. Therefore, in writing this section, my goal is to illustrate the many factors of assassination and not to answer any moral questions.

ORIGINS

In seventh-century India, many passers-by would be grabbed and strangled by the Thuggee (hence the word "Thug") in full view of the public. Centuries before that, many a Roman citizen would find themselves a prisoner of the Jewish zealots, who had a terrible habit of cutting the throats of their victims, again in public. During the 11th century the "assassins", a drug-crazed Shi'ite sect, would hide along the routes frequently used by their enemy and ambush and murder them. Similar acts can be traced to all continents throughout history, most of which were carried out to instil a sense of fear within the local community.

Modern-day assassination can be described as the planned killing of a person whose death would provide positive benefits for society as a whole – this is termed an "executive action". Assassination may or may not be morally justifiable, as it depends on the self-preservation of one element of society over another. In general, assassination has done little to change the course of history. Even where it has, the change is usually for the worse. The British SOE trained an assassination team that parachuted into Prague and killed the acting German Governor of Bohemia and Moravia, Reinhard Heydrich. Heydrich was a remarkable linguist, a wonderful musician and a superb bureaucrat; he was also a staunch Nazi. Nevertheless, his assassination in the spring of 1942 resulted in the deaths of thousands of innocent Czechs. Likewise, the assassination of Archduke Francis Ferdinand is reputed to have started the First World War.

If we are to believe what we read in the newspapers, President Bush signed an intelligence order in 2002, authorizing the CIA and related Special Forces to overthrow, capture or kill President Saddam Hussein. If the Americans can carry out an assassination, why can't anyone else? It is a subject that provokes all manner of debate, a debate that is hampered by society, laws and the will of its people. Some would claim that we should not stoop to the level of terrorists, while others argue that taking a life by assassination smacks of a "big brother" government. Terrorist organizations rely on this irresolution among the general populace to tie the hands of governments and restrict their ability to counter the terrorist problem. There is also the argument that, while assassination removes certain individuals within an organization, it does not guarantee the removal of the organization itself. Finally, assassination has the ability to bite back, i.e. you kill our leaders and we will kill yours. One nation that has continued to refine the skills of the assassin is Israel. They systematically hunted down all of those responsible for the Munich Olympic massacre in 1972 and assassinated them. Israeli policy on assassination continues to this day and many countries, including the United States and Britain, are requesting copies of the Israeli handbook on the subject.

For the most part, the general public as a whole is unaware that an assassination has taken place, being led to believe that the victim has died in an accident or of natural causes. In addition, it is sometimes difficult to differentiate between assassination and suicide. If the government version says suicide and there is no proof to say otherwise, then suicide it is. All the same, circumstances can be interpreted in several different ways.

CLANDESTINE BOMBING OF RAINBOW WARRIOR

▲ **It was 11.38 when the peace of the night was shattered as two limpet mines planted by the French divers went off, sending *Rainbow Warrior* to the deep.**

In order to cite an immoral clandestine operation, I quote the bombing of the ship *Rainbow Warrior*, the pride of the Greenpeace organization, an international body concerned with conservation and environmental issues. *Rainbow Warrior* arrived in Auckland and was tied up at Marsden Wharf. On the night of 10 July 1985 shortly before midnight, two high-explosive devices attached to the hull of the *Rainbow Warrior* detonated within the space of a few minutes. The force of the explosions was such that a hole 2.5 metres in size was opened below the waterline near to the engine room. The vessel sank within minutes.

Fernando Pereira, a crew member and the official photographer, was drowned while attempting to retrieve photographic equipment from his cabin. The later discovery of an abandoned rubber Zodiac dinghy and an outboard motor, and the sighting of a blue-and-white camper van, led to an interview with a French-speaking couple two days later by the New Zealand Police and their subsequent arrest on 15 July. Although they were initially identified as Alain Jacques Turenge and his wife Sophie Frédérique Clare Turenge, inquiries revealed their true identities to be Major Alain

Mafart, aged 35, and Captain Dominique Prieur, aged 36. Serving as commissioned officers in the French Special Forces, they had been detailed to assist members of the DGSE (SDECE) Intelligence Service to ensure that the much-publicized voyage of the *Rainbow Warrior* to French territorial waters to disrupt the French nuclear test program simply did not happen. The vessel had to be damaged to such an extent that repairs could not be completed in time for the voyage to begin.

Though the French operation succeeded in part, it turned out to be a publicity disaster, as the intelligence service had failed to extract Mafart and Prieur directly after the attack, although the French intelligence officers had apparently flown out the day before the operation. When their arrest was linked with information obtained by New Zealand detectives in New Caledonia, Norfolk Island, Australia, Switzerland, France and the UK, it proved without any doubt the major role played by the French Intelligence Service and Special Forces in the bombing and the subsequent death of Fernando Pereira. The positioning and successful detonation of the explosives indicated that those responsible were trained and expert in underwater warfare and it is believed that both French officers were serving members of the Commando Hubert Underwater Warfare unit.

MECHANICS OF ASSASSINATION

The mechanics of assassination are fairly simple. Intelligence agency executives see a clear case for disposing of a certain person or persons. Once the decision has been taken, the project is then handed over to the appropriate organization for action. Those responsible for carrying out the assassination will plan, organize and execute their orders.

The Assassin

The image of an assassin has changed dramatically over the past century. While many intelligence agencies employ a small section for dirty tricks – including certain types of assassination – these generally only carry out operations against other spies or agents. The death of a terrorist leader or a known activist is carried out by Special Forces personnel seconded by the agency.

Internal units within an intelligence agency will mainly consist of specialists who have a good working knowledge of specific assassination techniques, such as how to blow up a house and make it look like a gas leak, for example. These people are your ordinary nine-to-five civil servants who have shown an aptitude for such work and who treat it very much as a mundane job. However, when it comes to assassinating foreign agents, most of the clandestine work is carried out by Special Forces. They have the advantage of being highly trained in infiltration, camouflage and concealment and sabotage. For the most part, they are resolute, courageous, intelligent, resourceful and physically fit – attributes that make them ideal assassins. However, these people see themselves as professional soldiers and not assassins.

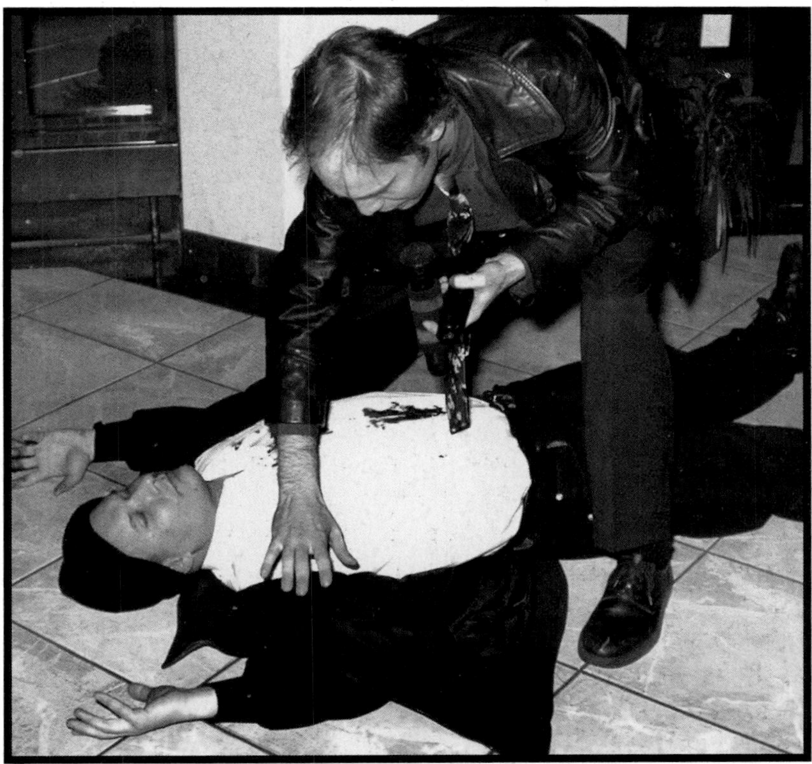

▲ The assassin.

Assassination Planning

Having taken the decision to assassinate a person, the powers that be will either authorize an individual or a team to carry out the task. At this stage, the issuing authority will include the method of assassination – covert or overt. In certain circumstances, these orders are given verbally. This ensures that the assassination can be denied if things go wrong. The team will then plan their operation and decide on the best course of action, based on the target location and profile.

A target may require the team to infiltrate a foreign country and the method must be established (*see* chapter on Infiltration). By far the most important aspect of any assassination is the target profile; this will establish his whereabouts, his movements and any projection or weaknesses. Much of this information should be readily available from the intelligence agency: photographs of the target, maps of the surrounding areas and aerial photographs of any building occupied by the target or his organization to name but a few.

The means by which the target is assassinated will also be taken into consideration, as this may require the team to carry specialist equipment. If the target is to shot by a sniper, then this will require both a sniper team and their equipment. If the target is to be killed in a road accident, then radio-controlled triggering devices will need to be fitted to the target's car.

Assassination is all about getting the target into a position where the assassination can take place. Here is an example in its simplest form: girls in Northern Ireland urged British soldiers to a room under the promise of sex – an IRA assassin was waiting. Not all targets are that accessible and many have bodyguards, but these problems can be overcome by using either the sniper option or by setting up a booby trap. Imagination is the key.

One of the most creative methods of assassination of recent times was seen when a perceived terrorist leader was murdered with a poisoned whip. The man, who was well known for his sexual appetite for young women and bondage, enjoyed being whipped before having sex. He ordered his men to find street prostitutes that specialized in his needs on a regular basis. The assassination team discovered this useful fact put it to good use, promptly visiting the cafe where most of the girls were recruited and placing their own female agent. Within a week, the girl was asked to cater for the target's sexual needs and promptly agreed. She was taken to the target's home and was searched for weapons before entering. An hour later, she left the property and made her way back to the cafe from where she was exfiltrated. The target died later that night as a result of a poison-soaked whip. The girl had made sure that the lashes of the whip had broken the skin, allowing the poison to enter the target's bloodstream.

Covert or Overt

In order to kill someone covertly, a spy's assassination plan will ensure that the result looks like an accident or a death by natural causes. When successfully executed, the death will cause little excitement and will only be casually investigated. In all cases of simulated accidents, the team will ensure that no wound or condition is attributed to anything other than death by natural causes. The most effective assassinations are those that have been carefully planned and that are simple to put into practice. If the target is to be shot, a spy will employ a very good marksman. If an accident is planned, an agent will make sure that it is organized correctly, leaving little or no evidence of foul play. The aim of the operation will be to kill the target. Briefly outlined below are some common methods of assassination that are used by agents in the field.

By Hand

It is difficult for a spy to kill someone with their bare hands; it is also very inefficient, especially when so many other objects could be used, such as a rock, a hammer or a kitchen knife. In all cases where a hand-weapon other than a firearm is used, the assassin must be in close proximity to the target. One of the failings of hand-held weapons is their instant-kill unreliability, as a stab to the heart or a blow to the head carries no guarantee of instantaneous death.

Strangulation is an effective method of assassinating a person with bare hands and it has been employed by many agents.

By Weapon

Providing an agent can get close to his target or if he has a clear line of sight, firearms offer the best solution for any overt assassination. Close up, the best type of weapon is a pistol. This is usually small, however, such as a .22 calibre weapon with a silencer fitted. Although this weapon is underpowered, the silencer makes it almost undetectable and several shots to the head or heart will guarantee a kill. If the target is well protected, then line-of-sight weapons, such as a sniper rifle, offer a good means of assassination. However, a spy will have to bear in mind that the greater the distance, the greater the chance of missing. Many of the "assassination manuals" available today claim that smaller calibre weapons are not suitable for assassination, but they have been the weapons of choice for many teams.

CASE HISTORY

In July 1973, it was believed that Ali Hassan, a Black September leader and the organizer of the Munich Olympics massacre, had been tracked down to the small town of Lillehammer in Norway. The Israelis immediately assembled and dispatched a hit team to Norway. Using an old photograph, they were convinced that they had located Ali Hassan, also known as the "Red Prince". Two days later on a Saturday evening, they shadowed their victim as he left the local cinema, together with a blonde Norwegian girl. The couple then caught a local bus that would take them to their flat on the outskirts of Lillehammer.

Author's Note: I interviewed Torill Bouchiki about the assassination of her husband Ahmed – this is her story. (She was seven months pregnant at the time of the husband's assassination.)

We left the cinema and walked down to the bus stop. At this stage the only thing I can recall is that Ahmed spoke of his brief conversation with another Arab he had met in the town; neither of us thought any more about it. The bus drove out of town to the wooded outskirts, where we got off at the stop opposite our block of flats. As the bus continued up the hill we crossed the road, heading for the small gravel drive that led to the ground-floor doors. We had gone no more than 20 metres, when, from behind us, there was a loud bang. We both stopped, turning to see what had caused the noise. We had not noticed the car that had rolled down the hill towards us, braking almost parallel; but the slamming of the door made us look. A man climbed out of the nearside, while at the same time, a woman got out of the other side. I thought, maybe that they were looking for directions, but then Ahmed stepped away from me, crying out, "No. No."

Then I saw the bright flashes coming from both the man and the woman. They were so close, but I couldn't hear any noise. Shocked, I watched as Ahmed's body twitched before falling to the ground. I dropped to the ground, hugging my arms around my swollen belly – waiting for death to come. The man stopped firing, but the woman walked up to Ahmed, who by this time had rolled over onto his belly as he tried to crawl away. She deliberately fired two bullets into the back of his neck. Then they were gone. To this day, if I close my eyes, I see it as if it was happening all over again.

Listening to Torill and watching her expressions, I felt sad. She had suffered so much with the loss of Ahmed, but the sadness did not come from that alone; it came from the loss of love, a love that had been stolen from her. Two weeks after his death and heavily pregnant, she was forced to return to work in order to support herself.

I wonder if the Mossad assassins would like to go and see the damage they have caused to an innocent family. At the time, very pleased with themselves, the hit team returned to Oslo and reported their success to Israel. The Mossad members that had actually pulled the trigger left that night, while the rest of the team planned to leave the following morning. It was the biggest mistake that Mossad has ever made – next morning six of them were caught. Although the Israelis were held for questioning and admitted to having made a mistake in murdering the wrong man, their prison sentences were reduced to two years, just because they were members of Mossad. Even though they admitted their mistake, Mossad have never paid a penny in compensation to Torill.

Disposal Team Operations

Many assassination teams are supported in their operation by a cleaning team, i.e. once the hit has been carried out then a "clean-up" team sterilizes the body and the surrounding area. A clean-up team may also respond when one of their own agents has been killed and the agency wishes to remove their body without any trace of the fact. Likewise, foreign agents who have been compromised are often set up for assassination and total removal. Spies who have died as a result of torture are often disposed of in such a manner. Such clean-up operations are normally left to a specialist unit. Their job is purely one of removing the body and removing any trace of the deceased, to make it look as if they had never existed. The two main aspects of a clean-up operation are disfigurement and disposal.

Disfigurement

One of the tasks of a clean-up team is to ensure that the body cannot be identified. This entails removing or disfiguring all body parts that may be on record, such as fingerprints, iris and retina scans, teeth or any other distinguishing body marks, such as tattoos, and full-facial scans. Any trace of one or more of these methods will allow the public authorities to identify the dead body. Total disfigurement is the only way to overcome these identity biometrics. The most common method is to use acid. If a strong solution of sulphuric acid is poured over the hands and face of the body, it will totally eradicate the facial structure, including the eyes, burning off the finger tips and eroding the enamel from the teeth. An alternative to acid is burning; before this is done, however, the teeth have to be removed with a hammer.

Disposal

In addition to disfigurement, the long-term disposal of a body is also desirable. This will be achieved in any number of ways, with the following methods top of the list.

- A shallow grave in an isolated area, preferably in a thickly forested area.
- In a *bona fide* graveyard, hidden in a legitimate, freshly dug grave together with another corpse.
- Weighted and dropped overboard, out at sea.
- Weighted and thrown into a large lake.
- Placed in the foundations of a new building or a motorway.
- Cremated down to ashes.

Explosives

Using a booby trap for assassination requires a lot of skill and a detailed itinerary of the target. Depending on the amount of explosive used, a well-thought-out booby trap stands a good chance of success. While letter bombs have been used by assassins for many years, they are not particularly accurate, i.e. there is no guarantee that the target will actually open the letter. If someone else is killed, all the assassin has done is tip off the target.

Home

Assassinations in the home will try to be passed off as accidents. These can be caused by gas leaks, fire, electricity or fatal falls. In most cases, assassinations in the home take place in large towns or cities. The target may be befriended by the team or team member using sexual favours. Once a team member has gained access to the target's home then any number of assassination ploys are possible. If, for example, the target is lured away from his home and plied with drink, a team member enters the

▲ Explosives can be an effective tool for assassination, as seen here when the IRA tried to kill members of the British Conservative party in a Brighton hotel.

premises and switches on all the gas appliances while he is out. Before leaving, the team member turns off the gas at the outside main incoming supply. The target returns home drunk and then goes to bed. Once the target is asleep, the team reconnect the incoming gas supply. At six in the morning, hungover and drowsy, the target wakes up and switches on his bedroom light – boom.

Getting someone very drunk is also a common spy ploy. After several hours, the target will become unconscious, leaving the assassination team to create a natural fire that gets out of hand and consumes both the room and the target. Alternatively, if the target lives in a block of flats, they could fall down the stairs or, better still, off the balcony. A fall is an efficient accident; agents will throw their victims onto a hard surface, but they will be wary of throwing people off bridges, as the victim may fall into water.

▲ Many victims of assassination have been found dead in their own swimming pools.

Vehicle

Killing someone in a hit-and-run accident is not a much-used assassination technique; it often fails to kill the target and, in many cases, the incident can be witnessed by others. Many other methods of killing the target in his vehicle have been tried over the years – from plying him with alcohol or drugs to wrapping him in cling film. A very effective method that has been used by spies is when they choose a spot along a route driven regularly by their target, like a sharp corner, a river bridge or a motorway. The spy gains covert access to the target's car and fixes a device that will blow off a wheel, lock the doors and increase the vehicle's speed. The spy will simply follow the target's car to the point of attack and then press a button. They will organize for a tow truck to be passing the scene several minutes after the accident and thus will be able to retrieve the car and remove any telltale signs of their device from under the nose of any police investigation.

▲ An assassination using a vehicle can be made to look like an accident.

Medical Accidents

Medical accidents, such as an overdose of medicine, can be used by agents to fake a suicide.

Likewise, an alcohol-induced coma offers the team time to suffocate a target and there will be little evidence of foul play.

Drugs have sometimes been used as a very effective method of assassination by spies in the past, but generally they are selected and administered by a medical professional. If the target is a heavy drinker, an overdose of certain drugs can be administered; the cause of death will be put down to acute alcoholism. Other drugs, such as LSD, have been used in the past to cause the target to committee suicide either of their own accord or with a little help.

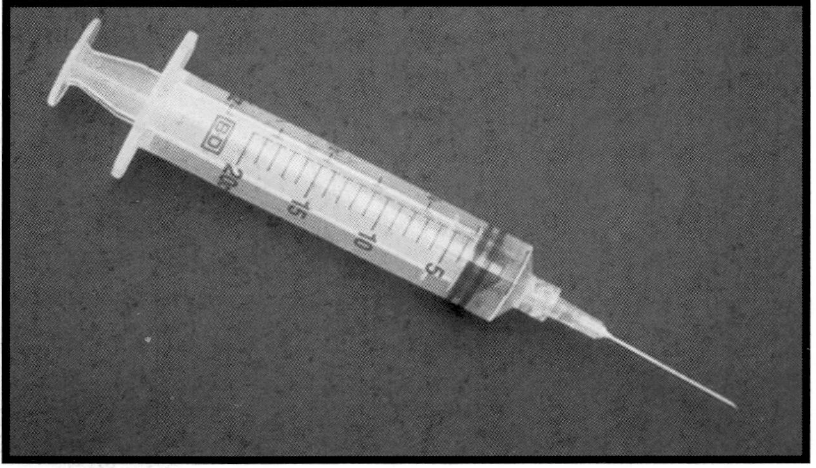

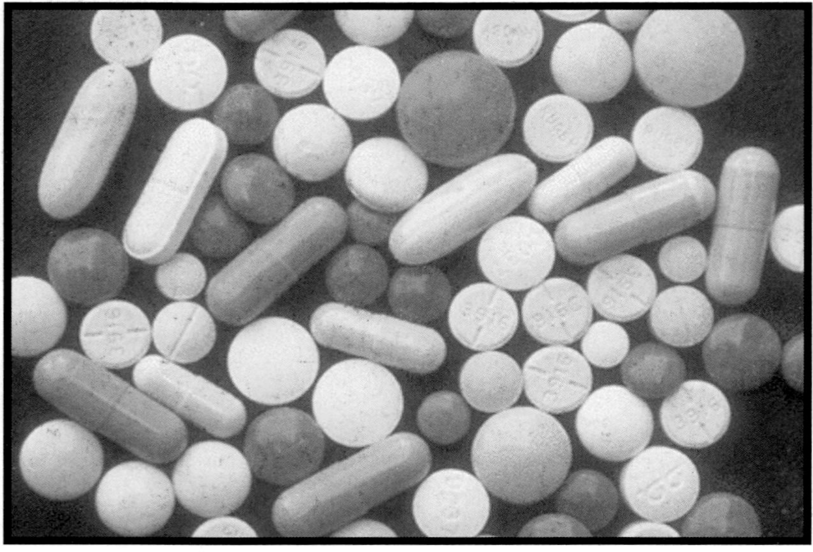

▲ Spies have used a variety of drug-related methods to kill their targets in the hope that the medical evidence will show no foul play.

CASE HISTORY

Some time after the Korean War, the CIA became obsessed with the idea that the Soviets or the Chinese might employ methods of brainwashing to recruit double agents or that they would find a way to manipulate an entire population. To counter this, the CIA initiated a series of programmes, one of which was Operation Artichoke. Artichoke involved the use of torture and drugs to interrogate people. The effects of substances such as LSD, heroin and marijuana were studied by using unsuspecting individuals as human guinea pigs. Artichoke also included the development of poisons that take immediate effect. These substances were later used in attempts on the lives of a number of foreign leaders, such as Abdul Karim Kassem (Iraq), Patrice Lumumba (Congo) and Fidel Castro (Cuba).

One of the leading scientists who was carrying out research in the field of biological weapons and who had been working for ten years in the biological warfare facilities at Maryland Camp Detrick (today Fort Detrick) near Washington DC, was Dr Frank Olson. Olson was a biochemist and occupied a leading position in Operation Artichoke. However, on 28 November 1953, Olsen threw himself out of the 13th floor of the Hotel Pennsylvania in New York City.

Before Frank Olson plunged to his death, others in the room say he exhibited symptoms of behavioural disturbance. His death was officially described as suicide due to depression. Only in the mid-1970s, when the CIA secret activities were scrutinized in the wake of the Watergate scandal, did the government admit to a certain degree of responsibility. Ten days before his death, the CIA had administered LSD to Olson without his knowledge. President Gerald Ford subsequently apologized to his family and the CIA paid compensation to his widow.

Outdoors

If an agent's target lives or goes on the water, be it a river or in the open sea, then various opportunities arise. Swimming accidents are common, although it can take a great deal of effort from the agent to make the death look natural. Likewise, boating accidents have been linked to assassination for many years as they offer a very good opportunity for assassination. A boat at sea can be sunk without trace by a spy and there is no limit to the possibilities and there are never any witnesses. If an agent's target has any hobbies, a spy will investigate them carefully to see if they present an opportunity for something that can be made to resemble death by natural causes.

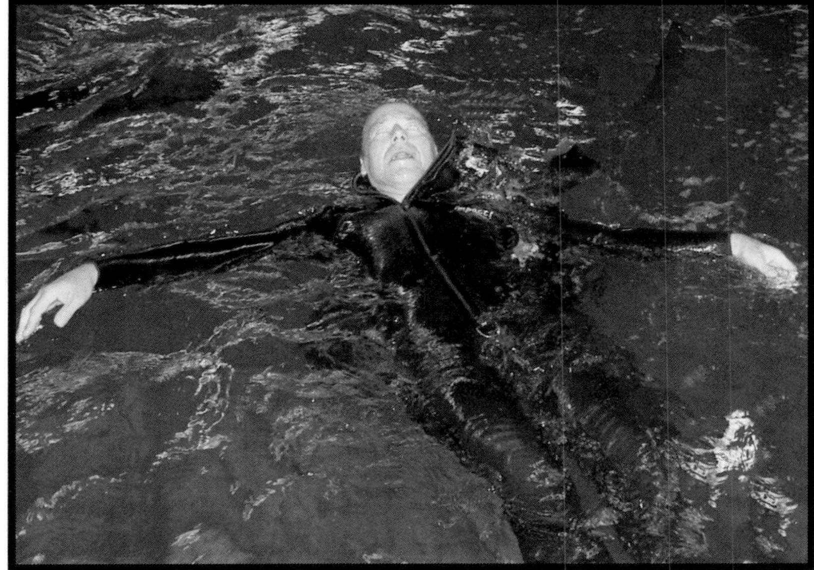

▲ Deaths at sea rarely show evidence of foul play.

WEAPONS OF THE ASSASSIN

In 1978 the KGB designed an umbrella with a poison-pellet secreted in the point. It was used to assassinate the Bulgarian dissident Georgi Markov in London. He was jabbed with the umbrella at a bus stop, an action that was easily dismissed as an insignificant accident. The jab delivered a metal pellet into which a small amount of ricin – a poison derived from castor-oil seeds – had been placed. The metal pellet was discovered after Markov was dead. The KGB had designed it to dissolve, but this had failed. Encouraged by Markov's death, the KGB went on to produce several versions, including pens that would fire gas and miniature .22 pistols.

Welrod Silenced Pistol

Built during the Second World War for the British SOE and for Special Forces covert action, the Welrod was designed as a single-shot, silent-killing/assassination weapon. With a 9 mm chamber , it is very easy to conceal, reliable and accurate up to 50 m (55 yards) in daylight or perhaps 20 m (22 yards) on a starlit night. Other variations developed during the Second World War at the Welwyn Experimental Laboratories were the Wel-Wand, a .25 calibre "Sleeve-Gun", a silenced single-shot device hidden in the sleeve of the assassin's overcoat; the Welfag, a .22 calibre firing device concealed in a cigarette; the Welpen, a firing device concealed in a fountain pen and the Welpipe, a .22 calibre firing device concealed in a smoking pipe. An updated Welrod is still available today.

▲ A silenced pistol is favoured by many assassins as it avoids body contact, almost guarantees a kill, and is silent.

Mobile Phone Gun

In its outward appearance, the modern device looks like a mobile phone. It separates in the middle to reveal four .22 calibre cartridges. Once loaded, the two halves simply click together and the gun is then armed by triggering a lever positioned at the base of the phone. Depressing any of the four top buttons on the phone fires a single shot. The gun is designed for close-quarter (three to five metres maximum) assassination, but its accuracy leaves a lot to be desired. These guns are thought to be manufactured in Eastern Europe and several have been seized by British, German and Dutch police forces.

Concealed Weapons

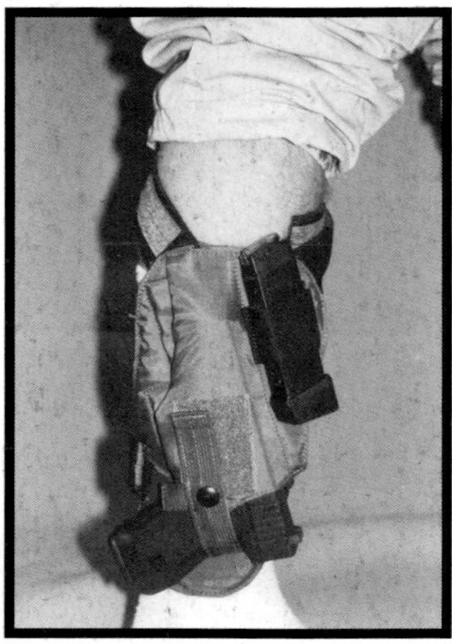

◂ There is often a need for the assassin to conceal his weapons.

Agents operating in foreign countries are sometimes required to carry a weapon, which, for the most part, would be concealed. These types of weapon fall into two main categories: knives and pistols. The amount of concealed weapons available would fill several volumes. Knives can be disguised as combs, keys and belt buckles, while pistols take the form of rings, phones and pens. A complete range of concealed weapons can be found in the *Manual of Prohibited and Concealed Weapons* published by Paradigm Partners Limited in Britain, or by visiting the FBI Guide to Concealed Weapons at the following website:

http://datacenter.ap.org/wdc/fbiweapons.pdf

Explosives

Explosives are also major assets for any assassin as they provide numerous ways of killing people (*see* section on Sabotage).

Operational Executive Action

Lawful killings can be carried out in several situations. For the most part, the actual incident can be predetermined, giving the operational team the time to plan ahead. For example, if a known terrorist leader is discovered at a certain place, such as a military check point, he could be shot while resisting arrest. If the terrorist is armed, all the better, if not, those that actually do the shooting simply state that they thought he was armed. The legal or illegal shooting of a suspect in a war zone generally causes little or no political problems for the intelligence agencies.

CASE HISTORY

In March 1988, information filtered through the security screen that the IRA was planning to detonate a bomb in Gibraltar. The IRA team consisted of three people, Sean Savage, Daniel McCann and a woman, Mairead Farrell, each of whom had a history of terrorist activity. The three, later acknowledged by the IRA as an active cell, had been spotted by British intelligence agencies, who had trailed them for months, recording many of their conversations. Surveillance paid off when the target identity was discovered – Gibraltar's British garrison. The method of attack was to be a car bomb. As events unfolded, the target was a ceremony with military bands parading. It was also known that the IRA had developed a device that could remotely detonate a car bomb.

In late 1987, a well-known IRA bomb-maker, Sean Savage, had been located in Spain. Another IRA suspect, Daniel McCann, was with him. MI5 spent six months watching the two, gathering information that they were certain was leading to a bombing. When, on 4 March 1988, Mairead Farrell arrived in Malaga airport and was met by the two men, it seemed likely that it was on. At this stage, the SAS were invited to send in an Increment team. The Gibraltar police were informed and were instructed that the IRA active service unit was to be apprehended. For a while, contact with the IRA cell was lost, but, by this time, the target had been defined. It was suspected that one car would be delivered onto the Rock and parked in a position along the route taken by the parade. This car would be clean – a dummy to guarantee a parking space for the real car bomb. The plaza where the troops and public would assemble was considered as the best spot to cause the most damage. This proved to be correct. At 2 pm on the afternoon of 5 March, a report was received that Savage had been spotted in a parked white Renault 5. There was a suspicion that he was setting up the bomb-triggering device. Not long after, another report was received to the effect that Farrell and McCann had crossed the border and were making their way into town. (CONT...)

▲ The bodies of Daniel McCann and Mairead Farrell, shot by the SAS in Gibraltar.

The Increment were immediately deployed and, once Savage was out of the way, an explosives expert did a walk past of the Renault. No visual telltale signs were observed – such as the rear suspension being depressed – that would indicate the presence of a bomb. However, if they were using Semtex, 15 kilos or more could easily be concealed from the naked eye. After consultation, it was considered probable that the car did contain a bomb. At this stage, the local police chief, Joseph Canepa, signed an order passing control to the SAS. Operation Favius, as it was known, was about to be concluded. The orders given to the SAS men were to capture the three bombers if possible, but, as in all such situations, if there is a direct threat to life, be it to the SAS or anyone else, they hold the right to shoot. It was stressed that the bomb would more than likely be fired via a push-button detonator.

The SAS men, dressed in casual clothes, were kept in contact through small radios hidden about their persons. Each soldier was also armed with a 9 mm Browning Hi-Power. Savage met up with McCann and Farrell and, after a short discussion, all three made their way back towards the Spanish border. Four of the SAS team shadowed the trio. Suddenly, for some unexplained reason, Savage turned around and started to make his way back into the town – the SAS team split accordingly; two with Savage and two staying on McCann and Farrell.

A few moments later, fate took a hand. A local policeman, driving in heavy traffic, was recalled to the station. It was said later that his car was required; to expedite his orders he activated his siren. This action happened close to McCann and Farrell, making the pair turn nervously. McCann made eye contact with one of the SAS soldiers, who was no more than ten metres away. In response to this, the soldier, who was about to issue a challenge, later said in evidence, that McCann's arm moved distinctly across his body. Fearing that he might detonate the bomb, the soldier fired. McCann was hit in the back and went down. Farrell, it is said, made a movement for her bag, she was shot with a single round. By this time, the second soldier had drawn his pistol and opened fire, hitting both terrorists. On hearing the shots, Savage turned to be confronted by the other two SAS men. A warning was shouted this time, but Savage continued to reach into his pocket – both SAS men fired and Savage was killed.

As the first news of the event hit the media it looked like a professional job, but the euphoria was short lived. No bomb was found in the car, and all three terrorists were found to be unarmed. Although a bomb was later discovered in Malaga, the press and the IRA had a field day. Allegations were made and witnesses were found who claimed to have seen the whole thing. The trio had surrendered; their arms had been in the air; they had been shot at point-blank range while they lay on the ground and so on. Once again, the SAS were held up as state-authorized killers. No matter that they had probably saved the lives of many people and dispatched three well-known IRA terrorists – they would stand trial.

In September 1988, after a two-week inquest and by a majority of nine to two, a verdict was passed of lawful killing. Although this satisfied most people, the story did not end there. The SAS soldiers that took part in the shooting in Gibraltar were taken to court by relatives of the three IRA members killed. The European Commission of Human Rights in Strasbourg decided, 11 votes to six, that the SAS did not use unnecessary force. They said that the soldiers were justified in opening fire, as they thought the IRA members were about to detonate a bomb.

Sniper

The lone sniper has long been used for assassination, the most famous case being the death of President Kennedy, on 22 November 1963 in Dallas, Texas and there have been many other attempts from lone gunmen throughout history.

▲ Records show some 26,000 VC were executed, many by sniper fire, during Operation Phoenix.

On the other side, literally, at the start of 1965, the American intelligence services in Saigon created a list of Vietcong cadre that it wished to dispose of. Special teams were drawn up; these were mainly recruited from the Green Berets or Navy SEALs and worked under the direction of the CIA.

A similar unit has been established in Iraq called Task Force 121. Their main task objective is to track down and capture hard-core Baathists who they believe are behind the insurgency against the US soldiers and their allies. Task Force 121 comprises elements of Delta Force, Navy SEALs and the CIA. The unit's priority is the neutralization of the Baathist insurgents by capture or assassination.

The sniper provides a long-range capability for taking out targets. In many cases, a sniper will carry at least two rifles, one for short distance (300 metres or less, with day-night capability) and one for long range (300–600 metres for daytime use only). The combination of sniper rifle and sights will depend on the individual. More recently in Iraq, there has been a demand for heavy calibre (.50) sniper rifles that provide extreme-range accuracy. Snipers wear camouflaged "Gilly" suits that blend with the surrounding terrain. At present, a new range of "stealth" clothing is being developed, which will allow the snipers to approach the target unseen to infra-red or night-vision equipment.

◂ Task Force 121 is a joint Special Forces operation to track down members of the hard-core Ba'athist party in Iraq.

Psychological Operations

◂ Psyops means winning over the will of the people. The influence of psychological operations is a serious aid to winning any conflict.

Psychological warfare, or "Psy-Ops" as it is better known, is used to mentally persuade an enemy to conform and surrender. Although the basic idea has been around for many years, its full potential was not recognized until the Second World War. For example, German propaganda played on the fact that American soldiers were having a wonderful time in England, having sex with the girls, while the British soldiers suffered on the front line.

When done professionally, Psy-Ops has the ability to influence an entire population. For instance, in 1970, after Sultan Qaboos ousted his father in Oman, the SAS operated a full-scale Psy-Ops war. This included the setting up of a radio station and the distribution of thousands of free radios to the Jebel people. Millions of leaflets – informing the rebels of the recent coup and offering them amnesty – were dropped by Shyvan aircraft across enemy-held locations. SAS Psy-Ops teams would also distribute T-shirts and flags for the children prior to the new Sultan visiting many of the outlying towns and villages. One SAS soldier, Corporal John Ward, who arrived in the regiment via 21 SAS, became so professional at his work that he remained in Oman to continue his Psy-Ops work.

▲ Win the hearts of the people and their minds will follow. Water, education, food and medical aid are all appreciated. This picture shows the locals picking up air-dropped leaflets.

"Hearts and Minds"

"Hearts and Minds" is a tactic that is integral to the way the modern SAS fights. It was a term originally coined by General Sir Gerald Templar, the Military High Commissioner in Malaya, during the "Emergency". In June 1952, he was asked whether he had sufficient soldiers for the job. He replied: "The answer lies not in pouring more soldiers into the jungle, but rests in the hearts and minds of the Malayan people." Templar took measures to win over the Malayans, with policies such as building forts in the jungle and winning over the indigenous aboriginal tribes. From 1953, the SAS participated in the building of these forts and lived with the aborigines, learning their language, their customs and their way of life. It soon became clear that medical facilities, however primitive, were integral to winning the trust of the locals – it is important to note that aid of any kind had to be real and beneficial; in no way were locals treated patronisingly. Thus SAS soldiers started to acquire midwifery and veterinary skills. A simple aspirin could cure a toothache and would make a friend for life. However simple this may seem, it worked in the jungles of Malaya, Borneo and in the deserts of Oman. Among the benefits of "hearts and minds" was the intelligence gained from the locals. Of course, living with locals could be infuriating and SAS soldiers had to learn the qualities of patience and tact.

It is now common policy for the SAS to conduct a "hearts-and-minds" campaign in all theatres of war, as it provides "eyes and ears" intelligence that is otherwise unobtainable and the rewards of which are incalculable.

Basic Propaganda Principles an agent will use:

- They will get the attention of the people. Organize rallies, marches and meetings and get media-friendly attention.
- They will be wary of supporting a weak cause, as the people will not follow and the agent will not gain media interest.
- They will make their issues clear and factual, and keep their propaganda peaceful, on the surface at least.
- Clearly target and identify their adversaries – the government, the army or foreign invaders.
- Always have answers prepared. If they are asked a question, they will turn it around by saying, "Yes, but first let me explain this," and then go into a rehearsed answer that puts across their point of view. Politicians have been doing this for years.

- Always condemn the enemy. Name the leaders and hold them personally responsible.
- Use insiders to pass them secret government information and use this at any major international press interview. Anything that is true or half true and can be testified serves to weaken a government.
- Research examples of previous government follies. They will use these generalities to accuse the government of stupidity, corruption and nepotism.
- Use facts about the government that frighten people. e.g the number of people the state intelligence agency has taken into custody and have simply disappeared. Agents could unmask a mass grave – covert subversion unit can easily organize this – and they will then blame the current government for human-rights violations.

SUBVERSION

Subversion is a difficult word to define, but in the context of clandestine operations it means subverting the people against their own leadership. For the agent or Special Forces unit, clandestine operations can involve supporting a guerrilla movement in its quest to overthrow its own government. While military training and equipment provide the muscle, the war is propagated by the use of subversion and psychological warfare. In order to succeed, the subversive organization must adopt a policy that is relevant to the current political situation. To do this, it will establish an overt body, such as a political party that openly subverts the people against the present ruling government. At the same time, it will also opt to organize a covert apparatus that, although hidden, controls the real power. This organization may well be an armed subversive group that is distant from the overt organization. On the surface, both parties can publicly denounce each other; in reality, they act as one.

CASE HISTORY

In 1997, the CIA released 1,400 pages of secret files on their first covert operation in Latin America. This operation had been such a success that it became the blueprint for similar CIA operations and many of the same techniques are used today. Today, in an atmosphere of openness, everyone is free to examine these documents and they should, for they expose the horrific details of what we would now call "acts of terrorism".

In 1952, Jacobo Arbenz Guzman became the second legally elected president of Guatemala. His first task was to change the rules under which a minority, select elite had previously governed the country. These changes included the recognition of the Guatemalan Communists and some serious land reforms that threatened US companies, such as the powerful United Fruit Co. The United States did not consider the democratically elected president to be an ally and set about organizing his downfall. This task was given to the CIA and a plan of action was developed that included assassination plots and sabotage. The CIA planned to attack Jacobo Arbenz Guzman from all angles, but the campaign was mainly aimed at undermining the backing of the Guatemalan military, which Arbenz needed in order to control the country. The CIA succeeded and, in 1954, Arbenz relinquished power to the military, the only power that the US deemed capable of maintaining order. The military leaders formed little more than a dictatorship. When a small insurgency developed, Guatemala's US-equipped-and-trained military would let loose a savage wave of repression that left thousands of peasants dead. The oppression lasted 40 years, totally destroying the fabric of Guatemalan society and causing the death or disappearance of almost a quarter of a million people. This type of story is not new. Ask any Special Forces soldier and he will tell you that they have all participated in similar scenarios.

"As a CIA operative, I trained Guatemalan exiles in Honduras to invade their own country and unseat the elected president... The coup I helped engineer in 1954 inaugurated an unprecedented era of intransigent military rule in Central America. Generals and colonels acted with impunity to wipe out dissent and garner wealth for themselves and their cronies... Later, I realized we weren't fighting communism at all, we were fighting the people." These are the words of Philip Roettinger, a retired US Marine Corps colonel and a CIA operative.

Implicit and Explicit Terror

Subversion uses both "implicit" and "explicit" terror in order to control the people. Implicit means the threat is unseen but always there. Explicit is when the subversive organization carries out an act of aggression to demonstrate its power. Both of these principles work hand in glove in any revolutionary war; control the people and you control the country. When supporting a revolutionary movement, it is always best for the agent to advise co-operation with the local people. For example, when a group of armed revolutionary soldiers enter a village, they can be viewed either as hostiles or as liberators, depending on their treatment of the villagers. Normal people live under constant threat of either collaboration with the revolutionaries or the government – the trick is to tip the balance in favour of the agent. This can be achieved through either armed propaganda or a hearts-and-minds campaign; inevitably, it finishes up with a mixture of both.

▲ **A small South African village being overrun by armed subversive elements.**

Agents' Armed Propaganda Techniques:

- Agents will initiate their arrival by arresting local police and any government officials before removing them to a safe place.
- They will release any political prisoners, but not criminals.
- They will cut the government lines of communication.
- They will ambush all roads in and out of the village.
- Establish the immediate needs of the people.
- Make friends with the local professionals, such as doctors, priests and teachers.
- Agents will use armed revolutionaries to help the people. They will mix with them and play with the children, giving them candy.
- Pay cash for anything they take from the village.
- If hospitality is offered, they will take it, thanking their hosts.
- Agents will not bombard the locals with too much propaganda.

Agents will let the people establish a local council and let them decide what should be done with any local police or government officials. They will hold a public trial, disperse their members among the people and encourage them to shout slogans. This is generally self-perpetuating. They will make enquiries about any government troops that have been seen: their numbers, the weapons they use, the routes they take and the frequency between visits to the village. Finally, they will encourage the young men and women of the village to join them in the struggle.

A good agent will explain to the people that the government is backed by foreign powers whose only interest is to steal their country's wealth. Also, they will explain that any foreign troops training and supporting the guerrillas are brothers in the fight for freedom. They'll use political, social, economic or religious differences to alienate the people from the government. They will highlight the scarcity of consumer goods for the general public and their availability to the privileged few. They will denounce the high cost of government polices and the tax burden that it places on the common people. They will express how powerless the people are without the revolution and their guerrilla army. Before leaving the village, they will congratulate the people on their strength in defying the government and reiterate that the agents are there for them.

Once the government learns of the agents' visit, it will dispatch troops to investigate. In reality, this will involve acts of reprisal, such as rapes, pillage, destruction, captures and murder. These reprisals for providing hospitality to the guerrillas only serve to alienate the people from the government even more.

Agents will then wait until the government troops have done their dirty work, and plan an attack. Once they have enough numbers to overcome the troops it will be time to send some of the recently recruited villagers to establish troop dispositions. During the attack, the agents will kill as many troops as possible, but not the commanders. They will place any senior officers on trial and then execute them. They will inform surrounding villages of government troops' atrocities and know that timely intervention helped save many lives. Careful agents will apply this same strategy within a given area until they are strong enough in both manpower and equipment to do serious damage.

A FARC guerilla group, well trained, well armed and experts in armed subversion.

An agent may also decide to play the tit-for-tat reprisal game. If the government hits a village that is friendly to them, they will hit the government back where it hurts and make sure that they know the reason for it. This can be done by attacking the government's assets – such as the military and their main sources of revenue. The abduction and execution of selective government ministers, court judges, state security officials and senior military personnel will all intimidate the government. Agents will, however, make sure that any official political government opposition members are left untouched, as this affiliates them with the guerrillas.

The full support of the common people is vital to any resistance campaign. This can only be done by entwining the revolution with the people. Agents will recruit from the people; use their sons and daughters to fight for the cause as family ties are always strong. Live, eat, and work with the people; find out what the people really want. Positively identify the revolution with the people, so that they feel part of it. Here are some dos and don'ts that agents use.

- Win hearts and minds.
- Show respect for human rights.
- Help protect families and homes.
- Respect religious beliefs and customs.
- Help the people in community projects.
- Protect the people from government attacks.
- In poor areas, set up schools for the people's children.
- Develop animal husbandry techniques in rural areas.
- Develop better hygiene to prevent diseases.
- Hold regular clinics.
- Never touch their women (other than for medical reasons).
- Never discuss military operations with the common people.
- Recruit trustees to act as spies in the towns and villages.

Subversive Tactics

Although most subversive groups work with only a minority support from the people, their existence will always be termed as representative of the people. For example, if a paramilitary group accidentally killed and maimed several people by mistake, the people would be against them. A political wing would endorse the people's feelings in order to gain public support for their movement. On the other hand, the political wing may request the paramilitaries to plant a bomb just prior to a crucial meeting with the government to improve their bargaining position. This approach encapsulates the benefits of an overt and covert subversive campaign.

One of the basic forms of subversion is agitation. The agitator picks on a subject and seeks to exploit it with the people in support of the overt movement. In Northern Ireland, this was a simple matter of asking the Catholic people, "Why are your lives controlled by the British government?" or "Why are there armed British soldiers on our streets in Belfast?" These are both comprehensible and irrefutable facts that the agitator will seize on in order to whip up support. They are facts that people can relate to; they create a mood of doubt, fear or hatred and awaken feelings of rebellion.

Once the seeds of rebellion have been planted, the next subversive stage is propaganda. Propaganda capitalizes on the fears of the people and seeks to convert a peaceful population into a controllable mob. The principle behind propaganda is to convince people that they are acting in self-defence, while in reality these actions are being dictated to them by the subversive group. People will often see these actions as a means of protecting their own society.

An example of this could be seen in Northern Ireland during the early 1970s. When an IRA gunman had taken a pot shot at a British patrol, he would then run for cover. Any chase by the British would be hampered by the local women, who would bang dustbin lids against the walls of their houses. Once started, almost every house in the area would take up the call. This allowed the gunman to run through the houses, dispose of his weapon and make good his escape. This simple system also brought the local people together in support of their armed resistance.

The above example highlights the definitive goal of the subversive group: to undermine the government and to demonstrate the solidarity of the people. This type of propaganda is commonly referred to as "white" propaganda – it is suggested and controlled by the overt group. "Grey" propaganda generally comes from the media. All instances of violence are classified as prime news, and while the some people may look on in horror at what they call an atrocity, those people subjected to the subversive group will hail the perpetrators as heroes.

OVERT SUBVERSION

Whenever a prisoner was taken during the Oman War, he was provided with the opportunity to join the ranks of the local militia; his other option was a bullet in the back of the head. The next stage in the process was to persuade the defector into showing the intelligence personnel his last-known location, when he was with the rebels. This was simply done by flying over the mountain area in a helicopter and letting the defector point to the location on the ground. Unbeknown to the defector, several attack aircraft would be quietly following the helicopter, ready to strike once the enemy location was known. This type of operation was known as the "flying finger". The technique was very successful when it came to locating and destroying enemy strongholds.

Russians Accuse Americans

Subversion comes in many disguises. For example, it would have been easy for the Russians to accuse the United States of using body parts reaped from street children in South America. What constitutes good subversion is a modicum of truth. For example, the bodies of many homeless children in Bogota, Colombia, have been found with their eyes surgically removed. One four-year-old child, who had had her eyes removed after being abducted, was found alive with a 500 peso note pinned to her dress and a note saying: "Thanks for your gift." There is a huge demand in the richer nations, such as the United States, for body parts paid for with ready cash. It is easy, therefore, to accuse the Americans as a whole of dealing in such a despicable trade. Where this may be true in a few cases, it serves to taint the whole nation. These and many other similar tactics have been used over the years to discredit an enemy.

FORGERY

Note: Forgery of documents is illegal and a criminal offence. Some spies do it but it should not be undertaken by members of the public.

Spies and agents engaged in subversive operations are often obliged to use false documents. These include passports, identity cards and birth certificates. Counterfeit money is also produced in large quantities and is used by many agents, often as a means of subversion. Most agencies have their own department of "artists" who acquire documents that can be tailored to fit the agent for any special operation. Of these, by far the most important document is the passport.

Passports

It is fairly easy for an agency to obtain blank passports in their own country; it is even possible to build a complete identity for the agent. However, this is not so easy to achieve when the agent is forced to operate with a foreign passport. Outside of the intelligence agency's specialized staff, it is not easy to make a forged foreign passport; the best method is to obtain a legitimate one.

A New Passport

The ideal way, and one that a spy will try to use on order to obtain a new identify, is to "steal" one from someone who is dead. The more recent the death, the better a spy's chances are of accomplishing this. They will scour the obituaries and look for someone of the same race, age and gender as themselves. They will try to look in a large city, where the death rate is greater than in, say, a country village. Once a spy has located a match, they will attempt to gather as much information about the deceased as they possibly can, and, if possible, obtain a photograph. The deceased's address can normally be gleaned from a newspaper, and if the death is very recent there is nothing to stop a spy from going along to the house and pretending to be an old friend. Once there, they will simply ask for a recent photograph as a keepsake. If a spy discovers that the deceased lived alone, they might try a little burglary; if they are lucky they might even turn up the passport or birth certificate (relatives normally dig these out when someone has died). But a spy will be careful not to steal anything else. Another scam that a spy will use is to pretend to be a representative of the local coroner's office – they will have a fake ID – and make an appointment to visit the family. If a spy does this, they will make sure that their telephone call is made just after the coroner's office closing time, so that no one can check up on them. They will mention that they will need to see any relevant documents the family can find, such as the social security number, passport or birth certificate etc. As most people rarely deal with the coroner's office, they will think that this is a normal procedure.

If neither a burglary nor a scam produce a birth certificate or a passport, then a spy will have to think about making and obtaining false documents. This is not as big a problem as it might seem. Once a spy has obtained a photograph of the deceased and has established their details it is a fairly simple matter; it is a task that comes with risks, however. They will need to obtain a legitimate copy of the deceased's birth certificate and then apply for a new passport, this time using their own photographs.

In many cases, the deceased may not look anything like the spy, but this is not a real problem. The spy will use a computer-morphing graphics programme. They will scan a facial picture of both themself and the deceased, then, using the morphing programme, merge them halfway. The final result should look something like the spy. They will then print out passport photographs using photographic quality paper and include these with their new passport application.

CASE HISTORY

In March 2004, two Mossad agents, Uriel Kelman, 30, and Eli Cara, 50, were jailed for six months in New Zealand for trying to obtain false passports. The plot was discovered when a passport officer noticed that a passport applicant was speaking with a Canadian or American accent. The clue led to an investigation that uncovered a complex conspiracy involving up to four Israeli agents. Using a fraudulent birth certificate, they were attempting to create a false identity for 36-year-old Zev Barkan, another suspected Israeli spy. Officers planned to arrest the spies as they picked up the completed passport. However, Cara had preempted this by having it sent by courier to an apartment block, where it was to be collected by a taxi driver and taken to a rendezvous with Kelman. Police surveillance caught Cara acting suspiciously, close to the central Auckland apartment block, while Kelman was arrested after fleeing the other rendezvous and throwing his mobile phone into a hedge. Both men were sentenced to six months in prison for their involvement in the plot.

Mossad has frequently been accused of using fake passports to launch its operations. An incident in 1997, in which Mossad agents used fake Canadian passports in an attempt to assassinate the Hamas leader, Sheikh Khaled Mashal, resulted in the expulsion of the Israeli ambassador from Canada until Israel promised to cease the practice.

If they managed to get a copy of the deceased's passport, they can change the identity by requesting a second one from the passport office. Many countries will issue a second passport for business purposes, but the spy will need to prove this. One way is to update their present passport with lots of fake travel visas. A spy will copy foreign visa stamps from one passport to another using simple copying methods.

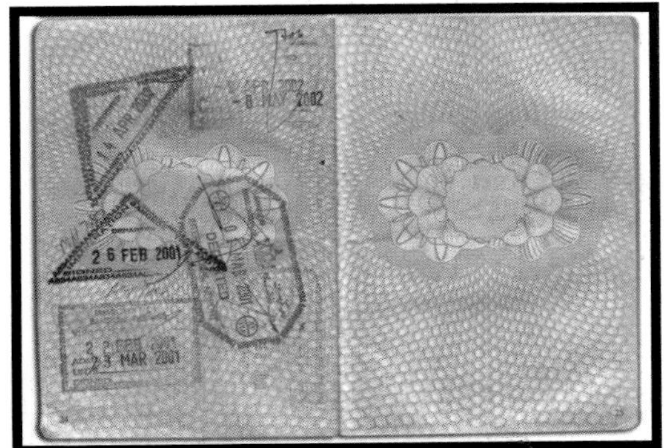

Using a block of gelatine, the visas have been copied from one passport to another.

A spy will assume the identity of the deceased. Providing they use their new identity in a foreign country, the chances of discovery are minimal. The spy will be able to easily open bank accounts, buy a home and so on.

There are many other methods that a spy has of obtaining a false passport. Stealing one while abroad is probably the easiest way, although this will be reported and cancelled and is, of course, illegal. Another way they may try is to purchase a flight ticket under a false name, and have some form of ID – but not a passport – with them. This is best done through a travel agent. The spy will then claim to have had their passport and wallet stolen. They will go to the local embassy with four photographs of themself and ask for a new one, stating that they are leaving the country the next day. They will go so far as to explain that their flight ticket is all the proof they have. With a little luck, they will get a new passport issued without too much hassle.

ID Cards

Identity cards, such as a driving licence, do not pose such a serious problem for spies, as they are easier to forge. There are many Internet sites offering a whole range of identity cards. Few of these are any good, and fewer are legal. A spy will no doubt be better off making their own, and all they require is a modern computer set-up with a scanner.

A spy will use roughly the same principle to make a fake copy of just about any paper object.

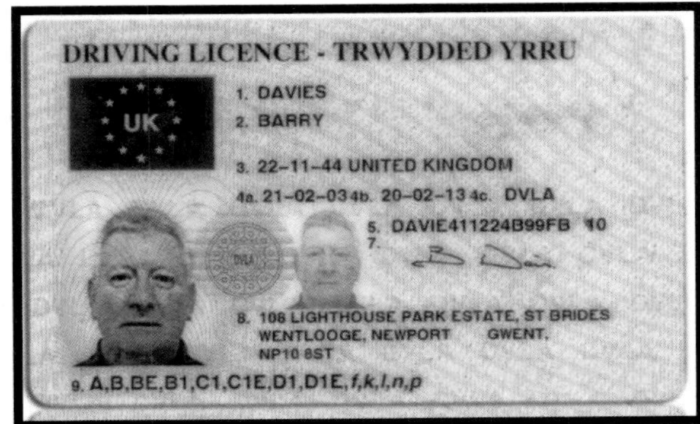

A driving licence picture could be changed using a simple graphics program.

They will scan, using a high resolution, and in colour. This will create a large file. Once a spy has made a decent digital copy, they will manipulate it to suit their needs. This may mean removing the other person's photographs, name or address and replacing it with their own details.

A spy will always ensure that they have the correct type of paper to print on. ID cards are normally printed on thick card, whereas birth certificates are on fine paper. Ideally, the paper used will be the correct weight, white and with no watermarks.

If the fake copy contains a watermark the spy will need to prepare the paper by embedding a watermark picture to the same density as that of the original.

The problem that the spy has now is to process their new fake so that it looks like an original. If it is an ID card type, it will need trimming with a scalpel and sealing in a plastic protective jacket. Machines for doing this can be found in most major office supply stores. Once completed, however, a spy will always check their fake copy against a real one.

A spy can age documents by placing a damp – not wet – cloth over the paper and iron over it several times. Next, they will place their document in the sun for several days. Once it has faded to their satisfaction, they will fold it several times then dust a little cigarette ash over the surface. They will then fold the paper several more times so that the ash falls into the creases. The document is now ready; and a spy will check their forgery against a real one once more.

Money can be made in the same way and while every effort is made to protect paper currency, it remains one of the easiest objects to copy. However, to make an undetectable copy requires a great deal of skill and very advanced machinery. One of the major problems that a spy who wants to indulge in counterfeiting, especially bank notes, is the use of Radio Frequency Identification (RFID).

Leaving paper in the sun causes it to age rapidly.

Radio Frequency Identification

RFID tags are regarded as either active or passive. Active RFID tags are powered by an internal battery and are typically used to track anything from pallets to dogs.

The white spots indicate the RFID. These passive devices prevent people from copying bank notes. Most modern computer graphics programs will not allow you to scan a bank note if it is tagged with an RFID, and will refer you to the appropriate country for authorization.

Passive RFID tags operate without a separate external power source and obtain operating power generated from the reader. Passive tags are consequently much lighter than active tags, are much cheaper to produce and offer an unlimited operational lifetime. One of their new uses is tracking bank notes around the world. The new European euro notes have the traditional metal strip, into which are placed two RFID tags. Each tag can trace its whereabouts from its origin to the present day. The absence of a tag means that the money is counterfeit. Similar tags can be found in ID cards, driving licences and credit cards.

CHAPTER 7

Sabotage can be a necessary evil that may pave the way for resistance and the deterioration of government.

SABOTAGE

Sabotage can be carried out by any member of an intelligence agency. It can be a single act carried out by an agent or it can involve the destruction of major facilities by Special Forces. Operations that require demolitions or sabotage are commonly known as "bang-and-burn" operations. Although not always necessary, the use of explosives increases the effectiveness of sabotage, and, providing the user has the imagination and training, almost anything is possible.

Many sabotage techniques have been gleaned from low-intensity wars, where guerillas have been forced to improvise in order to defeat an organized and well-equipped army. If manufactured landmines were unavailable, the guerillas would make "punji pits". While these punji pits lacked the power of a landmine, anyone stepping onto the sharpened spikes would still be hospitalized, as many an American soldier discovered during the Vietnam War.

Sabotage was used very effectively by the French Resistance during the Second World War. The felling of telephone poles and the placing of sugar or sand in fuel tanks were just a few of the tricks used by the Resistance. They also discovered that adding carborundum powder to the axle grease of French trains soon brought the German's supply system to a halt. Nonetheless, most of the damage was achieved by the use of explosives. This allowed them to destroy bridges and railway lines, as well as blowing up troop conveys.

Finding and recruiting people to carry out sabotage depends on the individual situation. If a country is in rebellion and if Special Forces personnel are assisting the guerrillas with training, it is often best to get civilians to carry out small, non-explosive acts of sabotage. Students are particularly good for this. With a few exceptions, the students of most countries are at odds with the government over one issue or another; it is simply a matter of infiltration and organization to get them to work. The best method is to use an agent who is compatible with the student fraternity and to task them with defining the militant elements within the student movement. Once this is done, it is simply a matter of organizing student riots into which guerrillas can be infiltrated. Once the latter start the ball rolling, the riot will be self-perpetuating. The government will react predictably with over-zealous violence that will lead to an escalation of the riots and the use of petrol bombs etc.

TRUE STORY

At 8.37 pm on 28 December 1968, several helicopters loaded with paratroopers took off – their destination was Beirut airport. As Beirut International Airport is situated to the south of the city some three kilometres from the sea, and is approximately 90 kms (55 Miles) north of the Israeli-Lebanon border, the flying time was estimated at 45 minutes. In 1968, the airport comprised of two runways crisscrossing in scissor-like fashion, in a north-south direction. The passenger terminal lay between the two lanes and there was an open area in front of it. Hangars and parking and maintenance areas for the planes were at the north-eastern and south-western edges of the runways. South of the terminal was the standby emergency services pavilion of the airport, where fire and first-aid stations were located.

Each of the helicopters carried a team of highly trained explosive experts; their objective was to destroy as many civilian aircraft as possible. Security for the airport consisted of some 90 security men, armed mainly with handguns. Back-up for a real emergency came from a Lebanese Army commando company situated some three kilometres away. Extra help was also available from the police in Beirut city, but it would take them a minimum of 30 minutes to reach the airport.

The aim was to confront the on-duty security officers and hold them while the bulk of the military and police would be prevented from approaching the airport by the helicopters, which, once they had deposited the soldiers on the airfield, would proceed to the approach roads, where they would drop nails and smoke. Several military vehicles tried to force their way through this barrier, only to be fired on by the helicopters.

As serious resistance was kept at bay, the disembarked troops set about fixing explosive devices to the aircraft parked on the airfield. Intermittent gunfire could be heard throughout the airfield, much of which were warning shots to frighten away the civilian maintenance workers. A total of 14 planes – mostly belonging to Middle East Airlines (MEA) – were destroyed at an estimated cost of $42 million. Those responsible for this assault – or act of terrorism, as it was claimed by many Western governments at the time) – were the Israeli military. This was their retaliation for an assault by PFLP on an El AL aircraft at Athens airport earlier in the year.

SABOTAGE TECHNIQUES (AS FEATURED IN THE CIA HANDBOOK)

Note: These acts are all used by spies. As they are illegal acts, however, they should not be used by civilians.

Felling Trees in Road: Felling a large tree in the right place can cause long delays and hold-ups. If these hold-ups include enemy troops, then a perfect ambush area is created by the spy.

▲ Rocks or trees on the road are effective.

A Potato up the Exhaust: A potato rammed into an exhaust will stop any vehicle after a few metres.

Sand or Sugar in Fuel: Placing sugar or sand in the fuel tank will stop a vehicle, although it will not do too much damage to the engine.

▲ Sand or sugar in a petrol tank will "kill" a car.

Tyre traps: Old nails, twisted in such a manner that they fall spike up when dropped onto the ground (known as "jacks"), are ideal for bursting a vehicle's tyres. A well-planned ambush site can stop a military convoy – the jacks are placed at night by the spy.

▲ Bent-up nails and heavy-duty tacks.

Create Waste and Drain Capital: In guerrilla warfare, locals can help the spy by draining the government's resources: leaving taps running, smashing and bursting water pipes, bringing down telephone lines, knocking out the local electricity substations, burning vehicles in the street, creating no-go areas for government troops etc.

Civil insurrection.

Spies can cut main and exchange telephone lines.

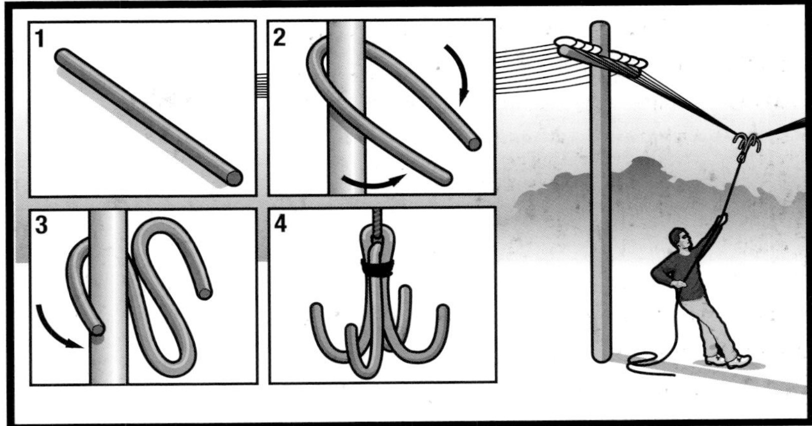

Telephone lines can be pulled down by the spy with a makeshift hook.

SPECIALIST SABOTAGE MISSIONS

Specialist sabotage missions normally take place in a war situation, with the intention to hit the enemy's war production capacity. Weapons and ammunitions factories, power stations, railroads, and MSR (Main Supply Routes) are prime targets. In order to ensure that the enemy facility is completely destroyed, a good knowledge of explosives and their placement is required. For example, the destruction of an enemy oil refinery that occupies a square kilometre plot may seem like an impossible task. For a well-trained Special Forces team, however, it is relatively easy.

A reconnaissance would take place during which the team would look for the Horton Sphere; this is a huge metal ball that can be found in every oil refinery. Once the sphere has been located, it is a simple matter of fixing two charges: the first is a basic, high-explosive cutting charge, and the second is an incendiary. The Horton Sphere contains thousands of litres of liquid gas and the idea is to utilize this by converting it into a bomb. The cutting charge punches a hole that releases the gas; an instant later, the incendiary ignites the gas. If this is done correctly there would be little left of the oil refinery, as the Horton Sphere would take out everything within a square mile with no difficulty.

Telephone communications also play a major role in any conflict. While the military will have their own radios, the civilian population rely totally on the phone system. This makes it a high-priority target. It is traditional for telephone exchanges to be destroyed by fire; the problem lies in the fact that the sabotage team has to guarantee that all the computer frames inside the exchange are destroyed. Even if only one is left intact, the engineers can quickly lash up an emergency service. One unique way of knocking out a telephone exchange is to destroy the ringing equipment. On older systems, these are two small generators; on newer ones, the sounds are created by computers and all that is necessary is to locate and destroy them. While the telephone system may remain intact, no one knows that there is a call. Both of the above examples are typical of specialist sabotage.

BOOBY TRAPS

Explosive booby traps are used extensively by both Special Forces and guerrillas in order to create panic and disorder among the enemy. They range from complicated manufactured devices to the plain opportunist variety. They can be triggered by pull, pressure, pressure release, trip, contact, motion sensor and heat. In many cases, booby traps are designed not to kill but to maim, thus placing an extra strain on the enemy's logistics. Most booby traps require some form of triggering device; these are best kept simple, as the following examples will demonstrate.

A pressure plate switch can be made from a catering-size can of baked beans or a similar product which can be found in the garbage bins of any hotel. The top and the bottom lids are removed by the spy using a can opener. On a flat wooden surface, using a hammer and a large nail, the entire surface of both is punctured with holes. A wire is fixed to each of the lids, and then one of the lids is wrapped in clingfilm – two layers are enough. Finally, both of the lids are placed together, with the serrated edges are facing each other. The clingfilm will stop moisture contact and prevent the plates from touching. This is placed on the ground and covered by a small amount of soil for camouflage. When someone steps on the plates, the pressure causes the serrated edges of the punched holes to penetrate the cling film and create a contact.

A cigarette is often as a timer for igniting the fuse. The cigarette will burn slowly enough to provide anything between a one- and ten-minute delay. The cigarette is simply attached to the fuse at the required position. As most cigarettes smoulder, rather than burn, a match will be attched by the spy, near to the point of ignition.

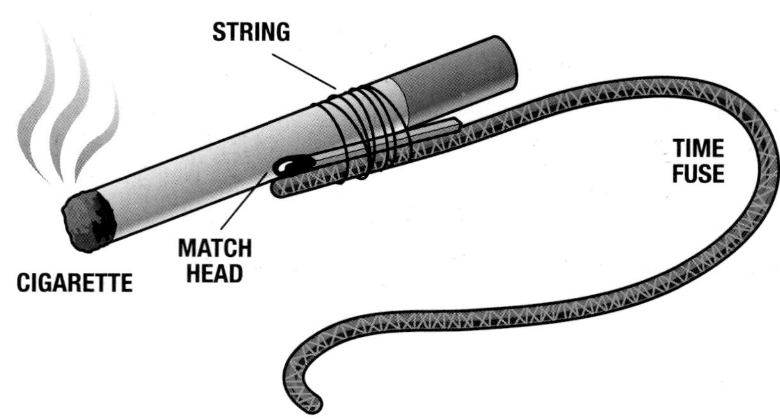

▲ A cigarette timer is one of the oldest methods of making a delayed fuse.

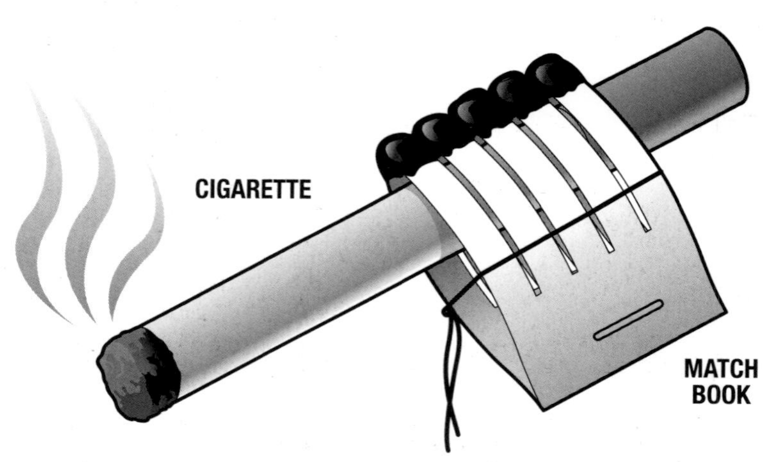

▲ Book matches can be converted into a delayed fuse or used as a friction fuse igniter.

A book of matches can also be used by the spy as pull-switch igniters. A strip of striking board is placed over the match heads and a piece of trip wire is attached in the path of the intruder.

One of the simplest triggers for any form of bomb is the clothes peg. This can easily be converted into a pull switch or a pressure-release switch.

Most DIY stores offer a complete range of switches, all of which can

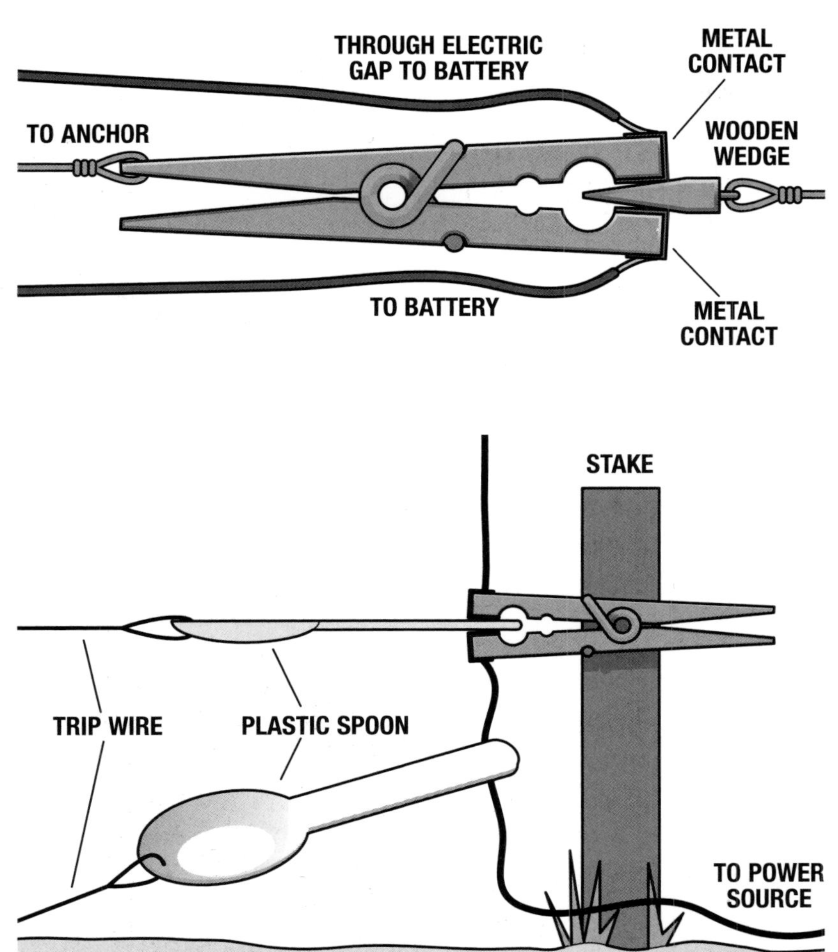

▲ The common clothes peg offers the explosive expert the means of constructing a very effective means of initiation. A string has been attached to a plastic spoon, which when tripped will allow the peg to close and cause a circuit to form. When the weight is lifted the peg will close and cause a circuit to form.

easily be adapted for sabotage by the spy. A simple magnetic door or window magnetic contact can quickly be wired into a booby-trapped room.

The trigger for a letter bomb can be made from any musical birthday or Christmas card. These are found in most card shops and are purpose-made for use by the spy. The music mechanism is replaced with a detonator and a small amount of explosive.

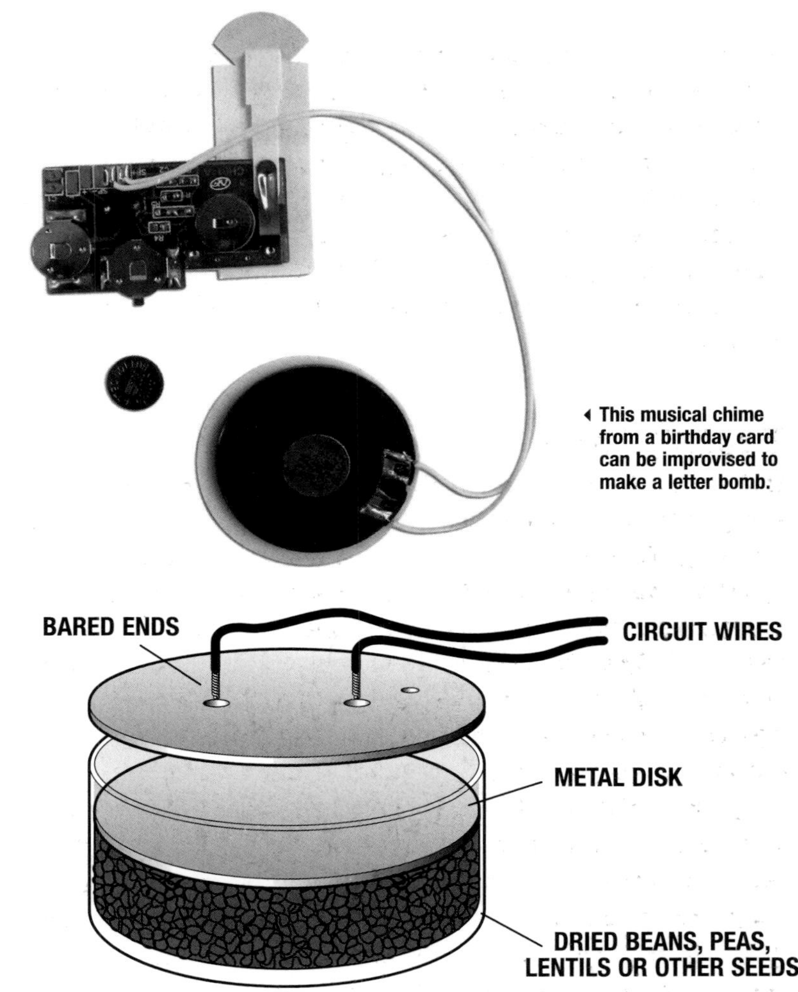

◄ This musical chime from a birthday card can be improvised to make a letter bomb.

▲ When water is poured over dried vegetables it causes them to expand; this can be used to create a delayed action igniter.

A makeshift timer can be constructed out of a tin and some dried beans, peas or lentils. Timers can be made by first placing the dried vegetables in a jar, adding a set amount of water and waiting to see how much they swell over a given time span. Once the expansion rate of the dried vegetables is established, it is a simple matter of wiring everything up.

Radio-controlled toys offer the spy the possibility of wireless controlled explosions. The receiver is removed from the toy and the wires that control the drive motor are used to fire the detonator in the explosive. One of the ways an agent will use such a device is to place both the receiver and explosives on the target's car and then hide the transmitter by the side of the road, on a sharp bend – a steep drop, bridges and tunnels provide further opportunities. The transmitter will be wired so that it is permanently on and provided that there is a good battery supply and if the timing is right, when the target passes the chosen point, the explosive will not only destroy the car, but will also send it off the road. By this time, the agent can be many miles away.

▲ Modern anti-personnel mines are highly sophisticated.

ANTI-PERSONNEL MINES

When operating in the field, especially in a war zone, it is always a good idea for any agent to have a working knowledge of mines. Mines are extremely dangerous and for the most part they are placed by inexperienced people who make no record of their location – the end result is often the loss of innocent life. In an emergency, however, they can provide a good defence or delaying tactic. While there are many forms of mine available, the agent is only required to concentrate on one type, the anti-personnel mine. If the agent is being pursued for any reason, either on foot or in a vehicle, the careful placement of anti-personnel mines will slow down any pursuers. The mines can be set in a dirt road or on a desert track. They are activated by any number of means, from straightforward pressure, to trip, pull, movement and vibration. Some mines can be set to disarm after a given period.

▲ The highly effective Claymore can be set up and removed many times. It is lethal.

The American-made Claymore mine is still widely used by many countries. It can be used by the agent to form a perfect perimeter defence or to ambush the enemy. The mine is easily deployed and, if not used, can be quickly disarmed for re-use at a later date. The mine itself is a moulded plastic case measuring some 7.5 cm high by 20 cm wide. The whole case is slightly curved with the words "Front Towards Enemy" embossed on the crest face. The mine is packed with a solid explosive into which thousands of small ball bearings are set. The base of the mine has two sets of spiked legs that can be adjusted for angle; the top contains two screw-cap detonator wells. The mine is exploded by command detonation, when a half-wave, handheld generator is depressed. One in five mines contains a testing device to show continuity along the command wire. The whole mine, including the wire and detonator, is housed in a lightweight carry satchel.

A-TYPE AMBUSH

An "A-Type" ambush is a series of unmanned explosive devices that are set up and left for the enemy to walk into. The explosive can vary from WP (white phosphorus) to hand grenades and Claymore mines, all linked by detonating cord into a single triggering device. They are mainly used on set routes used by the enemy for ferrying weapons. A-Type ambushes were laid by the American forces in Vietnam and by the British SAS during Borneo operations and during the Oman War. They are always clearly recorded and are removed if they have not been triggered.

LASER TARGET DESIGNATOR

This device is at the top end of sabotage and is only generally used by Special Forces or agents to destroy large targets. The development of the laser target designator enables the operator to "paint" a target so that an aircraft or a missile can destroy it. This eliminates the need to expose yourself on the target, and thus avoids compromise. The unit looks like a large pair of box-shaped binoculars and weighs less than six kilograms, yet it enables an agent to destroy a target from a considerable distance. Laser target designators allow agents to deliver airborne ordnance – such as Paveway or Pavetack Laser-Guided Bombs (LGBs) – onto ground targets with a high degree of accuracy. The agent will move into a position where he has an unobstructed view of the target. Once the sight has acquired the target, the agent can either call for an immediate air strike or he can programme the designator to activate at a predetermined time. The pilot will release his ordnance once the signal has been "locked", this can be up to 20 kilometres (13 miles) from the target. Provided that the laser target designator continues to paint the target, the ordnance simply homes in on the signal.

◂ A sophisitcated laser target designator in action.

SPECIAL ATOMIC DEMOLITION MUNITIONS (SADM)

The Special Atomic Demolition Munitions was a nuclear landmine with a yield of between one and 15 kilotons. It was designed primarily for deployment behind enemy lines and to destroy harbours, airfields, bridges, dams – or to effectively disrupt enemy troop movements. The complete unit (including the warhead) weighed less than 200 kgs and was deployed between 1965 and 1986. Delivery was normally by a specialist two-man team who would place the weapon package in an acceptable location. They would then set the timer and make good their escape. The timer delay could be set between one and twenty-four hours. For this reason, the insertion teams – some of which were parachute-trained – practised placement and retrieval procedures extensively. Most of the deployments took place in the former Soviet Union or in Europe.

▴ Special atomic munitions look deceptively simple.

The SADM used a gun-type principle, whereby two sub-critical masses of U-238 were fired through a precisely machined "doughnut" of uranium. The mine used a mechanical permissive action link to prevent unauthorized detonation. The basic philosophy behind the SADM programme was to attain predetermined targets that the USAF planes were unable to reach. Both the Russians and the Chinese had their own SADM programmes, and it is widely believed that the latter still does.

TERRORIST SABOTAGE TACTICS

Many terrorist attacks are similar in design to those carried out by Special Forces; the only differences between the two are motivation and target acquisition. Any sabotage causes damage to both human life and property, but when it comes to terrorist attacks, it seems as though the supporting necessity is for each new atrocity to raise the death toll in order to secure media attention. This escalating trend causes terrorist organizations to look to more powerful weapons and it is only a matter of time before they start using weapons of mass destruction. For the moment, however, they have many other sources of sabotage at their disposal.

To ascertain what and where the terrorist organizations will strike next, we must not only look to the past, but also at what is achievable. Remember the basic philosophy of war: who has the means and who has the intent. Nuclear bombs, nerve gas, suicide bombers, assassinations and even conventional warfare are all possibilities that are open to terrorist groups. In reality, most of these possibilities are restricted by governing factors. While it may be possible, in theory, to construct a nuclear bomb, in practice, it is almost impossible. Therefore, it will be a long time before we see a terrorist organization carry out this scenario. Unfortunately, the same cannot be said for biological or chemical weapons, some of which, although highly dangerous, are extremely simple to produce.

CYBER SABOTAGE

Many nations rely heavily on their economic infrastructure, much of which is entirely computer-based. It is hard to imagine everyday life without computers; it would almost be impossible to go back to the old days of paper business. The demands on a modern society are so high that it requires machines to control its functions. However, this very reliance on computers also makes them vulnerable.

Computers support the delivery of goods and services, aid manufacturing, governance, banking and finance. What would happen, say, if the stock exchange computers were put offline for several days, or if the banks could not issue money to their customers because all of the accounts had been wiped out? While both would have a continuous back-up system, it is feasible that someone in the know could, after years of research, also find ways of destroying those as well.

All political, military and economic interests depend on information technology. This includes critical infrastructures such as electric power, telecommunications and transportation. The information technology infrastructure is at risk not only from disruptions and intrusions, but also from serious attacks.

The military, in particular, rely heavily on computerized weaponry. Smart bombs and cruise missiles are guided to their target via GPS (Global Positioning System), as are many of the ground troops. If you could find a way of shutting down the 27 or so satellites the system uses, the US military would be blind in one eye. What if someone could get both access to and control of the nuclear missile system?

The type of people capable of hacking into military computer networks are already out there. Several have penetrated the American Department of Defence, as well as the CIA. True, these people have been tracked down and sentenced accordingly, but only after the event. For the most part, cyber warfare offers a cloak of obscurity to potential attackers. In addition, all they need is access to a computer and a telephone line.

CASE HISTORY

In March 2001, Japan's Metropolitan Police Department disclosed that a software system had been acquired with the ability to to track 150 police vehicles, including unmarked cars. It had been developed by the Aum Shinriyko cult – the same cult that gassed the Tokyo subway in 1995, killing 12 people and injuring 6,000 more. At the time of the discovery, the cult had received classified tracking data on 115 vehicles. Furthermore, the cult had developed software for at least 80 Japanese firms and ten government agencies. They had worked as subcontractors to other firms, making it almost impossible for the organizations to know who was developing the software. As subcontractors, the cult could have installed "Trojan horses" to launch or facilitate cyber-terrorist attacks at a later date.

THE INTERNET

The invention of the Internet and email has, in general, advanced mankind in a huge way. Information and basic knowledge on just about any subject is now available. Simply booking your holiday or sending flowers to your girlfriend can now be done with a few strokes of the keyboard. Billions of emails a week speed up conversation, save telephone charges and enable us to communicate rapidly around the world. This is why the Internet and email were designed. Unfortunately, the price we must pay for this service is high, not in monetary cost, but in the way in which both the Internet and email can be abused.

The Internet offers unlimited facilities to the saboteur: the knowledge on how to make home-made explosives or how to construct a bomb and any amount of information on a potential target. Email can be encrypted in such a way that no government agency can crack the code, thus allowing terrorist organizations secure communications on a worldwide basis. The same system allows them to contact other groups and to prepare joint operations. Business and bank accounts can be established over the Internet which provide money for weaponry and operations; if done properly, almost all these activities are untraceable.

BIO-TERRORISM

There is a perceivable threat from bio-terrorism, as both extremist nations and terrorist organizations have access to the skills required to cultivate some of the most dangerous pathogens and to deploy them as agents in acts of terror. In 1995, the Japanese cult, Aum Shinrikyo, released the nerve gas Sarin in the Tokyo subway. The Sarin had been manufactured by the cult's own chemists. Members of this group are also known to have travelled to Zaire in 1992 to obtain samples of the Ebola virus. However, the main causes of concern are anthrax and smallpox.

Anthrax is an organism that is easy to produce in large quantity and is extremely stable in its dried form. The effect of aerosolized anthrax on humans is highly lethal. In 1979, an anthrax epidemic broke out in Sverdlovsk in the Soviet Union. Sverdlovsk was also the home of a military bio-weapons facility. Some 66 people died, all of who lived within four kilometres of the facility. Sheep and cattle also died along the same wind axis, some as far away as 50 km. Anthrax also reared its head shortly after the 9/11 attacks in the United States. A strange white powder was concealed in the mail system that was later confirmed as weapons grade anthrax – as a result several people became contaminated and some even died. However, even anthrax slips into insignificance when compared to diseases such as smallpox.

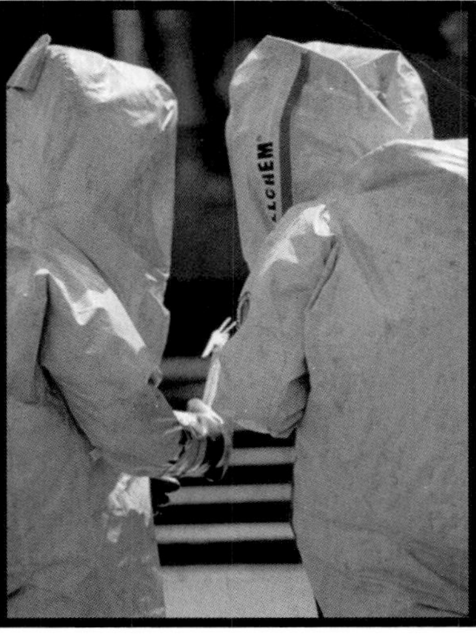

The effectiveness of explosive sabotage fades into insignificance when compared to bio-terrorism.

Smallpox is caused by a virus spread from person to person; those infected develop a characteristic fever and rash. After an incubation period of ten to 12 days, the patient has high fever and pain. Then a rash begins, with small papules developing into pustules on days seven to eight and finally changing to scabs around day 12. Between 25 and 30 per cent of all unvaccinated patients die of the disease. The terrorist potential of aerosolized smallpox is demonstrated by the outbreak in Germany in 1970. A German who had been working in Pakistan became ill with high fever and diarrhoea. He was admitted to a local hospital on the 11 January where he was isolated due to the fact that they thought he might have typhoid fever. Three days later, a rash appeared and by 16 January he was diagnosed with smallpox. He was immediately transported to one of Germany's special isolation hospitals, and more than 100,000 persons were swiftly vaccinated. However, the smallpox patient had had a cough and the coughing acted as a large-volume, small-particle aerosol. Consequently, 19 cases of smallpox occurred in the hospital – resulting in the death of one of the cases.

Two years later, in February 1972, a similar outbreak went undetected in the former country of Yugoslavia. It was four weeks before a correct diagnosis was discovered, by which time the original carrier had already died. Twenty million people were vaccinated. Some 10,000 people spent several weeks in isolation, while neighbouring countries closed their borders. By the time the situation was under control, 175 patients had contracted smallpox, and 35 had died.

CHAPTER

8

When working in a hostile environment, a spy may need to live by one basic law: kill or be killed.

HOSTILE ENVIRONMENT TRAINING

Today, a lot of emphasis is placed on hostile environment training. Aid workers in Afghanistan or Iraq and media personnel covering a live war situation are just two examples. For these individuals, hostile environment training makes their stay in these places more comfortable; for a spy working in a foreign country, such skills are literally a matter of life or death.

Hostile environment training teaches an individual about military combat, weapons, explosives and tactics. A modern spy must learn the safety drills, how the weapon operates, and be able to field strip the weapon in an emergency. Once these skills have been mastered, the student will move on to basic shooting skills, movement and room clearance drills.

The spy must know how to use both weapons from his country of origin and those of his enemy. Most weapons, irrespective of their origin, operate more or less along the same principles. If the spy can understand several in detail, it will provide an elementary understanding of how all pistols and submachine guns operate.

It is always useful for the spy to have a fundamental understanding of explosives and demolitions. A modern spy needs to know how to detect a bomb, deal with a bomb or how to make a bomb. In the normal case of events, specialist units, such as the SAS, will be brought in to perform demolition tasks. This unit has its own unique demolitions course that is restricted to the SAS officers only. The course teaches all the formulas for explosives, both commercial and homemade and their use in sabotage operations (*see* Explosives in MoE section). British spies learn their basic skills during the IONEC military week, when they get to work with the Increment (*see* Clandestine operations).

They must also learn resistance to interrogation. If spies and agents get caught, the information that they possess may be of vital importance to the enemy – if captured, therefore, a spy can almost always expect to be tortured. The modern spy also needs to learn escape and evasion techniques, how to evade dogs and how to stay free once he has escaped.

While these are essential skills for the spy to acquire, his first and foremost skill must be to assess the threat. This means spotting a dangerous situation before it comes to fruition, dealing with a situation that has arisen, and escaping from that situation.

◂ Working in a hostile environment.

AWARENESS

When living and operating in a hostile environment, the spy has to live on his wits. He must be aware of suspicious people or actions that occur at his accommodation or his place of employ. The spy must always be on the alert against an enemy attack. This requires vigilance, observing his immediate environment whenever he is awake. First and foremost, he must evaluate the geography of his location. For example: meeting and dealing with a group of thugs outside a pub in London may result in a good kicking; meeting a group of armed terrorist sympathizers in the back streets of Beirut will result in death. The list of awareness practice is inexhaustible, but the spy should always:

- Be aware of areas with a high-risk element.
- Maintain a fit state of mind; being drunk always makes him vulnerable.
- Change routine, be unpredictable.
- Walk on the right-hand side of the road if the traffic drives on the left. This gives him plenty of time to observe vehicles coming towards him, but makes it difficult for any surveillance following him.
- Avoid observable patterns of behaviour that would enable the enemy to predict his future movements; change his eating and drinking places on a regular basis.
- Vary his habits of catching a bus or a train from the same stop or station every day.
- Be wary of telephoning for taxis. The enemy may be listening in and may provide their own taxi. If meeting an agent he will get the taxi to drop him off several hundred metres away from his home. He will then walk away in the opposite direction.
- Be wary of revealing particulars of his movements to anyone he does not trust. Avoid pre-booking any travel. If he must pre-book, he will do it under someone else's name.
- When he is on public transport, he will seat himself where he can observe the other passengers and get a seat near to the door for a rapid escape.
- If he thinks he is being followed, he will get off and walk back the way he came and check if anyone is following.
- Have a back-up plan should things go wrong.
- Keep his car in a garage if he has one.
- Have photographs of the cars that are normally parked outside in the street and check for any newcomers.
- If he must park on the road, he will park in a place where he can see the car from the house.
- Fit a good motion detector alarm.
- If driving, keep the rear- and side-view mirrors clean.
- Never leave articles in the vehicle, they can be booby-trapped.
- Always carry important documents on his person and use a briefcase as a dummy.
- Keep away from dark or isolated areas, especially at night. Avoid walking through public parks late at night.

Timing is also important. The same back street in Beirut may be a peaceful market place during the hours of daylight, with the bustling streets offering a degree of protection and normality. At 2 am, the market traders will have gone home and the street will be empty.

The first question the spy must ask himself is, “Why I am here?” Assuming he started in a safe location, why is he now in a hostile one? No one simply walks into danger, but the activities of a good spy may require him to do so. It may be that he is going to meet an agent, or that he needs to obtain information about a person or a property. In planning his task, he must understand the dangers, both known and assumed, and make preparations for his safety. He needs to establish whether he should walk, drive, arm himself or have back-up units ready to assist.

The logic of both geography and time provides us with situation awareness; a spy must learn to react to it if he is to survive. Situation awareness is a mixture of visual and mental simulation triggers.

Example: Feeling – this is not a good situation. The area is known to be hostile. Normal activities have calmed down – the local population are moving for cover. Small groups of young men are loosely gathering around. The spy is the only stranger in the immediate vicinity. What should he do?

- Ideally, at the first signs of a situation such as this, he should casually walk or drive to the last known safe area and extract himself.

- If this is not possible, or if the way is blocked, he must look for an escape route. If none are available, he should prepare for an imminent attack, but keep moving
- He will aggressively confront those blocking his path.
- Fight and flee.
- Call for hot extraction. (The problem with calling for back-up is that he will blow his cover.)

A "hostile situation" is a term that is often used very loosely. Basically, it implies that something, usually unplanned, has happened, and that the spy now find himself in a totally unknown and unexpected environment from which there is no immediate prospect of extraction. If he is a suspected spy his life may be under threat. Physical fitness and his exact location at the time of awareness will to a large extent determine his reaction to any unplanned incident. The prospect of being killed or taken prisoner by an enemy must rank as one of the most frightening situations a spy must face. When the immediate fear of the unknown and the looming threat of death plays havoc with the emotions, the only channel open to the spy is to fight – to win.

THE BASICS OF SELF-DEFENCE FOR A SPY

Note: For civilians, it is permissible to use reasonable force to defend yourself and this force can extend to killing your aggressor if they present a real threat to your life or the life of another. Excessive force, however, beyond what is justified by the facts of the situation, must not be used. The best policy is to avoid, if possible, violent situations but to be ready to defend yourself, and others, appropriately if there is no alternative.

In the world of intelligence gathering, most premeditated attacks are carried out by religious zealots. As previously stated, the secret of avoiding any attack is awareness and preparation. Awareness will take away the element of surprise from a spy's attackers; preparation will help the spy defend himself.

In any confrontational situation, he will stay calm and stay ready. He will never allow reasonable behaviour to be mistaken for weakness.

He will defuse the situation by looking confident, always looking for avenues of escape. If the opponents have been drinking heavily or are under the influence of drugs, they will not be able to run very far before they are short of breath. If a fight looks imminent, he will get his blows in first, quickly and with all the aggression he can muster.

BALANCE

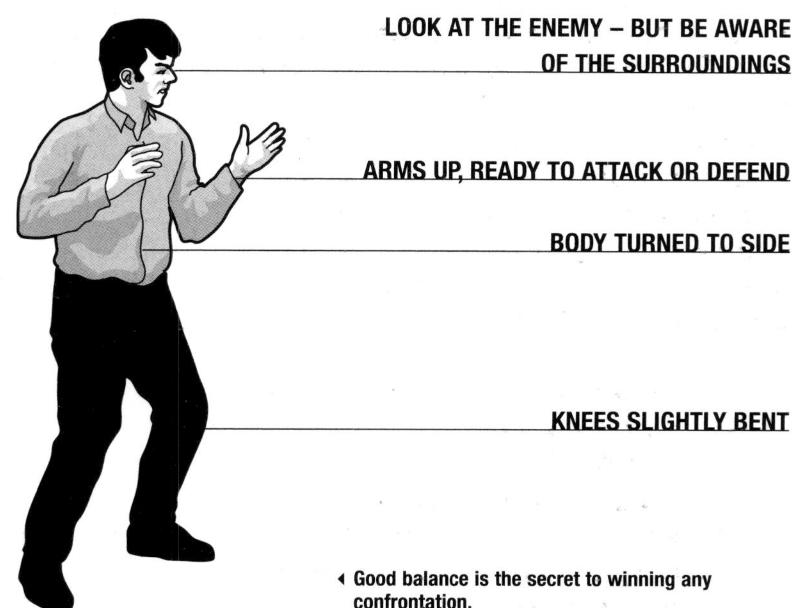

Good balance is the secret to winning any confrontation.

Fighting skills, no matter what form they take, all depend on one single factor, balance. To acquire the skill necessary to overcome any antagonist, there is one outstanding principle: "Without balance there is no strength."

If the body is not properly poised, and thus unbalanced, any struggle between two unarmed people will rely on pure muscular exertion – which means the stronger person will win. In order to win against a stronger person, the spy must adopt a positive mental attitude, coupled with speed and aggression. The "on-guard" stance will automatically put his body into a well-balanced position from which he can use his body strength to its full advantage.

ON GUARD

The best on guard position is taken when a spy is facing an opponent, with feet shoulder-width apart. One leg will be slightly forward and knees will also be bent. Elbows will be tucked in, and hands will be raised to protect face and neck. This can and should be practised by the spy – the agent will stand relaxed and then, with a slight jump, go straight into the on-guard position.

The spy will not stiffen and will try to feel comfortable. He will tell his body that it is a spring at rest. First he will throw out his favoured hand in a blocking motion – at the same time automatically placing the other hand in front of his lower face to protect his mouth and nose, but not obscuring his vision. Next, he will imagine that someone is about to punch him in the stomach. He will keep his stance, with elbows in tight and twist his shoulders from the waist. This puts the muscle of the forearm in a protective position, without having to move feet or upset his balance.

To practise keeping balance, he will move about the floor, first sliding one foot back and drawing the other one after it quickly, until, no matter how he moves, he can always stop instantly in balance without shuffling his feet into position, but with clean-cut, precise movements. When he has to move, he will flow. He will not lift his feet, unless he intends to kick. He will not cross his legs. He will move in the opposite direction to any attack. A good agent will practise the on-guard position with a partner attacking him.

VULNERABLE PARTS OF THE BODY

The human body is well adapted to taking punishment and may survive even the worst assault; this is one of the reasons we have progressed to the top of the animal chain. We can live with no arms or legs, without eyesight or without hearing, but life is a lot better with them. The most vulnerable parts of the body are as follows.

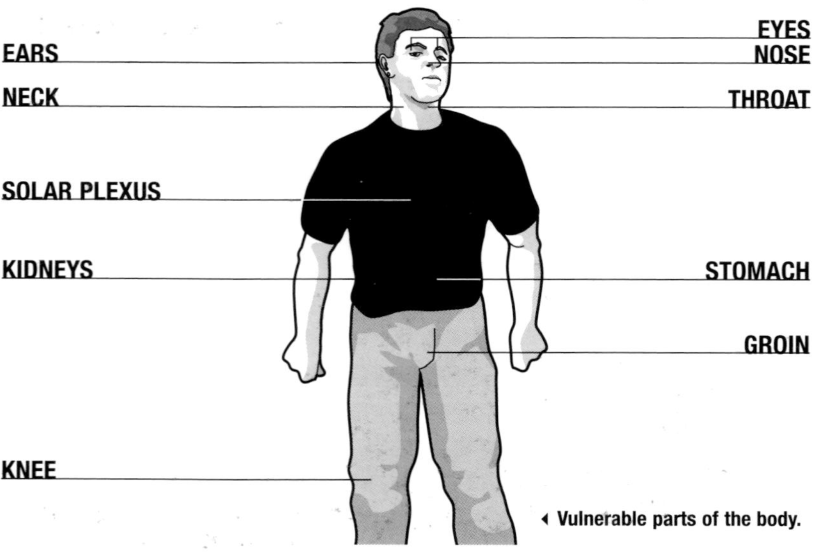

◂ Vulnerable parts of the body.

Note: Below is a list of vulnerable body parts and how a spy can make use of them. These should not be used by non-spy civilians. Members of the general public must only use reasonable force in defending themselves and should not take pre-emptive action.

Eyes

Without eyes the human being is pretty helpless. Damage to an opponent's eyes will cause temporary, or even permanent, loss of vision. This will allow the spy to escape any attacker.

Ears

The ears offer a good target. They offer themselves readily available to biting attacks. Sinking his teeth into someone's ear lobe will have the desired effect if a spy is being attacked. Clapping his open palms over both his attacker's ears will produce a nasty numbing sound to the brain, and has even been known to cause unconsciousness.

Nose

Like the ears, it protrudes and therefore offers a good target to bite or strike with his fist. The spy will use as much force as is deemed necessary to make his attacker break off the attack. Any upward blow will make the attacker lift his head and will offer his throat for a further attack. Even a gentle open-palmed upward movement by the spy to an opponent's nose will cause them to lessen their grip.

Neck and Throat

The neck and throat can be very vulnerable; it contains most of the vessels that keep us alive.

Stomach and Solar Plexus

A heart punch, aimed by the spy at the point where the ribs start to separate, will have a devastating effect on any attacker. Likewise, most people do not have a muscle-bound stomach; the same blow delivered with force will literally knock the wind out of a person.

Testicles

Although a good kick or blow to the groin will hurt a woman, it will cause triple the amount of pain to a man. It is also possible to grab and twist a man's testicles; while this procedure may repel a woman, it will produce the most amazing results.

Lower Legs

A backward blow against either knee joint is guaranteed to stop any attacker chasing the spy. The legs are also a good area to kick if the spy is being held in a bear hug or if he is being gripped from behind. Stamping down hard on the attacker's toes will have the desired effect.

DELIVERING A DECISIVE MOVE

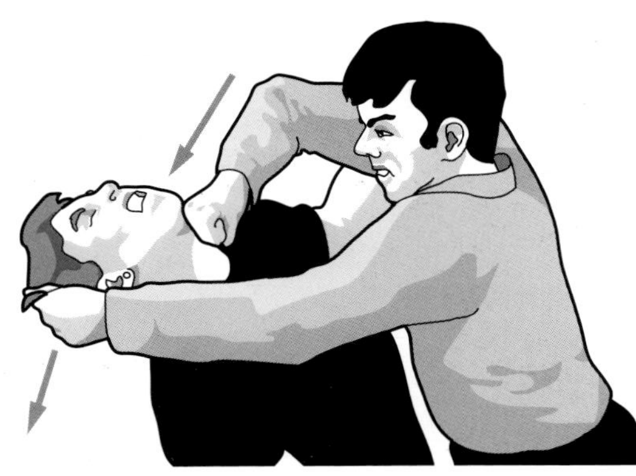

The spy will learn one effective move and use it. The one illustrated here is potentially fatal and would only be used if his life was in danger.

A spy will beat an opponent by learning to recognize the precise moment to strike. Sometimes just one blow, swift, sharp and accurate, will suffice. Other times, the spy may need a practised set move.

Note: members of the public should only use reasonable force in a self-defence situation and never pre-emptive action.

Example: In some cases, the attacker may block the spy against a wall and wait a few seconds before having a go at him. Should the attacker present himself side-on at any time or if the spy can manoeuvre himself into this position, he will take the following action:

- He will grab the crown of his hair and pull his head back sharply.
- This will unbalance the attacker and expose his throat.
- Bring his fist up into his windpipe with one hard blow.
- If he continues to pull backwards, his attacker should drop to the ground.

WEAK POINT

There is an old saying in the SAS, "Take hold of a person's hair and the body will follow." The secret is to maintain a grip from the rear and never let the opponent twist around.

- If the attacker has no hair to grip, the spy will use his hand like a claw and grab at nose and eyes, forcing the head back.
- Once free, the spy will kick, break and run.

USING THE BODY FOR FIGHTING

When in conflict with an attacker, and if no other aid is available, the spy must rely on his own body in order to fight. Surprisingly, this is not as bad as it sounds, as the human body offers much power and force.

Note: Once again, the rules are different for non-spy civilians. Civilians must only act in self-defence and should only use such force as is reasonably necessary in order to escape. Some of the methods below are quite drastic and will be criminal offences unless they are reasonable and in self-defence.

Balled Fist

It is normal for the human to fight with a balled fist. The spy will use his first punch to hit one of his attacker's vital target areas. He will aim for the nose, chin, temple or stomach.

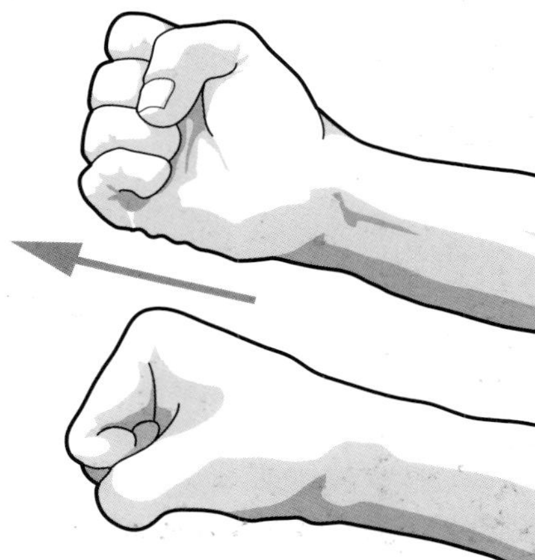

Fingers must be curled in tight with thumbs pointing forwards.

Open Palm

The spy slaps his open palms simultaneously against the ears, from the back or from the front, will cause damage to an attacker. Using a chopping motion against the side and rear of the neck can also be effective.

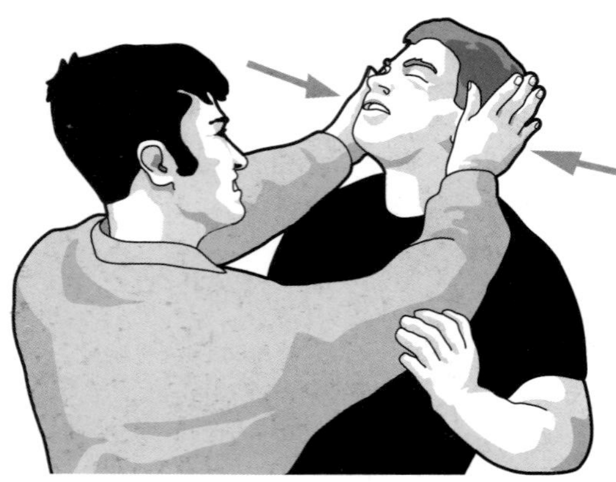

A quick sharp movement will be most effective.

Heel of the Hand

The chin jab is delivered by the spy with the heel of his hand, putting the full force of his body weight behind the punch. When attacking from the front, the spy will spread his fingers and go for the eyes. If attacking from the rear, he will strike the back of the neck just below the hairline for a very effective punch. As the head snaps forward, he will use his fingers to grab the hair and snap it back quickly. He is less likely to injure his hand if he uses heel-of-the-hand techniques.

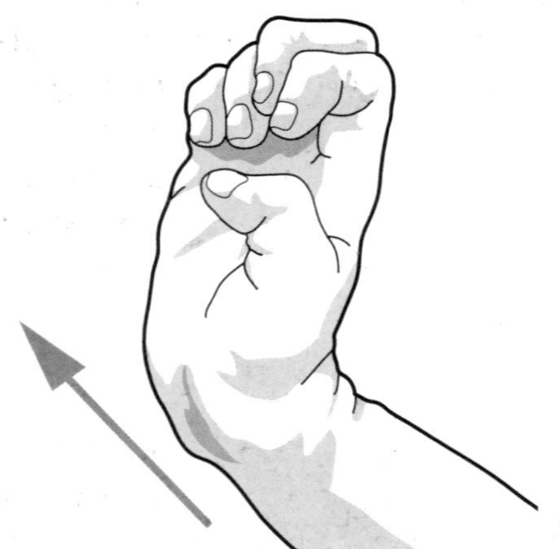

Also known as a "bear paw" punch.

Elbow

The elbow is a formidable weapon if the spy is side-on or if he has his back to the attacker. Jabbing the elbow into the attacker's stomach will usually drop him to the floor. If the spy has been knocked to the ground, he will try elbowing up into the testicles of his attacker. A well-connected blow from the elbow will give him enough time to break contact and run.

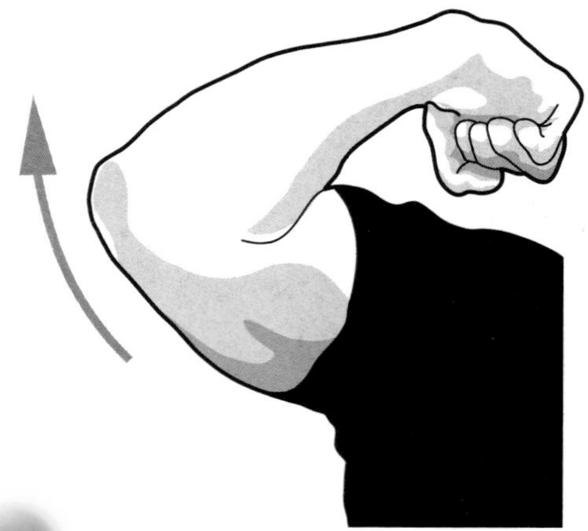

Getting the power of the hips behind an elbow blow can make it an incredibly powerful attack.

Knee

Although it is one of the body's more powerful weapons, it is limited by its movement; it can only be directed to the lower part of the attacker's body. However its battering-ram effect can cause severe damage when driven into the testicles or when aimed at the outer thigh.

Bringing target to knee makes an even more powerful attack.

Foot
A hard kick is as good as any fist punch, and can be used by the spy just as readily. Unless the spy has had some special training, he will keep his kicks below waist height. The moment he lifts his foot from the floor, he becomes unbalanced.

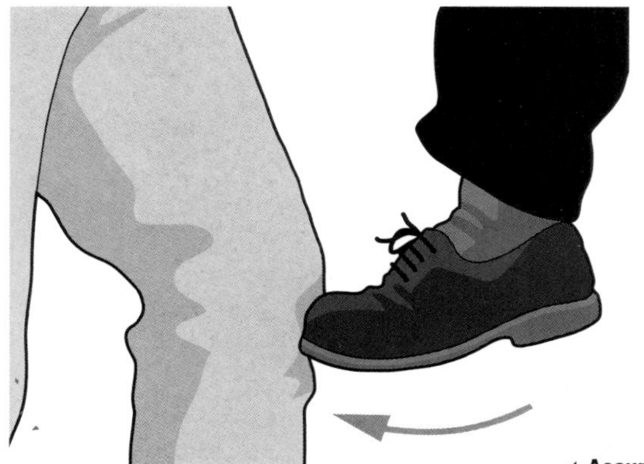

Accuracy helps, but is not essential.

Heel
The heel can be an excellent self-defence tool if the spy has been grabbed from behind. He will drive his heel down on to the instep of the attacker or stamp continually on his foot. Another effective way is to kick the attacker's anklebones.

The spy will swing the heel backwards if he is grabbed from behind.

Teeth
Biting into any part of the attacker's body will cause severe pain and discomfort. The spy will know that the ears and nose are the best places to go for, but any exposed skin will do.

Biting and tearing will cause maximum pain to an attacker's ear.

EVERY ITEM IS A WEAPON
Humans have perfected the art of killing; from the very first club to the cruise missile. While a spy may well be carrying a weapon, such as a pistol, circumstances may prevent him from using it. The spy will often carry a number of seemingly ordinary items that he can use as weapons.

Note: Civilians cannot carry weapons in a public place without good reason or authority. If they do so they are committing a criminal offence. This can extend to objects which are not always viewed as weapons but which the civilian intends to use as a weapon.

Comb
Any type of metal comb or hairbrush will cause discomfort if dragged quickly by the spy across the eyes of an agressor. Equally, just scratching the comb across an attacker's skin may cause them to release their hold.

Coins

A hand full of loose pocket change and formed a fist will greatly increase the force of any blow. Additionally, several coins tied into the corner of a handkerchief will form a very effective cosh. The spy can then swing it at the attacker's temple or general skull area.

Magazine or Newspaper

Any magazine or newspaper can be rolled into a baton and carried around by the spy. He will hold it by the centre to stab with, using either backward or forward thrusts. The end of the baton will be held to beat the attacker around the head. A rolled-up newspaper is a great defensive weapon for the spy to fend off any knife attack.

▲ A rolled-up newspaper or magazine makes a very effective weapon.

Pen

Most types of pen have a pointed tip; that means that they will penetrate skin if used in a punching manner. The pen will be held by the spy as if it were a knife and used against any exposed part of the attacker's body, such as the neck, wrists and temple. The harder the punch, the better the results.

Extendable Baton

This item offers excellent protection for the spy and can be disguised as a key holder. It can be used by the spy as a fencing sword to slash, and rain blows at the attacker's head and hard bone areas, such as the elbows and knees. This is a very useful tool if the spy is outnumbered by attackers.

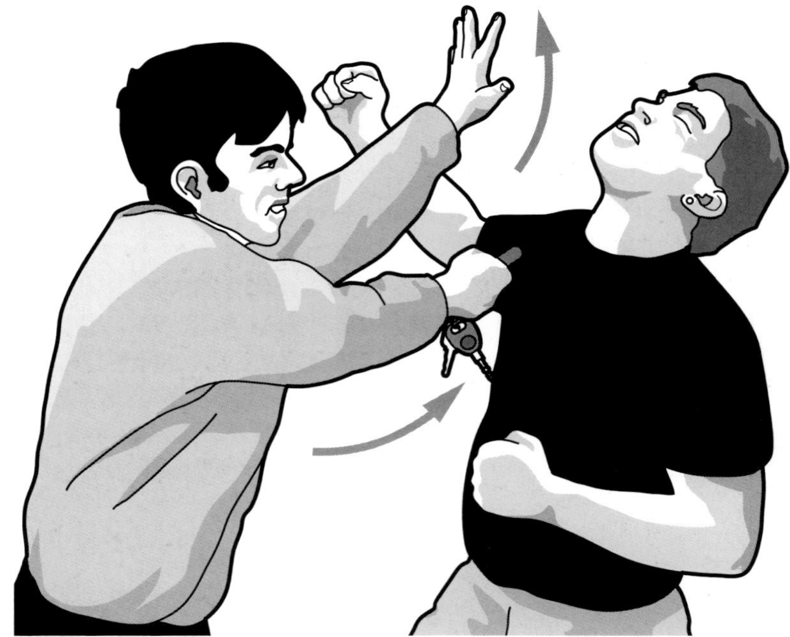

▲ A great weapon – the simple baton.

Ashtray

There is normally a plentiful supply of ashtrays in social premises (such as pubs and restaurants), some of which will be fairly full. Ash can be thrown by the spy into the attacker's face and followed up with the ashtray itself. Most ashtrays are round in shape and, irrespective of weight, can be used by the spy as a Frisbee-type missile.

Pool Cue

This has been a favourite weapon for many a thug over the years. If a spy is attacked in a club he may find that this is a weapon very close to hand and he won't hesitate to use it.

Bicycle

If a spy is attacked while riding a bicycle and is unable to escape, he will pick the bike up and use it as a shield, in the same way as he would use a chair. The bicycle pump is also very handy to use. If it is readily accessible, a spy may even use a bike chain – a steadfast weapon of the 1960s Teddy Boy era.

Boiling Water

This is a good defence if the spy attacked in his home. Boiling water splashed in the face will give him plenty of time to escape. Boiling water can come in any shape or form, a cup of hot coffee or tea, or even hot soup. In a restaurant, the spy may even use the coffee percolator. Most kettles or coffee machines in the home have a 1 m length of electric cable. In an emergency, this can be disconnected from both the power socket and the appliance and used as a weapon. The appliance end can be gripped by the spy and the plug swung at an attacker; it is extremely effective against the head. The same principle can be used by the spy in an office, e.g. computer and printer leads.

Boots and Shoes

All the spy's footwear should be comfortable but sturdy. Kicking is one of the basic defensive moves available to him and it is no good trying to damage an attacker with a pair of flip-flops. A good solid boot will damage an attacker wherever he is hit. The spy will know that it is best to concentrate on the attacker's legs.

Bottle

The favoured weapon of many a street fight, its design could have been made for fighting. The spy will not bother to smash the end of the bottle off; this normally results in the bottle disintegrating altogether. He will use the bottle as he would a club and strike for the head and temples. Being hit on the joints, such as the elbow and kneecap, is particularly painful.

Belt Buckle

Any belt with a good metal buckle will provide a good defensive weapon. The spy will wrap the tail end around his hand several times and then use the belt in a whipping action. He will concentrate his attack on the exposed areas of skin, such as the face, the neck and the hands.

SPY'S OUTFIT

When venturing into a hostile area, the spy will select his shoes with care. They will be light enough to run in, but hard enough to deliver a stunning blow.

Chair

The common household or cafe chair is a very formidable weapon. It can be held by the spy by gripping the back support with one hand and the front of the seat with the other. The spy will always try to attack with a chair if his attacker has a knife. The seat of the chair works as a shield, while the legs can be prodded into the attacker's head and chest.

Cigarette Lighter

If the spy finds himself pinned down or held from behind by a stronger attacker and if it is feasible to reach the lighter about his person, he will use it. The flame from a lighter will break even the strongest hold. Once he is free, he will grip the lighter firmly in his fist and strike against the attacker's temples.

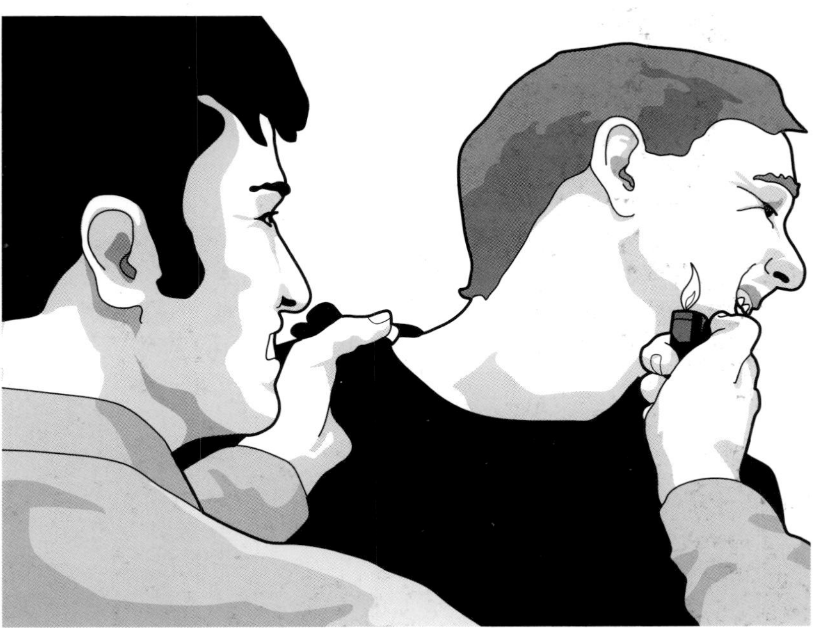

▲ A cigarette lighter can cause a lot of pain.

Coat

This is not so much a weapon, but more of a shield. If the spy is attacked in the street, he will remove his coat and use it in the manner of a bullfighter. Throwing the coat over the attacker's head may only give a couple of seconds head start, but the spy will run faster without it.

Deodorant Spray

Spray carried in a female spy's handbag can be sprayed directly by a female spy into the face of any attacker. Hair spray is particularly effective against the eyes or when sprayed directly into the mouth or nostrils.

▲ Spraying deodorant or similar aerosol products in someone's face will make them think twice.

Caution: Some self-defence books advocate using a cigarette lighter to ignite the spray from an aerosol can but it is rarely used by spies; there is more than a 50/50 chance that the can will explode in the hand.

Fire Extinguisher

Most homes and offices now have several fire extinguishers. The pressurized contents can be used against any attacker by spraying him in the face. Once the attacker is blinded, the spy can beat him over the head with the bottle.

Flashlight

It is common sense to carry a flashlight while walking out any dark night. Although expensive, the more modern Mag-light type torches are extremely good and make an excellent weapon for a spy. The spy will use the flashlight just as he would use a baton.

◂ Using a torch as a club or baton.

CLOSE TO HAND

The spy may carry a small plastic baton fitted to your car keys; this not only stops him from losing them, but also offers an excellent defensive weapon.

Keys

Keys can be used by a spy by laying the key-fob in the palm of the hand with the keys protruding between the fingers. This forms a crude type of weapon. The spy will direct his blows against the vital pressure points of his opponent's head and neck.

Rocks and Soil

If a spy is attacked outdoors, throwing rocks at his attacker will help to keep him at bay. Closer up, a handful of sand or dirt thrown in the attacker's face will temporarily blind him.

Scissors and Screwdrivers

These common household items are very useful for a spy. The spy will use them for jabbing and stabbing, held as a knife.

Socks

Silly as it may seem, a sock will readily make a very effective cosh for a spy when, filled with sand, chippings or soil. In the home, or if the spy is on the street, he may use loose pocket change. He will swing the cosh hard at his attacker's head.

OTHER PROTECTION DEVICES

It is fairly easy to make a wide range of protective devices that are quite effective – a spy may save his life with one; most only require a little imagination. In most countries it is illegal to carry any form of weapon in public, even if it is for the purposes of self-defence so a spy will try to hide the fact that he is carrying anything. This must not be done by a non-spy civilian.

Weighted Clothing

One of the best protective items is the cosh. This weapon has been around for many years and is often associated with old-time gangsters. There are several advantages for a spy to use a cosh; a hit in the right area with a well-made cosh will immobilize most aggressors who have attacked the spy. On top of this, they are easy to conceal about the person, although again, as above, note that concealed weapons are illegal in most countries.

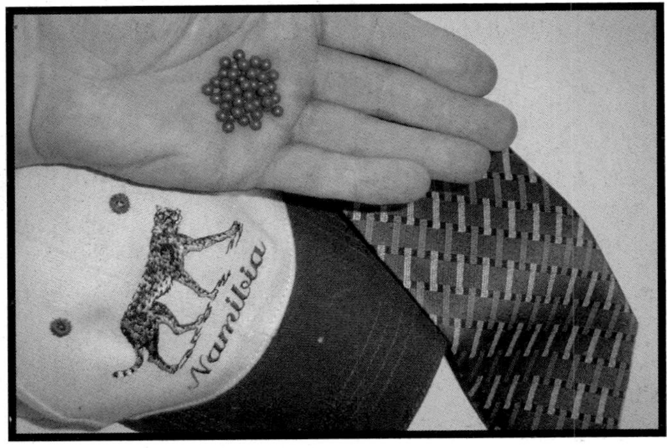

A spy can weight anything with lead shot.

Pepper Spray

Defensive sprays are banned in many countries and thus must not be used by civilians. However, an effective, but non-lethal spray can easily be made by a spy. Both pepper and curry powder offer an excellent deterrent against attacks in the home. In an emergency, it is possible for a spy to throw the dry contents directly into the face of an attacker. However, it is not easy to carry these around and the practicalities of using them out of doors are small.

DEFENSIVE MOVES

If a spy is attacked from the rear and the attacker's arms or hands are within range, he will try biting them. If he manages to get his teeth into a section of his skin, he will only bite a small section, however. By doing this, he will get a better grip and cause a lot more pain to the assailant. A small section is also easier to rip at; the spy will grind his teeth into it and try to come away with some flesh.

If the attacker has a low bear hug hold on the spy, with his arms more around the waist than the chest and thus making it difficult for the spy to slip out, he will try doing a rear head-butt. He will push up on his toes, bend forward at the waist and then slam his head sharply backwards. He will try to hit the attacker's nose. Also, by shifting his hips to one side, the spy may be able to hit the attacker's groin area.

A two-handed attack from behind can be dealt with.

If an attacker grabs him from behind using just one arm, the spy can take the following action.

- He will push his bodyweight forward, twisting in the opposite direction of his attacker's gripping arm.
- At the same time, he will raise his left elbow as high as possible in front of him.
- The attacker will automatically try to pull the spy back. He can use this by twisting back the opposite way, only this time using his momentum and that of his attacker, to bring his elbow back into the face.
- This move can be combined with a backward blow from the other hand, driving a balled fist into the attacker's testicles.

If the spy has been grabbed from behind in a bear hug with both his arms pinned at his side, he will do the following:

- Bend his backside into the attacker; at the same time link his fingers together.
- Bend his knees to drop his body height and try to slip down through the bear hug.

An attack from the front: the spy will block with his front hand and attack with everything else.

- With his fingers linked, he will swing his elbows out.
- Using a rocking, twisting movement, he will swing from the hips, driving his right elbow into his attacker's stomach.
- Follow through with a back head butt or a foot stamp.
- Once free, he will kick, break and run.

Most normal attacks will start from the front. If the spy is quick and recognizes that he is about to be attacked, he can take the following actions before he is held:

- Go into fighting stance.
- Block with his left arm and punch or chin jab with his right hand.
- Continue through the motion. Push back his attacker's head to unbalance him.
- Make sure that he is well balanced before he brings his knee up into the attacker's groin.
- Try to avoid the attacker holding on to him or any part of his clothing.
- Once free, he will kick, break and run.

An attacker may grab the spy around the throat using both of his hands in a strangle hold. He will generally force the spy to the ground maintaining this hold. If possible, the spy will try to relax; the strangle hold on him will not be as effective. Should he find himself threatened in this manner, he will take the following action:

- In the early stages, when his attacker has just gripped, he will bring his right hand, fist clenched, up to his left shoulder.
- With a backward swing, he will drive a back-fist against his attacker's temple (see devastating blow).
- If this is not successful, he will link fingers together between him and his attacker.
- He will raise his clenched arms in an "A" above his head and then drive them down, maintain the "A" by keeping his elbows lower than his hands.
- This will have the effect of either breaking the attacker's hold or, at worst, bringing his head forward.

- The spy will snap his forehead down on his attacker's nose as he brings his linked arms down.
- This procedure can be used either standing or lying down on the ground.

KICKING

Learning to kick properly is not something that many non-spies bother to study, but ask any martial arts expert or a Thai boxer and they will advocate the advantages of giving an attacker a good kick. Spies know that legs are much stronger than arms and they can deliver a really powerful attack. The secret is to keep kicks low; unless a spy has a clear line to an attacker's testicles, he will never kick above knee height. If he does, he puts himself off balance and possibly allows his attacker to grab his leg, at which time he will have control over him. Direct kicks to the side of the ankle or to the front of the knee produce good results.

STEPS AND STAIRS

Sometimes the spy will be attacked on, or near, steps or stairs. If he is being chased or forced up a flight of steps, he may carry out the following:

- Get in front of his attacker.
- Wait until he is are near the top, then bend down and grip the top step or handrail.

For a stair kick, the spy pushes back hard.

- As he leans forward he will bend his knee and then kick back with his foot. The hit will be around chest height; using this, a spy will try to knock his attacker down the stairs. He will chase after him and continue kicking until he can make good his escape.

GETTING UP FROM THE GROUND

Learning the art of falling is almost as important as staying upright, and the chances are that at some stage during a conflict a spy will get knocked to the ground. Therefore, it is something that he needs to practise. Falling in the gym is vastly different from being thrown onto the road or rough ground. Once down the spy becomes vulnerable, but not helpless. It is possible to fight from the ground, but the spy will try to get up as soon as possible.

Getting up.

This is the method to use to get up from the ground. All moves should be made in one continuous roll of the body:

- Turn over sharply onto the left side, with stomach facing downwards.
- Place both palms on the ground and push. At the same time, the right knee should be tucked under the body.
- The left leg is swung under the body until the foot is flat on the ground.
- From there, the spy can spring up and face his attacker.
- He will adopt the on-guard position.

The following method appears in a lot of movies, but with a little practice it will work:

- The spy will roll onto his back.
- He will bring his knees up to his chest and over his head in a rocking motion.
- He will rock forward using a rolling action.
- Favour either left or right hand he will place his palm down to spring back onto his feet.
- He will face his attacker.
- Then adopt the on-guard position.

DEFENDING AGAINST WEAPONS

Guns, knives and machetes are all very dangerous weapons; in most close-range attacks, they will cause serious injury, or even kill. In the event of a robbery, most people give up their possessions without any fuss. A suspected spy, however, may have little choice other than to defend himself. In truth, unless he is fully trained and confident in dealing with such situations, his chances of survival are slim.

It is very difficult to offer any defence against a person who is holding a gun: the spy has to assume that they will use it. An automatic pistol normally has a magazine that contains a certain number of bullets. The magazine needs to be in the pistol; it normally fits inside the handgrip. Once in position, a bullet has to be fed into the chamber of the barrel. This is done when the top slide is pulled back, cocking the pistol. At this stage, providing the safety catch is off, the weapon will fire if the trigger is pulled.

A revolver is different in as much as it houses its bullets in a round cylinder. When the trigger is pulled, a bullet is fired and the cylinder moves one place to the right, pulling a new bullet under the hammer ready to be fired.

There are techniques for disarming a person who is holding a gun on a spy, but these take years of practice and even then there is no guarantee they will work. If the spy is being threatened with a gun, and his death – or the death of another – looks imminent, he will think about the following:

- He will assess the person holding the gun. Could he take him if he was unarmed?
- Assess his actions. How close does he come? (A professional will keep out of striking range.)
- Look at the weapon. Is it an automatic or a revolver? Is the firing hammer cocked back?
- Is the safety catch in the on or off position?

With the gunman standing in front of the spy while his hands are in the air, a straightforward downward snatch at the gun with both hands may work. Once the spy has hold of the gun, he will grip it for all he is worth, using both hands to twist the gun away from him and towards his attacker. He will think twice before pulling the trigger. Given that he has good leverage on the barrel of the weapon, he may be able to wrestle it from his attacker's hands. If he gets hold of the weapon, or if it falls free, he will kick it or throw it out of range and continue the fight on a more even basis.

Both automatic pistols and revolvers will only fire a bullet that is in the chamber, immediately under the hammer. It is possible to prevent a second bullet being fired by holding the top slide of an automatic pistol or by gripping the cylinder of a revolver.

If the gunman has his weapon pressed into the spy's back and he is standing still, the spy will try twisting his body around suddenly when he feels the weapon pressed in hard. He will try a back-fist blow to block the attacker's weapon hand and follow through with a really aggressive action. He will grip and hold the weapon hand to stop the attacker from firing the gun. He will remove the weapon from his attacker's grip if possible.

If the spy manages to disarm his attacker temporarily, he will pick up the weapon. If he is unable to do this, he'll put some distance between himself and the gunman. Even 20 metres will suffice; it is almost impossible to hit a running man at this distance with a pistol. He will zigzag as he runs. He will not stop even if he feels a bullet hitt; if it is serious, he will go down anyway. He will put at least 50 metres between himself and the gunman; the attacker's aim may not be very good, but a lucky bullet can still kill.

A SHOOTING CHANCE

Having been shot twice myself, I know that the immediate effect is one of numbness, although it is still possible to operate. However, some 70 per cent of all bullet wounds occur on the limbs or on other non-fatal parts of the body.

FULL AUTOMATIC WEAPONS

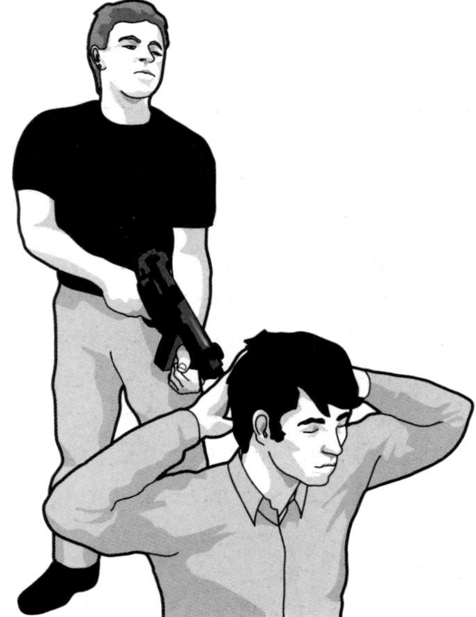

Little can be done against fully automatic weapons.

By nature, spies often operate in areas that are termed "unstable", that is to say areas in which there is some degree of violence. It is a sad fact of life that such areas are also flooded with automatic weapons. In most cases, these weapons are used by untrained and undisciplined people, many of whom are little more than children. Automatic weapons are used in war zones, for serious crimes, such as drugs and terrorist activities.

If a spy is confronted by anyone with an automatic weapon, he will do exactly what they say. The only true defence against an automatic weapon is to be armed and to shoot first.

KNIFE ATTACK

There are two types of knife attack. The first is committed by someone who is in dispute and a knife happens to be handy. This type of person is not likely to stab or cut, but will intend to use the knife in a threatening manner. This can be a good stage for the spy to call a halt to the conflict, by convincing the attacker of the consequences if they stabs him. This may not work, but people who are not used to fighting with a knife will sometimes listen to reason. In some instances, the attacker may use a knife to equal the odds, as he sees it, against a larger or more aggressive opponent. In this case, the spy will let the aggressor know exactly what he will do with the knife if he gets hold of it. Most will back down.

The spy using a chair to stave off a knife attack.

The degree of threat is related to the weapon and to the skill of the person using it. If a spy is involved in a conflict with a person who normally carries a knife, he may well back down. He will try to avoid the situation and run away if he can. Knives can – and often do – kill; if he is forced to fight, he will carry out the following:

- Look for a blocking object, such as a chair.
- Get some protection around one arm, such as a jacket or a coat.
- Stay away from the knife if the attacker is slashing.
- If he is using a stabbing action, take the blade on a padded arm.
- Use a stick, a broom or an umbrella to parry the knife hand.
- He will not try to kick the knife hand, but go for the lower legs.

CAPTURED

A modern spy operating in a hostile area faces the possibility of death or capture on a daily basis. Getting killed is a simple risk of intelligence work; getting captured is one of those unavoidable acts of war. Where men and women are sent to spy in enemy territory, the risk of capture is ever present. Although capture is sometimes inevitable, it should be remembered that, if there is even the slightest chance of avoiding this fate, then that opportunity must be seized.

The spy will never go enter into a hostile environment without some form of back-up or hot extraction plan. He will make sure his route in and out of the country are clearly marked. If he has communications, he'll check that they are working. Better still, he'll wear a hidden alerter that will transmit location. This will be hidden in clothing that the enemy is unlikely to take, e.g. shorts. It will be activated before his hands are tied if possible.

If caught, the spy cannot expect anything other than total hostility from his captors. While a soldier is protected by the Geneva Convention – the rules of which govern the treatment of POWs – more often than not the spy is on his own.

Being captured, means pain and possibly death.

Various factors will determine the spy's fate and his treatment will depend on the organization that eventually captures him. If his captors come from a radical religious sect, he will be of little use to them, other than as a means of demonstrating their religious zeal. Examples of this have recently been seen in Iraq where several captives have been beheaded. If, on the other hand, he is taken by the intelligence agencies of another country, he may well survive. Even if the spy survives, he must be prepared to encounter some hostility and torture, the intensity of which will vary from case to case.

THE ADVANTAGE OF AN EARLY ESCAPE

It is a recognized fact that more opportunities for escape exist during the first few hours of capture. Primarily, the spy will be closer to a familiar area. He will still be fit and may have items that will aid his escape about his person. The longer he waits, the deeper into enemy held territory he will be taken and the stronger will become his bonds.

If his captors have not blindfolded him, he should watch out for the opportunity to escape during transit. He will stay alert and take advantage of diversions such as road blocks or other stops. Even if escape is not immediately obvious, the spy should note his whereabouts and collect any useful items that may aid his escape at a later date.

If he does escape and manages to get free, he will do everything to stay free. If he is still in possession of his alerter, but has been unable to activate it – he will activate it.

THE PSYCHOLOGICAL EFFECTS OF CAPTURE

Even with the amount of sophisticated technology available today, just because the friendly forces can see the spy does not mean they are at liberty to come and get him. If he is captured, or if he is surviving alone for any length of time, without the promise of imminent rescue, various psychological factors will come into play and it is important to understand just how potent these can be.

It is a sad fact that man's psychological reactions to disaster or danger often make him unable to make the best use of his available resources. The spy's first step must, therefore, be to control and direct his own reactions to the current situation. These reactions include pain, fatigue, boredom, loneliness, and the effects of heat and cold, thirst and hunger. Either separately or in combination, they work to induce fear in the individual. Everyone has had some experience of all of them, but very few people have experienced them to the degree of that suffered by a captured spy. Recognizing these psychological factors and understanding how they affect survival prospects are the first important steps to ensuring survival.

TORTURE

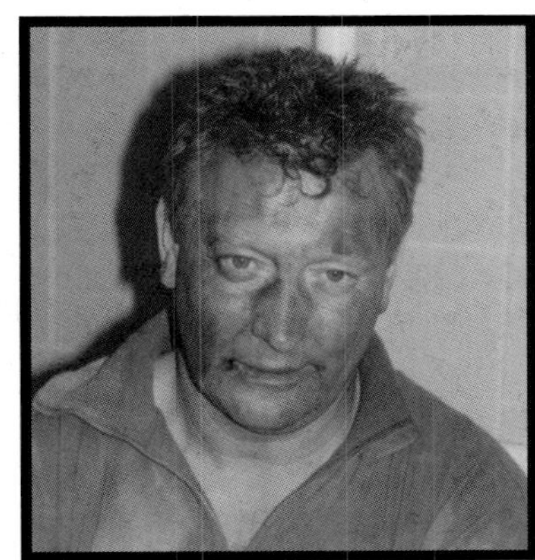

Modern torture techniques can be horrific and include at least a beating.

It is difficult for anyone who has not undergone torture to understand fully the extent of physical pain that can be inflicted upon a human body. Throughout the ages, man has tortured man, normally to extract information or to get a confession, but sometimes purely to satisfy the delight of the torturer. Hot metal has been used to burn or blind people, rocks have been placed on top of people to slowly crush them. During the Middle Ages, the rack was used to stretch people, resulting in unbelievable pain. Yet few of these come close to producing the degree of pain that can be delivered by modern standards. In addition to inflicting pain, most modern torture chambers employ doctors to help prolong not only the life of the prisoner but also extend the amount of pain the prisoner has to suffer.

Note: Torture is obviously illegal throughout the world, but nevertheless it is still carried out in many places.

A very successful form of torture involved dripping water on to a prisoner's head for days at a time. This rendered the prisoner susceptible to questioning. Another method using water is to cover the prisoner's head with a wet pillowcase – this caused the prisoner's mouth to be forced open, gasping for air.

The tools of choice for modern torture seem to be electric DIY tools. There is a horrific degree of pain that domestic tools can produce if they are used on the human body. However, such devices leave telltale signs that, if the prisoner is ever released, lead to accusations by organizations such as Amnesty International – a body with a powerful lobby.

Hence the use of electro-shock devices is much more common, as they leave little or no external evidence.

Electric shocks have been widely used for torture for several decades, but they were perfected during the Second World War by the Germans. To date, Amnesty International has documented the use of electro-shock torture on men, women and children in over 50 countries during the 1990s.

The devices range from cattle prods to state-of-the-art stun guns, the most modern of which are capable of inflicting temporary incapacity or inflicting horrendous pain. The shocks can be applied to moist areas of the body, such as the armpits, the abdomen or inside the legs. Reports have been verified that electro-shocks have even been put inside the mouth, on genitals and inside the vagina and rectum. While short-term application leaves little physical scarring, the long-term effect can lead to permanent mental disorders or heart failure.

PAIN

Pain is a natural occurrence; a normal way of making you pay attention to something that is wrong with your body. However, nature and mental strength also makes it possible to hold off pain for extended periods of time. The simple answer is for the spy to concentrate his thoughts on the pain itself. He will analyse where it hurts worst and try to calculate its severity. It is possible to make pain more bearable in this way. If, on the other hand, he does not attempt to combat it, the pain will weaken his drive to survive. Pain demands a special effort of thought and a will towards both optimism and mental activity. However, his body can only take so much pain before it automatically actives the "off" switch and he falls into unconsciousness.

COLD

This poses a far greater enemy to the prisoner than one would assume. The obvious threat posed by cold is the physical damage that it can inflict, but it is far more insidious than that. It numbs the mind as well as the body. It weakens the will and reduces the ability to think clearly. It can do this in such gentle stages that a positive attitude to resist it is essential before it takes effect.

HEAT

Because many of today's conflicts take place in the Middle East, many captives are forced to spend months in rooms that are little more than ovens. Dizziness, severe headaches and the inability to walk may result from the heat and emergency measures will need to be taken.

FATIGUE, BOREDOM AND ISOLATION

Fatigue arises from lack of hope or an absence of any real goal. It can build up from frustration, dissatisfaction or boredom. It may unconsciously be used as an avenue of escape from a reality that seems too difficult to contemplate. However, unknown reserves of strength can often be summoned if both the dangers and sources of fatigue are recognized and fought against. Boredom and isolation will all feed on the captive's mind. He is waiting and nothing is happening. His hopes and expectations have been dashed. He is alone night after night. He needs to estimate that it will take five years before he is are released; anything else is a bonus. He needs to remind himself that they could have killed him. He will talk to himself if necessary and make plans for the future. He will talk about the future after his escape and devise problems to keep his mind exercised and occupied. Active, positive thinking leaves no room for boredom or loneliness and helps fight off fatigue. The captive should make a long-term escape plan, think it through and make it happen.

ESCAPE

The knowledge of how a spy can escape does not remove the pain, the boredom and the loneliness, but it is a catalyst that invigorates the prisoner's brain into some positive action. All prisoners are normally confined within one or more type of structure. These structures need to be analysed and a plan needs to be made to defeat them. The first problem to solve is how to get out. Should the spy go under, over or through? The answer lies in the confinement's structure.

WALLS

Walls fall into five basic types: brick, stone, block, timber and reinforced concrete. The spy must study his place of confinement and search for an avenue of escape. The spy will do this systematically; check the floors, the walls and the ceilings, he will check the plumbing and any electrical fittings. He will study the guard's routine, such as when he delivers the meals, and check immediate surroundings if taken from the cell.

◂ The first brick is the hardest to remove.

More often than not buildings are constructed from bricks. Bricks are one of the easiest materials to break through. All brick walls get their strength from their bond. If the prisoner can break this bond he can break the wall.

The simplest method of doing this is to select the position where he wishes to exit. Starting at the middle, he can remove all the mortar from around a single brick. This is best done by continually scraping away at the mortar with a makeshift chisel. The process is likely to take a few days to complete. Therefore, work should only be carried out when the prisoner is isolated, with no guards present. Once the first brick is removed, the bond is effectively broken. However, he may have to remove several bricks before the rest are loose enough to be taken out by hand.

BREAKOUT

It may take days to remove the first brick completely. At the end of each session, the prisoner should collect all the powdered mortar scraped from between the bricks and wet it with water or urine and re-use the mortar to cover the work that he has done – adding soap to aid the rebinding. This should prevent any of the guards noticing what he has been up to. If possible, he will select an area that is obscured by some other object, a bed, for example. Floor dust against the wall will mask the work.

BLOCKS

Many of the buildings constructed in recent decades are built of large concrete blocks. These should be treated by the spy in exactly the same way as bricks, although they are more difficult to remove in one piece. However, there is an increased risk of breaking the block, especially those that are hollow internally. Walls constructed of single hollow blocks can be smashed through by a spy in a very short time using a homemade hammer and chisel. A short piece of steel pipe from the plumbing may also serve as an improvised sledgehammer. This is an excellent method of escape if noise is not a limiting factor.

◂ **Blocks can be broken through if noise is not an issue.**

STONE

Normally to be found in older buildings, stone walls are generally very difficult to penetrate because of their thickness. Although the same basic principle to escaping through brick walls is applied, it takes much longer to break though the several layers of different-sized stones. If the spy is in a room with stone walls, it is a good idea to examine the other openings in the room, in particular the windows and the doors. If the building is old, these may well have deteriorated to such an extent that they can be broken from their fixings.

TIMBER

Timber buildings, unless they are made of solid logs, do not pose a formidable problem. A length of metal piping, flattened at one end, can be inserted by the spy between the overlapping panels to force the timbers apart. In addition, panels with the nails removed can offer good escape holes. Escape via the roof of a wooden building should also be considered by the spy, as should the possibility of tunnelling, as some timber buildings are erected on a temporary basis and are placed directly onto earth foundations.

REINFORCED CONCRETE

Buildings made of reinforced concrete pose a major problem. However, these are normally only found in special buildings and in foundations, such as cellars. Escape through the walls is virtually impossible, so the spy will have to look for other means of escape, such as windows, doors, air vents or sewers.

FENCES

Fences come in several different forms, but for the spy, they are either used as a temporary enclosure measure or as a secondary perimeter barrier. All fences need to be meticulously studied to ascertain the wire type, the manufacturing construction and the thickness of the wire.

◂ **Razor-wire.**

Knowing how the wire has been constructed is vital, as some manufacturing methods will allow for a certain number of links to be cut in order to collapse a large section of fence. The thickness of the wire is also important, especially if the spy intends to cut the wire. The spy may also wish to climb the fence, in which case he must be sure that it will bear his weight. The type of wire will influence the spy's decision on how to tackle the fence. For example, if it is razor-wire, then the spy will require some padding if he intends to climb the fence. As with walls, he will study the problem and the construction before deciding on how to escape. Is it best to go over, under or through?

Most fences are made by weaving together metal links; cutting the links in a set pattern will reduce the number of cuts that have to be made and shorten the escape time. On the other hand, solid mesh metal fences such as the ones used in more modern prisons are best climbed, using some homemade claw grip. This is easy to make: the spy can heat a six-inch nail and drill it through a four-inch length of broom handle. When this is done and the nail is still warm, he can bend over the end 5 cm from the tip.

▲ A simple Batman cloak of tough material will get a prisoner over most wire fences.

Fences that can be climbed are often protected by a secondary barrier at the top, these can include razor wire, barbed wire and rolling drums. In the case of razor wire and barbed wire these can normally be crossed by employing the "Batman cloak". Any thick matting, such as carpet or heavy canvas can be fashioned into a Batman-type cloak, prior to climbing. The cloak will not normally get snagged as the spy climbs, and it is a simple matter of throwing it over his head and releasing it from his neck to achieve protection from the hazardous wire.

OVER THE TOP

If the spy is in a prison that is surrounded by a wire fence on top of which is a continuous stretch of drum-shaped tubing, he should forget going over the top. These drums were designed as a result of government tests on prison escapes. They make it literally impossible to climb over, as the drums rotate and, once activated, trigger an alarm.

ELECTRIC FENCES

Very few electric fences are used to house prisoners, but the spy should check if he is not sure. This is simply done by placing a small blade of grass against the fence, making sure he doesn not directly touch the fence with any part of his body. He will hold the blade of grass in his hand and touch the tip to the fence; if nothing is felt, he should advance the blade of grass on the fence and bring his hand closer to it. If, by the time his hand is within 3 cm of the fence, and he feels no tingling sensation, the fence is not live.

Note: On some modern installations, the fences are electrified by intermittent pulses. The pulse cycle may be short, with brief intervals between each one.

TUNNELS

Although tunnelling was a very popular means of escape during the Second World War, it relied on several factors: firstly, the number of prisoners required to dig and distribute the tunnelled earth and secondly, the time that tunnels took to construct. In modern warfare, this method of escape would still be possible, but because modern warfare tends to involve shorter conflicts, it would be best to use short tunnels under fences that can be dug by one person in a single night.

LOCK PICKING

During the Second World War many doors were opened using skeleton keys and by picking the locks. It is said that the prisoners in Colditz had roamed freely round the castle via this method of escape. The principle of picking locks is fairly basic and the tools required can be made easily or improvised; the problem lies in the skill. It can take many years to perfect the fundamentals of lock picking and it requires constant practice to get the "feel". (An outline of lock-picking skills can be found under the MoE section.)

INVENTIVE METHODS OF ESCAPE

In the last 50 years there have been some dramatic escapes. These have been carried out by people who were desperate, and, in some cases, they risked not only their own lives but also those of their families. The most outstanding example was the man who flew his family to freedom from the former East Germany into the West. He did this using a platform and a homemade hot air balloon. They made one abortive attempt. The second time, however, clinging to their homemade platform, the hot air balloon lifted them silently over the mines and fences and across the border to freedom.

ESCAPE TOOLS AND AIDS

One of the major difficulties of confinement is boredom. This can be alleviated by making some escape tools or any other items that may improve the spy's living conditions while he is in captivity. Even a small stick, with its end crushed, will serve as a toothbrush, and will be an aid to health. While making items, a spy will always remember to look after the ones he already has; that includes his clothes and boots. The most important thing of all is to look after the body.

He will be presented with many opportunities to escape during long-term imprisonment. It takes time to adjust to any environment, but the human body is very good at adjusting. The first thing is to analyse the immediate surroundings. What is he actually seeing? Is there a bed in the room? Does the bed have springs? Can these springs be used to make a flexible escape ladder? No matter what items he chooses to make, the spy should use his mind; ingenuity and resourcefulness are the key words.

Food

The spy will always eat any food that he receives in captivity. If he is are planning an escape, he will try to keep some food in reserve. Sugar, for example, can be kept and turned into a solid energy bar; the addition of a little water to dissolve it and then heat will form it into a solid block. All products with a high sugar and salt content have longevity and are ideal for survival escape rations. When possible, any tinned foods issued should be kept for escape rations.

Maps

▲ The basis of a good escape and evasion kit, a silk escape map, gold coins, a miniature compass and lock picks.

The spy should get a map, make a map or steal a map. If he intends to escape, one of the first things he will need is a map. If he cannot find one, he should draw it on the inside of his coat, jacket or shirt. As a last resort, he can keep the map in his mind. When he is escaping, he should look for any type of map, regardless of scale or size. These can be found in cars, telephone boxes, on dead soldiers and many other places.

Lock Picks

Lock picks can be made from an assortment of items, such safety pins, wire flattened at one end, or even cut from hard plastic. If the spy has access to a machine shop, then a good lock-picking set can be made from a set of heavy-duty feeler gauges (*see* Lock Picking).

Chisel

A chisel can be made from any metal substance. Its primary function will be to scrape the mortar from between brick joints. Sources can include anything from the metal tip of a boot to kitchen utensils and piping from any plumbing.

Compass

Escaping is just one part of the problem, evading and travelling to safety is another. To help with this, the spy will need a compass. All that is needed is a magnetised needle and some way to balance it; this will allow it to point to the north. This can be achieved by placing the magnetized item on water or by floating it in the air. Modern plastic razors offer metal strips that are an ideal size.

Bones

All animal bones can be useful. They will provide needles for sewing, buttons for clothing and handles for homemade tools. Bones of all kinds are easy to fashion.

Tyres

Vehicle tyres of any type will provide an excellent raw supply of material for making a number of items: shoes, belts, and, in an emergency, fuel for a fire. A burnt tyre will supply an endless amount of wire for traps and snares.

Note: Burning tyres creates a vast amount of black smoke.

EVASION

How and when he escapes will depend on the individual and their escape opportunity. The spy must take advantage of everything, even the weather. A dark stormy night may not seem ideal, but it will offer him concealment and, more than likely, it will divert the guard's attention. If the storm is strong enough, it may well knock out the local power supply. The spy will face many problems; it may require days or even weeks to find his way to safety. During this time he will have to use all of his survival know-how: he will have to gather food, locate water and stay warm and healthy. Finally, he may have to travel great distances through hostile terrain.

Once he has escaped, the idea is to stay free. A recaptured spy will at best be beaten and at worst killed. Once clear of his immediate confinement, the escapee has two options. One is to lie hidden until the initial search has died down; the other is to clear the area as swiftly as possible. The answer to this is normally dictated by the surroundings and how far it is to safety.

▲ Evasion means staying hidden.

It is more than likely at this stage, that the spy will be totally surrounded by hostiles, with both the military and civilian population on the lookout for him. Therefore, immediately after his escape, it would be wise for him to avoid all contact with the local population and remain unseen. This may involve travelling only at night, under the cover of darkness, or by using some disguise to travel under. A successful evasion after escape will rely on the following:

- Preparation prior to the escape. This means making a workable plan and preparing both mentally and physically. He must decide on the direction and route that needs to be taken. He should cover as many of the "what ifs" as possible and consider all the things that can go wrong. It is important to be both patient and confident.

- Escape and survival equipment. He should use every opportunity to conserve food and where possible turn it into escape rations. He will never throw anything away; even animal bones from food can provide tools.
- He will remember and observe the basic military rules of covert movement. Make full use of camouflage and concealment techniques. If possible, he will select a route that offers the best cover. If he must travel in the open, he will move only at night or when sure that it is safe.
- He will not take any chances. Stay alert. If he thinks that his recapture may result in death, he will try to arm himself.

DOGS

For any escaping spy, the threat of dogs can come from two directions. First, his presence in an area could be compromised by domestic dogs; the second, and by far the biggest threat, is the detection, pursuit and capture by professional tracker dogs and their handlers.

Man has used dogs for military purposes for thousands of years. The Egyptians, the Huns and the Romans all resorted to the use of guard and tracker dogs and the evasion tactics employed by escapees then have changed little.

Police or military dogs must conform to certain requirements, irrespective of their breed. They are physically strong, weighing between 25 to a 50 kg, with a good turn of speed over short distances. This basically means that they can run faster than a human and, if asked, take them to the ground. The best type of dog should have a good temperament, be intelligent, courageous, faithful and energetic. The following breeds fit this category: Alsations, Dobermanns, Rottweilers, Mastiffs and Labradors.

Sensory Characteristics

A dog relies very little on its sight during day-to-day activities; its attention is aroused by movement, and, if it is interested by it, it will then make use of its hearing and smell. There is no evidence that a dog's night vision is any better than that of a man, although its low position to the ground may help, as it will give objects a better definition.

A dog's hearing is twice as sensitive as that of a human, and a dog can be attracted by a noise that its handler cannot hear, although its sense of hearing may well be governed by the weather, in particular wind and rain.

Dogs also have an amazing sense of smell. It is estimated to be some seven to nine hundred times greater than that of humans. It can track microscopic traces of a substance, or vapour that lingers in the air, on the ground or that has come into contact with other objects. A dog can also detect minute disturbances on the ground that may alter the "scent picture".

The Scent Picture

The scent picture is analysed in two ways: from the "air scent" and from the "ground scent". Air scent is comprised mainly of an individual's body scent, clothing, deodorants, toiletries and the chemical aid that is used when washing clothes. The total amount of body scent given off by a human will depend on his constitution, the activity he is undertaking and his mental state. As a prisoner runs along, this scent is suspended in the air for a short while before falling to the ground.

From the dog's perspective, the ground scent deposited will consist of two pictures: the body scent and the disturbance made in the environment as each foot hits the ground. This results in crushed vegetation, dead insects and the breaking of the ground's surface, which releases a gas vapour. Ground scent can last up to 48 hours or even longer in ideal conditions.

Certain factors will affect the scent picture: moist ground conditions, vegetation, humidity, forest areas and light rain, mist or fog will all act to make favourable scent picture. Unfavourable conditions include arid areas, sand, stone, roads and city streets, high winds and heavy rain.

The Guard Dog

Guard dogs are normally employed to detect intruders, locate them and physically apprehend them. In other words, they are used to protect both the property and the handler. They can be employed in several different ways:

- Loose in a compound.
- On a running wire.
- On a lead with their handler.

The Tracker Dog

The tracker dog is employed to find and follow a prisoner's scent as he progresses on foot. They work mainly on ground scent, unlike a guard dog that would work primarily on air scent. The dog will normally follow the freshest scent, and a lot will depend on teamwork between the dog and the handler. The dog is trained to follow a distinct track; it is up to the handler to ensure that it follows the correct one.

Dog Evasion

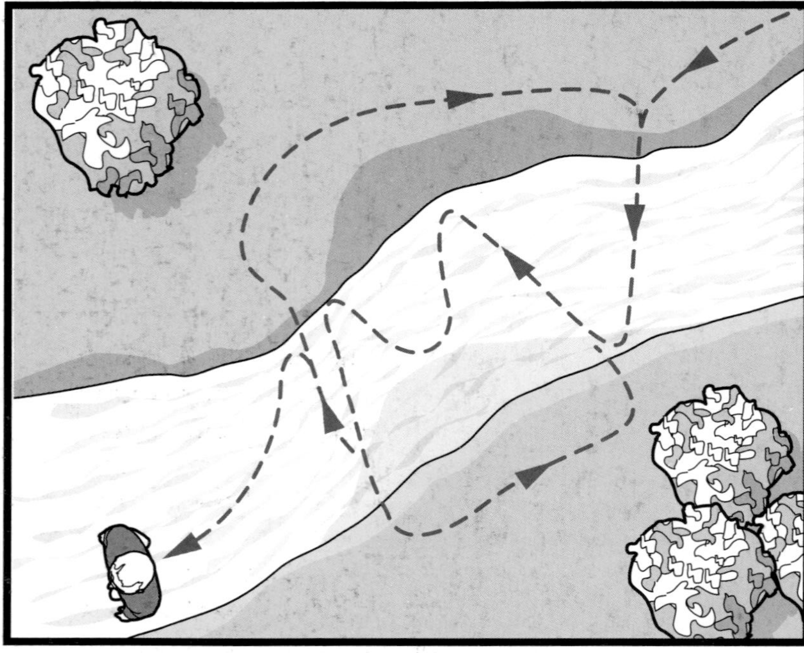

▲ Dog Evasion is not easy, but a spy should be able to fool the dog handler.

If a dog has spotted a moving man, it may lose interest if the man freezes. In immediate pursuit the only thing a spy can do is defend himself. In a delayed pursuit, even if the delay is very short, there are several counter-measures that can be taken. The main aim is to increase the distance between himself and the dog. The spy should:

- Run steadily.
- Climb up or jump down vertical features.
- Swim rivers.
- If he is in a group, split up.
- Run downwind.
- Do things to confuse the handler.

Note: If a spy is being tracked by a dog and its handler, he should cross an obstacle, say a river, and walk some 200 m downstream and cross back over. If this pattern is repeated several times, the handler will think the dog has lost him and call the dog off. In reality, all he has done is confuse the handler.

Attacked by a dog

▲ When attacked by a dog the spy will kill it or it will kill him.

An attacking dog will attempt to paw down any barrier placed in front of it so a strong stick to bar his path could help. The dog will normally wish to take a bite and "lock on" to the spy. If this is the case, the spy will offer a padded arm to the dog. Once the dog has taken a grip, the spy will stab it in the chest or beat it on the head with a rock or a stick. He will make sure that whatever he does to the dog, the injuries caused are permanent; otherwise it will just be even more annoyed. If the handler is not present and the spy has no other weapon, he can try charging directly at the dog with arms outstretched and screaming. Given the size of a human being compared to that of a dog, and the sudden unexpected nature of the attack, the dog may break. A dog's confidence and security can be weakened.

The spy should not use any chemical substances, such as pepper, to put the dog off the scent, as this will only increase the scent picture. If cornered by both dog and handler, he should give up unless armed.

CANINE EVASION

If a dog is charging at an escapee, he should try to break the momentum that it will need to knock him to the ground. This can be achieved by standing next to an object like a tree until the dog is just a few feet away. He will move rapidly behind the tree at the last moment. The dog will be forced to slow in order to turn and the spy can take advantage of this.

WEAPONS TRADECRAFT

▲ Every agent needs to have a good understanding of weapons.

SAFETY RULES

Weapons, especially pistols and submachine-guns, have a nasty habit of being accidentally fired when in the hands of an untrained person, the result of which is often death. The barrels of both are extremely short and therefore even a slight shift of the hand can turn a weapon through 45 degrees or more. Even for a spy the best safety rule is to always check to see if a weapon is loaded or unloaded. A spy will always check:

- Whenever he picks up or puts down a weapon.
- Whenever someone passes him a weapon or he gives someone else a weapon.
- When he signs out or returns a weapon to an armoury.

Here are some simple rules he will follow:

- He will handle the weapon in such a way that the barrel is pointing in a safe direction, either at the ground immediately in front of him, in the air at a 45-degree angle or into a weapons inspection pit.
- He will check the safety catch is turned to "safe" position.
- He will remove the magazine.
- He will cock the weapon and lock back the working parts. This will eject any round in the chamber and will also allow him to see inside the chamber to confirm it is "clear".
- He will release the working parts, set the safety catch to "fire" and, with the weapon pointing in a safe position, squeeze the trigger.
- He will set safety to "safe" and put the weapon down.

Tradecraft requires that all spies are proficient with many basic weapons, both from their own country of origin and foreign ones. Tradecraft training normally starts off with pistol handling, and, irrespective of the weapon used, the basic procedures are always the same. Safety is the first priority, followed by stripping and assembly and then on to basic shooting. At first, the spy will shoot facing the target, but, as he develops his skills, he will learn to shoot from different positions, and will eventually learn to engage more than one target at the same time.

Practice is the key to good responsive shooting, and constant practice, even after mastering the basics, should be encouraged. As well as individual shooting skills, the spy should also be well versed in how to operate under a diverse number of situations. Once the basic pistol has been mastered, the trainee will then move on to the more advanced techniques using automatic weaponry.

WEAPONS

It was rare for a spy in the past to be armed. Spies operating in countries such as Russia and China could be arrested for such an offence – the last thing a spy needs. However, modern spies often work in hostile and dangerous environments, and that makes carrying a weapon essential. The following are a cross section of weapons used by various Western and Eastern intelligence agencies.

SIG Sauer P226

▲ The Sig 226 a modern and powerful covert weapon.

Specification:	Pistol
Calibre:	9 mm x 19 Parabellum
Weight:	750 g
Muzzle velocity:	350 m per second
Magazine capacity:	15- or 20-round box

This pistol is made by one of the oldest Swiss weapons manufacturers, SIG (Schweizerische Industrie Gesellschaft), which was founded in the 1800s. SIG's weapons have always had a reputation for being expensive, but that is because they have such an excellent record for accuracy; mainly attributed to the length of the bearing surfaces between the slide and the frame. In the early 1960s, SIG entered the international market with a new range of pistols, bypassing Swiss arms export laws by making a marketing agreement with a German company. The SIG Sauer P226, with its 15-round magazine, is widely used by Western Intelligence agencies.

Walther PPK

▲ The Walther PPK may be old but it remains the ideal weapon for personal protection.

Specification:	Pistol
Calibre:	7.65 mm or 9 mm Short
Weight:	568 g
Muzzle velocity:	280 m per second
Magazine capacity:	7-round box

Originally designed by Walther as the Polizei Pistole Kriminal, it was intended for undercover protection work. The weapon operates on a well-made, double-action, blowback system. While the PPK is relatively old, it remains a favourite with many intelligence agencies for use as a concealed weapon. It is very reliable, but many doubted its stopping power. The PPK's design has influenced many pistol manufacturers around the world and its original features are often seen in other weapon designs.

Armalite-Colt

The AR15 and AR18 series both achieved substantial commercial success and some notoriety as a favourite weapon of certain terrorist groups. It is the US military version of the AR15, the M16 series, that has become one of the world's premier combat weapons and certainly ranks alongside the Kalashnikov as one of the most widely used. The original design by Eugene Stoner for Armalite, manufactured by Colt, entered service in 1961, but the best-known version, the M16A1, was only introduced in 1966 after field experience in the Vietnam War. The M16A1 is a gas-operated rifle that fires 5.56 mm rounds from 20- or 30-round box magazines in either single shot or fully automatic mode with a cyclic rate of up to 200 rpm. To avoid gross ammunition wastage, a selector was eventually fitted, allowing a three-shot burst. The later M16A2 had a heavier barrel, which allows the use of the more powerful NATO SS109 5.56 mm round, increasing the effective range from 310 m (340 yards) to 500 m (550 yards). The M16A3 is simply an M16A2 with a removable carrying handle, which leaves a more substantial mounting for the larger and more advanced scopes. All M16 variants can be fitted with the M203 40 mm grenade launcher beneath the barrel, which allows for the use of a range of fragmentation or smoke grenades. The M16 series are often fitted with laser-sights, telescopic sights or passive light intensifiers. A further variation, the M15 Colt Commando, had a shorter barrel and retractable butt and was designed for combat in a restricted space, whether it be in the jungle or urban warfare. The latest offering from Colt is the M4A1.

M4A1

◂ **Heavy firepower is supplied from the newer automatic rifles such as the M4.**

Specification:	Assault rifle
Calibre:	5.56 mm NATO
Action:	Gas operated, rotating bolt
Overall length:	838 mm (stock extended); 757 mm (stock fully collapsed)
Barrel length:	370 mm
Weight:	2.52 kg without magazine; 3 kg with magazine loaded with 30 rounds

The M4 modifications include a rail interface system (RIS) instead of the standard handgrip, which allows for a number of different sighting arrangements. These include telescopic sights, reflex red-dot, detachable back-up open sights and laser pointers both visible and infra-red. The weapon can also be fitted with a detachable sound suppressor (silencer) and a modified M203 40 mm grenade launcher. It also incorporates a shorter barrel and a telescoped, four-position stock. In all other aspects, it remains very similar to the M16A3 rifle.

Heckler and Koch

Heckler and Koch produce some of the finest machine guns in the world, and they have become an icon in the battle against terrorism. The company was founded in 1947 by three former employees of Mauser. To begin with, they did not make weapons, but, by 1959, they returned to their original trade and had their first success when their G3 assault rifle was adopted by the West German army. The MP5 developed from the G3 and shares many of its characteristics, especially its relatively light weight. It was first used by German border police, but now can be seen slung around the necks of any half-decent anti-terrorist team. In fact, it almost seems to represent those that fight against terrorism, just as the AK47 has come to represent those that cause it. Most Heckler and Koch weapons are variations upon one model, making various parts interchangeable between models. Also, the stripping and assembly of most models in the range is much the same – for example, the three-pin system is similar in most models, including the infantry weapons and sniper rifles. This makes learning the safety aspects of the range slightly easier. The MP5 uses a closed bolt system which means the round is chambered and ready to be fired. Pressing the trigger simply releases the firing pin. This system has the advantage of keeping the weapon steady while firing.

MP5: Heckler and Koch

▲ The MP5 has been in service for over 30 years yet it is unrivalled in its role, and is used by intelligence agencies around the world.

Specification:	Submachine-gun
Calibre:	9 mm x 19 Parabellum
Weight:	2.55 kg
Muzzle velocity:	400 m per second
Magazine capacity:	15- or 30-round box

This is the weapon of choice for many of the world's anti-terrorist units, including the SAS. It was the weapon used by the SAS during the Iranian Embassy siege in 1980. Its closed-bolt mechanism makes it the most accurate submachine-gun currently on the market. However, these weapons are not cheap. There are various versions of the MP5, including one with a telescopic metal stock and another with a short barrel.

Firing the H and K MP5

- The right hand holds on the pistol grip and the left hand on the forward handgrip.
- The thumb of the right hand sets the selector to "safe".
- The cocking handle is pulled to the rear with the left hand and hooked into the retaining notch.
- A full magazine is inserted into the housing and clipped home.
- The left hand is used in a chopping motion to release the cocking handle.
- The right thumb is used to change the selector to single shot or automatic.
- The gun is aimed and fired.
- When the magazine is empty, the working parts stay closed. This process can be repeated.

Shoulder Holster Rig

▲ The MP5K in a shoulder holster.

Designed for covert use, the shoulder holster rig comprises a shoulder holster and a double magazine carrier used to conceal a 9 mm semi-automatic such as the MP5K. Manufactured in water-resistant soft leather, the harness is designed to be worn for long periods with maximum comfort. The holster and magazine carrier are fitted with loops so that it can be secured to the wearer's belt. The weapon can either be completely withdrawn or fired while still attached to the rig. The SAS favour such holsters when they are engaged in bodyguard work and VIP protection.

The MP5K fitted in a specially designed briefcase.

H and K make a wide variety of weapons, many of which are specially manufactured for covert work; the MP5K briefcase model is a good example. The briefcase is purpose made to take an MP5K (short barrel). The weapon is pre-loaded with a full magazine and the weapon is clipped into place using a set of clamps. The barrel is aligned with a hole in the side of the briefcase. Once assembled, the case is closed and the weapon's functions, such as safety and fire, can be selected by a switch and trigger in the briefcase handle.

Accuracy International PM

Accuracy International produce some of the greatest sniper rifles.

Specification:	L96A1 PM
Calibre:	7.62 mm x 51 NATO Match
Weight:	6.5 kg with sight
Muzzle velocity:	850 m per second
Magazine capacity:	6-round box

The PM is a bolt-action, 7.62 mm sniper's rifle with a free-floating, stainless steel barrel. It is unusual because it has a fully interchangeable and adjustable trigger system that can be switched between rifles. The bolt is cleverly designed to ensure that the head moves neither during its operation nor through the recoil cycle, thus allowing continuous observation of the target. The rifle is equipped with a bipod and a retractable spike on the rear of the butt that effectively creates a tripod for use during long hours of surveillance. This is considered to be of great value by the SAS SP (Special Project) teams. It has a box magazine holding 12 rounds and, with scopes such as the Schmidt and Bender 6 x 42, has a lethal range in excess of 620 m (700 yards). The 7.62 mm PM or Counter-Terrorist (L96A1) can also be found chambered in .300 Winchester Magnum and 7 mm Remington Magnum. It is currently considered to be the best available sniper rifle in its class.

Heckler and Koch PSG1 Sniper Rifle

The H & K PSG1 sniper rifle.

Specification: PSG1
Calibre: 7.62 mm x 51 NATO (.308 Winchester match)
Weight: 9 kg with sight
Muzzle velocity: 820 m per second
Magazine capacity: 5- or 20-round box

The PSG1 is a semi-automatic 7.62 mm sniper's rifle with a free-floating bull barrel and a single adjustable trigger. It is a heavyweight weapon, at around 8 kg, and is therefore most often used for precision kills from a fixed position. The stock has an adjustable cheek pad while a pistol grip and butt plate all help extend stability and the sniper's comfort zone. Equipped with a bipod and either a five- or 20-round box magazine, the PSG1 has an enviable reputation as an excellent sniper's weapon. It is equipped with a sight, such as the Hensoldt Wetzler 6 x 42, which is adjustable from 100 m to 600 m and also has an integral battery-powered illumination unit for the crosshairs in low-light shooting situations. This sight also is very fast in engaging multiple targets.

POPULAR TERRORIST WEAPONS

KALASHNIKOV

Mikhail Kalashnikov's original design, though influenced by the German assault rifles that appeared towards the close of Second World War, became a triumph of military practicality, through its ease of mass production and its reliability. Since the first version, the AK47 achieved widespread use in the early 1950s. The design has constantly spawned new variations, produced both in Russia and throughout the world. The AKM, a simplified design, is capable of manufacture in relatively unsophisticated industrial facilities. Both were chambered in the short Russian 7.62 mm round, with 30-round curved magazines and had a cyclic rate of 600 rpm. Kalashnikovs are the standard infantry weapon of the former Soviet Union and are also widely used by other countries. It is a popular weapon in many Third World countries because it is relatively cheap, extremely robust and will operate under almost any conditions. After World War II the Soviet Union carried out a full analysis of infantry battles. The results showed that most fighting took place at close range. The AK47 was designed around this research, making it one of the most combat effective weapons in its class.

AK74

◂ The AK74 assault rifle.

Specification: Assault rifle
Calibre: 5.45 mm x 39 Soviet
Weight: 3.6 kg empty
Muzzle velocity: 900 m per second
Magazine capacity: 30-round box

Developed from the older AKM 1974, the 5.45 mm AK47 is a re-chambered version. Lighter and with a higher cyclic rate of fire at 650 rpm and an effective range of 500 m (550 yards), it has already appeared in a number of variations from the standard with fixed stock; the airborne/Special Forces version, with folding stock; the squad automatic weapon, the RPK-74 with a 40-round magazine and the AKR submachine-gun. This latter variant is very similar to the AKS-74, but with a shorter barrel and an effective range of only 100 m (110 yards).

Dragunov SVD

Specification: Sniper rifle
Calibre: 7.62 mm x 54 rimmed
Weight: 4.3 kg
Muzzle velocity: 830 m per second
Magazine capacity: 10-round box

The Soviet army discovered the value of snipers during the Second World War and for many years they used the old bolt-action Moisin-Nagant, the heritage of which dates back to the 1880s. The Dragunov first appeared in the early 1960s and was partly based on the Kalashnikov. The SVD differs because it uses a short-stroke piston to operate the bolt carrier, which is more appropriate to the needs of a sniper rifle as the long stroke of the AK could affect both the stability and the accuracy. In combat conditions, many of the AK family parts can be interchanged with the SVD. The SVD chambered in 7.62 mm full power was introduced in 1983 and has a 10-round box magazine. Equipped with either a PSO-1 telescopic sight or the NSPU-3 image-intensifying night sight, this Russian weapon is one of the world's most widely used Special Forces sniper rifles and is credited with a range of at least 1,000m.

Norinco Type 64/67

Specification:	Silenced pistol
Calibre:	7.65 x 17 mm rimless
Weight:	1.18 kg
Muzzle velocity:	205 metres per second
Magazine capacity:	9-round box

This Chinese pistol is produced exclusively in silenced form. It has two forms of firing, manually operated single-shot and self-loading. When the choice selector is pushed to the left the breech is locked, allowing only a single shot. The breech block must be hand-operated in order to fire a second round or change self-loading. The second option is achieved by pushing the choice selector to the right. The weapon is extra silent in single-shot, locked-breech mode. The pistol fires a 7.65 x 17 mm rimless round unique to this pistol. As with all silenced weapons, the gasses are discharged into a large tube-like attachment that is fitted to the end of the barrel. In this case, the sound is broken down by a combination of rubber grommets and wire mesh. It is essentially an assassination weapon.

COMBAT SHOTGUNS

Both the Americans and British favour the Remington 870, 12-gauge pump-action shotgun. Shotguns are not new to intelligence services and have proved highly effective in close-quarter actions. Shotguns can be used for various purposes – from blowing open non-armoured doors to dispersing gas. Deadly at 40 m, most combat shotguns are extremely useful in hostage rescue operations or anti-hijacking assaults. Early combat shotguns were merely modified civilian weapons, but, the newer variants are designed purely for the military, especially as a close-range assault weapon.

SPECIAL AMMUNITION

Enhanced capability ammunition is produced for a variety of small arms regularly used by Special Forces. High-penetration rounds are produced to deal with terrorists equipped with protective body-armour, such as the KTW-round, high velocity bullets made of bronze alloy and coated with Teflon. Another bullet, the Glaser round, is filled with shot in a copper case sealed with Teflon and is designed to penetrate plaster walls or wooden partitions and then to fragment, causing devastating flesh wounds to the target. One of the advantages of this type of round is that there is little chance of a ricochet injuring a member of the assault team or an innocent bystander.

HATTON ROUND

The Hatton round is a 12-bore cartridge that ceases to be a missile on impact. It is primarily used to remove hinges and locks from doors. The British SAS employ Hatton rounds by firing them from a Remington shotgun to ensure rapid entry during an anti-terrorist assault. The muzzle of the shotgun is placed directly against the hinge or locks and is then fired; this allows for most doors to be opened without harming hostages who might be on the other side. The shot is a compound of micronized gas that is released after smashing off the door hinge.

STUN GRENADE

◂ The effect of a stun grenade in a totally darkened room is outstanding, allowing the assault team members the vital seconds they need.

The first stun grenades were originally designed and made in the United Kingdom at the request of the British SAS. Today, they are a formidable tool and can be found in the armoury of most intelligence agencies. The SAS needed a weapon that could provide them with vital seconds to come to grips with terrorists. The Royal Ordnance experimental unit made various devices and eventually came up with the stun grenade. It consists of a G60, which makes a loud noise (160 Db), combined with a high light output (300,000 cd) that does not produce any harmful fragmentation. The effect is similar to a flashing strobe in a disco but a million times stronger. Anyone in close proximity to a stun grenade when it goes off will be stunned and unable to move for about three to five seconds.

SPECIAL OPTICS AND OTHER SIGHTING DEVICES

One of the first problems encountered in a Special Forces operation is darkness or restricted visibility. This can be caused by smoke, because the power has been cut at some point in an enclosed CQB (close-quarters battle) or simply as a result of the time of day set for the operation. A wide range of advanced low-light or fast-acquisition optics is now available either for use on weapons or attached to helmets or worn as goggles.

For snipers, the efficiency of light-enhancing optics can provide the difference between the success of the mission and the life or death of the hostages. Various laser-targeting devices are used; these are mounted on the weapon and, when activated, they place a small red dot on the target at the point where the bullet should strike. It has its uses in rapid-target acquisition scenarios and in bright light conditions, the laser spot has a range of 100 m (110 yards).

GAS

Over the years, both the military and intelligence agencies have developed a wide variety of gas products for one purpose or another. Capsules containing cyanide gas were given to spies and agents to provide them with a means of suicide should they get captured. Similar cyanide devices with a remote electronic triggering device have been made for assassination. However, gas in all forms remains a double-edged weapon when poorly used. Any gas usage requires the operator to wear a protective respirator.

The most common form of gas currently used is CS. This is an irritating, or harassing, agent, more commonly described as vomiting or tear gas; it is a sensory irritant. Its action is usually rapid enough for it to be used as an incapacitating agent in hostage rescue situations. Its effects are usually comparatively brief, but in extremely high concentrations or in very confined spaces, it can be lethal.

Some agents cause a temporary flow of tears and are known as lachrymators; some, called sterutators, induce uncontrollable sneezing or coughing; some agents, called orticants, cause severe itching or stinging to the skin, and others, if swallowed or inhaled, cause bouts of violent vomiting.

Many of the wide range of agents now available were developed during the First World War and these include CN (Chloroacetophenone), the "classical" tear gas and DM-Adamsite, which is slower acting than CN, but which also causes severe headaches and nausea. The faster-acting and more effective CS, named after its discoverers BB Corson and RW Stoughton and otherwise known as Orthochlorobenzylidene Malonbuitvise, dates from 1928, but was only really developed for military and police use in the mid-1950s by the British War Office (today's Ministry of Defence). CS in any concentration higher than 2 milligrams per cubic metre is likely to cause anything from a severe pricking sensation behind the eyes to an uncontrollable flow of tears, coughing, streaming nose, retching, vomiting and a gripping pain in the chest. In normal circumstances, an individual is likely to be incapacitated within 20 to 40 seconds of contact with the gas and to suffer the after-effects for up to ten minutes, even after exposure to fresh air.

◂ The black respirator provides protection against gas, but it also has an intimidating effect.

CASE HISTORY

During the evening of Wednesday, 23 October 2002, 50 Chechen guerrillas – 32 men and 18 women – stormed a Moscow theatre, taking some 700 hostages. The rebels had massive amounts of explosives, which they threatened to detonate, and kill both themselves and the hostages.

A few days later at 5.30 am, a potent gas was released into the building through the air conditioning system of the theatre. This gas, which has now been identified as an opiate-based anaesthetic, quickly put those inside to sleep before any explosives could be detonated. An Alpha team of the Russian Special Forces then stormed the building, shooting and killing all of the Chechens and bringing out the hostages. Gunfire and explosions were heard for approximately 15 minutes before the all clear was sounded. Unfortunately the gas proved lethal for some hostages with heart or respiratory conditions and 115 died as a result of the rescue. A further 42 remained seriously ill in hospital.

NEW WEAPONS IN THE WAR AGAINST TERRORISM

There have been several new developments in the war against terrorism. One is a new type of stun grenade that is thrown into a room prior to an assault and whose detonation is controlled from the weapon of the soldier who threw it. Instead of having the stun grenade detonate automatically on impact, the person who threw it has the opportunity to evaluate the situation before reacting, and the operator may choose a different option. For example, if the room turns out to be only occupied by women and children or non-combatants the grenade may only emit smoke or flare a bright light. If, on the other hand, the room contains armed hostiles the grenade can be detonated, causing a disabling effect on the occupants. While this seems like a softly, softly approach to terrorism, the "hearts and minds" benefits in not killing innocent people has really paid off in such places as Iraq.

Another serious development is the Belgian FN P90 PDW (Personal Defence Weapon). This compact but full-powered weapon was designed primarily for military personnel including communications specialists, drivers, and the like. However, it has built itself up a reputation with many counter-terrorist units, as the weapon is ideal for operating in urban and other close-quarter battle scenarios and environments. By design, the P90 is one of the most ergonomic guns in the world. The extensive use of composite materials contributes to the light weight of the weapon system, and the balance of the gun, whether used by a left- or right-handed shooter, is not compromised. The mechanism of the P90 is quite simple, and without tools the gun breaks down for field stripping into three major assemblies, in addition to the magazine, in about five seconds. The P90 features a blow-back mechanism and fires from a closed breech, thereby combining the reliability of the simplest operating system with the accuracy potential of a full-size weapon.

FN P90 PDW

Specification:	Sniper rifle
Calibre:	5.7 mm x 54 mm rimmed
Weight:	4.3 kg
Muzzle velocity:	830 metres per second
Magazine capacity:	10-round box

CHAPTER 9

A spy, agent or not, must be able to look after his own personal security. There are certain basic points that facilitate this.

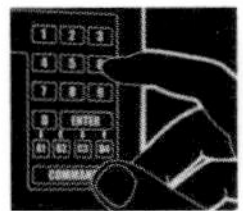

SELF-PRESERVATION

Nobody likes to learn that they are being watched, listened to, or followed. Unfortunately, governments and other institutions these days have the power to hold significant records on individuals. However, there are many means at a spy's disposal for keeping a very low profile, or even ducking out of the system altogether. As well as this, any individual may want to learn how to avoid being "attacked", be it physically or via electronic means: banking, billing and the like.

Author's Note: I have always been fascinated by the way that people put a label on individuals who pertain to be spies, secret agents, assassins and executioners. The label appears to elevate them, as if they exist in a different dimension. Yet they are all human; they have mothers, fathers, wives and children. Most people who work for intelligence agencies do so in the belief that they are helping to protect their country. A member of an Israeli "Kidon" team may fly to Paris to assassinate what they term to be a Palestinian terrorist and then fly back to Israel and spend the weekend playing with his children. For some 18 years, when I was a member of the British SAS, I always seemed to have a weapon in my hand. On one occasion, the prime minister sent me and a colleague to help free the hostages from a hijacked Lufthansa aircraft. Five days later, three of the four hijackers were dead, and most of the hostages were released alive. I just went home to my wife and two young children. This was not an isolated incident. I have always carried a weapon and used it in many countries. Ask me if I am ever worried that my past will one day catch up with me and I will answer not really. Nevertheless, I keep a weapon handy and I do take some basic precautions. So, a spy, a secret agent, an assassin, executioner or just plain John Doe, should take precautions to protect yourself in everyday life.

Note: "Kidon" is the name widely used to identify an Israeli assassin. Kidon is the executive arm of Mossad and is based in the Negev Desert. It is a small unit of around 50 people, a handful of whom are women. Years of protecting Israeli interests have made them highly skilled at assassination techniques. Kidon operators normally work in teams of four and, while they can call on the Mossad structure for support they rarely do.

SECURITY IN THE HOME

A spy is at his most vulnerable when approaching or leaving his home. Anyone looking for him will know that at one time or another he can always be found there. Home is where he relaxes and drops his guard; it is also a place where he holds most of the documents and information that establish his identity. Home is also a place he shares with his loved ones. He will keep this in mind and anticipate any intrusion into his personal life and home. Above all, he will always – always – listen to his senses and gut feelings – if something does not feel right, then it usually isn't. He may think about the following self-preservation points:

▲ **The ultimate guard dog.**

- Get a dog with attitude. Better still, get two.
- If permitted, always have some form of weapon handy. A baseball bat is a good option.
- Construct a safe room within his house. Make this impregnable for at least five minutes. He will make sure that he can activate an alarm from this room and that he has means to telephone the police.
- When not in use, he will make sure his car is always garaged, even in the day time.
- Always lock the garage and set the alarm.
- Fit sensor-activated cameras and record all activity around his home.
- Fit a very noisy alarm system.
- Fit mortise deadlocks to all outer doors.
- Fit wrecker bars to glazed doors and windows.
- Protect weak and vulnerable entry points with magnetic contacts or glass-breaker sensors.
- Use a key box for all of keys and make sure he knows who holds any keys to his home.
- Fit lightproof curtains to all windows. This avoids assassination from outside at night.
- Fit good lighting to all dark areas around the house.
- Always leave a light burning at night.
- Have emergency spot lighting that is controlled from inside the house.
- Have emergency lighting, such as gas lanterns and torches, easily accessible inside the house.
- Make entry and exit difficult for any assailant, with the aid of a high fence or a wall around the garden.
- Remove any house number and his name from the letterbox.
- Never answer the door automatically – always check who is there first.
- Put a chain on the door.
- Insist on seeing identity cards from anyone who needs access to the home, such as meter readers or work people.
- Never leave his home while strangers are present.
- Always lock doors and windows, even if only leaving for a few minutes.
- Ask friends to telephone him before coming over.
- Treat all visitors after midnight as suspicious.
- If he is leaving home for any length of time, he will cancel any regular deliveries and have a trusted neighbour empty the mailbox.
- Never tell anyone about his business or the fact that he is going away.

Preparation is the key to protecting both himself and his family, but the spy cannot live under constant fear. I have found it advantageous to anticipate the types of attack that may be directed against my family and our home. For example, shooting involves line of sight, even for a sniper, and a person using a pistol needs to get within a few feet of his target to be certain. Therefore, the spy is fairly safe when he is at home. An explosive attack is more likely to be against his car, but letter bombs delivered to the home are also effective. In some countries, there is a real hazard from suicide bombers, not just in the home but also while the spy could be out socializing. A professional assassin will almost certainly get to the spy if he needs to, so there is little point in getting paranoid. The spy will take a few simple precautions and follow his gut feelings in an effort to survive.

▲ If a spy has a weapon around the house, he'll make sure it's handy. Some spies may even sleep with a gun under their pillow.

I no longer keep sensitive material in my home, but, as a writer, I do hold a lot of valuable material. Both sensitive and valuable material should be protected. The best idea is to invest in wall safe, and most DIY stores now stock a wide variety of them. A spy may use a box folder for such things as family identification, birth certificates, marriage certificate, passports etc., and another for any personal papers that he deems to be sensitive or valuable. These should be placed in a safe place under lock and key and only removed when necessary. Avoid doing this when strangers are in the home. A spy will never keep sensitive material that is no longer required in his home; he will destroy it. It is best to burn documents and then flush the ashes down the toilet.

He will always back up any important material from his computer. Personally, I use a removable hard drive, rather than disks, and remove this every night. Make sure that this hard drive is put in a safe, dry place. Computers are vulnerable to attack and it is a simple matter for people to hack into it and download all information. Additionally, a computer stores a record of all your activities, including everything you download from the Internet. Computers should be purged by formatting the internal hard drive every four to six weeks. While this may seem drastic, it works. I use my back-up hard drive to reinstall important work. If email is used, a spy will always make sure that it is encrypted, and send important documents hidden within a digital picture (see Secret Codes).

While many telephones are fitted by private companies, most telephone systems are controlled by the state. This means that the state can listen to any conversation at any time. Additionally, telephones can be bugged or used to trigger another hidden bugging device (see Surveillance). A home telephone should be used as little as possible and never for important business. A spy will assume that a third party is listening in to his conversation. That way, he will not say anything he should not. He will take the telephone apart and check if it has been tampered with, although it is almost impossible to tell these days. He will have a separate, "clean" telephone locked away and only plug this in when he needs to talk to someone special. Mobile phones are cheap and easy methods of temporarily making and receiving anonymous calls.

We all receive mail. For the most part we open the letterbox, take out the mail and open it in our homes – bad move. Letter bombs are easy to make (see Sabotage), yet most people never give this a second thought. Most of us recognize our mail, the familiar bank statements, bills and volumes of junk mail. Occasionally there is one that stands out; it looks interesting and so we rush to open it. A spy will always consider there may be a bomb-related risk. Was I expecting this letter? Do I know who sent it? Is the letter bulky, more than two sheets of writing paper? Are there any lumps or hard pieces? If he is not sure, he may use the follwing trick.

A very thin piece of wire can be carefully pushed through the bottom of the envelope. The wire is looped and fastened to a length of string. Most letter bombs only contain a small amount of explosive, so a three-metre length of string should be enough. The envelope should be laid on the ground and secured carefully with a weight – not enough to crush the letter. Then, from a safe distance, the wire should be pulled to rip open the bottom of the envelope. If it does not go bang, the letter can be picked up, bottom uppermost. Many letter bombs are activated by the top flap being opened or by the contents being removed. Both of these methods can be assessed by opening the bottom of the letter. It is a good idea to be suspicious of bulky greeting cards that have musical chimes.

▲ **Why take the chance? If he suspects a letter bomb, a spy will open it with wire and string from a safe distance.**

A spy's car is an extension of his home. It is the means by which he travels to and from home. This makes it equally vulnerable to attack. Many people have been killed by car bombs and there will doubtless be many more. It is a destructive form of attack and one that is fairly simple to achieve. Car bombs can be triggered by pressure, pull, speed, breaking or any electric device within the car, such as turning the radio on. They can also be triggered by various radio devices that are remote from the car.

A professional assassin would practise on a similar make and model of vehicle to that used by his target, to ensure that when he places the explosives, they are almost impossible to find. These basic rules will minimize the threat.

▲ **When checking for a car bomb, the most likely place is around or near the driver's seat.**

Most assassins who use car bombs always place the explosive close to the driver's seat, so the spy will make sure that he always checks this area thoroughly. He will always garage his car when it is not being used. He will always check his car before getting in. He'll check the bonnet, underneath the car and under the seat. He'll go to both windows and look at the opposite door for signs of tampering or for any wires. He'll carry out a sweep every time he uses his car, because if he is under observation this approach will often deter anyone from planting a bomb. The enemy can attack the car in four different ways:

- Using a device placed directly on the vehicle that is detonated on entry or ignition.
- Using a device placed on the vehicle that is detonated while in transit by radio control.
- Placing a large bomb along the route the spy will travel – in a drainage ditch or on an embankment.
- By firing a rocket-propelled grenade at the vehicle.

Finally, if the spy ever gets attacked in the home and manages to gain the advantage over his assailant, he will make sure that they never come back a second time. Self-preservation means fighting back and winning.

GLOSSARY

CQB – Close-Quarters Battle. Hand-to-hand or weapon combat that occurs at very close range.

Echelon – A powerful intelligence-gathering organization. It captures huge volumes of information from cellular, microwave, satellite and fibre-optic sources and processes them for security purposes.

EDX – Electronic Data Exchange.

FARC – Revolutionary Armed Forces of Colombia (Fuerzas Armadas Revolucionarios de Colombia). A terrorist organization formed in 1957, the guerilla arm of the Communist Party in Colombia.

GCHQ – Government Communications Headquarters in England. Part of the government, it is an intelligence and security organization.

GIGN – National Gendarmerie Intervention Group (Groupe d'Intervention de la Gendarmerie Nationale).

GIS – Geographic Information System.

GPS – Global Positioning System. A satellite-based navigation system.

GSM – Global System for Mobile communications. The European standard for digital cellular communication.

HUD – Heads up display. A glasses-or helmet-mounted display usually used in airplanes.

IONEC – Intelligence Officer's New Entry Course. Run by British secret services for new officers.

JARIC – Joint Air Reconnaissance Intelligence Centre. A Defence Agency, part of a British governmental branch that analyses imagery and intelligence.

MexE – Mobile Station Application Execution Environment. A framework designed to ensure predictable environments for third-party applications for GSM and UMTS handsets.

NSA – National Security Agency. A branch of the United States government, it is the US's cryptologic organization.

OSS – Operation of Strategic Services. This department was the forerunner of the CIA (Central Intelligence Agency) from 1942–1945.

GLOSSARY

RDX – A solid usually used to make explosives.

RF – Radio Frequency.

SEAL – Sea, Air And Land. A special forces branch of the United States Navy.

SIS – Secret Intelligence Service.

SOE – Special Operations Executive. The British secret service that was active during World War Two.

Spetsnaz – A branch of Russian special forces. They are seen as the elite and ultimate force in Russia. Originally formed to conduct secret combat operations behind enemy lines.

BIBLIOGRAPHY

References and facts in this book were ascertained from the following sources:

- Adams, James; ***The New Spies***; Hutchinson 1994.
- Andrew, Christopher & Gordievsky, Oleg; ***KGB: The Inside Story***; Hodder & Stoughton 1991.
- Bamford, James; ***The Puzzle Palace***; Sidgwick & Jackson 1983.
- Bar-Zohar, Michael & Haber, Eitan; ***Quest For The Red Prince***; Weidenfeld & Nicolson 1983.
- Davis, Simon; ***Big Brother***; Pan 1996.
- Geraghty, Tony; ***The Irish War***; Harper Collins 1998.
- Hagar, Nicky; ***Secret Power***; Craig Potton Publishing 1996.
- Harclerode, Peter; ***Secret Soldiers***; Cassell & Co. 2000.
- Hollingsworth, Mark & Fielding, Nick; ***Defending The Realm***; André Deutsch 1999.
- Hollingsworth, Mark & Norton-Taylor, Richard; ***Blacklist: The Inside Story of Political Vetting***; Hogarth Press 1988.
- Jenkins, Peter; ***Advanced Surveillance***; Intel Publishing 2003.
- Melman, Yossi & Raviv, Dan; ***The Imperfect Spies***; Sidgwick & Jackson 1989.
- Porter, Bernard; ***Plots and Paranoia***; Unwin Hyman 1989.
- Ranelagh, John; ***The Agency***; Sceptre 1988.
- Urban, Mark; ***UK Eyes Alpha***; Faber & Faber 1996.

BIBLIOGRAPHY

In addition, many of the techniques found within this book can be examined in greater detail by obtaining the following American Military publications.

- FM 5-31 Booby Traps
- FM21-75 Combat Skills
- FM21-150 Combatives
- FM90-8 Counter Guerrilla Operations
- FM 31-21 Guerrilla Warfare And Special Forces Operations
- FM 34-5 Human Intelligence And Related
- FM 34-56 Imagery
- TM 31-210 Improvised Munitions Handbook
- FM 34-7 Intel Sup To Support Ops And Stability Ops
- FM 34-52 Intelligence Interrogation
- FM 34-8-2 Intelligence Officer's Handbook
- FM 2-27 Intelligence Reach Operations
- FM 2-50 Intelligence Systems
- FM 34-25-1 Joint Surveillance Target Attack
- FM 2-33-6 Military Intel Command And Control
- FM100-20 Military Ops In A Low Intensity Conflict
- FM 34-44 Signal Intelligence
- FM23-10 Sniper Training
- TC23-14 Sniper Training & Employment
- FM31-20 Special Forces Operations Doctrine
- FM31-20-5 Special Forces Recon Tactics
- FM34-36 Special Ops Intel & Electronic Warfare
- FM21-76 Survival Evasion And Escape
- FM 2-22-7 Tactical Human Intelligence And Counter
- FM 34-54 Technical Intelligence
- FM 34-40-5 Voice Intercept Operations

INDEX

INDEX

INDEX

INDEX

INDEX

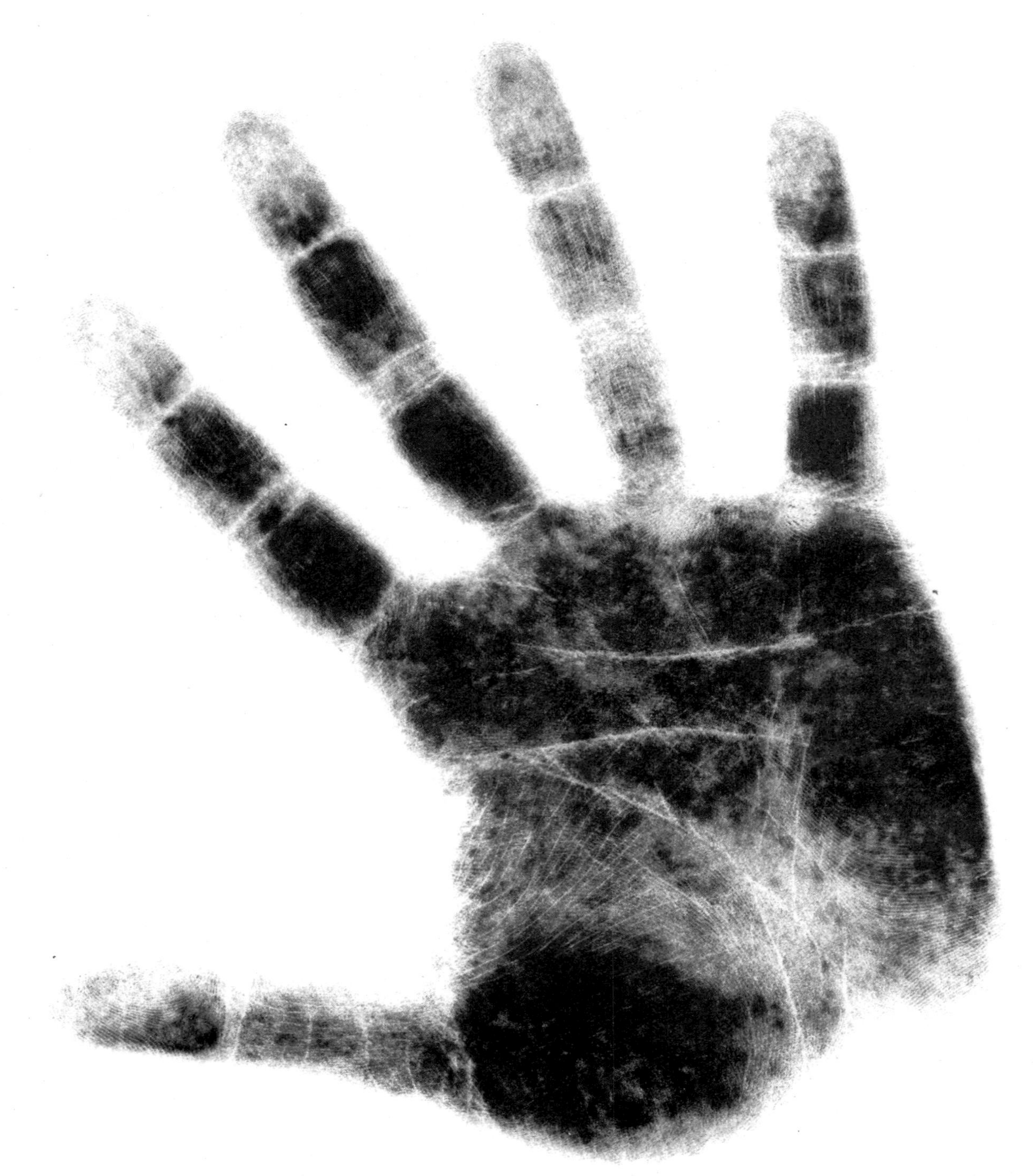